1979

PHILOSOPHY EAST/PHILOSOPHY WEST

Philosophy East/Philosophy West

A Critical Comparison of Indian, Chinese, Islamic, and European Philosophy

Ben-Ami Scharfstein
Ilai Alon
Shlomo Biderman
Dan Daor
Yoel Hoffmann

NEW YORK
OXFORD UNIVERSITY PRESS
1978

© Basil Blackwell 1978

First published in the United Kingdom by Basil Blackwell, Oxford

Published in the U.S.A. by Oxford University Press, New York

Library of Congress Cataloging in Publication Data
Main entry under title:

Philosophy East/Philosophy West.

   1. Philosophy, Comparative—Addresses, essays,
lectures. I. Scharfstein, Ben-Ami, 1919–
B799.P47   109   78–18473
ISBN 0–19–520064–0

Printed in Great Britain

Contents

Preface

This book is meant to be an introduction, though a serious one, and we ask no more of its readers than a reasonably good general understanding of European philosophy. We have been determinedly selective. That is, we have tried to penetrate into the subject, not by aiming at an impossible completeness, but by establishing the necessary backgrounds and then by taking up particular representative examples. The whole second part of the book is therefore devoted to extended examples of comparison. There are, of course, many interesting problems that we have not been able to take up here. We hope to continue our comparisons in a subsequent volume on political, social, historical, and aesthetic theories.

Although we have all read and approved of this book as a whole, each of us is primarily responsible for certain chapters or chapter sections, the titles of which are marked by the names of their respective authors. The Introduction, the first two general chapters, and the chapter on the *cogito* are mine, as are introductions in the second part. Elsewhere, the primary responsibility for Islamic thought is that of Ilai Alon; for Hindu thought, of Shlomo Biderman; for Chinese thought, of Dan Daor; and for Buddhist thought, of Yoel Hoffmann.

I may add that I have acted as editor of the book as a whole; and I must add that I owe a debt of gratitude to Prof. S. Pines, of the Hebrew University, who read an earlier version of the first two chapters and gave me equally helpful encouragement and criticism. I also want to thank the editors of the *Journal of Chinese Philosophy* for the few pages in 'Modes of Argument' that are repeated from an article written at their invitation.

We have tried our best to play fair with the reader and the subject, but much of what we have written is necessarily subjective. We have therefore not tried to avoid the natural use of the pronoun 'I'.

Ben-Ami Scharfstein

Note on Transliteration: We have not found it necessary to use the special symbols for transliterating from foreign languages. The one perhaps inconsistent exception is the ś, pronounced *sh*, used in the transliteration of Sanskrit words.

Introduction

Soon, after this Introduction is done, each of us, the authors, will be speaking for himself; but before we are reduced to almost unrepentant individuals, we should like to express the attitude that the five of us, who are colleagues and friends, hold in common towards the subject of comparative philosophy. We can begin to express it by stating the implications of the title (including the subtitle) we have chosen for our book. The title, as we see it, has three major implications. It implies that philosophy is not confined to the West; it implies that the Indian, Chinese, European, and European-allied Islamic traditions are worth comparing and are similar and different enough to make the comparison intellectually profitable; and it implies that the comparison ought to be critical, by which we mean, factually careful, analytically close, and as intelligent as its authors are able to make it.

This justification of our title may be more persuasive if each of its three parts is itself explained or justified.

Take the first point, which may not seem worth arguing. It is true that there have been Western philosophers with a serious interest in Chinese, Indian, or Islamic philosophy. The interest in Islamic philosophy was mostly confined to the Middle Ages, when Chinese and Indian philosophy could only have been distant rumours. Later, however, in the seventeenth century, there was a moment during which Leibniz hoped that China would give him the universal logic for which he was searching. During the eighteenth century, French thinkers half-invented an ideal China, the kingdom of the philosophers, the better to criticize a Europe that appeared to them to be as absurd as it was cruel.[1] Still later, Kant and Hegel, though they may not have given the Chinese and Indians a high cultural rank, studied what they could of their thought, while Schopenhauer, who read the Upanishads every night before going to sleep, made his own synthesis of Indian certainties and Kantian doubts.[2] In the twentieth century, the American philosopher, Santayana, more than once compared his own so-to-speak Platonic naturalism with Indian mysticism. Still more recently, Jaspers devoted a good many pages of his book, *The Great Philosophers*, to Buddha, Confucius, and Nagarjuna.

Yet these and the other examples that could be cited have never been enough to convince very many Western philosophers that philosophy, in the sense they most appreciate, exists outside the Western tradition. By and large, they seem to have believed that Eastern thought was either pre-philosophical or extra-philosophical, that is to say, either composed of traditional, perhaps superstitious rules of conduct, or of formulas for mystical salvation. They seem to have found it incredible that non-Westerners should have engaged in the constructive intellectuality, adventurous reasoning, and logical analysis that is identified with philosophy in the West.

They are wrong, of course. The reason for their error, if we may speak bluntly, is either cultural myopia or personal ignorance. Both stem from an insufficient education. Western education, whether that of philosophers or others, has never been seriously concerned with the thought of anyone or anything not long assimilated into the Western tradition.[3] Consider the education of the professional philosopher, which we, along, we suppose, with some of our readers, have enjoyed or been subjected to. The professional philosopher may have studied logic and philosophy painstakingly, he may have read and practised linguistic analysis, which is nothing if not painstaking, and he surely has read, with painstaking attention, such books and articles as his teachers have regarded as essential. He has probably learned a second and perhaps a third European language. And he has, in addition, studied a number of the great philosophers—Plato and Aristotle, Locke and Hume, Spinoza, Leibniz, and Kant, not to speak of the contemporaries who interest him. At this stage he may well begin to attempt serious original philosophizing, or, if his interests run that way, serious scholarship relating to philosophy. Absorbed in his attempt, he can no longer spare the time or summon up the desire to study philosophers from other traditions. What, at this stage, could inspire him to sit down again like the callow student he once was, who learned with a sense of revelation what Plato meant by an Idea and Aristotle by Substance, and study the strange concepts, transliterated from unknown languages, of philosophers from puzzling, distant cultures? Out of curiosity, he might leaf through the *Analects* of Confucius or through a paperback edition, in pseudo-Biblical English, of some Upanishads, and he might even find rational ethics or poetically stimulating religion in them; but these would no longer have the power to transform him as a philosopher. He would be likely to assume that the rest of Chinese and Indian thought was approximately the same, and so he would not attempt the later, more complex books. For now he would be feeling, not the student's curiosity, but the professional's mastery, and he would be unlikely to delay or humiliate himself by becoming a student again. A young philosopher on the verge of his career is apt to assume that what his teachers never required of him cannot be of any importance. Then, when he himself becomes a teacher, he perpetuates the attitude he has learned, and the beginning is never made.

The first point will not be argued any longer. Like the others, its plausibility must rest on the evidence we bring in the body of our book. The second point, that the traditions we have chosen are worth comparing and similar and different enough to make the comparison intellectually profitable, must be worked out slowly and by example. We shall try to characterize each of these more or less self-sufficient cultures so that each becomes more visible by way of contrast with the others. Over and again, we think, a clearly analogous technical device will be seen to serve a different cultural end; and at least somewhat analogous cultural purposes will be seen to be served by different technical devices. Each of these traditions has its sacred writings and revered philosophers, and, during long periods of time, everything that is said in them appears to be said by reference to such writings and philosophers; but sometimes there is open denial of the writings and always there is a process of surreptitious change from them, conscious or not. Arguments become more keen and better elaborated, paradoxes are raised, and scepticism or sophistry begins to flourish. It has often been noted that the great philosophical systems of China, India, and the West (to which Islamic philosophy may be said to belong) were all in part developed in answer to the potentially destructive paradoxes of men who seem to have taken pleasure in wielding the instruments of the logic they had discovered. The great systems all incorporate something of the scepticism they combat. Śankara is something of a Buddhist, and so is Chu Hsi; and the Buddhist himself has a touch of philosophical nihilism. Likewise, Plato incorporates Gorgias, Descartes incorporates Montaigne, and Kant incorporates Hume.

If you continue to compare, you find formal or at least formalizable logic in India, including a Buddhist theory of syllogisms, which looks not un-Aristotelian, except that it has an existential qualifier. You find elaborate lists of fallacies and discussions of modes of sound and unsound argument, including Indian analyses of the types and the validity of evidence. It is possible that Śankara, the ancient Indian, depending in this upon the 'school' of Mimamsa, has a view of evidence like that of Karl Popper, namely, that no hypothesis can, in the positive sense, be proved to be true, but can only be shown to have successfully resisted the attacks levelled on it. Incidentally, one branch of the Mimamsa (that led by Prabhakara) teaches a Kant-like morality, for it contends that religious precepts should be carried out, not for possible reward or punishment, which are morally irrelevant, but for the sheer consciousness of duty performed. Furthermore, in Indian and Islamic philosophy, matter, time, and space are atomized, in both familiar and unfamiliar ways, while the Chinese, we are told, unify the world by means of quasi-field theories. The European problem of causality, which will be compared with the Islamic, receives a hundred Indian and a few Chinese forms, reminiscent, respectively, of the Epicurean, Stoic, Neoplatonic, Humean, Kantian, and Hegelian forms. Bertrand Russell appears to be anticipated and answered. The great Scholastic debaters of Nominalism and Realism have their peers. Briefly, there is a wealth of thought and experience concentrated in philosophical abstractions.

We now come to our third point, that the comparison we are undertaking should be factually careful and analytically close. Even though five of us are collaborating on this book, we are, individually and collectively, aware of how much there is that we ought to know but do not. But we take our relative ignorance to be a cause, not for despair, but for the attempt to be explicit about our evidence and careful in interpreting it. Too much of the study of comparative philosophy has been motivated by nationalistic pride or shame, too much of it has assumed just what it ought to have found evidence for, and too much of it has been intellectually slack. We hope that we are taking a genuine step out of our own provincialism and towards the world in which the different philosophical traditions exist as equals and together express the single humanity of them all.

PART ONE

BACKGROUND COMPARISONS

1

Cultures, Contexts, and Comparisons

Ben-Ami Scharfstein

First things first. Before the comparisons that are the object of this book are begun, the general difficulty involved in making them must be considered. It is not unreasonable to begin by doubting whether a critical intelligence can profit from them much. One does not have to indulge in nominalistic doubts whether anything is genuinely comparable with anything else in order to recognize that we are dealing with cultures the differences between which may qualify the thinking of all their members. As there will be occasion to point out, it is only too easy to lift ideas out of their cultural contexts, to translate the terms in which they are expressed into familiar ones, and to come to plausible but misleading conclusions.

Such conceptual difficulties can be made clear by making them concrete, that is, by giving examples. Two philosophically interesting ones will be given. The first will be a discussion, relatively casual, of cultural differences in the perception of time. The second will be a discussion of the possible effect of differences in language on thinking, and then, more narrowly, the effect of the presence or absence of the interesting verb, 'to be'.

It should be remembered that these two examples are merely preliminary and illustrative. After they have been given, a necessary moral will be drawn and a constructive reaction to the problem of comparisons will be suggested.

Personal and Cultural Variations in Time[1]

The sense of time furnishes an old if problematic illustration of the point that everything is both personally and socially conditioned. Even such a fundamental mode of experience, in which we grasp ourselves, the world, and our continuity and discontinuity with others, varies, within limits, of course, from one age of life and person to another, and from one culture to another.

Suppose that, to simplify, we forget the sheerly personal qualities of temporal experience and think only of its varying speed in the course of an ordinary human life. This ordinary, subjective time-experience is certainly not identical with the public time of clocks and calendars. Not only do we recognize the difference between subjective and public time, but we measure each in terms of the other. In terms of subjective time, public time passes quickly if we are absorbed in what we are doing, and slowly if we are not. But once we have finished whatever it is that we have been doing, a reversal generally takes place. The time that passed quickly becomes subjectively full and memorable, while the time that passed slowly because of boredom leaves few if any distinguishable traces in the memory and becomes a time that has passed quickly.

The subjective speed of time seems to be related to age as well. To older people, subjective time passes with increasing speed. So, at least, it appears when it has already passed. The reason may be that what ordinarily happens in an old person's life so resembles what has happened before that no event stands out for long against the background of the past. It has been speculated, furthermore, that time passes more quickly as we age because our internal physiological mechanisms work with increasing slowness in relation to clock time, which appears correspondingly quicker. Perhaps, too, each day passes more quickly because it is a relatively shorter and shorter addition to a longer and longer experience; or perhaps the desire for time grows increasingly strong as one realizes that there remains increasingly little of it. Of course, beyond its simply changing speed, subjective time has, or rather is a whole spectrum of related qualities that we experience and that, in a sense, constitute us. It is never, as clock time is or seems to be, something separate and immutable. (As a matter of fact, research makes it appear that the notion of a single 'subjective time' is too simple. When we undergo the biological disturbance caused by flying to a distant place, different biological processes recover at different rates. 'In the body each physiological mechanism tends to have its own biological clock.')[2]

Yet, despite all this, we tend to belittle subjective time, at least in our public lives, and to live by clock time—with such increasing precision that scientists have officially adopted a caesium-atom-defined second having 9,192,631,770 parts. We tend to acknowledge that time is uniform and only seems to pass quickly or slowly. Perhaps, believing that only public, clock time is real and that reality is directly experienced, we believe that we do, in fact, sense time as an even flow from the past, into and through the present, and towards the future. Perhaps, given our modern, clock-ruled life, we believe that we intuit time in the same way as we conceive of it abstractly, that is, as a flowing continuum of uniform hours that is added to uniformly and used, saved, and wasted. By this public, clock time we organize all our lives. Inability to orient oneself by clock time may even be regarded as a symptom of insanity.

Our acceptance of clocklike time is neatly embodied in the three chief tenses, past, present, and future, that are shared by at least the Indo-European languages. Do we speak in these three tenses because, as we are immediately tempted to say, reality demands them? Or is it possible, as some have thought, that language may clothe reality in its own nature? Or are reality and language so involved in one another that they cannot be clearly distinguished? Unfortunately, none of these clear-cut alternatives has a simple answer. Which of them, taken simply, would explain the strange or strange-seeming disproportion between grammar and reason? That is, although the past, present, and future are given approximately equal grammatical status, reason finds the present to be a curiously elusive vanishing point between the past and the future, yet a vanishing point that seems real, as against the unreality, the mere existence-that-has-been and the existence-to-be of the past and the future.[3]

It is at least possible, then, that the quality or sense of time is affected by language; but we may postpone this theme, which immediately becomes difficult, in order to point out the unquestionable ways in which our sense of time has been affected by technology. Now, we are obliged to live by clocks and calendars. In classical Greece, in contrast, hardly anyone but the astronomers divided the day into hours; and the astronomers' hours varied with the seasons, each hour being the twelfth part of a day or night that changed in length as daylight grew longer or shorter. For the ordinary Greek, 'the time of full market' was accurate enough; and medieval Europe remained equally permissive, so far as the hours went. Mechanical clocks, powered by hanging weights, were invented in the thirteenth century, but long afterward, in the sixteenth, they were still scarce and unreliable. People met 'about sunrise' or 'about sunset'. Often they did not know how old they were—subjectively speaking, this knowledge might in any case have been misleading.[4]

Finally, commerce, technology, and developing scientific thought made the idea of endless, uniform time appear natural. Hard as the remaining literary evidence is to judge, it appears that time and space were not always considered to be neutral and uniform containers. To Hesiod, in the eighth century B.C., the universal container was fearful chaos; to certain Pythagoreans, it was air. The Greek atomists were the first European thinkers we know of to distinguish the infinite void from the matter it contained. Aristotle, for reasons he elaborated cleverly, refused to accept the idea of the void or vacuum, which he regarded as a pseudo-entity constructed by the imagination to help it to picture how bodies shift.

Towards the end of the long dominance of Aristotle's view, bold attacks were made on it by such Renaissance philosophers as Franciscus Patritius and Giordano Bruno. They argued that there was a single general space, an immense, penetrating, enveloping void. Then Newton assured the victory of the now familiar idea of an absolute, uniform medium in which motions take place relative to the fixed centre. The counterpart of such space is, of course, the absolute, uniform time that we, or the naïve pre-Einsteinians among us, are tempted to regard as intuitively known and metaphysically true.

Non-European cultures, however, may have different senses of time, more nearly akin to that (or those) of the ancient Greeks and the medievals. These time-senses are public, as they must be, but, as measured by clocks, they are erratic and subjective; just as clocks, as measured by them, may be rather arbitrary. Anthropologists in particular have discovered examples of non-European, non-clock methods of estimating time. To these we turn for a moment.

How could a clock or calendar (rather than an odorometer) have helped the Andamanese islanders, who, living in the jungle, located themselves in time by the odours of the different flowers as they came into bloom? These flower-time signals were useful to them because they marked the changes in climate, vegetation, and animal life that they needed to know.

The Balinese, in contrast, have had two calendars, a lunar-solar one, and one that depends on independent cycles of day-names. Given briefly, the description of the Balinese time-sense may be obscure, but it does exemplify a non-European attitude and perhaps experience:

The cycles and supercycles are endless, unanchored, uncountable, and, as their internal order has no significance, without climax. They do not accumulate, they do not build, and they are not consumed. They don't tell you what kind of time it is. . . . In general, the lunar-solar calendar is more a supplement to the permutational than an alternative to it. It makes possible the employment of a classificatory full-and-empty, 'detemporalized' conception of time in contexts where the fact that natural conditions vary periodically has to be at least minimally acknowledged.[5]

The Nuer, who live in the Sudan, conceive of time by means of whatever affects their food supply and the lives of their cattle, and by their own movements from villages to camps and back again. An event is usually placed in time by the Nuer, not by the month in which it occurs, but by the ruling activity, such as the harvest, that coincides with it. 'The daily timepiece is the cattle clock, the round of pastoral tasks.' A man says, for example, 'I shall start off when the calves come home.' Time, in our sense, changes its value, for it is different in periods of rain and drought. 'In the drought the daily time-reckoning is more uniform and precise.'

Given such regulation of time, it is natural that

the Nuer have no expression equivalent to 'time' in our language, and they cannot, therefore, speak of time as though it were something actual, which passes, can be wasted, can be saved, and so on. . . . I do not think that they ever experience the same feeling of fighting against time or of having to coordinate activities with an abstract passage of time, because their points of reference are mainly the activities themselves, which are generally of a leisurely character.[6]

Like the Nuer, the American Indians did not compute the year in days. Their year was chiefly marked by the recurrence of winters. One's age was given, not in years, but in the sequence of memorable events. This is how tall I was, the Indian would say, when the great famine struck, or when we won the victory at the square bluff. It ought not to be argued that this is a mistaken or useless way of reckoning time. For the individual, size may be a more accurate measure of his approach to adult stature than the number of astronomical years he has lived. The great famine locates him effectively in his tribe's annals. Given an astronomical calendar, he would still, like us, have to jog his memory and think of what had happened and how he had felt at a particular 'time'.[7]

To these Indians, morning was 'before the sun came out from under the trees', after which the time became 'red shining in the treetops', and, later, 'when the sun hangs in the treetops'. Day was light and work; night, darkness and sleep. Time was not the rhythm of the clock, but the falling of the poplar leaves, the freezing of the water, and the recurring tribal ceremonies.

The anthropologist Benjamin Lee Whorf has gone so far as to contend, in a celebrated group of articles, that the Hopi Indians quite lack our sense of a uniform stream of time. His evidence is their language, which, he contends, has none of our tenses. Instead of the future, the Hopi, he says, have verb-forms that indicate expectation. Instead of the past and present, verb-forms indicate that such-and-such is the case. In Hopi, *I will* is analogous to *I expect to* or *I intend to*, and *I am* or *I was* is analogous to *It is the case that I*. Unlike us, the Hopi, says Whorf, do not objectify temporal processes. We think of *summer, year, month*, and *day* as 'things' that approach and recede, that are many or few, that we are close to, at, in, or far from. But such temporal nouns are expressed adverbially by the Hopi. That is to say, our *morning* is their *while morning is occurring*; and *this winter* is *winter recently* or *winter now*, because winter is not an object that can be, so to speak, pointed at.[8]

As summarized here, Whorf's description of the Hopi language may well be unclear. Assuming, however, that it is accurate, it may not be sufficient in itself to prove that the Hopi experience or understanding of time is utterly different from ours. Whorf's claim has generally been discounted and, in its extreme form, apparently discarded, yet it has played its part in stimulating, not only linguistics, but the currently active research into possible cultural differences in perception and cognition. Some psychologists have come to emphasize that perception is dependent upon so many factors and is so subject to illusion that it is reasonable to regard it, in each instance, as a hypothesis influenced by personal and cultural expectations.[9]

In any event, we cannot take it for granted that the Indians, Chinese, or Muslims, experienced, imagined, or conceived time just as we do. Does the desire, evident in some Indian philosophy, to transcend time indicate anything basic about Indian, or some Indian character? How can we grasp the peculiar logic that has been claimed to characterize both Chinese speech and life? Does Muslim 'atomism', 'derived from the apperceptions of the Arabs in ancient times', really dominate the Muslims' temporal experience? Even when the time-expressions used in these cultures seem intertranslatable, it cannot be assumed, without evidence, that we have a good understanding of what the terms refer to.[10]

Languages in General

Consideration of the issue of time has led to the possibility that different languages embody different forms of understanding. This possibility is of crucial importance to the whole enterprise of comparative philosophy. There are, it may be assumed, two extreme ways of judging the possibility. The first may be termed the metaphysical-aesthetic, and the second, the logical. The first tends to regard each language as a unique, relatively closed universe of discourse, the second to regard it as only one of the countless possible variations of a universal logic.[11]

What is the case for the uniqueness of each language? Those who accept it say that a language is not simply a neutral medium in which to think and communicate. Its structure, they say, is its own, its vocabulary makes unique distinctions, it has its own method of combining word-fractions and words, it has its own parts of speech (if it has them at all), and it expresses temporal relations in its own way. Furthermore, its lilts and sounds have their own peculiarly aesthetic nature. Given all these characteristics of uniqueness, a language may be supposed to function for those who speak it much as Kant assumed that the categories of thought function for human beings in general. If they do, a language may be said to constitute the very thoughts it conveys, just as mathematical language constitutes and conveys mathematical ideas. It is in agreement with such a view that a French expert in the languages of Africa has claimed that the scientific study of these languages requires 'radical cultural adjustment'. Europeans, he writes, have mistakenly tried to read their grammar into non-European languages:

This misguided universalism has produced too many so-called African grammars, done by European and African amateurs, where we find the paradigms of the French language down to the last details, even including the obsolete second form of the conditional and the pluperfect subjunctive . . . In brief, these writers have tried at any cost to take a normative description of French (usually grossly incorrect) and to force into this framework the particular structures and forms of the African languages they thought they were describing and even regulating . . . Each language constitutes a system which can be described only in reference to itself. . . .[12]

Whorf, who accepted this rather old view of language, therefore said:

We dissect nature along lines laid down by our native languages. The categories and types that we isolate from the world of phenomena we do not find there because they stare every observer in the face; on the contrary, the world is presented in a kaleidoscopic flux of impressions which has to be organized by our minds—and this means largely by the linguistic systems in our minds. We cut nature up, organize it into concepts, and ascribe significance to it largely because we are parties to an agreement to organize it in this way—an agreement that holds throughout our speech community and is codified in the patterns of our language. The agreement is, of course, an implicit and unstated one, but *its terms are absolutely obligatory*; we cannot talk at all except by subscribing to the organization and classification of data which the agreement decrees . . .

This rather startling conclusion is not so apparent if we compare only our modern European languages, with perhaps Latin and Greek thrown in for good measure. Among these tongues there is a unanimity of major pattern which at first seems to bear out natural logic. But this unanimity exists only because these tongues are all Indo-European dialects cut to the same basic plan . . .

When Semitic, Chinese, Tibetan, or African languages are contrasted with our own, the divergence in analysis of the world becomes more apparent; and, when we bring in the native languages of the Americas, where speech communities for many millenniums have gone their ways independently of each other and of the Old World, the fact that languages dissect nature in many different ways becomes patent. The relativity of all conceptual systems, ours included, and their dependence upon language stand revealed.[13]

The European languages themselves have been considered to be unique even in relation to one another. For example, it has been suggested that German is relatively animistic, and that French is relatively logical and abstract. That is, German (like Dutch, and, to a lesser degree, colloquial Norwegian) continues to classify non-living things as if they belonged to three genders. This animistic classification has been dropped, it is pointed out, from English, Danish, and Swedish. The assumed orderliness and logicality of French have been attributed in part to the disappearance of case-endings, which has strengthened the need for the fixed logical order of subject, verb, and object. The essential trait of the French vocabulary has been said to be 'the fear of the concrete word', a fear perhaps inherited from medieval scholasticism. As compared with German words, French words have been said to be more dependent on context for their meaning. The reason given is that French has relatively more general terms, each with different, sharply distinguishable senses, and more homonyms. French is closer in this respect to Chinese, though not generally as close as English.

The differences between the vocabularies of the different languages are more subtle than they may seem at first sight. Languages, as is evident, have vocabularies of different degrees of richness, a richness it is best to measure, not by the mere number of synonyms, but by the number of significant combinations the words in question can enter. The words cannot be considered in isolation, for they affect one another through the network of their associations. Each word is bounded, entered into, communicated with, and joined by similar and opposed words. This similarity and opposition can be of sound, sense, history, or of all three. Therefore, no two words of the same language, though regarded as synonyms, are exactly alike. It is all the more true that no two words of different languages are exactly alike in associations or intimate meanings.[14]

In comparing languages, it has been found illuminating to regard their words as having what may be called field properties, the fields into which they are organized being called, as one chooses, linguistic, conceptual, or semantic. A semantic field is an alliance of words so ordered as to categorize and express a distinct area of experience. Because the words in a field are ordered, the meaning of each is dependent on that of the others, just as the pictorial function of each tessera of a mosaic is dependent on that of the other tesserae. It stands to reason that analogous semantic fields in different languages are different, and therefore, by means of their emphases, associations, and inclusions and exclusions, tend to constitute different conceptual worlds or world-fragments.[15]*

The spatial system, the colour system, and the system of basic elements or kinds are clear examples of semantic fields. A word on each may be helpful.

To simple tribal groups, the number system may consist of no more than 'one, two, several'. But however limited or unusual, number systems are linguistically unique in that they can be translated exactly into one another. Yet, though technically intertranslatable, they are different in actual manipulation, and different to imagination and perception. For example, compare the decimal system with its chief competitor, the system with a base of twelve. It does make some difference, though not an arithmetical one, if the tens or twelves are regarded as whole numbers, in the same way as it would make some difference to our historical imagination if we dated events, not by centuries, but by units of 120 years. As will be pointed out, the very conception of number has suffered changes, or, rather augmentations. If religious, philosophical, and magical associations are taken into consideration, number systems vary far more, of course, than has been suggested here.

Spatial systems tend to some uniformity, but it is far from

* 'The Humboldt-Trier-Weisgerber conception of semantic fields has been criticized repeatedly on the grounds of vagueness and subjectivity, yet even critics seem willing to grant that there is something of semantic and psychological importance underlying the general conception. The theoretical task, therefore, is to try to formulate these ideas more clearly in the hope of dispelling some of the uncertainties and misunderstandings that surround them.' G. A. Miller and P. N. Johnson-Laird, *Language and Perception*, p. 240.

complete. Temporal and spatial concepts are intimately related, and it is significant that although English verbs do not necessarily show in their form what shape or spatial relation they express, each of their forms has an obligatory tense. Spatial systems enumerate cardinal directions differently. To the Zuni Indians, there were seven directions—our four, plus above, below, and centre. To the Chinese, there were five—our four, plus the centre. As is usual in every culture, the Chinese associated spatial directions with particular aspects of nature. The East, for instance, was associated by them with the left side, with green, spring, growth, the rising sun, the increasing male force (the yang), the activity of building, the act of forgiveness, and good luck. The right was the opposite, and unlucky and dishonourable. The translator of the New Testament into Chinese was therefore faced with a dilemma. To translate the sentence that says that Jesus is seated at the right hand of God, he had to play false either to the word or the intention of the Bible.[16]

As for colour systems, it appears that none of those traditionally embedded in any language gives a neutral, even relatively complete account of the colour differences that can actually be perceived. It is said that some languages have only two basic colour terms, one for dark and the other for light colours, with added distinctions, such as *blood* for red and *fresh leaves* for green. The term for red may refer to what we call *red, orange, yellow, brown,* or some or all of these together. Blue and green are often not distinguished by special terms, in Greek, for example. On the other hand, our twofold division of blue and green is sometimes increased to a basic threefold or fourfold division. Natural associations with colour may obviously make the response to them different. A number of African languages have no word for snow, so the missionaries who translated the Biblical phrase, *white as snow,* into these languages had to use an African simile, such as, *white as egret feathers,* the tactile and emotional associations of which are not very similar.[17]

The system of basic elements or kinds enters directly into each of the traditional philosophies. The Greeks and medievals, as we know, believed that the universe was made of earth, air, fire, water, and ether. The Chinese, on the other hand, believed it evolved in fire phases, miscalled 'elements', of earth, metal, fire, water, and wood. Obviously the 'elements' that correspond in name play a systematically different role in the physics or cosmology of the Indians, Chinese, and Greeks.

As a kind of challenge to you, the reader, I, the author, ask you to compare the different associations, by which I mean the position in their respective semantic fields, of the concept of *haham* (wise man) in ancient Israel, of the *guru* in ancient India, of the *ju* in ancient China, of the *sophist* or *philosopher* in ancient Greece, of the *philosophe* in eighteenth-century France, and of the *philosopher* in twentieth-century America or Europe.[18]

To Be *in Particular*

What has been said about languages in general can be tested in relation to the philosophically critical verb *to be*. The English forms of this verb have had a complicated history. They seem to have been derived from four different Indo-European roots: the form *be* comes from a root having the associated meanings of *exist* and *grow* and, in the future tense, *come to be*; the forms *am* and *is* come from a different root meaning *be*; the form *are* comes from a merely conjectured root; and the form *was* comes from a root with the associated meanings of *delay, dwell, stay the night*.[19]

The complex origin of the verb is compatible with its subtly, perhaps misleadingly related uses. Its grammatical power is unmistakable, for its presence as a mere copula, without any clearly separate meaning at all, is often enough to turn a group of words into an acceptable sentence ('This is a sentence'). It expresses or helps to express many kinds of states or relationships, including identity ('We are whoever we are'); membership in a class ('We are members of the human race'); existence ('We are'); property ('We are curious'); location in space or time ('We are here', 'The meeting between us is now'); and possession ('These opinions are mine; the reactions to them are yours'). Regardless, however, of all the verb's interrelated uses, those which have been of philosophic importance have been of two main kinds: the indication of existence, reality, occurrence, or life; and the linking of subject and predicate, the indication, that is, of what sort, or where, or how the subject is.

This joining of the existential and copulative functions in the same verb is characteristic of the Indo-European languages, such as Greek, Latin, French, German, and English, but other languages are said generally to assign the different functions to different verbs, or even to ignore one or another function, as if there were no particular need to express it. Surely, in the Semitic languages, such as Hebrew and Arabic, there is no verb that combines the two functions. The most nearly equivalent Hebrew verb (*hayah*) expresses meanings such as *develop, become, be caused*, and *exist*. It is not used, at least not in the present tense, as a mere link or copula. The English sentences, 'The wind is strong', 'The house is here', 'He is a good man', 'This sand is white', become, in a Semitic language, 'The wind (or, The wind it) strong', 'The house here', 'He good man', 'This sand white'.

Why, in a language such as English, does 'The wind is strong' appear to be a complete sentence, while 'The wind strong' appears to be only a phrase? From a purely grammatical standpoint, the answer is that we have adopted the convention by which the verb *to be* is a sentence-forming link. But from the standpoint of psychology, the answer is that we unconsciously assume what most Western philosophers have assumed since Aristotle, namely, that the *strong* we mean is a quality that exists in, resides in, or occurs to the wind. We think of the man to whom the quality of goodness has been added, of the house that possesses a certain quality of location, and of the sand to which the quality of whiteness adheres. Without the *is* as the link of possession, a sentence seems to be broken or unfinished; but to require the link is to risk confusing it with the *is* that asserts existence. In the *Sophist*, Plato was already trying to analyse the different functions of the verb, and perhaps even to distinguish between its existential and copulative use; but the confusion continues to bedevil us.[20] It is easier to analyse the confusion in relation to a circumscribed problem than to shift a whole deeply eroded channel of thought. But Chinese, as will soon become evident, is different, and Japanese makes a clear distinction between the one *is* and the other.*

* The Japanese verb *desu* functions as a copula in 'equational' sentences such as, 'This city is San Francisco.' *Desu* is derived from the existence-denoting verb *arimasu* (*desu* = *de*(*arima*)*su*), but it appears only in equational sentences and is thus intuitively grasped as *be* in its copula-function.

In Japanese, the idea of existence is expressed by two different verbs, *aru* and *iru*. Both are translated by *be*, but there is a significant semantic difference between them. *Aru* is used with non-living things and denotes the location of an object or the simple fact of its existence; but *iru* is used when the subject is a living

Beginning with Aristotle, the fateful duality of the verb *to be* became an integral part, even a dogma of European philosophical reasoning. Aristotle was convinced that everything that existed could be classified as either a subject or that which belonged to a subject. This distinction between substance and attribute, to use Aristotelian terms, was later equated, in a not really Aristotelian way, with that between substance and accident. In distinguishing between substance and attribute, Aristotle must have been influenced by the structure of the Greek sentence, with its natural separation into subject and predicate. He was also influenced, no doubt, by the nature of the Greek definite article, which allowed an abstract concept to be formed from an adjective or verb—an adjective like *good* was easily transformed into the noun, *the good*, which might then be thought of as some kind of independently existing substance.[21]

That the subject-predicate form is not necessary to language, and therefore not to thought, is proved by the nature of Chinese, especially in its classic form. The nature of Chinese also proves that it is not essential to suffer the ambiguity involved in the transformation of adjectives into nouns. We of course cannot now undertake to explain the Chinese language, but we can give some broad indications to clarify what has just been said.[22]

Imagine a language in which the words are unchanging root-words, which cannot be inflected or have prefixes or suffixes, or, therfore, show tense, number, gender, person, or case. This should not be so difficult to imagine if we think, not of our ordinary language, but of the language of mathematics and logic—we do not inflect numbers or give them tenses. The word-

---

thing, and it suggests living movement or activity. In certain cases, both verbs can be used with a living subject. *Watashi wa otōto ga aru* and *Watshi wa otōto ga iru* are both translated, 'I have a younger brother', or, 'As for me, there exists a younger brother.' In using *aru* the speaker suggests the simple existence, the 'objective being' of his brother, whereas *iru* suggests the life or activity, the 'subjective being' of his brother. The use of *iru* implies that the speaker is to some extent identifying himself with the subject's own mode of being.

Strangely or not, there appears to be a somewhat analogous distinction in the Bantu languages. The form *liho*, it is said, implies that the existent in question is present and will cease to exist. It refers only to a living being. In contrast, the form *baho* applies to actual and continuing existence. It can be used only when the idea of living is excluded. A. Kagame, 'The Empirical Apperception of Time and the Conception of History in Bantu Thought', in L. Gardet *et al.*, *Cultures and Time*.

roots or idea-symbols of Chinese are not unlike the theoretical roots of Semitic words. They have even been compared with the Jungian archetypes, because, while remaining the same, they can assume so many different meanings. English has lost so many of its inflections that, compared with Latin, French, or German, it is relatively Chinese. In English, for example, the word, *drive*, serves as a verb (retaining this form except in the third person singular), as a noun, and as an adjective (in the compound, *driveway*). Of course, plurality can be indicated in Chinese when necessary, by the proper number inserted into the proper place, and tense, when necessary, by the insertion of words such as, to indicate the past, *past day* or *finished*.

Strictly speaking, Chinese has no fixed classes of words, though its words have been broadly separated into terms of designation, like our nouns, and terms of action, like our verbs. Proper nouns and (in our terminology) personal pronouns can be used as we use verbs. So, sometimes, can numbers. For example, the Chinese of Confucius's *Analects* (14/18) reads, 'One rectify heaven under.' Because the character 'one' functions here as 'to make one', the translation of this phrase reads, 'United and rectified the whole kingdom.'

In a summary comparison of Indo-European languages and Chinese, one might say:

Indo-European singular and plural help to distinguish noun and verb from each other and from other parts of speech and to show the verb's dependence on the subject from which it takes its number; such word forms illuminate the structure of the sentence and the different and interacting functions of its parts. The Chinese sentence, on the other hand, is a featureless series of unchanging words the interrelations of which defied analysis until very recently; Chinese has had lexicography from an early date, but, unlike inflected languages such as Greek, Sanskrit and Arabic, scarcely any study of grammar... The Chinese sentence can be indefinitely expanded and contracted, rendered as precise or vague as the speaker pleases.[23]

The devices that make Chinese clear are, in principle, simple enough. Because its words, that is, word-roots are unchanging, and because the same word both designates a thing and expresses the process relative to it (the equivalent verb), the relationships between the words, and therefore their meanings, are established very largely by their order, which is to say, by their placement either before or after the word or words they are related to.

On the assumption that the reader knows no Chinese, these last paragraphs are unlikely to convey anything clear. Under the circumstances, generalities, supplemented by a few clarifying examples, will have to suffice. The Chinese language, like the Chinese philosopher, favours what has been called 'correlative logic', in which the meaning of one word is completed by its opposite. 'For example there is a passage in the chapter *Refutation of Twelve Philosophers* in *Hsün-tzu* (3/16A/8) which begins "TRUST TRUST TRUST *yeh*". Taking the sentence by itself, even the syntax is doubtful. But the next sentence is parallel: "DOUBT DOUBT ALSO TRUST *yeh*". At once the syntax orders itself: "Trusting the trustworthy is trustworthiness; doubting the doubtful is also trustworthiness." Hsün-tzu could have put the thought into a more complex and clearer sentence, like that which his commentator Yan Liang (preface date A.D. 818) provides as a paraphrase: "Trust in what deserves trust and doubt of what deserves doubt; although as attitudes they are not the same, both belong to trustworthiness." But Hsün-tzu's aim is not precision but gnomic force, and parallelism serves to organize the sentences and restrict their meaning just to the degree he needs.'[24]

As this passage shows, the emphasis in Chinese is on relationships or coordinations, and not on substance and attribute, or on an adjective that can be turned into a noun. Thus a Chinese philosopher will ask the question, 'Which of the many parts of the body are the servants, and which are the rulers? Or are they', he will ask, 'rulers and servants in turn, each adapted to the other?' The world, he implies, is a symbiotic shifting and coalescence of elements, not unlike the shifting and coalescence of the Chinese word-roots themselves.

Differences Between Chinese and Indo-European Languages and Philosophies

The differences between languages are hard to conceptualize exactly, and it is harder still to judge to what extent these differences are reflected in the very nature of thinking. What will be said here about the reflection of language in thought will therefore be conjectural. But the subject itself is of pervasive importance, so that, conjectural or not, an attempt will be made to summarize the differences in emphasis between Chinese and Indo-European philosophies, in so far as the differences may be assumed to result from those between the respective types of language. The differences in question can be divided into four groups: those that may result from the presence or absence of the word *be*, that is, of a single word having both the basic senses that have been discussed; those that may result from the presence or absence of word-inflection; and those that may result from the presence or absence of time, number, and gender.

First, the troublesome word *be*. In the Indo-European languages, the presence of the copula *be* and its tendency to be confused with the *be* of existence, lead to the creation of a substance-attribute distinction more easily than in Chinese (and, though to a lesser degree, in the Semitic languages). The absence of the *be* of existence in Chinese may make for a more variegated attitude towards what we call, with global indiscrimination, 'being' or 'existence'. Without particular guidance, a translator from Chinese may quite rightly hesitate between, 'is equivalent to', 'amounts to', 'consists in', 'will endure', 'is fundamental', and the like. He may well feel a need to resolve the ambiguity of the encompassing European *be*. Absence of a full equivalent in Chinese makes ontological arguments difficult to put and implausible on their very faces. The importance of ontological arguments of various types in European philosophy makes their absence in Chinese philosophy a fundamental difference, though it must be conceded that some such arguments became known in China when imported together with Buddhist polemics.[25] The absence of ontological arguments can be taken to be an advantage. Speaking of a translation of Hegel into Chinese, A. C. Graham remarks sardonically, 'It is curious to watch Chinese translators struggling to reproduce Western fallacies in a language which, whatever its defects, does not permit one to make these particular mistakes.'[26]

The absence of the Indo-European *be* in Chinese also makes it easier to regard the 'elements'—earth, metal, fire, water, wood—as specific powers rather than kinds of matter. In this relatively non-substantial view of the 'substances', however, the Chinese were not very different from the pre-Socratic philosophers of Greece or from Indian philosophers.

Second, the differences resulting from the presence or absence of adjectives recognized as such. There are likely to be two closely related results. In the Indo-European languages, as has been said, adjectives have a separate status and are easily granted the function of a noun. 'The man is conscientious' is easily transformed into, 'The man has a conscience'. Qualities are therefore emphatically and formally separated from that which they qualify, and are prepared for the status they are assigned in Realistic, that is Platonic, metaphysics. In addition, the Indo-European languages find it easy to express a verb as an adjective, so that, for example. 'The man thinks', becomes, 'The man is thoughtful', which then, by transformation of adjective into noun, becomes, 'The man shows thoughtfulness'. Seeing that he shows this laudable quality, philosophers may conduct a metaphysical search for its source, as if it were a certain something, like the fire that Prometheus stole from the gods, that men had to get or be given from some non-human source. By metaphorical extension, Chinese philosophy did transform the ordinary word *tao* or *path* into the metaphysical Tao and the ordinary word *t'ien* or *sky* into the impersonal force or being that ruled the universe; but verb-like concepts seldom became purely nominal ones, and truth, like many other such abstract concepts, was not easily promoted to metaphysical status, because, like them, it was compounded of a pair of opposites, which were, in its particular case, *shih fei*, *rightness-wrongness*.[27]*

Third, the differences resulting from the presence or absence of word-inflection. These may create a different attitude toward logic and grammar and, in consequence, a different kind of thought-structure. To be more specific, the necessary concern of the Indo-European languages with grammatical structure helps to create an interest in thought-structure as such, or, in other words, in the correctness of the form of a statement irrespective

* In classical Sanskrit, it is said, 'the verb tends to be eclipsed by substantive and adjectival expressions . . . The well-known "substantive character" of classical Sanskrit, with its juxtapositions, repetitions, etc., and the predominance given passive rather than active verbs shows a preference for static over dynamic relationships, a certain primacy of being over becoming; it reflects a tendency to eliminate action as such. It is noteworthy that most nouns expressing static qualities have an intrinsic positive value, whereas nouns which express movement and change possess a pejorative value.' B. Bäumer, in L. Gardet *et al.*, *Cultures and Time*, p. 79.

of its factual content. In Chinese, on the other hand, the concern is with the correct application of names, by which is meant the correct application of a word to that which it is taken to signify, or of a statement to the state of affairs it was taken to signify. To a Confucian, it was important that the name *king* be applied only to a person with the proper Confucian attitude towards his function as a ruler; otherwise, the concept would be degraded and degrade social life. To a Legalist, it was important that an official should not talk big and accomplish little, because this lack of correspondence would make efficient government impossible. To a Taoist, it was important to point out that the Confucians and the others were always trying to circumscribe the uncircumscribable *tao* by naming, that is, characterizing it definitely.[28] Given this kind of concern, intuition and practical and historical experience play much larger roles in Chinese thought than explicit grammar or logic.

Lacking inflection, Chinese, to remain clear, needs far more repetition or pairing of words or phrases. As the brief example from *Hsün-tzu* has already shown, the structure of Chinese language and thought demands repetition, a doubling or parallelism, in which words, phrases, and thoughts are always being weighed against other, related ones. This lays the stress, as has been said, on relationships: no idea seems complete until related to another that balances it. Indo-European languages lay the stress more on the connection of the subject with its predicate, or, in other terms, of the substance with its attribute, and on one-directional, linear rather than reciprocal causation.[29] Compare the kind of thinking we are most likely to practise with the thinking exhibited by Confucius when his disciple asked him why his first advice to a ruler would be to rectify names. Observe how the reasoning is carried on by successive instances of parallelism when Confucius, the Master, says:

> If names be not correct, language is not in accordance with the truth of things. If language be not in accordance with the truth of things, affairs cannot be carried on to success. When affairs cannot be carried on with success, proprieties and music will not flourish. When proprieties and music will not flourish, punishments will not be properly awarded. When punishments are not properly awarded, the people do not know how to move hand or foot. Therefore a superior man considers it necessary that the names he uses may be spoken *appropriately*, and also that

what he speaks may be carried out *appropriately*. What the superior man requires, is just that in his words there may be nothing incorrect.[30]

Fourth, and last, the differences resulting from the presence or absence of time, number, and gender. These are perhaps the most subtle of all. Their omission in Chinese may or may not result in greater ambiguity, but it surely often results in greater generality. For example, the first line of a poem by Tu Fu, taken literally and word for word reads: 'State (*or*, a state, the state, states, the states) is (*or* are, was, were, will be, *etc.*) mountain (*or* a mountain, the mountain, mountains, the mountains) river (*or* a river, the river, rivers, the rivers) survive (*in any person or tense*).' There is a prose translation of the line that reads, 'The state may fall, but the hills and streams remain'; but every reader is free to prefer his own variations in definite or indefinite articles, number, and tense. It should be remembered, however, that the practised Chinese reader may be perfectly satisfied with the line in all its generality. For him, the poetry may not require any further specification of number, time, and so on, than it already has. For philosophers, who may be suspected of courting generality, this is likely to be a very satisfactory linguistic situation.

It is evident that much that we have to say, the qualifications that we have to make in order to express ourselves at all, are unnecessary in Chinese. From a Chinese standpoint, the speakers of European languages have to say too much in order to say anything at all. In spite, therefore, of its chronic ambiguity, which comes from its natural sparseness in its classic written form and from its dependence on associations, Chinese resembles mathematics and symbolic logic. Some commentators stress the ambiguity, others, the logicality. This is not surprising, for Chinese has them both.

The Matter of Comparison

Before going on to the comparison of philosophies, it may be helpful to think for a moment about comparison as such. It is obvious that whenever we perceive or think, we compare, that is, respond to similarities and differences. To perceive is to respond to the perceptual similarities and differences that are relevant, as we have learned, to our lives. Analogously, to think (as we are now thinking) is to relate ideas to one another in keeping with their similarities and differences, the object being to arrive at patterns of intelligibility that will clarify things for us and, in so doing, give us what might be called, not unambiguously, intellectual pleasure.

Such an abstract characterization may become persuasive if we turn to particular examples. The perception of colour makes an especially good because especially perceptible example. Think of red. We perceive red surfaces as identical with or very like other red ones, as rather like orange surfaces, as distinctly unlike blue surfaces, and as antagonistic to, meaning, unblendable with green surfaces. It may appear strange at first thought that the impression made by red, or by any colour, may be weakened by the presence of an identical or similar one and strengthened by the presence of a different one. But this is only to say that contrast increases visibility. The redness of red and the blueness of blue accentuate one another and simultaneously bring out the separate identity of each colour and the difference between them. Without differences of colour, colour in the most general sense, nothing at all, of course, can be seen.

In establishing that comparison is essential to perception and thought, it is necessary to keep in mind that concepts such as 'identity', 'similarity', and 'difference' are interdependent. To be considered identical in a not merely logical sense, 'identical' things (or elements, or qualities) must be different from one another at least in time or place. 'Similar' things, to be considered so, must exhibit distinguishing differences. And 'different' things must be similar to one another, because, to make out their difference, they must be compared in the same dimension or sense. Red and blue, different as they are, are at least the same in being colours. That is, different things can be distinguished as such only because they are compared, and they can be compared only because they can be perceived or thought by means of the same act, the act that established the dimension or sense of the comparison. Put in the paradoxical language that some philosophers, Eastern and Western, have favoured, similar things are different and different things are similar; or, more succinctly, similarities are different and differences are similar. Less paradoxically, the fact is that similarities can be made out only because there are differences, and differences, because there are similarities. In other words, the similarities and differences essential to thought are interdependent, as are the concepts 'similarity' and 'difference'.

Most of our comparisons are made in the normal course of perceiving and thinking, without much conscious intervention on our parts. But the history of thought has often forced particular problems of comparison on the attention of scientists and philosophers. The history of the concept of number serves as a good illustration. On a first, naïve view, it might seem that, of all concepts, numbers are the most easily and naturally comparable with one another. Yet history shows that the naïve view is mistaken. The very names assigned to certain types of numbers, such as 'natural numbers', 'rational numbers', 'irrational numbers', 'real numbers', 'imaginary numbers', 'complex numbers', and 'transfinite numbers', should lead to the verifiable suspicion that it was not historically easy to establish that all these were genuinely comparable and all worthy of the status of 'numbers'.[31]

A word on the history of some of the problematic numbers may make this observation clearer. For a long time, it was difficult, surely in Europe, to accept that the zero, a mere nothing, with its own strange arithmetical properties, was a number. The number one was also regarded in a special light. The Pythagoreans, Plato, and Aristotle considered it to be not a number, but the unit or principle of number. Euclid defined 'a unit' as 'that in virtue of which each of the things that exists is called one', and defined 'a number' as 'a multitude composed of units'.[32] As for 'irrational numbers', which are not ratios of integers, but are expressed as infinite, non-repeating decimals, they were said, in the sixteenth century, not to be numbers at all, because they 'flee away perpetually, so that not one of them can be apprehended precisely in itself'. Both Pascal and Newton held that the square root of three and the like could be grasped only as geometric magnitudes, not as genuine, arithmetical numbers. Negative numbers, which were accepted rather early in India and China, were rejected as numbers by most European mathematicians of the sixteenth and seventeenth centuries. Negative numbers could not, they held, be roots of equations and were, briefly, 'absurd'. It was not till the nineteenth century that a unified theory of numbers was finally constructed. But even in the 1870s and 1880s, Leopold Kronecker, the father of mathematical Intuitionism, felt able to accept only the whole numbers as 'the work of God', and he tried to rid mathematics of irrational, imaginary, and transfinite numbers.[33]

The conclusion is that the basic likeness between the different types of numbers has not necessarily been obvious. The transfinite excepted, they were assimilated into the same continuum, but only with great difficulty and over a prolonged period of time. Their assimilation to one another took place as the end result of hesitation, conflict, redefinition, and clarification. This process was fertile for mathematics. What must have been decisive in the long run was the repeated demonstration that it was mathematically useful to include different types of numbers in the same continuum, on the assumption that they belonged together both functionally and theoretically.

If the history of the number continuum can serve as a guide, it seems that the comparability of things, their likeness that repays careful attention, sometimes becomes evident, not as the result of immediate, intuitive understanding, but of the prolonged effort of many persons. In any case, history shows that the question as to whether something is or is not genuinely comparable with something else is likely to be answered by the interests of the person, group, or circumstance that decides.

Consider this matter of interests. Suppose that an imaginative ethologist, with his own interest in differential biology, had asked himself about the relativity of environments, and suppose that he took an oak tree as a convenient, limited example of an environment. But having fixed on the example of an oak tree, his first question would surely be, 'An oak tree to whom or to what?' The question might be accompanied in his mind by the images of, say, an imaginative little girl, who might like to play in the oak's branches; of a superstitious peasant, who might see it as the residence of an evil demon; of a fox, which might lie among its spreading roots; of an owl, which might perch on it; of a squirrel, which might climb its branches and gather its acorns, and of a bark-boring beetle. Each of these creatures would find the same tree to constitute a quite different environment; yet it would be absurd to ask which of them was right. The most adequate answer would undoubtedly be that given by the imaginative ethologist himself, the only one of the creatures able to grasp the tree as a summation of the different environments, or as the structure common to them all. His very demonstration of the environmental differences would also be the provision of a common framework for them, which is to say, of a means for comparing them.[34]

This conclusion allows us to identify what seems to have been an error in perspective made by those who contend, for example, that the time sense that prevails in different cultures may not be comparable, that the colour sense may have striking local variations, or that languages may be so different that no adequate translations from one into another may be possible. The whole discussion of possible differences in time perception presupposes that we know what we are talking about, for, to talk about its differences, we must assume that the same time which is the subject of our discussion is being stretched, contracted, or otherwise changed in different cultures for a variety of reasons that we attempt to analyse. The whole discussion is intelligible only if we have assumed some common time, which we may as well consider to be clock time. This time is surely structurally common to all subjective or culturally local times, and something in it is surely physiological. When an illness, such as Parkinson's disease, affects the ability to perceive time or space uniformly, one becomes shockingly different from other people, whatever, it may be assumed, the culture in which they live. To give an explanation and an example:

Parkinsonian patients often make 'macro-' or 'micro-gestures' —gestures of the right *sort*, but on the wrong scale (too large, too small, too fast, too slow . . .); these they may perform completely unwittingly, unaware that the gesture is inappropriate in scale. I am often able to show a beautiful example of such 'kinetic illusion' when I demonstrate Aaron E. . . . to my students: 'Mr. E.', I say, 'would you be kind enough to clap your hands steadily and regularly—*thus*?' 'Sure, doc', he replies, and after a few steady claps is apt to proceed into an incontinent festination of clapping, culminating in an apparent 'freezing' of motion . . . This demonstration (when it works! . . .) . . . is literally shocking, because of the clarity with which it shows that what Aaron E. clearly perceives in others he cannot perceive in himself; that he may use a frame-of-reference (or coordinate-system, or way of judging space-time) which departs from 'the normal' in an ever-increasing and accelerating way; and that he may be so enclosed within his own (contracting) frame-of-reference, that it is unable to perceive the contracting scale in his own movements.[35]

So, too, with differences in language. The linguist who tries to explain in just what ways a certain language, that, perhaps, of the Hopi Indians, is totally untranslatable into what he calls Standard Average European comes near to contradicting himself. That is, his explanation either makes no sense or he is, in fact, making a partial translation, by explaining in Standard Average European just what characteristics of Hopi make it impossible to translate and by accompanying his explanation by examples to show what he means.*

The ethologist and the linguist, not to speak of the person engaged in comparative psychology or philosophy, can, at the least, try to discover common conditions, relationships, or principles of explanation. It should not be assumed, without further evidence, that linguistic differences are necessarily paralleled by great differences in action or understanding, and it should certainly not be assumed that such differences necessarily create impassible epistemological barriers to comparison. To give a modest example of misleading verbal differences, two investigators who studied the Kpelle tribe of North-Central Liberia concluded from the analysis of Kpelle temporal expressions that the Kpelle perceived time intervals less accurately than Westerners. Actual tests showed, however, that the opposite was the truth.[36] To give another, less modest example, an investigation into cultural differences in the naming of colours has concluded that they are the result of a more or less uniform process of social evolution. More exactly, the analysis of basic colour terms in ninety-eight languages is said to have shown that the terms,

* A more analytical reaction to Whorf advocates 'focusing on attempts to delimit more sharply the types of language behaviours that do or do not show the Whorfian effect as well as the degree and modifiability of the Whorfian hypothesis'. J. F. Fishman, 'A Systematization of the Whorfian Hypothesis', in J. W. Berry and P. R. Dasen, *Culture and Cognition: Readings in Cross-Cultural Psychology*, London, Methuen, 1974, p. 84.

A recent survey of research says that systematic psychological investigation shows that the Whorf-Sapir hypothesis is mistaken in both its strong and weak forms, but that there is evidence 'that language influences memory in terms of the encoding system it provides for organizing data', and may therefore influence cognition. The author of the survey argues that cross-cultural research into perception and cognition should begin from the local models by which experience is organized, but should assume the possibility that some factors in perception and cognition are universal. B. B. Lloyd, *Perception and Cognition: A Cross-Cultural Perspective*, Harmondsworth, Penguin Books, 1972, pp. 43–4.

which number, depending on the culture, from two to six, can be arranged in a sequence of complexity that accords with the general social complexity of the culture that uses them. In other words, there is a universal pattern of development of colour terms, which, at every step, reflects the universal human pattern of colour perception. All the so-called 'landmark colours' are universal.[37] If this is true, colour terms as such determine nothing in perception, but follow from a common physiology and the complexity of the need for distinguishing between one colour and another. There is no epistemological moral except, perhaps, for a bias in favour of a theory of social evolution.

None of this is meant to minimize the problems of comparison; but there are rational ways of approaching them. When faced with the endless differences between things in fact, Aristotle hit upon the solution of an identical form immanent in never-identical matter. His solution appears to be a metaphysical variant of contemporary attempts to understand 'pattern perception'.[38] These attempts find practical expression in machines designed to read addresses for post-offices. To do so, the machines have to respond to that which is common to all forms of the same letter and, as far as possible, to all the broken forms of the letter. Aristotle and pattern-perception machines strengthen my conviction that opponents of the kind of comparison I have been suggesting may simply be shying away from unfamiliar territories or unwanted intellectual difficulties. Surely, to claim, in advance of any serious effort and for no more than impressionistically stated reasons, that the philosophies of different cultures cannot be compared is to defy common sense, common experience, and an analytical understanding of the situation. A single careful analysis of the difficulties is worth more than any number of casual dismissals on more or less *a priori* grounds.

The truth is that the whole discussion for and against the possibility of comparative philosophy pales in the face of the history of thought. For the truth is that actual contacts have been made and influences exerted by cultures that might have been supposed to be incompatible. Some of these influences are literally visible. In Greco-Roman-Indian art one can see how Apollo becomes Buddha. In characteristic Persian miniatures one can see dragons and clouds that come from China. A Persian miniature bears a quite Chinese flowering branch with a Chinese bird perched on it.*

One can see how, in the late sixteenth century, Japanese merchants or warriors who want to be in fashion and want, perhaps, to ensure their good luck, wear Portuguese clothing and crucifixes; and one can see how Japanese prints, which remain quite Japanese, assimilate European perspective, while, later, European paintings, which remain quite European, adopt principles of composition discovered in Japanese prints.[39]

Our concern, however, is not with art, but with philosophy. For philosophy, the point can be made with the help of a review of the process by which philosophy was in fact transmitted from culture to culture. History shows that the problems of translation arose, sometimes in their most extreme form, and that they were solved in time. The transmission of Greek to Latin philosophy will be sketched in terms of these problems, then the transmission of Greek to Arabic and Hebrew philosophy, of Greek (through Arabic and Hebrew) to Latin philosophy again, and of Latin to French philosophy. Somewhat more attention will then be devoted to the case that concerns us particularly, which is the transmission of Indian to Tibetan and Chinese philosophy.

Translators in Fact: Greek into Latin, Arabic, and Latin Again

Translation has always been a difficult art; but its difficulty has always been most acute during the initial meeting of two languages, before experience has taught how the expression of the one can be adjusted to that of the other. Greece and Rome appear to us to constitute a nearly single, classical culture, yet their joining was a prolonged, sometimes rancorous process.[40] A conscientious translator did not find his task easy. When Lucretius

---

* To be more scholarly, a strong 'Far Eastern influence occurs in the Rashid al-Din landscapes with the introduction of Chinese-type mountains and a greater sophistication in the use of planes and of drawing techniques. The groupings of personages also bear the earmark of Far Eastern painting, as do certain types of clothes, certain facial features, and the ubiquitous cloud forms. These themes all remain in the "Demotte" *Shah-Nama* and the Istanbul *Kalila and Dimna* in the sense that clouds, mountains, trees, certain flowers, groupings and personages, and certain spatial arrangements based on a series of lines continue to be derived from Far Eastern art.' O. Grabar, 'The Visual Arts, 1050–1350', in J. A. Boyle, ed., *The Cambridge History of Iran*, vol. 5, Cambridge, Cambridge University Press, p. 655.

and Cicero set about transposing Greek into Latin philosophy, they complained of the inadequacy of Latin. Lucretius, a pioneer translator in both the linguistic and cultural senses, said, as classicists well remember, 'It is a hard task in Latin verses to see clearly in the light the dark discoveries of the Greeks, above all when many things must be treated in new words, because of the poverty of our tongue and the newness of the themes. . . .'[41]

In the absence of a technical vocabulary, Lucretius borrowed Greek words directly, but he more often created technical equivalents out of words already in use. Cicero, on the other hand, preferred to invent equivalents, *individua*, for instance, for *atomoi*. The different associations of the Latin equivalents must have caused misunderstandings. The Greek word, *arete*, implying harmonious integration, became the Latin *virtus*, implying manly self-control. The Greek *logos*, meaning 'word' or 'reason', became the Latin *ratio*, meaning 'reckoning' or 'calculation'. And the Greek *theoria*, meaning 'viewing' or 'contemplation', was translated by the Latin *comtemplari*, meaning 'to observe carefully' for the sake of augury, or by *considerare*, meaning 'to observe' the conjunctions of the stars, also for the sake of augury. What could a fastidious philosopher have said except that Greek philosophy was untranslatable?[42]

The problem that faced the translators of Greek philosophy into Arabic was, however, distinctly worse, for the languages were very different structurally. Arabic is often characterized as atomistic and linear, meaning that one element in it is simply added to another. It lacks the Greek sense of superordination and subordination, and it lacks the nuances made possible by the concordance of tenses. For the early translators, the inadequacy of the Arabic vocabulary was glaring. Still another difficulty was that the translations often had to be undertaken in stages, the first of which was Syriac. The Syriac translation itself was often obscure because the translator might not have understood the Greek original very well; and when he would come on a Greek word for which he knew no Syriac equivalent, he might merely transliterate it. A translator from Syriac into Arabic could therefore often do no more than approximate the approximation from which he began.

'Arabic translations', it has been said, 'seem to represent the earliest large-scale attempt known in history to take over from an alien civilization its sciences and techniques regarded as universally valid, while other manifestations of the civilization, which were supposed to lack this kind of validity, were more or less neglected.'[43] But though the borrowing was distinctly selective, the difficulties of translation, which have been no more than hinted at, were great. The proliferation of terms must have created a bewildering situation at first.[44] Yet a consistent enough philosophical vocabulary, none of which had existed before, was created. Much of it was was modelled on Syriac terms, and it contained words borrowed outright from Greek and Persian—*jawhar* (or *jauhar*), the philosophical equivalent of *substance*, the Greek *ousia*, is an example of borrowing from Persian. It became clear that word-for-word translation was inefficient and seriously misleading, for two reasons, an Arabic commentator said. 'First,' he explained, 'it is impossible to find Arabic expressions corresponding to all Greek words and, therefore, through this method many Greek words remain untranslated. Second, certain syntactical combinations in the one language do not always necessarily correspond to similar combinations in the other; besides, the use of metaphors, which are frequent in every language, causes additional mistakes.'[45] Finally, as the result of the kind of effort and thought that have been described, Aristotle could be read and clearly understood in Arabic. Translation of Greek philosophy into Hebrew followed a similar course, with similar results.

The passage from Greek into Arabic philosophy underwent sometimes precarious situations, perhaps the most dramatic of which, in retrospect, is described in a story of its early transmission. Greek philosophy is often said to have ended with the Alexandrian academy, which was transferred to Antioch, where it dwindled almost to nothing. The last two students of the last professor at Antioch became teachers themselves, and one of them taught the great ninth-century Moslem philosopher, al-Farabi, from whom this story is derived.[46] The truth is that the process of translation was generally dependent on the ambitions and precarious fortunes of such patrons as were willing to support the study of a subject that seemed no less alien than dangerous to many faithful Muslims.*

The Islamic success in translating did nothing to ease the prob-

* The possible debt of Islamic to Indian philosophy will be mentioned later. What is known of the connections between Islamic and Chinese culture is sum-

lems of the Christians who first tried to become acquainted with Greek philosophy by means of translations or retranslations from the Arabic. In the beginning, there were few if any translators who know both Arabic and Latin. One translator would therefore turn the Arabic into literal Spanish, and another the Spanish into Latin. It appears that the translators often did not understand the meaning of the texts, at least not clearly. Despairing of their ability to translate Arabic terms, they often merely transliterated them. Yet the cultural transfer was made, and made effectively, and the channel that had been opened from Greece to Islam was opened to medieval Europe as well.[47] The time came when translations were made directly from the Greek. Thomas Aquinas took William of Moerbeke as a linguistic adviser and persuaded him to translate both Aristotle and Aristotle's commentators. The end of the process of translation was, once more, substantial success. Medieval European philosophy assimilated the Greek, Latin, and Arabic texts perfectly well for its own needs and could reach a considerable level of insight into these, its philosophical sources. Thomas Aquinas, who did not know Greek, understood whatever Aristotle was available to him exceedingly well.

When Latin began to give way to the new languages of Europe, the problem of translation arose again. To those who, educated in Latin, used French in the sixteenth century, it was clear that French was insufficient for accurate philosophizing. The critical abstract words were missing. There were no *absolute* or *relative,* no *abstract* or *concrete,* no *causality,* and no *concept. System* did not exist yet, and *deduction* meant only 'narration'. Syntax was too simple, too vague, and too irregular for accurate philosophic purposes.[48] Yet philosophy arose in French, too. Montaigne philosophized in it in his wayward fashion, then Du Vair and Charron wrote their more regular philosophy in French, and then Descartes found it apt for his purposes.

Excursus: The Translation of Socrates into Arabic
(Ilai Alon)

The 'translation' of the title just above is an intentional pun,

marized in Needham, *Science and Civilization in China,* vol. 1. pp. 214–19. Needham cites the description of a Chinese scholar who learned to speak and write Arabic in five months, and who became able to translate (Galen) faster than the text could be read to him.

having both the linguistic sense in which it has so far been used and the sense of 'transferral', that is, transferral from one culture to another. In the following chapter-section, something will be said about the translation of Buddha and Buddhism from Sanskrit to (or into) Chinese. Here, the subject is the translation of Greek thought, in which Socrates was displayed as a paradigmatic philosopher and human being, from Greek to Islamic culture.

The Greek influence on Islam was channelled through three main streams: science, philosophy, and popular ethics.[49] Science, which won the support of interested political authorities, came first in time. It was transferred to Islam by way of the sometimes faithless, sometimes faithful translations, the nature of which has already been described.[50] The translations dealt, for the most part, with medicine, pharmacology, astronomy, astrology, mechanics, and other useful sciences.[51]

The second stream of Greek influence was that, as I have said, of philosophy. At first, the term 'philosophy' connoted only Aristotelian thought, but was later broadened to include the thought of other schools. The translation of philosophical texts seems to have been an almost incidental accompaniment of that of scientific texts, either because of the affinity in subject-matter, or even because of the occasional presence of a philosophical book in the same manuscript as a scientific one. Perhaps, too, if this is a reason, philosophy was translated because, like science, it was there waiting to be picked up.

Philosophical translations were more often of the earlier than of the later Greek thinkers. Some were verbatim, many were paraphrastic; still others were simply inauthentic, that is, falsely attributed to the famous Greek philosophers. Thus, of Plato's dialogues, only fragments in verbatim translation have survived, of Aristotle's works in such translation, rather more.[52] Paraphrases of the writings of Greek philosophers, in particular those which had commentaries, are more common than direct translations. Paraphrased philosophers include Plato, Aristotle, Galen (as both philosopher and commentator), and others.[53] As for the falsely attributed writings, they were considerable in their importance. They include the *Liber de causis (Book of Causes)*, said to have been written by Aristotle, but in fact an adaptation of Proclus's *Elements of Theology,* and *The Theology of Aristotle,* a paraphrase of the last three Enneads of Plotinus.[54]

The third stream of Greek influence I have enumerated is that of popular thought, primarily ethics. It is significant in that it represents an oral, popular, rather than learned, tradition, and conveys the mood of the times it represents. A considerable body of such popular, aphoristic literature has come down to us, either in separate collections, or in books, which include sayings attributed to Greek philosophers and sages, dedicated to various topics that might be presumed to interest their readers. In spite of the fact that Greek literature abounds in gnomological collections, of which those of Diogenes, Laertius, Stobeaus, and Plutarch may be mentioned, it is significant that so far no Arabic collection has been found that is a direct and full translation of a Greek source of this kind.[55] Furthermore, even of the aphorisms and anecdotes identified as having their origin in Greek literature, only a minority are given in a direct and exact translation. The majority are given in more or less accurate paraphrase. Their paraphrastic nature may be presumed to be the result, not of scribal error, but, for the most part, of oral transmission.

What was it, or who was it in the Greek tradition that interested Muslims of all kinds, not excluding philosophers and theologians? Socrates makes a good example. He was chosen because he was perhaps the best known of the Greek philosophers, because he had, conveniently, written nothing, and because his basic ideas could be presumed to coincide with those favoured by Islam (Plato, had he met him in his Muslim guise, might have had trouble in recognizing him). Islam believes in the existence of 'national' prophets or messengers who preceded Muhammad, and although I have not been able to find any reference to Socrates as such a messenger, many Muslims, I am sure, would not have flatly rejected the description as blasphemous.[56]

In Muslim terminology, the Socrates we are dealing with is a 'primitive Muslim'.[57] I use this term to describe a man, preceding Muhammad, who strove against paganism, who believed in the one God, who led a life of true modesty, and who, though not obeying all the formal commandments of Islam, followed the basic moral and religious ones in its spirit. The patriarch Abraham, for example, was taken to be a man of this kind.

That Socrates, too, was considered to be a kind of 'primitive Muslim' may be inferred from the sayings attributed to him and from the Islamic terms, such as 'idols' and 'Allah', that occur in them. It is true that the philosopher al-Razi (d. 932?) maintained that the popular view of Socrates was, at best, a partial one, and that Socrates had in fact led a full life, not that of a hermit.[58] But the consensus of Islamic opinion was that Socrates had been an ascetic, who avoided an excess of food and drink, opposed having possessions, dressed in a torn mantle, lived in a barrel (this detail, like others, obviously borrowed from Diogenes the Cynic), and uttered sayings in favour of monotheism and asceticism. It seems that Socrates was recruited by the Muslims in order to lend philosophical, 'scientific' authority to the religious and ethical views they held. They sometimes even used him to fight their personal wars. Al-Razi's description of Socrates came in response to the accusation that he, al-Razi, had been living a notably unphilosophical life.

What I have been saying must be qualified. It was not unanimously believed that Socrates had, in effect, been a Muslim. On the contrary, there were those who looked on him as an atheist and a symbol of heresy.[59] However, even this less widely accepted opinion judged him from a religious, Islamic point of view, and so marked his importance in popular thought.

The material for Socrates's life and for the aphorisms attributed to him was not invented by the Muslims, but was chosen, with a real though perhaps unconscious selectivity, from among the vast Greek literature, many of whose aphorisms were left untouched as uninteresting or unfitting. The translation of the sayings from a Hellenistic environment and their reworking in an Islamic one did not, however, lead to a quite unified conception of Socrates. Aphorisms and anecdotes were attributed to him because the Muslims knew him so well, even though the same aphorisms and anecdotes were attributed in the Greek collections to other persons, of whom ordinary Muslims knew little or nothing. An instance of such a transfer from an obscure to a famous person is the story that Socrates asked the (unspecified) king who had offered him all he wished, simply to move out of the light of the sun.[60]

The subjects on which the Islamic Socrates expressed his views were basically those on which he expressed himself in the popular Greek literature, in Stobaeus, for example. The subjects in question were such as talking and silence, possessions, education, women, and whatever else was characteristic of popular wisdom. To give an instance of this wisdom, Socrates is said to have looked at a woman who had made up to go to town and to have said to her, 'I think that you go to town not to see it but rather to have the town see you.'[61]

Although there is no full, one-to-one correspondence between the Socratic aphorisms and anecdotes in Arabic and Greek literature, the spirit in both is the same. In terms of historic accuracy, the Arabic, of course, suffers from disadvantages, one of which is lack of familiarity with Greek culture, and another, a pervasive religious-ethical interest; but the correspondence is nevertheless close.

In summary, one can say that the popular philosophy of Islam proves to be still another link in the chain of ideas and attitudes that connected ancient Greece with medieval Europe.

Translators in Fact: Sanskrit into Chinese

It is evident that, in spite of all its internal differences, the Greek-Latin-Arabic-Hebrew-Latin chain of transmission constitutes a substantially single philosophical culture (or civilization)—a judgment that will be defended at the start of the following chapter. Now we turn to another philosophical culture, the Indian, or, rather, to the Buddhist fraction of it, in its passage from India to Tibet and, above all, China. As in the previous instances, the history is one of difficulties finally overcome and of a kind of philosophizing finally transmitted to territory that had previously been alien to it.

To begin with Tibet, Buddhism was introduced there, it seems, during the seventh century. It was then, during the reign of a Buddhist king, that an Indian alphabet was adapted for the Tibetan language. Tibetan grammar was explicitly and not very naturally constructed on an Indian model. At the risk of their lives, Tibetan translators travelled to Nepal and often on to India, where Indian teachers expounded the chosen texts to their scrupulous translators. 'Using entirely their own linguistic materials (Direct borrowings of Sanskrit terms are very rare indeed), they produced a highly complex religious and philosophical vocabulary, capable of rendering in faithful translation the whole vast range of Sanskrit Buddhist literature, and usually so accurate that modern European and Indian scholars are able to produce an adequate reconstruction of any lost Indian Sanskrit work from its Tibetan translation. This is made all the easier in that, by the early ninth century, the Tibetans had drawn up lists of fixed equivalents for the translation of Sanskrit Buddhist terms into Tibetan; in order to ensure absolute conformity they retranslated into Tibetan all the texts previously translated that did not conform to the new rules. From then onwards the conventional equivalents, carefully taught by one generation to the next, have been used unerringly up to the present day.'[62]

Buddhism first reached China in the first century **A.D.** It was brought by missionaries, not from India itself, but from Serindia, that is, central Asia. Its first adherents in China may have been strangers, such as official envoys to China, political refugees, and merchants. Buddhism came denuded of its cultural background and accompanied by its notion, strange to the Chinese, of universal suffering and the need to escape it, and the equally strange notion that all passions had to be suppressed.[63]

At first, Buddhism seems to have been taken as an exotic form of Taoism. A story was invented that the great teacher, Lao Tzu, who was known to have disappeared in the West, had reappeared, incarnated as Buddha, in India, where he had converted the Indians to the Taoism that they were now bringing to China. Early translations made the acceptance of Buddhism easier by their neglect of basic doctrines, those of the 'four noble truths', the chain of causation, and the like. Instead, like the Taoists, they stressed particular techniques of breathing and meditation. Reasonably enough, the Chinese supposed that the Buddhist belief in the cycle of rebirths implied the immortality of the soul, and they therefore made a quite fatal error from the Buddhist standpoint. But the Buddhist's presumed quest for immortality created a further resemblance with Taoism. It was several centuries before the Chinese were in a position to understand Buddhism in its authentic specificity.

No wonder, then, that the early translations of Buddhist scriptures made liberal use of familiar Taoist terms. The word *tao* itself, the Chinese *way*, with a whole rich set of Chinese associations, might be used to translate the Indian *dharma*, the associations of which clustered around the meaning of 'teaching' or 'doctrine'. *Tao* was also used to translate *enlightenment (bodhi)*. The Taoist kind of *pure man* or *immortal (chen-jen)* was assumed to be the same, for translation purposes, as the Indian *worthy one* or *saint (arhat)* who, while still appearing in his normal bodily form, has attained nirvana. For *nirvana* or *śunyata (nirvanic emptiness)*, the Chinese translators substituted the not obviously identical Taoist term, *non-action (wu wei)*. And the Indian *morality (śila)* was translated by the Chinese *filial submission (hsiao-hsun)*. The actual proportion of Taoist terms in the translations might not have been high, but the terms were important ones. Comfortable as a Taoist reader might have felt with a translated Buddhist text, the meaning he got out of it could hardly have been a Buddhist one.

In India, sacred texts were usually transmitted by memory. The early translations were therefore often made from the recitation of a foreign monk. Someone else, perhaps, translated the recitation orally into Chinese, and still someone else wrote it down in Chinese. Stories were told of prodigious feats of memory on the part of the reciting monks, though the feats were sometimes marred by serious lapses:

> In 380 Samghadeva, a monk from Kashmir, translated from memory a text which in the Chinese version contained more than 380,000 characters. Prodigious though his memory was, it appears that he had forgotten a chapter. It was added later from recitation by another monk from Kashmir. In 407 two Indian monks wrote down a text which they knew by heart. It took them a full year, but it was not until six years later, in 414, that they had learned Chinese well enough to be able to translate the text into Chinese. We know of at least one instance in which the Chinese decided to put the memory of an Indian monk to the test. This was in 410 when Buddhayashas was invited to learn by heart, in three days, forty pages of prescriptions and census registers. He was able to recite them without making any mistakes in the weight of a drug or census figure. After having been tried in this way Buddhayashas orally translated a text, which in Chinese ran to more than 630,000 characters.[64]

The earliest translations were in the main paraphrases or excerpts. In either case they were made obscure by technical terms whose meaning had not been clearly fixed and by language devoid of the form so necessary for comprehension in Chinese. It is hard to imagine what the Chinese, still innocent of Buddhist doctrine, could have made of them. But the process of translation became more elaborate and careful, the translators became better versed in whichever of the languages was, to begin with, foreign to them, and bureaus of translation were set up under imperial patronage. The perennial issue of good style, to which the Chinese were peculiarly sensitive, as against literal faithfulness, came into the open. A champion of faithfulness would oppose the subjectivity and the non-Buddhist concepts that crept into the work of the more literary translators. He would warn against the preference for literary grace over substance, against the tendency to skip repetitions, chanted verses, and long explanations, and he would warn that it was difficult to transmit the profound sense of truths that had been preached a thousand years earlier.

Two, perhaps, of the great translators may be mentioned by name. The first of them, Kumarajiva, lived in the late fourth and the early fifth centuries. Opposed to literal translation, he mourned its loss of elegance. 'Though one may understand the general idea,' he said, 'one entirely misses the style. It is as if one chewed rice and gave it to someone else; not only would it be tasteless, but it might make him spit it out.'[65] But though against literalism, Kumarajiva was careful to get the basic meaning right.

The master held the text in his hands and proclaimed its meaning in Chinese. He would explain the foreign text twice, taking great pains to select the exact phraseology to convey the meaning of the original. If some pages were missing from the text he was using, he tried to obtain another copy of the same text to supply the missing portions. In the meantime the audience of monks was discussing the meaning of the passages and passing judgment on the literary style. If there were any doubtful points in the Chinese reading, Kumarajiva checked them with the original. When no more changes were to be made, he then had the translation written in its final form.[66]

A disciple said, 'Kumarajiva had superhuman capacities; he penetrated mysteriously into the domain of the truth and attained exactly "the center of the circle".'[67]

The second of the great translators, Hsüan-tsang, lived during the seventh century. He made a famous epic journey to India and back in order to collect Buddhist scriptures for translation. With a good knowledge of both Chinese and Sanskrit, he was tireless in his pursuit of the right word and the fitting style. His translations, made with the help of a team of twenty-three specialists, are more detailed than those of Kumarajiva—he translated formulas of *politeness* and dogmatic clichés quite literally. He worked sometimes with a more developed Indian version. Nevertheless,

Kumarajiva's principles of translation were more widely adopted. Kumarajiva's translations are said to be so lucid and fluent that a number of them have become part of the literary heritage of China. It was his translations that transmitted the thought of the great Indian philosopher Nagarjuna to the Chinese. Where the Sanskrit original still exists, it is possible to judge the nature and quality of its translation into Chinese. A scholar who compared Kumarajiva's Chinese with the Sanskrit says that, except for mishandling of logical terms, the translations are generally adequate to convey the meaning of the originals. In an evaluation of Kumarajiva as a translator, the scholar writes:

'It is apparent from the best of his translations that Kumarajiva must have known both languages very well. His technical terminology was adequate in most respects. . . . Chinese is capable of conveying all the significant lexical and structural meanings of a Sanskrit original. Even with regard to the difficult problem of "cultural meanings", Kumarajiva and his associates realized the nature of the problem, and utilized the device of interpolated glosses to explain Indian matters that translation did not make clear to the Chinese reader. They might have exploited this device more than they did.

'In actual fact, blemishes that need not occur are frequent in Kumarajiva's translations. They are due to haste in translation, too many collaborators, and too little attention to re-checking the edited copy against the original. The damage is not serious in most instances, but where mistranslation confuses the epistemological, ontological, and logical levels, it prevents the Chinese reader from grasping the formal precision which is one of the finest qualities of the original. In this respect, it must be admitted that defects in translation materially hindered the assimilation of Madhyamika in China.'[68] (Madhyamika philosophy, that of the philosopher, Nagarjuna, will be expounded in later chapters.)

The problems of the Chinese translators of Indian texts might have led us to consider those faced by the Europeans who first translated Sanskrit and Chinese into European languages. It would have been interesting to tell something of the linguistic and conceptual tribulations of the Jesuits in China, or of such a man as the German Jesuit, Heinrich Roth, who settled in India in the mid-seventeenth century and learned Sanskrit well enough to hold disputes with the Brahmins in their own language.[69] But we have been discussing the translators not simply because they have had interesting difficulties, but because they have provided us with the proof that philosophies, whatever their origins, can be transferred from one civilization to another. Such transfers, by their very nature, require profound cultural comparisons and adjustments.

Theory, it is said, is one thing, and fact another. No theoretical or aesthetic subtleties should be allowed to obscure the fact that the gaps between different languages and civilizations have often been crossed. The differences that function as barriers raise a challenge, and, the challenge having been raised, they can function as bridges as well. Impulses that attract us to the exotic need not always be resisted. The moral advantage in understanding civilizations that appear alien at first, may be accompanied by an intellectual advantage, for it stands to reason that the effort we make to understand the others, who are so different from us, may help us to understand ourselves more clearly. We and they may be like the red and the blue that are intensified and clarified by their contrast with one another.

2

Three Philosophical Civilizations: A Preliminary Comparison

Ben-Ami Scharfstein

A Word of Caution and a Word of Explanation

Comparative philosophy needs careful analysis of the abstractions of which philosophy itself, whether Eastern or Western, is constructed. Before the analysis is undertaken, however, some background seems necessary. The social background of philosophy has usually been taken for granted, but it has been so different in India, China, and the West that it is reasonable to begin by describing and comparing a number of salient traits of the three civilizations, especially those, of course, that are immediately relevant to the nature of their philosophies. In the case of each civilization, therefore, something preliminary will be said on the usual life and goals of its members; on the social imperatives and religious faiths that philosophy is likely to express and perhaps modify; on the social class or classes from which philosophers have been drawn; on the process of education by which philosophers have been formed; and on the frame of mind in which philosophizing has been undertaken.

There are no doubt readers whose interests in philosophy itself makes them impatient with preliminaries. I should not like to delay them, and I suggest that they turn at once to the chapters that draw their attention. The philosophy they find there may very well raise questions in their minds that will prompt them to return to the preliminary background. If they do not return, they should keep in mind that when the context of philosophical inventions and disputes is unknown, these may appear, quite misleadingly, to be unmotivated and therefore perhaps trivial. I think that a sense of fairness toward such faraway inventors and disputers requires us to know more about them than their bare abstractions. So, I should say, does curiosity.

Before going on to describe and compare, I and my collaborators should like to add a word of caution, to ourselves no less than to our readers. The civilizations we are dealing with have all had a complex history and a practically infinite internal variety. The very unity that allows each of them to be called a civilization may sometimes be questioned, though it becomes more evident when they are compared, that is, contrasted with one another. No single person is competent—surely we, the authors, are not—to give a definitive account of these civilizations. Even a serious though undefinitive account would have to be a complex, massive synthesis. Not only can we not pretend to offer such a synthesis, but we can give very little here of the historical dimension, in the absence of which much that we discuss may not be precisely enough located in time and space or precisely enough qualified. The need for such location is driven home if sheer numbers are considered. For long periods of time, each of the three civilizations has comprised perhaps one fifth of the population of the world—if we choose an arbitrary but convenient date, such as A.D. 1600, it can be estimated that each had roughly 100 million inhabitants of the 500 million total of all human beings then in existence.[1] (I omit Islam because it is not considered separately in the source from which this estimate is taken, Braudel's *Civilisation matérielle et capitalisme*. 'Indian civilization' at this date of course includes a large number of Muslims.)

The difficulties and the numbers just mentioned, which teach caution, need not forestall an account of certain basic traditional features of each civilization, or forestall the attempt to make a preliminary global comparison of their philosophies. Not everything in the description will be relevant in a narrow sense to philosophy, but the object of the description is anything but narrow. In any case, it serves as a beginning, not an end.

So much for the word of caution. The word of explanation with which I should like to preface this chapter is on the relation of Islamic to Western civilization. As the title of the chapter shows, I have counted the civilizations I will be comparing as three, not four, in number, on the assumption, which has already been voiced and to some extent justified, that Islam belongs philosophically to the Western tradition. I admit that in reducing the number of 'philosophical civilizations' to three I have been motivated in part by the desire to keep a complicated comparison from growing more so; but I should not have made the decision without what appears to most scholars good reason.

Let me explain myself. The Islamic world is clearly just as worthy of demarcation as the Greco-Roman, Indian, Chinese, or later European worlds. Like the others, the Islamic world was a synthesis drawing on many sources, in its case, Greek, Jewish, Christian, and Iranian, all these unified by its religion, its traditions, and its revered language, Arabic. It ought to be added, to emphasize the physical dimensions of the synthesis, that the Islamic empire at its height was far greater than the Roman.[2] In relation to philosophical thought, however, the Muslims were basically dependent on the Greeks. Unlike the Greeks, or, for that matter, the Indians or Chinese, they did not have to create philosophy *ex nihilo,* for history had already provided them with a beginning, Greek, or, rather, Hellenistic philosophy, which they exploited, varied, and sometimes extended with great energy and talent.

If one paid attention only to the geographic boundaries of Islam, which in time included much of India, its primary dependence on Greek philosophy might be surprising. Why should Islamic philosophy not have been nourished as much by Indian as by Greek philosophy? To the extent that a clear answer can be given it begins with the Islamic acknowledgement of kinship with Judaism and Christianity, both of which resisted and yet absorbed Greek thought. Like Judeo-Christianity, Islam accepted monotheism, the Bible (according to its own understanding), prophecy, the world to come, reward and punishment, and religion as the source of justice. Not surprisingly, the kinship between Judeo-Christianity and Islam is visible in Quranic stories and ideas, which are often close to those in the Bible, and in *hadith,* that is, Islamic oral tradition.[3]* There is also a visible kinship, both in form and content, between Christian and early Islamic theological reasoning *(kalam).*[4]

---

* Both the Old and the New Testaments are accepted by Islam (Quran 12/46) as manifestations of the divine book, of which the Quran is taken to be the authentic, Arabic version. Differences between versions in the Old and New Testaments, on

This sense of kinship was not, on the whole, extended to Hinduism or to any other Indian doctrine. The Muslim in India considered himself to be part of the great Islamic community, and he preserved what he could of its heritage. The continuing foreignness of Hindu and Muslim has been expressed in two simple sentences: 'The Hindu felt no kinship with the Arab past which the Moslem hugged to his bosom. The Moslem did not feel at home in Vedic India.'[5] Yet Islamic thought was inevitably influenced by Indian thought, and there have been scholars who have judged the influence to be strong. The bold though distinctly atypical al-Razi has been supposed to owe a good deal to Indian influence; the atomism of Islamic theology, *kalam*, has been supposed to have been largely borrowed from India; and there was certainly some interaction between Islamic and Indian mysticism. But even a partisan of Indian influence is likely to agree that it did not change Islamic philosophy in any basic way.[6]

The relationship between Islamic and Greek philosophy is far more evident and powerful. The Arabic word for 'philosophy', *falasafah*, meaning, essentially, Aristotelianism (with Neo-Platonic interpolations), indicates where Islamic philosophy originated; and even *kalam*, which polemicized against the Aristotelian philosophy, would have been impossible if not for Greek ideas and philosophical techniques. Al-Kindi, the pioneering ninth-century philosopher, justified his dependence on Greek philosophy with the words,

We ought not to be ashamed of appreciating the truth and of acquiring it from wherever it comes from, even if it comes from races distant from us. For the seeker of truth nothing takes precedence over the truth, and there is no disparagement of the truth, nor belittling either of him who speaks it or of him who conveys it.[7]

An eleventh-century Arab scholar writes, 'Greek philosophers belong to the highest class of human beings and to the greatest scholars, since they showed a genuine interest in all branches of wisdom'; and a Judeo-Arabic scholar explains how it came about that ' "philosophy" and "Greek" became synonymous.'[8]

The verdict, which surely holds for philosophy, must be that

the one hand, and the Quran, on the other, are accounted for by the charge that the Jews forgot or concealed parts of the divine book. See, e.g., the Quran, 5/16, 3/64, 6/91, and, for *hadith*, Bukhari, *Shahadah, bab* 29.

the civilizations of Greece and Rome, the Christian West, and Islam (including Judeo-Islamic thought) 'are branches of the very same tree'.[9] The 'Western' of my 'Western civilization' is no doubt misleading; but the decision to confine the comparison to three, not four, philosophical civilizations is clearly justified.

India: Diversity, Suffering, Holiness[10]

Constant comparison of the three civilizations might give a picture that was too fragmentary and confusing. I therefore propose to begin with Indian civilization, and, having described it without any break, to use it as background and compare it, relevant feature by relevant feature, with the civilizations of China and the West.

India is a subcontinent and a cosmos. Geographically, it is everything. On one side stand the icy walls of Tibet, five miles high. These enormous mountains shrink, as one enters India, to rugged hills, and the hills smooth out into plateaus and descend to plains. Along the way there extend wet forests and rocky barrens, silt-heavy rivers and dessicated plains waiting for the monsoon to break, and deserts that are slowly being transformed into salt marshes.

The human diversity is equal to that of the terrain. There is a settled population living in crowded cities, in many hundreds of thousands of villages, and in tiny hamlets; and there are bands of nomads of all sorts moving on restlessly with their bullocks, buffaloes, and donkeys. Every profession, formally divided and subdivided, is here, and, it seems, every religion, sect and subsect. Here, too, are every human face and figure (though hair is usually black), every coiffure and bangle, and every colour and degree of dress, down to outright nudity. Mingling with the human population, there are cattle, elephants, tigers, panthers, snakes, birds, monkeys, dogs, and insects. Life is gregarious and loud, so much so that isolation, even if only internal, is an accomplishment. The very dogs can be fierce enough to justify the suspicion, first voiced by the Greeks, that they had been crossed with tigers. The insects are fiercer than the dogs. The fiercest of all, often, are the men and the elements.[11]

The geographical and zoological multiplicity of India has been reflected in the atomization of its history. From time to time, it is true, there arose a conqueror who dominated much of its territory and gave substance to the Indian dream of the Universal Monarch. But India usually consisted of hundreds of different states, joining and separating as if taking part in an intricate, fateful dance. Swept up into the patterns of this dance, or left, perhaps, stubbornly immobile within them, there was the individual human being. He might be the respected priest, the elegant cosmopolitan, the rich landowner, or the trader, rich or poor; but he most often was, as he still is, the peasant, to whom India has, on the whole, been less than kind.[12]

I say this of the Indian peasant although I know of no detailed, careful assessment of his history. I say it although it has been reported that for a long period, ending, it may be estimated, about 500 B.C., India was generally prosperous, with plenty of food, clothing, and shelter.[13] I say it although it has been claimed that the endemic poverty of the Indian peasant was imposed on him by the selfishness or negligence of foreign conquerors, whether Muslim or British. I am also aware that it is easy to project the recent into the distant past. I have no choice, however, except to judge in the light of such history as I have read and to welcome any reasonable correction. Ignoring the early periods, which were probably different for most of the inhabitants of India, it appears that the Indian peasant has always worked very hard and earned extremely little. If he has owned a home, it is unlikely to have been more than a poor hut. Inside this hut, he has hardly had more than a few clay vessels, a sickle or two, and something, maybe, of brass; his wife may have treasured a few silver bracelets, and he, a stunted cow. The Indian peasant has learned to survive on incredibly small quantities of food, which can eke out with boiled leaves, shrubs, roots, and the like. His standard of living, it has been said, is lower than that of Western livestock. An Indian writes:

> For these men Nature, so far as it has been subjugated, is like their cattle—starved, twisted in the tail, and goaded; and so far as it is wild, is like the wild beasts—for then it means flood, dust storms, cyclone, creeping weed or sand, and locusts. They live at the mercy of nature, get very little from it, and take their revenge by making ceaseless war on it.[14]

When the rains fail badly, as they always do, unburied corpses dot the countryside; and when, as often happens, the rains are

too heavy, the rain-swollen rivers carry their victims away.
Describing a famine, an early seventh-century writer says, 'Rob-
ber bands multiplied, and people ate one another's flesh. Human
skulls, white as cranes, rolled on the ground . . . Villages, cities,
whole districts, were deserted.'[15] Describing a famine caused by a
sudden snowfall, which destroyed the rice crop, a twelfth-
century writer says, 'Tormented by hunger, men forgot the love
of wife, the affection of the son, the kindness for the parent,
modesty, pride, and high birth. Fathers abandoned sons, sons,
fathers.[16]

Famine is not the only possible disaster, of course. Diseases
have always exacted a heavy toll; and so have landlords,
moneylenders, and tax-collectors, who have held innumerable
peasants in debt-slavery, especially in the later periods of Indian
history. Even in a relatively early period, however, we hear that
the financial burdens of peasants could be so heavy that all the
inhabitants of a village would flee elsewhere.[17] Tigers, ghosts,
evil spirits, and demons, whose natural medium is the night,
have haunted the day as well, and the recitation of a *mantra*, the
sacrifice of a goat, or a cow-skull with a red rag set between its
horns may not have sufficed to ward them off.

Where there is so much suffering, it is only human to shut
one's eyes to it. People help one another, naturally, but the
helpers and the helped are likely to be in almost the same condition. Those who are much better off, generally insulate themselves against the irreducible press of misery. The dregs of fate
are left to it. Bolder or luckier men manage to accumulate wealth,
while men with an opposite ambition train themselves to become
indifferent to suffering. Because poverty is in any case endemic, it
may be easier to renounce the little one has than to acquire what
one does not have. 'We Hindus', writes an Indian I have already
quoted,

look upon the millionaire as the natural complement of the Sadhu . . . We
deny ourselves every comfort, contemptuously rejecting the Western
notion of improving the standard of living, in order to lay by and leave a
fortune at death, so that we may not be poor in future births . . . I am
inclined to think that the notion that a Hindu considers the world to be
an illusion, in so far as it has not been foisted upon us by Vedantizing
Occidentals, is only an antidote devised by the Hindu moralists to cure
us of our desperate clinging to things mundane.[18]

In the villages of India, money, and its stable, grimly-held equivalent, land, are the subjects of incessant talk and worry. Even when one has enough, misfortune, especially in the incurable form of old age, reawakens anxiety. In the words of an illiterate villager,

While youth lasts, passions rule the actions of man. While property lasts, the glitter of gold makes a man blind. But in old age, man laments for what he did in his youth. With his dim vision, he can no longer see the maddening glitter of gold. Then his thoughts turn to religion.[19]

In India, evidently, the most usual remedies for the human condition are property and holiness. Up to a point, the two have been similar. Like wealth, merit, it is believed, can be stored up, by living according to the prescribed ritual, that is, by performing the right acts, or, when necessary, hiring the priest to perform them. In the latter case, the priest's fee, like the alms given to a beggar, purchases lasting merit. To act so as to store up merit means, among other things, to venerate holy men and holy places, to worship the gods and the powerful forces of the universe, especially fire and water, to obey caste laws, and to show worshipful respect to all living things, except, in practice, to ordinary men, who are too numerous and difficult.

Holy men fall into three broad categories, of the priest, who is the Brahman; of the religious guide or preceptor, who is the Guru; and of the ascetic, who is the Sadhu. The holiness of the Brahman is the result of his hereditary functions, not his personal virtue. Only he can conduct the traditional ceremonies of birth, marriage, and death. Only pure Brahman hands can gather and twist cotton for the sacred thread with which the Brahman invests boys of the upper castes in order to mark their second, spiritual birth. It is the Brahman who draws the horoscope of the new-born child and compares the horoscopes of a prospective bride and groom. He decides the astrological moment when a journey should be undertaken or a crop sown. He tries to avert threatening planetary influences. He blesses new houses, wells, and reservoirs, and he purifies polluted ones. Briefly, he is indispensable—even the statue of a god is animated only by means of his spell. His blessing must be sought and his curse avoided.

The Guru, the religious guide or preceptor, is often but not necessarily a Brahman. Families usually have or share a Guru, who settles religious problems for them and prepares a boy to assume his religious duties. Castes may appoint Gurus as their supreme judges. The founder of a sect, too, is considered a 'guide', 'master', or Guru. A man of great, at least local, importance, he may come to be regarded as a saint, whose words and person are sacred. His devotees may assimilate his sacredness by eating the remains of his food or drinking the water he has washed in. The most attractive of the Gurus have been the poet-saints who taught loving faith rather than ceremonial duty. Like the Brahman, the Guru is imbued with power, and his blessing or curse is assumed to be able to change one's fate.

The Sadhu or ascetic goes under many names, 'Lord of His Passions', 'One Without Attachments to the World', 'Seeker of Union', 'Renouncer', 'Mendicant', or 'Itinerant'. Some of these names are essentially synonymous, others are not, but they may all be comprised under the title of Sadhu, the holy ascetic. There are Sadhus who go naked or who dress in rags, but many wear clothes dyed in a shade of yellow-orange. If the Sadhu belongs to a particular sect, this fact is marked by a sign drawn, usually, on his forehead, by his hairdress, and by the rosary he carries. Considered socially dead, with no further obligations except, perhaps, simple sectarian ones, he lives on the alms he begs. He may settle down in some cave, or by a temple or sacred tree, and then the villagers bring alms to him. He may practice one of the Indian forms of self-torture, which range from dragging heavy chains to walking in spike-lined shoes, to holding an arm up continuously until it atrophies, and to staring at the sun until his eyes are blinded. Strange as it may seem at first, in a country in which there is so much inescapable suffering and in which the maimed are so numerous, it is thought good to increase one's suffering artificially and to maim oneself deliberately.

Tradition teaches that towards the end of life all one's ties should be renounced, and therefore men whose worldly success has been shadowed by the feeling that the world and their success in it are unreal, may join the ranks of the Sadhus when they grow old. As Indians recognize, there are worthy and unworthy Sadhus, the latter being often no more than vagabonds. There are also more than a few psychotic Sadhus. One gives alms to a Sadhu not so much in order to help him as in order to increase one's own merit; but one also feels that acting rightly, which means giving alms, helps to keep the world in its proper state. Besides, refusal to give alms risks the Sadhu's dangerous curse.[20]

There is some analogy between the reverence paid to a holy man and that paid to a holy place. The memory of a great Sadhu sanctifies a place; the presence of a large number of Sadhus affirms its sanctity. Many Indians vow to make a pilgrimage if their prayer is granted. Others undertake it as a penance, or as a fulfilment of a lifelong ambition. Enormous, suffocating crowds gather at holy places at designated times. When the pilgrimage is difficult, the merit it confers is correspondingly great. The pilgrimage to Amaranth in Kashmir may be taken as an extreme example. Its goal is a freezing cave 13,000 feet above sea level, inhabited, it is supposed, by the god, Śiva. The last stages of the eight-day journey need, or used to need until not so long ago, the stamina of a mountaineer; and yet it has been attempted every year by women, children, and men weak from illness. Many of the pilgrims have died what they have believed to be their meritorious death on the way up to Śiva's cave.[21]

One's home, too, is a sacred place. To a Brahman, it is there that lives the fire whose continuity ensures that his line will not be extinguished. Every day he must mention in his prayers the three or five clan-ancestors, including ancient, perhaps mythical sages, of the family. Ceremonies commemorating ancestors unite the dead with the living and the living with one another. To everyone, home is also the residence of the family god, who is respected and courted with offerings of incense, flowers, and water, and with prostrations and prayers. The great gods of the Hindu pantheon, especially Vishnu and Śiva in their many permutations, are known everywhere. But ordinary people are more concerned with local gods and powers, regarded as more likely to do harm. A country proverb therefore gives this advice: 'Pay reverence once to a benign god, for he may do you good, but twice to a malign power in order that he may do you no harm.'[22]

The gods and the powers can grant security, especially when they are, like fire and water, basic constituents of the universe. All worship seems to demand fire and water. 'O Sun!' goes a daily prayer, 'fire is born of you, and from you the gods derive their splendour; you are the eye of the world and the light of it!' Fire and water, the water of even every well and spring, protect against sinful uncleanliness. In his daily prayers, the Brahman fixes his thoughts on the seven holy rivers, and he imagines that his ritual bath is taking place in the most holy of them all, the Ganges. He washes off his sins with the water he sprinkles on his head. As for the peasant, the holiness of water is proved to him each year. In the dry season, the peasant longs for water as he longs for life.

When, after a long drought, an abundant rain brings hope to the despairing husbandman by filling the great reservoirs for the irrigation of the rice-fields, the inhabitants at once flock to them and with signs of joy exclaim, 'The lady is arrived'; and they bow with hands clasped towards the water which fills the reservoirs, while he-goats are sacrificed in its honour.[23]

The lady, water, is thanked with money, with cloth, with jewels, and with food. She who is so bountiful must herself suffer no want.[24]

India: Caste[25]

The gods and powers are able to grant cosmic security, but this is not enough. There remains the problem of security among men, for the sake of which the institution of caste has been invented. Its broad purpose is easy to make out, but its development has been very complicated. It is supposed to conform with the traditional division of Hindus into four social orders, of Brahmans, of warriors, of farmers and traders, and of craftsmen and labourers. The last order, of craftsmen and labourers, is distinctly inferior to the other three. Its members are not privileged to undergo the spiritual rebirth that fits Hindus for the study of their scriptures. Because the term for social order is literally 'colour' (*varna*), it is supposed that the lowest social caste was first made up of the dark-skinned 'aboriginals' who were conquered by the light-skinned Aryans. The distinction between the four orders is of unequal importance in different regions. In South India, for instance, the Hindus are usually either Brahmans or Śudras, members of the lowest order; that is, only two orders are prominent.

While the Indian social orders have often been referred to as castes, it is more useful to confine the term 'caste' to an Indian word meaning, literally, 'birth' (*jati*), in the sense of 'species' or 'kind'. Traditional Hindu law pays little attention to *jati*, which it assumes, implausibly, to have been the result of intermarriage between members of the different social orders. But it is the *jati*, not the social order, which is of immediate importance to most Hindus. It is the caste, in the sense of *jati*, that has its special gods, ceremonies, priests, and discipline, and in which one is born, lives, works, worships, marries, and dies. A caste is evaluated in terms of its rank in the scheme of social orders, so that an ambitious caste may cultivate its holiness by, for example, vegetarianism, or by keeping its distance from other, low castes. It may hope, by cultivating its holiness, to rise in social esteem and be ranked in a higher order than before. The number of castes is naturally great: it is not unusual for a single village to contain members of fifteen or more castes. Not very long ago, the number of castes in India was estimated as about three thousand.

Along with many contemporary Indians, Westerners are inclined to condemn the caste system. Castes are by nature discriminatory, and their laws are certainly cruel to the 'unclean', who include hunters, butchers, tanners, potters, washermen, sweepers, garbage collectors, and others. Not to speak of the outcastes, the lowest caste of Śudras in Bengal has been considered so impure that its touch would pollute the very Ganges. Yet, together with such other basic institutions as the family and the village, it is caste that has given India its stability. Over and again, foreign groups have been absorbed as castes, on condition that they adopt a few universal practices and acknowledge the ritual dominance of the Brahmans. Caste has given India its specialized abilities and its technical training. It has also given self-government unaffected by the rise and decline of kings. The caste system has therefore been called the Hindu form of social synthesis.

To the individual, caste has been all-important. Even the usual outcaste, despite this name, belongs to a caste. For most Indians, social recognition depends on caste. When a traveller enters a village, he states his and his father's name, his caste and his village, and then everyone knows how to react to him. His caste endows him with his place in life.

One's place in life can be lost, however. To call a person 'casteless' is a deadly insult. Expulsion from one's caste, an extreme disciplinary measure, suspends a person from society.

In losing his caste he loses not only his relations and friends, but often his wife and his children, who would rather leave him to his fate than share his disgrace with him. Nobody dares to eat with him or even give him a drop of water. If he has marriageable daughters, nobody asks them in marriage, and in like manner his sons are refused wives. He has to take it for granted that wherever he goes he will be avoided, pointed at with scorn, and regarded as an outcaste.[26]

The situation has been changing. Caste laws are no longer observed on city streets. They are still powerful in family life, however, and in the more conservative villages they have continued without much essential change. Where it has taken effect, the new freedom from caste has demanded its own penalties. A Brahman unable or unwilling to live up to his tradition is likely to feel guilty and vulnerable. If he does, it is also because his identity, in today's language, has become obscure to himself.[27]

India: Life as the Matrix of Philosophy

The description I have so far given of Indian life may be interesting in itself, but its relevance to Indian philosophy must still be unclear. I hope the relevance will soon become clearer. The general object of the description is to display Indian life as the matrix in which Indian philosophy, with its life-induced problems, dogmas, insights, and solutions, was formed. Furthermore, as I shall try to show, Indian philosophical thought was carried on and preserved in 'schools' that were necessarily congruous with the forms of Indian life and with the roles that could be assumed by teachers and disciples.

To make the congruity of Indian life and philosophy more evident, I want to borrow something of the accuracy of anthropological research and to turn, therefore, to two, presumably typical Indian villages in which anthropologists have carried on their observations. The description, like the previous one, will be put in the specious anthropological present, which may or may not give an accurate reflection of life just now. I in no way wish to imply that Indian philosophers were villagers, but only that Indian character, as revealed in research carried on in villages, can be plausibly related to the attitudes that condition Indian life in general and so condition Indian philosophy as well.

The Indian village life I shall describe shows, I think, at least seven characteristics that are compatible with Indian philosophy and that perhaps help to explain its nature. These characteristics are: the villagers' striking cooperation and interdependence; the pervasive hierarchy among them; the everyday distance, varying with social rank, between professed ideals and actual behaviour; the identification of goodness with extreme self-restraint; the presence in many persons of strong latent anger and suspicion; the coexistence in many persons of opposite ideals; and the provocative unconformity of some sects and individuals.

Let me begin with the interdependence of the people in a certain South Indian village, of which we have a good anthropological description.[28] These villagers help one another to repair roofs and build houses, to weed and harvest fields, to observe ceremonies of marriage and death, and to cope with all emergencies. Such cooperation is merely neighbourly; but intercaste cooperation establishes a far more complicated web of traditional duties. For example, certain families of farmers have their plough and other implements repaired every year by a certain carpenter; a certain potter gives certain farmers their earthenware; a certain weaver gives certain farmers a few yards of cloth and a few saris for the women; a certain barber cuts the hair of certain farm families, whose clothes are washed by a certain washerwoman. In return, the farmers give all those who have served them a traditional share of the harvest. Money is neither asked nor paid for these services, although exceptional work, like the making of a bullock cart, must be paid for. The system is one of old family-relationships, and it is hard to change. Every family already has its traditional craftsmen, and a family that dismissed any one of them would find his fellow caste-members unwilling to replace him.

Everyone must know his place and cooperate. In the village council, the minority always gives in. In the family, the hierarchy is headed by the aged, the ranking relatives, and the males. Family ideals are maintained most rigorously by those on the upper social levels. No self-respecting Brahman would imitate the 'animal-like' ways of his social inferiors. The lower one goes on the social scale, the more merely theoretical the ideals become. On the lowest social level, age and kinship can be ignored in everyday life, women are rather free, sexually and otherwise, and they can return a husband's blows or leave him and take another husband.   .

At every level, theoretically, it is the man who rules. His wife touches his feet in homage, washes his clothes, and eats the food he has left in his plate. He is likely to suspect that she is faithless, and he has the right, for any reason, to scold and strike her. She, on her part, wants him to earn enough and to show a friendly firmness; but she hardly hopes that he will always be faithful to her. As for the children, after the age of six, they are expected to act properly and soberly. Their father grows increasingly severe with them.

The attitudes of the different castes toward one another are, on the whole, resentful. The reputation of the farmers is good. They are regarded as hard-working and essential to the whole community. But the Brahmans are regarded as two-faced, and the traders as cowardly, untruthful, and stingy. The villagers say that if a fly falls into the milk, the rich man throws away both milk and fly, the poor man throws away the fly, and the trader throws away the fly after he has squeezed the milk out of it. Educated people think that the others are brutish and, like bullocks, fit only to be goaded, while the uneducated complain that schoolchildren learn penmanship instead of ploughing and crookedness instead of simplicitly.

Religious attitudes are variable. Everyone takes part in the great festivals and ceremonies, enjoys the retelling of the holy legends, and is concerned when misfortune proves that the gods have grown angry or the malevolent spirits have been at work. Otherwise, the young are too busy to pay much attention to religion. The duty of recalling the creator each day is left to the older people. But though it is the aged who repent and go on pilgrimages, very few even of them are religious enough, in the Indian sense, to abandon their homes and property. After they have done what they can to help themselves, the villagers indulge in a characteristic fatalism; but they continue to believe that if they act rightly, their futures, in this life and future lives, will be better. They do not entertain the theological and philosophical notion that souls should be emancipated from the endless process of rebirth. They are concerned, instead, with the hell to be suffered or the heaven to be enjoyed between the time of their death and the time of their subsequent rebirth, and, of course, with the status into which they will be reborn.

These people are noisy, easily angered and mollified, and, though helpful to one another, quite suspicious. Innocent remarks are given a hostile interpretation. No open signs of sexual love are exhibited, praise is restrained, and, of the strong emotions, only anger is given free expression. Personal relations are unstable or ambivalent enough to make the stability of tradition very precious. The villagers think that the old, divinely ordained ways are permanently good. They establish everyone's position, and establish, in particular, the persons to whom he should rightly submit and those over whom, in turn, he should rule. The Brahmans and warriors may dispute for leadership, but within their competence the Brahmans are the lords; and the rich are lords over the poor, the upper over the lower castes, the men over the women, the mothers-in-law over the daughters-in-law, and the older over the younger children. Everyone both submits and rules, except, maybe, a little untouchable girl, who can only submit; but she too will grow up.

The above observations, made, as I have said, in a South Indian village may be supplemented by the more intimate ones made in a north-western Indian village by a psychiatrist born in India and able to speak the local language, Hindustani.[29] His special interest was to penetrate into the mentality of the three upper social orders, the Brahmans, the warriors (in this village, Rajputs), and the traders (in this village, Jains).

If we begin by observing the life of a newly married couple, we find that the couple, as usual in India, remains for a time in the husband's family. This creates difficulties. The husband and wife are not supposed to be openly affectionate to one another, and the man is not supposed to show affection even to his own little children.* He may not keep these injunctions very well, but it is

* Speaking of India in general, an anthropologist says of the young wife, 'Laughter above a demure titter would be a sure sign of frivolousness, and to walk rapidly or unrestrainedly would be a clear indication of boldness or even sexual looseness . . . A man should take no public notice of his wife except to display his complete authority over her. She, in turn, must never give any public display of intimacy and must demonstrate to the world that she regards her husband as a god, deferring to him and fulfilling his every desire . . . A young wife's position in the household remains difficult until she gives birth to a male child. From that time on she is treated with the respect accorded a mother, but her relations with

considered disrespectful of him, while under his father's roof, to demonstrate an emotional, and especially a sexual, life of his own.

A son is born—a daughter might be, but she is regarded as less important. The mother is typically very indulgent to him for the first two years or so, but afterward she begins to repulse him emotionally, because she is concerned to show him that she belongs to the father, not to him. The father, who was or was supposed to be aloof from the start, assumes his authoritarian role more completely. The son, it should be remembered, has great power over his father, because only he performs the rites meant to rescue a dead father from hell; but while the father is alive, the son must suppress his own desires and emotions and submit to him in every way. This relationship between son and father is more or less repeated in the student's to his Guru and the man's to his god. Before father, Guru, and god, one dwells on one's submission, helplessness, and sacrifice of pleasure. This surrender and sacrifice are meant to compel the father, Guru, or god to give whatever is requested of him.

To be moral in this village, as in India everywhere, means to be clean and sexually restrained. After contact with an untouchable, a man of an upper caste, especially a Brahman, will immediately bathe and change his clothes. Cleanliness is not next to holiness, but is holiness itself, although, to complicate matters, a good deal of plain dirt is tolerated. Sexual restraint, which is also regarded as a kind of cleanliness, cannot be absolute, for one must satisfy one's wife and, above all, have children. Hindus suppose that indulgence in sex is easily destructive to both morality and health. They believe that only the man who conserves his semen can be strong, long-lived, and radiantly healthy. Sexual restraint therefore preoccupies upper-caste Hindus, except, perhaps, for the military, whose specific tradition conflicts with it.

To the horror of the conventional Hindus of the village, there are secret cults, joined mostly by Śudras, that hold meetings in

the mother-in-law are never easy. The mother-in-law will accuse her of spoiling the child or, conversely, of punishing it too severely. With the passage of time the wife may gradually acquire considerable power and authority in the family, badgering her husband and effectively dominating him privately if not publicly.'
S. A. Tyler: *India: An Anthropological Perspective*, p. 89.

which the holiest of rules are deliberately broken. At these meet-ings, cult members of both high and low caste eat from a common dish, and, it is reported, the flesh of the sacred animal, the cow, may be served to them. The climactic act of worship, in which god is felt to manifest himself, is intercourse between the men and women, who participate on equal terms. The village also contains a class of holy beggars who try, by sheer force of contradiction of religious law, to compel God to accept them. For this purpose they eat mud and excrement, drink urine, gnaw dead men's bones, and live, in all good conscience, in filth.

The Brahman, warrior, and trader each has his characteristic outlook. It is naturally the Brahman who takes the orthodox rules most seriously. More than the others, he accepts the need to restrain himself, to submit, and to remain scrupulously pure. Restraint may come easier to him because he thinks himself born closer to redemption than other men; but even if he is lax in religious practices, he remains sure of his holiness.*

In contrast with the Brahman, a warrior boy is taught what a soldier must know, the uses of weapons and, traditionally, rid-ing. While a young Brahman used to be sent away to study sacred texts and practices, a warrior would usually get his book-learning from a local Brahman. The warrior is exhorted to be proud, brave, decisive, and soldierly. It is his prerogative, as ruler and soldier, to kill, drink liquor, eat meat, and keep concubines. This preroga-tive conflicts so clearly with orthodox Hindu values that he may suffer internal conflict.

Like a warrior, a merchant of the village may be troubled by contradictory standards. His goal in life is to become rich, and he literally worships a god of financial success. To a religious mer-chant, all the same, the contrast between his own interests and the orthodox detachment from worldly things can be painful. He must suffer not only the dislike of Brahmans and warriors, but his

---

* The same researcher from whom I have drawn this description says in a subsequent research, conducted in another village, that Brahman men showed relatively few symptoms of psychiatric distress. However, six of the seven male psychotics he observed were Brahmans. Despite the researcher's explanation (which I know only from a review of his book), the connection between the Brahmans' relative psychological health and high rate of psychosis remains obscure to me. See G. M. Carstairs and R. F. Kapur, *The Great Universe of Kota: Stress, Change and Mental Disorder in an Indian Village*, London, Hogarth Press, 1977.

own dislike of himself. In compensation, he may be fitfully generous to beggars, liberal to public undertakings, and interested in social reform.

As a rule, the inhabitants of the village are polite and agreeable. Once a quarrel starts, however, their voices rise to a shout, their eyes grow bloodshot, and their whole bodies quiver with rage. They grow extraordinarily, unreservedly angry. This failure of the self-restraint they have been so painstakingly taught expresses the effect of a constant latent anger. In the life of most individuals, there was once an indulgent mother, but she turned cold after a while, and this inexplicable coldness was, in the child's emotion, the first and greatest betrayal of its life, and the harbinger of the betrayals it must expect. The child has learned to feel, all at once, dependent, beloved, omnipotent, abandoned, and deceived. The mother, who has proved herself to be both protective and treacherous, adorable and shocking, appears to be resurrected in the grown man's goddess, who is the true mother of her sons who love her abjectly, but is also Kali, black and demonic, dancing on the man she has decapitated and drained of blood. It has been noted that 'Hindu myth is replete with imagery relating to fantasies of both omnipotence and dependence, which can be traced to their common origin in pleasure of receptivity and privileged freedom during earliest years . . . The effects on Indian culture of the deep-seated maternal attachment are of profound importance to our study . . . The commonest sublimation is intense mother-goddess worship and worship of womanhood in the abstract. But the total cultural pattern turns full circle again in the form of contempt, uncertainty, and distrust of the woman, her continued restriction, and a secret dependence upon her.'[30]

The father, too, has proved difficult to bear. In the early lives of most persons, there had been a cold father, who had added aggression to coldness when he took the mother away. Yet this is the very father one obeys and, if a son, replaces and imitates, the very father that one becomes in time. When father and son are so nearly identified, it is hard for the son to hate the father clearly—tradition says that it is inconceivable for him not to respect and cherish his father. But neither identification nor tradition can kill the anger, which lies hidden in wait for a suitable time and victim.[31]

In summary, the basic experience of the people of this village makes it hard to rely on anyone. Their parents, the emotional prototypes of all other human beings, have been either indulgent and faithless or cold and imperious. The unreliability of people infects the physical world with unreliability, because, rather directly to a young child, and unconsciously to an adult, the emotions that respond to people and to things remain similar. Suspicion is therefore deeply implanted in the inhabitants of the village, and the suspicion is quickly followed by rage. Their world has a paranoidal tinge.

As is usual everywhere, theology and philosophy are left to specialists; but people are sure that each of them is living in one of a series of rebirths, and that their position in the series has been determined by their actions during an indefinitely long past. Individuals as such are of little importance, they think. In keeping with inbred suspicion, the material world is assumed to be only a shifting illusion, from which, after an indefinite number of rebirths, one hopes to be finally released.

Granted these feelings and ideals, moral success has two impressive embodiments. One is the dignified, serene Hindu family that has succeeded in making its difficult adjustment. The other is the genuine Sadhu. Calm, steadfast, detached, undesiring, he has all the qualities whose lack most troubles the ordinary Hindu of the village. Both embodiments are interestingly alike. The one makes its renunciations for the sake of social life, the other tends to renounce social life itself, but does so in a way that confirms the traditions on which this life is based.

And so, I argue, two small, reasonably typical villages, containing no philosophers, can serve as a human background for philosophy. In saying this, I mean to imply nothing about cause and effect. I do not pretend to know whether the kind of life described here had much part in creating the philosophy, or whether the philosophy had much part in creating the life, or whether, as is most likely, both developed in interdependence. But although I do not want to press the issue of social determinism, I am convinced that the life described and the philosophy go together at least fairly well, and that philosophy has earned whatever plausibility it has had in Indian life by virtue of the manner in which it has analysed, confirmed, and extended the experience of life typical to Indians, whether villagers or not.

To be more specific, the ordinary village Indian, like the philosopher, learns the old dogmas of the transmigration of souls and of the effects of a person's deeds on his future, and even, in some villages, the dogma of possible total emancipation from rebirth. The emancipation the philosopher teaches can take root only in an appropriate soil. If the villages I have described are really typical, and not only of the present but also of the past, it is possible to conclude that personal relations in India have encouraged the feeling that the world is disappointing and deceptive. This feeling makes it relatively easy to judge the world to be an illusion from which one should, if possible, escape. The most ancient Indian evidence, that of the Vedic hymns, tells of a different life and different attitudes. But the idea that ordinary existence is deceptive and, by nature, disappointing, is so usual in traditional Indian philosophy, from the Upanishads onwards, that it suggests that the basic deceptions and disappointments found in a modern village are as old as Indian philosophy itself. This suggestion is supported by the traditional rules of conduct that have come down to us in India.

All philosophical traditions have developed in response to characteristic tensions. The predominant tension in India has been that between impulsiveness and sensual gratification, on the one hand, and self-control and asceticism, on the other. This tension surely exists in all human societies. But it seems particularly powerful in India, where hot and cold, emotionally, coexist in sometimes the starkest way.

The combination of the ideal of extreme eroticism and the ideal of extreme asceticism is especially clear in the ancient mythology that tells of the god, Śiva, who, the epitome of chastity, is the natural enemy of lust (the god, Kama), but also, sometimes, the perfect illustration of lust. 'Where Western thought insists on forcing a compromise or synthesis of opposites, Hinduism is content to keep each as it is; in chemical terms, one might say that the conflicting elements are resolved into a suspension rather than a solution. The aesthetic satisfaction of the myth lies here, where the god seems to savour fully and perfectly both of the extremes . . . By refusing to modify its component elements into a synthesis, Indian mythology celebrates the idea that the universe is boundless, that everything occurs simultaneously, that all possibilities may exist without excluding one another.'[32]

In India, emotional 'coldness' or difficult self-restraint has been felt to give one power, in the beginning over one's father, and then, in Indian thought, over reality. This power allows one to dissolve the deceptive vision of the world and identify oneself with reality as such, utterly stable, infinitely satisfying, and as devoid of particular, identifiable signs as the complete ascetic is devoid of particular objects of desire.

So far the 'good', the conformists. But when the strain of life is great, it is possible to sacrifice not, so to speak, oneself, but conformity, and to gain the sense of power by indulging in everything that the conformists have forbidden. The aim of the conformists is to be so clean in the contaminating world that none of the world will cling to them; but the non-conformists try to transcend the contaminating world by wallowing in it and proving that it cannot harm them. Indian philosophers often insist that to be beyond contamination and careless of it is, in the end, identical. This is the sort of paradox of identity they often favour.[33]

In traditional India, therefore, holiness is chasteness and chasteness is power; but holiness and power are also often explicit sexuality. Sexuality, theology, and philosophy are not easily separated in India (or elsewhere, not infrequently). The proper order of things is hierarchical; but it is often, in natural response, emotionally egalitarian. Interdependence is urged and practiced; but so is withdrawal from social life, sometimes before social life has more than begun, but more often in the old man's weary withdrawal from obligations maintained as long as society has formally demanded them of him. In India, human dignity urges that every expression of human love for adult human beings should be muted; but unmuted love for a god or godly man becomes the source of new religions and philosophies. Detachment from the world is advised, but a detailed philosophy of profit is developed, with or without a sense of its incongruity, just as in the life of the merchant. Living things are respected as embodied souls, but a philosophy of ruthlessness is developed, with or without a sense of its incongruity, just as in the life of the warrior. Money and poverty are both holy, and killing and mercy are both prescribed.

The themes that relate to ethics will not be taken up in the present book; but it may have been helpful to indicate how the tensions of Indian life suggest dominant qualities of Indian philosophy, with its asceticism and sensuality, fantasy and realism, selflessness and selfishness, and conformity and rebellion.

India: Gurus, Brahmacharins, and Sadhus[34]

In India, it is the Guru who teaches everything venerable and potent, including philosophy. Therefore, in order to understand the atmosphere in which philosophy has been taught and practised, the Guru and his relationship to his disciple must be understood.

The word *Guru*, meaning 'teacher', implies particular prestige and weightiness—'weightiness' is its original, etymological sense. The Guru's function was, and still is, to teach the sacred writings and traditional conduct of life so as to fit a Brahman for the condition to which he had been born. The word *Guru* became synonymous with *Acharya*, meaning, 'He who knows and practices established tradition', and with *Upadhyaya*, meaning, 'Teacher of the sacred Veda'. His student was known as the *Brahmacharyin*, meaning, 'The disciple imbued with the force of brahman,' or, 'He in whom the brahma-state has been produced by the teacher, the Acharya.' The relationship between teacher and disciple was sacred, for it was the Guru who initiated the disciple into the ceremony of spiritual rebirth, which transformed the disciple into a superior, 'twice-born' person and made his salvation possible.

Rules for this relationship were already laid down in the Upanishads and the old books of ritual law. The rules had many variations, but the spirit of the relationship and many of its details were preserved. Learning by oneself was considered inappropriate and even dangerous. The impression given in the Upanishads and elsewhere is that the truth one learns is a traditional secret. Therefore the relationship between teacher and disciple cannot be casual or impersonal. On the contrary, the disciple must be respectful, serviceable, and trustworthy, while the teacher must be a father who forms the character of his adopted son before he burdens him with the power of the truth.

I do not think that the relationship between an already mature man and his teacher had a really standard form, but it must have been influenced by the rules prescribed for every boy of a higher caste. The boy, the would-be disciple, was supposed to approach his teacher with firewood in his hand, as a sign that he was ready to serve him and keep his sacred fire burning. An impressive ceremony followed, of the adoption of the disciple and of his rebirth as the teacher's son. The disciple was formally granted his uniform, consisting of a staff, a girdle, a piece of cloth, and, in the case of a Brahman, the skin of a black antelope. As part of the ceremony, the teacher touched the disciple's heart and said, 'Your heart shall dwell in my heart; your mind shall follow my mind; in my words shall you rejoice; may Brihaspati [priest of the gods and god of inspired speech] join you to me.'[35]

The standard period of study, or rather, discipleship, lasted twelve years. During all this time, the disciple was a member of the teacher's family and served his teacher humbly.

We are told in an early source,

Every day, he should put his teacher to bed after having washed his feet and rubbed him. He should retire to bed after having received the teacher's permission. He should not stretch out his legs toward the teacher . . . If the teacher stands, the student should answer after having stood up. He should walk after the teacher, if the latter walks; he should run after him, if he runs. He should not approach the teacher with his shoes on, or with his head being covered, or with implements in his hand [except during a journey, if he sits at some distance from the teacher]. He should approach his teacher with the reverence due a deity, without telling him idle stories. He should keep his face turned towards the teacher, should sit neither too far from nor too near the teacher, but at such a distance that the teacher may reach him with his arms without rising.'[36]

The disciple's chastity was regarded as extraordinarily important, as was his diet, the details of which need not be repeated here. The student was required to be attentive throughout the whole day and never to allow his mind to wander while he was studying. Religious tradition was the all-important subject, with all that it implied of a well-stocked memory, fortified with mnemonic devices, of ritual customs, of grammar and chant for the sacred text, and of interpretations handed down from the teacher's teacher.

As the sacred text itself repeated in a refrain, one must study and teach, study and teach. One must also, it said, be right and true, restrain one's desires, control oneself, be tranquil, tend the fires, make sacrifices, receive guests, be humane, and beget children; but one must study and teach.[37]

No one who has known students and teachers, whether sacred or secular, can believe them capable of literally fulfilling all these ideals. My own relatively informal education, anarchic by Indian standards, has made me smile more than once while I repeated the old Indian regulations. But these ideal regulations were undoubtedly potent. The traditional system of education, which was already taking hold during the period of the earlier Upanishads, helps to explain a possibly puzzling characteristic of Indian philosophy. In India, unlike modern Europe, the open flaunting of originality has been rare. As a rule, tradition has been invoked and original ideas have been attributed to it. The Indian philosopher has no doubt wanted the support of some traditional community. But he has also had a deeply personal tie to his teacher. For him to speculate in open contradiction to his teacher would be to convict himself of a personal betrayal. It would not be very much of an exaggeration to see Indian philosophy as consisting of long chains of disciples, each of them at least pretending faithfulness to his teacher, the whole chain beginning in a sacred, or godly or quasi-godly figure. In later generations, respect for the Guru sometimes turned to worship. The followers of the theologian-philosopher, Ramanuja, have believed that he and the Gurus who inherited his position were manifestations of God, whose presence in them could redeem their disciples.

The Guru may also be the Sadhu, the ascetic. Ramanuja was both in the same person, and so was Śankara. According to tradition, Śankara discovered that the ascetic order he joined was in a bad condition, so he reorganized it thoroughly, dividing it into ten different groups, each headed by one of his disciples. He is said to have given the orders of ascetics a respectability that had earlier been denied them by conservative Brahmans.[38] Each initiate into the order was given and, I suppose, is still given a staff and a new name. He was told that he might wander, by which was meant that he should not stay in any one place more than three days, that he should beg his food as he went, and that he should visit the famous pilgrimage sites. He might also live in a monastery. A book published in 1920 says that the Sadhus of the highest level in a Śankaran monastery 'are almost always well-versed in philosophical literature, and are expected to carry on disputations and to preach and teach.'[39]

India: Philosophical Education and Educational Institutions[40]

The descriptions that have come down to us make it appear that Indian philosophical education was also a religious education of sorts. If we are to believe the idealizing, prescriptive literature, the adherents of each Indian philosophical system had their own educational principles. They thought of philosophy

as something to be lived, like religion, as truth to be realized. It was studied as a means for attaining the highest truth or *mukti*, emancipation which one is to attain by stages of experience, each representing a specific degree of conquest over the body and the material world. A system of philosophy is a system of Release. Thus philosophical study is bound up with a system of discipline.[41]

The description just given is too general and in some ways perhaps misleading. For a closer view, it is possible to draw on a contemporary scholar who has visited traditional Indian schools and who describes the more intellectually oriented education as we suppose it to have existed centuries ago. He reports that the student of the more analytic or intellectual method, though he memorizes a great deal, does so less than is expected of a more purely religious student. He says,

There are various ways in which a child may begin in this method. A favourite way is to start him out with Sanskrit grammar. . . . He will be expected to memorize the rules and to learn to apply them. To watch children applying these rules is something utterly fascinating . . . At each step the child justifies what he has done by quoting the pertinent rule. . . . Often there are conflicting rules or a choice of various methods of explanation. The constructions then are like the problems of geometry. They require not only memory but imagination and ingenuity. If a child can stand this training for the first year, he usually comes to enjoy it, and one can see these young grammarians testing each other after the teacher has turned away from his class. There is more honesty, more patience, and more true teaching in these antiquated *tols* than there is in the Westernized colleges of India, at least to the extent that I have been able to observe them.

The teaching of logic and philosophy proceeds in much the same way. The basic texts offer as it were a map of the universe. All the categories and the major types of relations are there precisely defined. The student is then tested with various sets of circumstances which he is asked, as one might say, to fit into the map. One student will take one point of view, another another, and at each step justification is given by reference to the rules of the game. A senior student acts as umpire with occasional reference to the master. On special occasions, that is, on holidays or on the visit of some great *śastri* [a teacher by the analytical method] from another city, there will be a more formal debate with advanced students and even masters taking part.[42]

The method of mutual questioning has been used systematically in Tibetan theological-philosophical education, which came to Tibet, together with Buddhism, from India. Thubten Norbu, the brother of the present Dalai Lama, describes it in relative detail. He tells us that he chose to be educated in the monastery faculty that stressed logic. In the basic course, he says, the students were taught by means of lectures, not books, and they were required to give quick, clear answers to simple questions. Then came the stage at which the students were set to questioning one another.

Two adversaries would be chosen; the one would squat on the floor, now wearing the pointed yellow hat, and the other would plant himself before him and ask him a question, which the seated student had to answer as rapidly and cogently as possible. One question would follow the other in this way until in the end the quicker and more intelligent of the two would reduce the other to silence. Then the roles would be changed, and he who had to answer the questions would now rise to ask them of his rival. During this kind of exercise we would be working in pairs all over the Chöra, hurling question and answer at each other's heads, often to the accompaniment of a tremendous babble, because a raised voice was regarded as a perfectly legitimate means of plunging the enemy into confusion. The questioner was also entitled to use movements and gestures to press home his attack, though he was not allowed to touch his rival in any way.

In the beginning the question would refer to the simplest things of everyday life and to the common vocabulary of everyday speech. Things and conceptions had to be defined and their application circumscribed . . . Many of these exercises, both simple and complicated, are recorded in the textbooks and can be learned by heart, but presence of mind and quick repartee can be perfected only in constant practice.

These subtly developed exercises aimed at sharpening our intellects were known as . . . roughly 'Intellect Sharpeners'. They were certainly very helpful to us in our efforts to think rapidly and logically.[43]

Such mutual questioning was kept up until the fifth class, in which each student had to take an examination in which he faced all the students of all the classes, each of his fellow-students being allowed to question him on any subject for up to about half an hour. The examination might last, Norbu tells us, for five or six days. He himself took it when he was about eighteen years old.[44]

The love of debate is ancient in India, and so is the formalization of debating rules. In much of ancient Indian literature, whether political and economic, legal, or aesthetic, a dialectical style is used, the possible argument of an opponent being anticipated and refuted at every step. In a general classification of types of debates, the 'discussion' (*vada*) is distinguished from the 'disputation' (*jalpa*) and the 'wrangle' (*vitanda*). The discussion, though conducted in debating style, is primarily meant to establish and impart the truth, the disputation to gain victory, and the wrangle, I suppose, to wrangle.[45]

I cannot go into detail, but at least the atmosphere of Indian debating, with its carefully prescribed rules, may be conveyed by the following description, which is couched in the historical present:

When the debate is to be conducted in a highly formal manner, it is decided at the very outset as to what particular language is to be used, whether a change in language is permissible or not, whether the debaters should as a rule speak in prose, which particular *pramanas* [means of knowledge] are to be recognized as independent sources of valid knowledge, whether the [problematic] Mahavidya syllogisms could be employed or not, whether the arguments are to be necessarily put on paper, whether symbolic gestures, writing on the ground, etc. are to be avoided or not, whether one should urge all the *nigrahasthanas* [formally-recognized 'checks'] that could be detected in the other party's argument or the exposure of one of them would suffice, how much of the opponent's argument is to be reproduced, how many members of a syllogism are to be put forth, or whether each party should follow the practice of his school and so on and so forth.[46]

To continue in the historical present, a formal Indian debate is opened by the umpire or judge, who states the point at issue. The first of the debaters then puts his thesis, which he supports by means of positive proof and the recognized logic of hypothetical reasoning (*tarka*). He does his best to anticipate and answer in advance the objections he supposes his opponent will raise. The first stage of the debate ended, the second stage is opened by the opponent, who demonstrates his understanding of the argument that has been put, by reproducing it completely or, if so agreed beforehand, in part. He then tries to apply a 'check' [a concept I will not stop to explain] or discover a fallacy in reasoning. In the third stage, the first debater, whose turn it is, repeats his opponent's statement of position and tries to find weaknesses in the opponent's charges. In his refutation, he takes the opponent's basic assumptions for granted and convicts him, if he can, of self-contradiction. 'And thus the argument proceeds from stage to stage till the debate comes to an end and the final result is announced by the assembly or council'.[47]

Elaborate formal debates were no doubt held in India, but an account such as the above assails me with a feeling of unreality. I find it particularly hard to believe in a realistic distinction between 'discussing', 'disputing', and 'wrangling', though I concede that there must have been instances of all three then, as there are now, in and out of India. Surely, when all a philosopher's pride was concentrated in the sharpness of his intellect, more than the truth might be at stake. To exemplify what I mean, I will allow myself the luxury of an evocative though not necessarily true story, its crisis caused by logicians' argumentativeness and pride, and its resolution by their mutual love of truth, at least in the sense of mutual recognition of the true victor of a contest. The story concerns the philosopher Raghunatha (*c.* A.D. 1475–1550). Raghunatha, who was blind in one eye, went to study with an illustrious logician, Paksadhara by name. One day, Raghunatha refuted an epistemological theory held by his teacher, who lost his temper, called him a one-eyed infant, and ordered him out of the class. Renewed a few days later, the debate was again terminated by the teacher's insult, this time accompanied by the jeers of the other students. Raghunatha then decided either to force his teacher to admit defeat or kill him. That night, sword in hand, he stole into the house of the teacher, who, as it happened, was out on the terrace, enjoying the full moon with his wife. Talking of the moon, the teacher said to his wife, 'There is one thing, my dear, which is quite as bright, even more so. All evening I was thinking of such a thing. A young logician, who has been troublesome for some time at Mithila, has come from Bengal. This morning he vanquished me by an obstinately conducted argument. In my opinion, his intellect is more luminous than the full moon itself.' Overhearing these remarks, Raghunatha involuntarily dropped his sword and fell at his startled teacher's feet. Paksadhara forgave him and embraced him warmly. Next morning, before all the academy, he confessed himself beaten by the young Bengali logician. This triumph, it must be added, entitled Raghunatha to confer degrees. For anyone who may be troubled by the problem of the historicity of the above story, it may be stated that it is possible from a chronological point of view, and that several writers of the time confirm that Raghunatha was, in fact, one-eyed. In relation to what I have said about Indian teachers, it should be remarked 'that Raghunatha himself never mentions the name of any teacher. Such silence is almost unique among Indian philosophers of his time. One is tempted to ascribe it to his pride.'[48]

If we investigate Indian philosophical education historically, we find many traces in Indian literature of institutions in which philosophy might have been taught in an organized way. Some institutions were apparently attached to temples or endowed by religious brotherhoods. Thanks to the descriptions left by Chinese and Tibetan pilgrims, the best known of the institutions are the Buddhist ones. We also read of spectacular religious disputations sponsored by kings and followed by the mass conversion of the adherents of the losing side. The seventh century translator and philosopher Hsüan-tsang was the hero, his biographer tells us, of one such disputation.

'There were present kings of eighteen countries of the five Indies; three thousand priests thoroughly acquainted with the Great and Little Vehicle, besides about three thousand Brahmans and Nirgranthas and about a thousand priests of the Nalanda monastery. All these noted persons, alike celebrated for their literary skill, as for their dialectic, attended the assembly with a view to consider and listen to the sounds of the Law; they were accompanied with followers, some on elephants, some in chariots, some in palanquins, some under canopies . . . The

Master then began to extol the teaching of 'the Great Vehicle', and announced a subject for discussion. . . . He also caused a placard to be written and hung outside the door of assembly, exhibiting the same to the whole people, and adding, 'If there is any one who can find a single word in the proposition contrary to reason, or is able to entangle (the argument), then, at the request of the opponent, I offer my head as a recompense.'

No one was bold enough to accept Hsüan-tsang's offer. 'Unbelievers of the Little Vehicle, seeing he had overturned their school, filled with spleen plotted to take his life,' but the king intervened. 'From this time the followers of error withdrew and disappeared'.[49]

The monastery of Nalanda, mentioned in the account of Hsüan-tsang's disputation, is the only one of the five Buddhist universities in India of which we know much. It was at the peak of its fame in the seventh century, entered into a decline about the ninth century, and came to an end in the thirteenth. Hsüan-tsang's biographer says that it had ten thousand students and one thousand five hundred and ten teachers; but the figure of three thousand students, given by another Chinese visitor, seems more probable. Students came to it from far away, from China, Korea, Mongolia, Japan, Tibet, Tokhara, and the East Indies. Entrance was by test.

The keeper of the gate proposes some hard questions; many are unable to answer, and retire. One must have studied deeply both old and new (books) before getting admission. Those students, therefore, who come here as strangers (i.e. intending entrants), have to show their ability by hard discussion; those who fail compared with those who succeed are as seven or eight to ten.[50]

The University of Nalanda, as we may call it, was open to everyone who could pass the entrance examination, but the students who did not intend to become monks either paid for their board or did some work to repay the university, 'All possible and impossible doctrines' were taught, not only those of Buddhism. The Vedas were studied, as were the subjects of logic, grammar, and philosophy; nor was magic neglected. But the principal studies must have been Buddhistic, that is, concerned with Mahayana and with the 'eighteen rival sects'. Boys of no more than six to eight might be admitted. They began with

Sanskrit grammar and went on to compositions in prose and verse, and to metaphysics and other subjects. There were many simultaneous lectures. 'Within the Temple they arrange every day about 100 pulpits for preaching, and the students attend these discourses without any fail, even for a minute (an inch shadow on the dial).'[51] In Hsüan-tsang's words,

The day is not sufficient for the asking and answering of profound questions. From morning till night they engage in discussion; the old and the young mutually help one another. Those who cannot discuss questions out of the *Tripitaka* [the Buddhist Scriptures] are little esteemed and are obliged to hide themselves for shame. Learned men from different cities, on this account, who desire to acquire quickly a renown in discussion, come here in multitudes to settle their doubts, and then the streams (of their wisdom) spread far and wide.[52]

At the end of their studies, which were not, it seems, of any prescribed length, some men,

to try the sharpness of their wit, proceed to the king's court to lay down before it the sharp weapon of their abilities; there they present their schemes and show their talent, seeking to be appointed in the practical government. . . . When they are refuting heretic doctrines all their opponents become tongue-tied and acknowledge themselves undone. . . . They receive grants of land, and are advanced to a high rank; their famous names are, as a reward, written in white on their lofty gates. After this they can follow what occupation they like.[53]

The life of individual philosophers seems often to have involved travelling from teacher to teacher. It was the life of a contestant, with (the stories tell us) dramatic conversions and victories and defeats. As an example, we may take the life of the enterprising Kumarajiva, mentioned earlier as one of the great translators of Buddhist texts into Chinese. His mother, who became a Buddhist nun when he was seven, took him along with her, and he spent the years between seven and nine studying Buddhist texts. She then travelled on with him to North India, where he studied Buddhist philosophical texts under a notable teacher and participated in public debates against non-Buddhists. Moving on with his mother, he came to Kashgar, where he studied for over a year, the subjects of his study being a famous Hinayana text, the Vedas, and the five sciences (grammar, logic, metaphysics, medicine, and arts and crafts). He was then converted to Nagarjuna's Mahayanist position. With his mother, he left Kashgar, on the way winning a debate against a famous teacher. At twenty, 'he received full ordination,' but continued to study. When his old Hinayanist teacher came from India, Kumarajiva converted him to Mahayana. He lived in the King's New Monastery in Kucha; but in the year 383, a Chinese expeditionary force took Kucha. Kumarajiva was taken as a captive to the Chinese court (of the Later Liang dynasty), where he studied Chinese for some twenty years. 'When Later Ch'in conquered Liang, he was escorted to Ch'ang-an and welcomed there in 401. He enjoyed the favor and support of Yao Hsing, the King of Ch'in, and spent the rest of his life in Ch'ang-an instructing an illustrious group of disciples and translating a large quantity of scriptures.'

Buddhist monks were apparently often magicians and gave demonstrations of the powers of illusion. Kumarajiva, e.g., often demonstrated them by swallowing needles before large audiences.[54]

To return to the subject of Nalanda, in 1351, after teaching there had come to an end, Tibetans founded a monastery in their own country bearing the same famous name. It contained 'a school for philosophy'. As I have already said, the traditions of Buddhist doctrinal and philosophical education were transferred to Tibet. Only very recently, as Thubten Norbu has explained, an advanced student could choose between monastic 'faculties' of meditation, mysticism, medicine, or logic and debate. Another Tibetan has described his own examination for the degree he considers to be the equivalent of a European doctorate. The seats at the examination, he writes, were filled with scholar-monks. 'These took an active part in the examination which was in the form of a dialectical discussion: the candidate was first required to answer any question the monks shot at him, then in a return attack to put his own question to the scholars. I am told', says the Tibetan, 'that similar practices prevailed in Christian monasteries during the Middle Ages. The examination lasted for three days. . . .'[55]

Although Buddhist institutions of higher learning were destroyed in India, similar Brahman institutions, some of them specializing in logic, were founded. 'Colleges' were often

attached, as I have earlier said, to temples. At these colleges the
Vedas, philosophical systems, and, sometimes poetry and
drama, were taught. How they were taught we can already
guess.

India: Life-Negation and Its Limits

I do not think that the description I have been giving supports the
old, stereotyped idea that Indian thought has been basically
directed against pleasure and against life itself; but this idea is
very persistent, and its direct examination seems to me important.

It has already been noted that Indians have tended towards
asceticism more often and more naturally than modern Westerners, and, to judge them from an alien standpoint, toward an
ideal resembling psychic suicide. Some of them have committed
actual suicide as the fitting end to a life of renunciation. It is, to be
sure, begging the question to condemn ideals as negative unless
we can refute the conception of reality on which they depend; but
even granted, for the sake of argument, that asceticism and
withdrawal from life are negative, it does not follow that Indian
thought as a whole can fairly be characterized as negative.

Indian tradition asserts that life has three ends, which may be
loosely and briefly translated as virtue, utility, and pleasure. It
was usually assumed that virtue preceded utility, and utility,
pleasure. But, as we might suspect even without knowing the
fact, there were persons who argued that pleasure, meaning
pleasure of the senses, and expecially sexual pleasure, was the
source of the other two. In the great Indian epic the *Mahabharata*
(12/167) it is forcefully argued that desire in all its forms is the
basis of all other human ends. Obviously, the argument goes,
people are motivated by the desire for wealth and success, but
religion itself is based on the hope that the person performing a
rite will be rewarded; and, it is further argued, the ascetic himself
would not try to be delivered from the world if not for his desire.
There were also thinkers who argued that utility, meaning especially political and economic utility, was the basic end, and the
source of the others. There were still other, conciliatory thinkers
who argued that the three ends should be cultivated harmoniously, or at their natural times, that is, pleasure in youth, utility in

middle age, and virtue in old age. There were also those who took the convenient view that the pursuit of virtue could be general only in a different, better, cosmic age.

Deliverance from the round of rebirths might be regarded as a fourth end. But deliverance, regarded by some as an inexpressible 'Nothingness', was in certain philosophical systems a condition of superlatively intense existence, akin to earthly love though inexpressibly beyond it. It was also believed, though not, to my knowledge, as part of a specifically philosophical doctrine, that men who had been delivered from the round of life and death could return to earth in a body free of the influence of previous existences.[56]

But not all Indian thought aimed at deliverance of any kind. We know of the widespread acceptance of sceptical and materialistic philosophies, the sophisticated counterpart of the Indian peasant philosophy that says, 'The world is the touchstone. There is no Heaven and Hell after death.[57] The old secular literature is full of humour whose victims are Brahmans and believers.[58] The *Mahabharata* has protagonists who advise, in different ways, that we should make the best of our one brief earthly existence.

Whoever contends that Indian thought is predominantly negative must therefore neglect the traditional, natural, and widely pursued ends of utility and pleasure, and, with them, the detailed Indian philosophies of erotics, politics, and law, and neglect, furthermore, those forms of mysticism that make metaphysical and cosmogonic elaborations on the ideal of sexual union.[59] He must also close his eyes to the historical importance of scepticism and materialism, whether literary or philosophical, and forget the pre-scientific but often complex physics, the theories of perception, some of them, in the philosophical sense, realistic, and intense, hair-splitting debates on the nature and validity of the different kinds of evidence. Even the philosophers who ended with a negative conclusion may sometimes be suspected as making the bow to virtue that allowed them to enjoy the preceding, unvirtuous pleasures of sheer philosophizing. One scholar, who has made a penetrating study of a group of Buddhist philosophers, says that the greatest among them seem to have been freethinkers.[60]

India: Tolerance and Its Limits[61]

One last problem remains to be dealt with among these preliminary generalizations on the life and thought of India. The problem is that of tolerence, the prevailing nature of which, it need not be said, has a deep effect on philosophy. Contemporary writers on Indian thought have often described India, some Moslem rulers apart, as highly tolerant. This judgment is misleading. I have no idea what a statistical comparison of Indian with European tolerance would show, nor is such a comparison really feasible. It is true that there was never a systematic Inquisition in India, nor a dogmatic creed from which it was a crime to dissent, but India was hardly ever a single country, that is, one with an effective central authority. Besides, given India's cultural and political variety, what reasonable conqueror would multiply his difficulties by trying to impose religious uniformity on everyone? There were Islamic persecutions of Hindus, to which I shall soon refer. On the whole, however, the political extremes varied from limited sectarian persecutions, on the one hand, to, on the other, a conscious ideal of tolerance. A pair of Indian kings are especially notable for their tolerance. One of them was Aśoka, who favoured Buddhism, and was exceptionally, though not quite universally, tolerant. The other was Akbar, a Moslem by birth and training, who was not only tolerant, but who tried to establish a new religion uniting the best features of those he was familiar with.

To know the theoretical limits of Hindu tolerance, it is necessary to turn to the Hindu law books. These prescribe that a ruler should support all religious sects that concede the authority of the Hindu scriptures. The most influential of the law books, the *Laws of Manu*, proclaims that

all those traditions and all those despicable systems of philosophy, which are not based on the Veda, produce no reward after death; for they are declared to be founded on Darkness. All those (doctrines), differing from the (Veda), which spring up and (soon) perish, are worthless and false, because they are of modern date.[62]

The 'despicable systems' referred to include Materialism, Buddhism, and Jainism. Their argumentative partisans are called 'logicians', and the Brahman is enjoined 'not to honor, even by a greeting, men who follow forbidden occupations, men who live like cats, rogues, logicians (arguing against the Veda), and those who live like herons'.[63] A believing Hindu is ordered not to visit countries in which rival beliefs are prevalent, nor to accept as a guest anyone who denies the scriptures. 'Let him', the believing Hindu, 'not live', says the *Laws of Manu*, 'in a country where the rulers are Śudras [farmers or labourers] nor in one which is surrounded by unrighteous men, nor in one which has become subject to heretics, nor in one swarming with men of the lowest castes'.[64] 'Deniers' are not legally qualified as witnesses. The *Laws of Manu* even prescribes that the king should expel those who engage in immoral occupations, who are cruel, or who belong to heretical sects. It says, 'Gamblers, dancers and singers, cruel men, men belonging to a heretical sect, let him instantly banish from his town.'[65] No one knows how often these rules were enforced. They suggest an austerity to which India has not generally been equal, for India has been incurably prolific in languages, faiths, and professions. Yet the *Laws of Manu* does codify some admixture of unknown proportions of Indian ideals and practices.

Hindu law books are also severe toward foreigners, literally 'stammerers', defined as those who live in countries where the system of the four social orders is not maintained. Not only were these countries not to be visited, but their languages were not to be studied. The 'stammerers' who came from them were not to be spoken to. For the purposes of ritual purity, they were the equivalents of outcastes, and Hindu mythology predicted that the god Vishnu would destroy them all at the end of the present cosmic age. In the instance of foreigners, too, the evidence is that the laws were not generally observed in all their harshness. Hinduism could never have influenced neighbouring lands as it did if such rules had been adhered to faithfully. There was also the practical consideration that when foreigners were invaders, the prescribed antipathy might stimulate too sharp a revenge.

Within Hinduism proper, caste gradations have always required intolerance. To the Brahmans, 'confusion' of the social orders was a dangerous crime threatening the whole social fabric, and they measured a king's quality by his efforts to maintain the purity of the orders. In the earlier times, however, 'confusion' was not unusual. Some Indians thought the whole system was a sham. Considering the effects of passion, they remarked, no one could be sure he was pure-bred.

Intolerance between sects was common, though people did not always care to which sect, if any, they themselves belonged. Groups of naked but expert 'fighting ascetics' have been common in India for many centuries. Some of them may have been organized in defence against the Muslims; but they have in effect constituted private armies, and the ascetic troops of Vishnu and Śiva have fought pitched and not at all bloodless battles against one another.[66] Nor were hostilities engaged in only by such professionally militant ascetics. In a description of the early nineteenth century, it is said that groups of Vishnuites and Śivaites might curse and rail at one another and finally come to blows. Vishnuites were told in their authoritative texts to regard the followers of Śiva as if they were outcastes or Śudras.

The intolerance of sectarianism could affect philosophers and rulers alike. 'Śankara, according to Anandagiri, did not hold any discussion with the Kapalikas, as their views were professedly anti-Vedic and their rituals offensively anti-Hindu. He simply had them chastised and whipped.'[67] Ramanuja's teacher Yadvaprakśa is said to have grown jealous of him and arranged to have him thrown into the Ganges; but Ramanuja found out in time, the story goes, and he escaped with the help of a kind hunter and huntress. We hear that the king of the country in which Ramanuja settled was a bigoted follower of Śiva. 'It seems that because of some important conversions, Ramanuja was summoned to appear in court.' Luckily for the philosopher, a disciple was willing to impersonate him at court, while Ramanuja himself fled in disguise.[68] The king is reported to have had the eyes of two of Ramanuja's stubborn disciples put out.[69]

The record of Hindu intolerance also includes the 'Heroic Śivaites' who, for the sake of their faith, resorted to murder. A book written about a generation ago records that a festival is still celebrated in Madura 'which commemorates, under the name of the "impalement of the Jains", the execution in the seventh century A.D. of 8,000 Jains by the slow torture of impalement, under the orders of a king who had been a Jain but had been converted to Śivaism.'[70]

The problem of tolerance in India requires a separate account of the relations between the Hindus and the Muslims, who invaded

India, and who conquered a substantial part of it as early as the eighth century. The negative reaction of at least one remarkable Muslim can be gathered from the words of al-Biruni, the tenth-eleventh century historian and scientist. Usually broad-minded and objective, al-Biruni could not stomach Hindu exclusiveness. It hurt him especially that the learned Hindus concealed from him the knowledge he was so eager to gather. In reading his reaction, it is well to remember that he had entered India in the wake of a ruthless Muslim conqueror, and that he was supported by this conqueror's son and successor. Whatever the traditional or immediate reason for their exclusiveness, they maintained it consistently, he reported. In his own words:

They are by nature niggardly in communicating that which they know, and they take the greatest possible care to withhold it from men of another caste among their own people, still much more, of course, from any foreigner. According to their belief, there is no other country on earth but theirs, no other race of men but theirs, and no created beings besides them have any knowledge or science whatsoever. Their haughtiness is such that, if you tell them of any science or scholar in Khurasan and Persis, they will think you both an ignoramus and a liar. If they travelled and mixed with other nations, they would soon change their minds, for their ancestors were not as narrow-minded as the present generation is.[71]

Indians converted to Islam for a variety of reasons. Some converted to escape the poll tax imposed on non-Muslims or to escape persecution, some to escape the caste system, and some, it may be assumed, simply because they were persuaded. Islamic polemical literature found much in Hinduism to denounce: gods who were really demons, responsible for the schisms that led to the institution of castes; gods who were both licentious and impotent, as attested by Hindu mythology; worship that was obscene, meaning, phallic; and doctrines, such as metempsychosis, that were demonstrably false.[72] The Muslim mystics, the Sufis, who were especially eager to convert Hindus, told of Sufi saints who overcame yogins in contests of flying and other miraculous activities.[73]

Hindu image-worship struck the Muslims as idolatrous, and justified, in their eyes, the destruction of Hindu images and temples, certainly in time of war. The eleventh-century Muslim invader, Mahmud of Ghazna, was deeply moved by the beauty of the temples, but not at all tempted, in wartime, to preserve them. Although the number of surviving medieval temples suggests their policy to have been laxly enforced, Muslim rulers discouraged the repair of old Hindu temples and, in theory, refused to permit the buliding of new ones.[74]

Faithfully Hindus reacted to the presence of the Muslims in two opposite ways, by the strengthening of mystical, often egalitarian cults, which resembled Sufism, and by the intensification of ritual, hierarchical orthodoxy. The reaction was also often violent, whether in revolt, massacre, or anti-Muslim vandalism.

The account of intolerance ended, that of tolerance may be undertaken. Some of the Muslim rulers, especially among the Mughals, whose empire survived from the sixteenth to the mid-eighteenth century, practised a notable tolerance. I have already remarked on the outstanding example of Akbar, who married a Hindu princess—in the long run, princesses—and whose abolition of the 'infidel's' poll-tax remained in effect for almost a century and a half.[75] (Later in life, and in violation of his own principles, he grew rather antagonistic to Islam and intolerant of some of its practices.)

There were also forces of tolerance at work among the Hindus, sometimes only in relation to other Hindus, and sometimes in relation to everyone. Sects that were intolerant to one another could be internally tolerant and promise women and low-caste Hindus the salvation otherwise reserved for Brahmans. There were groups of Śivaites and Vishnuites that relaxed caste rules; and there were those that denied all caste rules, together with Brahman supremacy, and so, in effect, dissociated themselves from Hinduism. The adherent of a 'natural' (Sahajiya) sect went as far as to say, 'I understand that the Vedas and their *śastras* [versified teachings] all are false, and that the dharma [law] which the Brahmans and the others follow is all false.[76]

A different tolerance, and intolerance, was shown by the religious monists who practised the joint worship of a number of formerly independent gods. They claimed all these gods to be manifestations of the same essentially indescribable reality. Philosophers, too, learned to reconcile themselves to rivals, but mostly by way of a method that favoured themselves. Thus the Jains granted that rival philosophers had grasped real, but only partial, truths, while they, the Jains, had grasped the whole truth, expressible as a kind of sum of partial ones. Indian philosophers came to favour arrangements of systems, from the lowest, which embodied a mere trifle of truth, to the highest, always, for some reason, their own, which they took to embody the whole superlative truth. The analogy with the hierarchical relations and temperaments of Indians generally is quite striking.

Finally, there was a poetic, religious literature that taught a simple version of monism in which, as in some philosophies, God was believed to be identical with the human soul, while matter and plurality were believed to be illusions. In this basically tolerant literature, each sect naturally regarded itself as superior to the others; yet Śivaites were often satisfied to accept the religions of others as equal in value to their own or as essentially identical with it.[77]

Such tolerance may have been common at times. A ninth-century philosopher, Jayanta, declares that many of his contemporaries believe that all religions have the same goal, all are liberating streams flowing into the same ocean. Indian poetry sometimes makes use of this theme of tolerance in order to attack the Indian forms of social inequality. A widely-known South Indian poem reproaches the Brahmans in these words:

> In the various lands of the Ottiyas, Mlecchas, Hunas, Sinhalese, the slender-waisted Jonakas, Yavanas, and Chinese, there are no Brahmans; but you have set up in this land a fourfold cast-division as if it were an order distinguished in animal nature . . . Who can see any unlikeness of form between men as there is between bull and buffalo? In our life, our limbs, our body, hue, no difference is revealed . . . Does the rain in its descent avoid certain men, or does the wind as it blows leave aside certain? Does the earth refuse to bear their weight, or the sun deny its warmth to certain? . . . Fortune and poverty are the fruit of our own deeds, and death is the common lot of all children of earth; one is their race, one their family, one their death, one their birth, one the God whom they revere.[78]

Through the translator's prose one hears the poet sounding the note of all humanity. To all of us, I hope, this is the most pleasant note on which to end the series of generalizations on India and Indian character and thought.

China, Islam and Europe: Society[79]

For the sake of brief and rough comparison, which is all that I can attempt here, I can do little more than point out that China, the Islamic empire, and Europe, like India, have each constituted a geographical and human cosmos. The geographical and human differences between them should not be allowed to obscure fundamental likenesses. One such likeness is the long dependence of all four on farming. As in India, in China, Islam, and Europe it has been the grubbing farmer, whom we are accustomed to call, with a tinge, perhaps, of derision or pity, the peasant, who has fed the rest of the population. A serious recital of what is known about Chinese and European peasants in comparison with the Indian would not be appropriate here. Instead of attempting it, I will concentrate on the peasants' troubles, of which, even on optimistic accounts, they were rarely free, and which will allow me to arrive at a pertinent observation.

The Chinese peasants, who cultivated their soil with great intensiveness, depended on two silt-carrying rivers, the Yellow River and the Yangtze River. Each year these two rivers and their tributaries distributed life or death or both with their waters, the danger of drought alternating with that of flood. The maintenance of a system of dykes was so important that it accounted in good measure for the development of a strong central government. South China had more rain, and its dependence on the whims of nature was therefore different from that of the North; and there was also the dry land of the steppes across which the nomads came.

How should the register of fortune and misfortune be kept? To what extent does dramatic misfortune conceal the existence of quiet, undramatic contentedness? Even in the nineteenth century, when overpopulation led to a painful shortage of land among peasants, travellers reported that in certain areas of China they found the peasants to be rather prosperous, or at least happy and contented.[80] Yet the register of misfortune is impressive. Someone has calculated that more than 1,800 famines have been recorded in China during the last 1,800 years. To the everyday hazards of life, there were added the disasters of drought, flood, typhoon, locust infestation, plague, and war. Surviving victims might sell their children into slavery, bind themselves to creditors, become what in Europe were called 'serfs', or join a band of outlaws. If not outlaws, the peasants had to pay yearly taxes in crops and work. These were onerous, and binding oneself to a landlord to ease their immediate pressure did not, in the end, make life much easier. 'Despite a certain progress, the thirteenth-century texts still describe the peasant's existence as wretched: with only a plot of land 10 metres square, which he cultivates with the hoe, he slowly raises and lowers the long handle, while in the distance the drums beat out the inexorable rhythm of work in the rice fields. Only the feast days, when everyone spent all his savings, relieved the monotony of life, bounded only by the ties uniting the owner with the worker, sometimes tempered with paternalist kindness and sometimes marked by patriarchal enforcement.'[81] As in India and, for a long time, Europe, the local power was the landlord, for land, which included the peasants who worked it, granted him influence along with wealth and security. It was mainly the tax-collector and the local magistrate who reminded the peasants, who lived in more or less self-governing villages, that the government bureaucracy, though distant, also governed their lives.

It should not be supposed that the peasants of Europe were necessarily better off. The whole population of Europe grew, regressed, and grew again in keeping with biological rhythms that are not well understood, but that may have been broadly the same as those that governed Asia. Perhaps these rhythms were basically climatic; but they were also the rhythms of plague and famine. Plagues persisted in Europe until the eighteenth century, the most terrible among them, the Black Death, a visitant from Asia. To give an example of the incidence of plagues in a place and time we know relatively well, there were forty outbreaks of bubonic plague in the city of Besançon, it has been estimated, between the mid-fifteenth and mid-seventeenth centuries. This illness, a seventeenth-century writer said, made him and the others more cruel to one another than if they had been dogs.[82]

Food was always a matter for concern. There often was not enough of it, and what there was of it was not good enough to maintain an even moderate state of health. The great preoccupation of many, perhaps most, persons was hardly more than to avoid hunger.[83] French historians have made a count of the extensive famines in their country up to the eighteenth century, when the famines ended. There were ten, they say, in the tenth century, and sixteen, the sixteen last, in the eighteenth. It is not hard to match descriptions of Asiatic with those of European famines. In the words of an eleventh-century witness, 'When men had eaten wild animals and birds, under the impetus of hunger, they collected carcasses and things too horrible to speak of . . . Raging hunger made men devour human flesh.'[84] In the words of a modern historian, 'It was not unusual to find people dead at the roadside, their mouths full of grass and their teeth sunk in the earth.'[85] When a famine struck, starving peasants would invade the cities, where they were put to forced labour or left to die in public squares.'[86]

Plague and hunger did not spare the Islamic empire, even during its prosperous heyday, which lasted from the eighth to the mid-tenth centuries.[87] Intolerable taxation led peasants to flee from their land. When they were caught, they were heavily fined, scourged forty lashes, and nailed, I have read, to a wooden yoke.[88]

Whatever prosperity might have eased the lot of peasants at better times or places, it seems to me no exaggeration to say that for the overwhelming majority of the people of China, Europe, and Islam, no less than for those of India, life was often brief and often cruel.* The human response could be cruel or stoically apathetic, but it was also expressed in the huddling together of families for mutual self-protection, in the demand that children obey their parents implicitly, and in the many instruments of salvation devised by the holy and the profane. The Indians and Chinese, especially, chose the family, with its venerated ancestors and anticipated descendants, as an instrument of salvation.

---

* I hope that I do not sound too dogmatic. I realize that economic and demographic history is full of pitfalls and of conclusions drawn on insufficient evidence. It is generally agreed, for example, that from the twelfth to the mid-fourteenth century, the population of Western Europe rose substantially. Prosperity is the simplest explanation of this rise. Yet a scholar judging the evidence for England believes that, despite the thirteenth-century agricultural boom, the poorer English villagers became worse off. Conversely, although agricultural productivity fell during the late fourteenth and the fifteenth centuries, the condition of these villagers, he believes, improved. M. M. Postan, *The Medieval Economy and Society*, p. 142.

Priests, monks, and other holy or magical men preferred their own traditional or untraditional instruments.

Anxiety multiplied objects of fear, and each specific fear, each transgression or demonic threat, had to be answered in a specific, sometimes elaborate way. Each person and each important object and undertaking had to be protected by blessings, charms, or auspicious astrological conjunctions. In view of future life or lives, as of temporary or final hell and heaven, or hells and heavens, pious Hindus, Buddhists, Taoists, Christians, and Muslims lived with prescribed, lifelong care. Only the Confucians, with their down-to-earth attitudes, avoided eschatological anxieties, though they were not exempt from others.

Such facts must be recalled if we are to understand the need, individual and social, for salvation. This need was answered first by religion, but philosophy, too, answered it, and codified its answers with more basic intellectual rigor.

If we turn from the almost universal need for salvation and try to compare social structures, we see that the caste system was unique to India. But Europe and China exhibited other forms of stratification. Even in Athens, with its freedom and philosophy which we still celebrate, the population was divided into citizens, foreign residents, and slaves. In medieval Europe, feudalism provided another form of stratification, which may possibly have been echoed in the stratification of medieval philosophy, just as the Hellenistic social hierarchy, with a ruler-god at its head, may possibly have been echoed in the hierarchy of Neo-Platonic philosophy. For its own adherents, Islam was relatively unhierarchical, but it did make a fundamental distinction between Muslims, on the one hand, and the 'protected' People of the Book (Jews, Christians, Sabeans, and, later, Zoroastrians), on the other, and it did distinguish both of these categories from idol-worshippers and the like, and it did accept slavery.[89]

It is unnecessary to remind Western readers of the changes in social stratification that followed the Middle Ages, or to dwell on the changing degrees of social mobility in European society; but it may well be necessary to remind them of the essential facts of Chinese stratification.[90] The Chinese traditionally classified themselves as scholars, farmers, artisans, and merchants, the merchants being regarded as the lowest, because the least productive, group. A still broader and no less important division was made between 'gentlemen' (*chün-tzu*) and 'little men' (*hsiao-jen*), the former primarily the scholars who had been given official standing, and the latter most of the others. As will shortly be explained, the scholars with official standing were considered to be a superior sort of men, exempted from the others' tax in physical labour, exempted from the corporal punishment that magistrates inflicted, and, in general, legally favoured. The lowest group of all, almost outcastes in the Indian sense, were the 'mean people', the government messengers, slaves, prostitutes, entertainers, policemen, and 'lazy people', who, with their children, were excluded from the examinations for government service. They were not allowed to marry even 'commoners', that is, ordinary Chinese.

The fundamental, legally enforced allegiance of every Chinese to his family required that each family member be responsible for the others' actions; and the same kind of responsibility could be extended to the families living together in the same community, each person and family becoming likewise responsible for the actions of the others. Within the family, the hierarchy was clear: the men were superior to the women and the old to the young. Parents had what amounted to the legal power of life and death over their children of any age.

The family itself was conceived as extending back to its oldest known ancestors, who were honoured by means of the Confucian ancestor cult, and extending forward to all its still unborn members. Everyone was supposed to be respected or 'loved' in keeping with his position in the family and in society. The ruler was considered to be related to his subject as father to son, and a higher to a lower official, or any official to any ordinary person, as elder to younger brother. There was also a special, well-defined relationship between husband and wife, and another between friends. This family structure, like that of Chinese society at large, was one that we, here and now, would stigmatize as authoritarian. Its great virtue was filial piety, in both the broad and narrow sense, and personal, especially familial, loyalty.

Within the individual family, the situation was rather the same as that within the Indian family.[91] This judgment applies not only to the rule of men over women and old over young, but to the few years of indulgence granted a child, followed by years of increasingly rigorous discipline. In the Chinese family, too, the indulgent person was the mother; but her loyalty was not suddenly and completely transferred, as in India, from child to husband. It was therefore characteristic of the Chinese to feel lifelong emotional closeness to their mothers. The father, however, was supposed to be the distant, stern disciplinarian. A Chinese boy might very well dislike his father as a result, but, like an Indian boy, he was under social pressure to identify himself with him and eventually take his place.

The likeness described between the early family life of the Indians and Chinese may possibly explain whey the Chinese have also often been described as easily falling, alone or in a group, into uncontrollable anger. The normal Chinese sense of propriety, though different from the Indian, was as strong; actual self-control under pressure was as weak as the Indian; but the sense of suspicion of everyone and everything appears to have been much less developed in China than in India. How much of this difference in suspiciousness was the result of a difference in maternal consistency? I do not pretend to know, and I cannot easily guess at another explanation. It remains true that although the world of the Chinese was often difficult, it was rarely false in their eyes. Buddhism made it easier for them to see the world, including themselves, in an Indian, illusionistic light; but a Chinese Buddhist usually remained a Confucian and Taoist as well. His feeling that life was an illusion was less simple negation of his personal existence, it seems to me, than regret at its brevity.

Perhaps because we know more about it, it seems harder to generalize about European family life than about Indian or Chinese family life.[92] Europeans, it has often been said, used to live in 'extended', clan-like families, not unlike those of India and China. It is now contended, however, that the small, 'nuclear' family has always been the most prevalent, a judgment that has been made for China as well, where reality may not so often have matched the expansive ideal. It is clear that aristocrats, perhaps especially in France, were often organized into large families, the power of which the civil and religious authorities were interested in weakening; but it does not appear that ordinary people were usually organized so. In any case, the pattern of dominance, like that in India and China, made the male superior to the female and the old person to the young. This pattern of dominance was not, however, as prolonged for the European children, who ceased to be bound to their parents after a certain age, while Indian or Chinese children remained in a child's status during their parents' entire lifetime.

In Europe, children were for a long time taken to be little more than adults still too small and weak to assume normal adult responsibilities, which were thrust upon them relatively soon. Unlike those of the Indians and Chinese, their lives did not begin in nearly total indulgence. On the contrary, discipline was apt to begin close to the beginning of life itself; and treatment of children seems often to have been unfeeling and even cruel. But, in time, the individual began to be more valued as such, and humaneness was urged in its own right. Montaigne pleaded for a more understanding, more humane education, in behalf of which Rousseau, Pestalozzi, and others later made effective propaganda.*

How a European child's upbringing may have been the cause or partial cause of the characteristic mentality that animates European philosophy, I, of course, cannot pretend to know. It may, however, be speculated that the cause was a difference in upbringing that strengthened the tendency to break free of parents, families, and other authorities, and to think independently. Maybe the sending of children to boarding schools and universities weakened parental authority. Maybe parental indifference led to filial indifference or criticism, or, to choose an opposite possibility, the growing tendency of parents to centre their lives on their children persuaded the children emotionally that they were important enough to decide things for themselves. Maybe the East-West difference should be ascribed especially to the

---

* A recent study of family types and attitudes in sixteenth- through eighteenth-century England contends that the sequence there was roughly as follows: First, among the aristocrats, there came the 'open lineage' families, concerned with family honour and estate. Peasant families, too, were basically concerned with land holdings. To such families, aristocratic or peasant, individual happiness was of no great concern. Children were generally treated callously, with the result that most people found it very hard to establish close personal relationships. The 'open lineage family' was suceeded by the 'restricted partiarchal family', based on the authority of the father. Children continued to be badly treated, and, like women, regarded as easily replaceable. Then came the rise, between 1660 and 1800, of the 'closed domesticated family', and, with it, greater intimacy between husband and wife and parents and children, each person coming to be regarded as valuable in himself. L. Stone, *The Family, Sex and Marriage in England 1500–1800*, London, Weidenfeld & Nicolson, 1977.

upbringing of the Indian and Chinese sons, whose independence was restrained, it seems, by stronger family pressures, by a strong, though in India highly ambivalent, love for their mothers, and by a strong early identification with their fathers, whose lives they were meant to continue. These are all, I grant, only speculations, which some reader may be able to pursue more successfully than myself.

The mention of the relative independence of individual Europeans leads easily to that of a social institution that furthered their sense that they were individually capable of thinking and acting for themselves. This institution, to use the word in an extended sense, was the Western city.[93] Cities in India, China, and Islamic lands were often large and socially complex, and they fulfilled many functions, military, administrative, and commercial. 'In the Muslim world', I have read, 'the whole of civilization was found in the town.' But though there was a period, between, roughly, 500 and 200 B.C., when some Chinese cities were sufficiently independent to issue their own coins, by and large, Far and Near Eastern cities never became noticeably independent of the central authorities, who never allowed the development of the sort of city-dwellers whom the English call 'burgesses', and the French 'bourgeois'. The Western city, in contrast, could struggle for and obtain its own charter, legal status, laws, and civic code. Its walls, often represented on its seal, ensured physical and symbolized judicial autonomy. This city, it has been said, was a non-feudal island in the feudal seas, a place where a man's status was not fixed within some rigid hierarchy. In Europe, a man who wanted to be free fled to the city, whereas in China he fled to the village. The relative autonomy of the city naturally fostered that of its citizens, especially the merchants. Like the autonomy of the medieval university, it stimulated the Western readiness to debate political and social issues, without great deference to the political or ecclesiastical authorities.

When India, China, Europe, and Islam are compared, the greater political and cultural continuity of China stands out. This obvious continuity should not obscure the subtle continuities of the other cultures. India has had Sanskrit as the language of holy tradition, and derivatives of Sanskrit as later spoken languages, as Europe has had Greek and Latin as its learned languages, and languages derived mainly from Latin to serve each country alone.

Islam has had Arabic as its sacred language, and, in a non-Arabic-speaking land like Persia, as its administrative language. India has also had its pervasive religious traditions and customs, not to speak of its systems of interrelated castes; Europe has had its varieties of Christianity, its memories of an embracing Empire, and its socio-economic relations that did not end at the borders of any particular state; and Islam has had its traditions spread, as I have emphasized, over an enormous and enormously variegated territory. Yet the unity of China has been more apparent, prolonged, and, in certain ways, influential.

The unity of China can, it is true, be exaggerated, and the divisive pull and richness of its various regions can be forgotten. In a sense, its unity was superimposed upon it by its Confucian bureaucracy. But it was just the members of this bureaucracy or their social likes who were responsible for the Chinese philosophy we possess, or responsible at least for situating it within a single tradition, which they preserved and enlarged to the best of their abilities. Although China went through a period, between the third and sixth century A.D., which the Chinese call the Age of Confusion, and which may be compared with the Dark Ages of Europe, the old culture neither died nor was split as in Europe. Perhaps China's greater geographical unity, denser native population, unifying written language, or effective political ideal were responsible for restoring the Chinese empire, whereas the Roman empire remained shattered. Whatever the reasons, from about the beginning of the seventh century A.D. to about the beginning of the twentieth century, the political and cultural unity of China overcame all threats to its existence. This unparalleled unity was largely the creation of its civil servants, recruited by means of a series of examinations. A relatively small number of these men, their memories stocked with the Confucian classics and other Chinese literature, their bureaucratic instincts and social consciences nourished on historical records, held China and Chinese culture together. They continued to keep much of China alive in their own present, and made their tradition of learning and of art richer and more powerful than a Westerner can easily appreciate.[94]

China, Islam and Europe: Students, Teachers, and Schools

In China, where learning and government were so close, learning had great prestige.[95] In spite of the advantages of students who came from rich, influential families, any able youngster, supported often by the pooled resources of his relatives, might pass the successive government examinations. Even minor success gave considerable rewards, and major success, which could be granted to very few, could lead to an influential position in the central government.

In primary school, set up, perhaps, by a group of families, the beginning student, stimulated by exhortations and not a few blows, would be set to memorizing the classic writings prescribed for children. The village teacher was often, in fact, despised, but teachers were supposed to be honoured, and the more advanced among them were. The relationship between student and teacher was based on filiality, but it did not have the religious associations of India, with its near-worship and menial serviceableness. 'In China,' a cynical nineteenth-century observer says, 'the relation between teacher and pupil is far more intimate than in Western lands. One is supposed to be under a great weight of obligation to the master who has enlightened his darkness, and if this master should be at any time in need of assistance, it is thought to be no more than the duty of the pupil to afford it. This view of the case is obviously one which it is for the interest of teachers to perpetuate, and the result of the theory and of the attendant practice is that there are many decayed teachers roving about living on the precarious generosity of their former pupils.[96]*

* A comparison with traditional Jewish education is in place here. 'Since very early times, Jewish teachers and their students maintained a relationship which was in many respects indistinguishable from that of father and son. Scholars would not only address their pupils as sons, but would often love them all like their own children. Indeed, in terms of the respect and honor due to them, the master enjoyed precedence over the father [cf. *Kid.* 32a; for a similar attitude in the New Testament, cf. *Matt.* 8/21f. and 10/37]. . . . The reason for the preferential treatment to be accorded to the teacher was that "his father brought him (only) into this world, but his teacher who taught him wisdom brought him into the world to come" [*Mishnah B. M.* 2/11]'. M. Aberbach, 'The Relations Between Master and Disciple in the Talmudic Age', in *Essays presented to chief Rabbi Israel Brodie on the Occasion of His Seventieth Birthday* (reprint without date or publisher).

Local and provincial schools were set up by government order, together with a central school of higher studies, the Chinese counterpart of a university. The subjects varied from period to period. During the T'ang Dynasty (A.D. 618–A.D. 906), the subjects, apart from the Classics, included calligraphy, etymology, and ceremonies. There were separate schools for law, calligraphy, mathematics, medicine, and Taoist studies. In the long run, however, it was the Classics and the narrow range of subjects fixed for government examinations that established the nature of the curriculum.

As a parallel to the etiquette with which an Indian student was instructed to treat his guru, the following recommendation written by a T'ang director of the Imperial School may be cited. It should be kept in mind that in this instance, as well, the description is ideal:

When the student first meets his teacher his presents should include a bundle of dried meat, a jar of wine, and a garment-length of cloth of a color suited to the teacher's use. The teacher, coming out of the central door, should be invited to take his seat. The meat offering should be cut, and three cups of wine poured. Then the student, taking his copy of the classic from its case, should, holding up his gown, step forward and request the teacher to explain the general meaning of the text. Thereupon they enter the room. There should be two sessions, morning and evening. At these sessions the teacher should inculcate the principles of propriety, conduct, loyalty, faithfulness kindliness, and friendship. Every ten days there should be examinations, with recommendations at the end of the year.[97]

The principles of gravity, dignity, good character, and respect for the teacher are upheld in this recommendation just as emphatically as they are in traditional India. Just as in India, the teacher is not to be contradicted. But there is no hint of intellectual combat even as an exercise, no hint of the development of critical, sheerly intellectual analysis.*

---

* In Jewish higher education, the great respect demanded for the teacher was not supposed to keep the student from probing and questioning. The student was supposed to greet his teacher with formal respect and walk behind him. Instruction was usually free and repaid by the student's services. 'Many students were impecunious and had to dine at their master's table or subsist on his charity or on an allowance provided by him—or else depend on contributions collected by the master for them . . . Students would not hesitate to question their teacher when

Philosophy, as we know it, demands the critical use of the intelligence. In this respect, medieval Islam and Europe resembled India far more than China. Yet the situation of philosophy in Islam was unique, because Islamic lands, unlike India, Europe, and, in a sense, China, did not recognize philosophy as a profession.[98] There were centres for the translation and study of Greek learning, including philosophy, by which was meant, as I have said, Aristotelian philosophy with Neo-Platonic modifications. But during the entire creative period of Islamic philosophy, from the ninth to about the fourteenth century, philosophy was absent from the curricula of the Muslim institutions of higher learning. Theology (*kalam*), which could be dialectically very keen, was widely taught, but its explicit object was to uphold the Islamic faith, and it used philosophy primarily as the object of refutation. About the fourteenth century, philosophy was finally adopted into the curricula of higher schools, but even then in a theological context. The educational recognition of philosophy is said to have been most usual in Persia, where classical Islamic philosophy is still taught in traditional schools.[99]

Characteristically, the trade of philosophers was medicine. Unlike European philosophers, who were usually university teachers, the Muslims were free from university censorship, though not from social pressure. It seems to have been the ambiguity of their position that made them concerned with defining the philosopher's true social and political function and the duties that accompanied it.[100]

Informal classes in philosophy would sometimes be organized and philosophers would sometimes, of course, meet in groups, but philosophy was generally studied in private. As in medieval Europe, everything began with a text, which had to be commented on. Sometimes the teacher, if there was one, would dictate his own commentary. There are striking and, no doubt, essentially true stories of the devotion of Muslim philosophers to their study. The freethinking al-Razi says,

his actions seemed to contradict his teachings or when his behavior appeared unseemly. Halachic discussions between teacher and pupil were often keen-edged to the point where they could be depicted as "enemies". Such hostility, born out of the vehemence of the argument, was, however, short-lived: "They do not move from there until they come to love each other" [*Kid.* 30b]'. M. Aberbach, op. cit., pp. 13, 14, 3, 4, 20.

So great in fact have been my endeavours and endurance, that in a single year I have written as many as 20,000 pages in a script as minute as that used for amulets. I was engaged for fifteen years upon my great compendium, working day and night, until my sight began to fail and the nerves of my hand were paralyzed, so that at the present time I am prevented from reading and writing; even so I do not give up these occupations so far as I am able, but always enlist the help of someone to read and write for me.[101]

The great Ibn Sina (Avicenna, A.D. 980–1037) writes dramatically of the trials he imposed on himself as a young man. He says that he entered into a set of files a painstaking analysis of each proof he studied, and that when he was baffled, he would visit the mosque and pray that the difficulty be solved. He goes on,

At night, I would return home, set out a lamp before me, and devote myself to reading and writing. Whenever sleep overcame me or I became conscious of weakening, I would turn aside to drink a cup of wine, so that my strength would return to me. Then I would return to reading. And whenever sleep seized me I would see those very problems in my dream; and many questions became clear to me in my sleep.[102]

The great al-Ghazali (A.D. 1058–1111), who was led to abandon philosophy in favour of a perhaps ambivalent mysticism, writes,

From my early youth, since I attained the age of puberty before I was twenty, until the present time when I am over fifty, I have ever recklessly launched out into the midst of these ocean depths, I have ever poked into every dark recess, I have made an assault on every problem, I have plunged into every abyss, I have scrutinized the creed of every sect, I have tried to lay bare the inmost doctrines of every community. All this I have done that I might distinguish between true and false, between sound tradition and heretical innovation.[103]

In medieval Europe, where philosophical teaching was institutionalized, stress was laid on an increasingly subtle and academic method. This, the Scholastic method, had been formulated in part by the codifiers of canon law and influenced by the controversies between the adherents of the Emperor and the Pope. Granted the alert, critical temper of medieval scholars, an ordinary commentary could not probe any issue very far. The desired probing could begin with the analysis of an issue into one or more pairs of contradictory arguments, each argument supported by apparently valid reasoning. Issues analysed in this manner were often disputed in public. A tentative solution was offered to the audience, whose members, speaking in the order of their academic importance, made their comments on it. The bachelor who was offering the solution defended it. At a later session, his master coordinated objections and answers and set the form in which the issue might be published. The most exciting of the Scholastic tournaments took place when a master offered to give impromptu solution to any problem whatsoever raised by no matter whom. While the ideas generated might themselves be important, such disputes were exercises in rational combat, sometimes almost for its own sake.[104]

At its best, the Scholastic method bred precision of thought, and fairness in at least the desire to give full expression to every contender and argument. As at Nalanda, only a relatively small number of the students who undertook to study in a medieval university finished it. The purpose of the university, in a social sense, was to educate doctors, lawyers, and the civil servants of Church and state.[105] In this purpose, the medieval university was like the Chinese institutions of higher education and like Nalanda, if the words I have quoted on the rewards of the sharper-witted Nalandans express a general practice.

Higher education in medieval Europe, like that in China, offered an able student the chance to overcome the disadvantage of birth in a poor family. It taught him how to analyse issues into their constituent parts, how to build up an argument systematically, how to marshal evidence for and against the argument, and how to think in consonance with even formal logic. Although such pioneers of modern philosophy as Bacon and Descartes were reacting violently against Scholasticism, they needed it as a foil, and much of their argumentation was not more than an idiosyncratic, often lax, version of what the Scholastics had said before them. Galileo, too, owed the Scholastics something, and so did Kant, by way of the intermediaries, Leibniz and Wolff.[106]

My impression is that Scholastic argument at its best was as full and keen, though not as varied, as Indian argument at its best. The fact that the Scholastics provoked anti-Scholastic thought and, in this way, the beginnings of modern philosophy, while Indian thought provoked mainly renewed versions of its old self and emotional reactions to its own contentious complexity, may or may not be related to something inherent in the respective methods of education. Surely, however, the advent of modern science and technology in the West, a subject that will soon be returned to, made a difference in the employment of the analytical intelligence that had been so painstakingly evolved there.

I forbear discussing philosophical education in Europe after the Middle Ages. It has been too little studied for me to attempt any summary remarks. I can only repeat that, in time, as everyone knows, philosophers became increasingly independent of tradition and increasingly individual, though not always in every country, and never completely independent or simply individual.

China, Islam, and Europe: Tolerance and Its Limits

Like India, China, Islam, and Europe have given stimulation and shown tolerance enough to allow the development of many clashing ideas, but, like India, they have limited the tolerance, often severely. In the ancient European and Middle Eastern world, some Greek cities, notably Athens, enjoyed a unique freedom of thought for a while. It seems reasonable to speculate that this Greek freedom was possible because of the absence of a centralized priesthood. (China, where scholars rather than priests exercised many of the 'religious' functions, was likewise usually uncoercive in matters of religious or metaphysical belief.) In Greece, a polis priest was sometimes elected; and in the Hellenistic period the office of priest was publicly sold. But although the relative freedom of religion in Greece allowed relatively great freedom of thought, it cannot be forgotten that Socrates was condemned to death, and that an impressive, though perhaps not wholly accurate, roll has been compiled of other Greek thinkers who were fined, suffered banishment, or fled. The roll includes Anaxagoras, Diagoras, Protagoras, Aristotle, and Theophrastus.[107]

The subject of Islamic tolerance, which concerns larger territories, a longer span of time, and more numerous human conditions than does Athenian tolerance, is naturally more complicated.[108] The account of Islamic tolerance in India has shown something of its positive and more of its negative side. To begin with the positive, the Muslims prided themselves on their essential equality with one another. The individual worth of Muslims depended, they believed, only on the degree of their piety. Instead of a hierarchical Church, like the Catholic, with a fixed, embracing dogma, they had the informal consensus of the learned (and powerful). They tended to accept any variation in belief that respected the common Islamic tradition and that did not have unacceptable political implications. To go on to the negative (from our standpoint), Muslim consideration for women and acceptance of the worthy among them into paradise, did not keep the Muslims, any more than it kept the Indians, Chinese, and Europeans, from consigning women to a distinctly inferior social position. Nor did the theoretical equality of all Muslims keep those of pure Arab descent from regarding themselves as superior to new, non-Arab converts. Slavery, as I have said, was accepted, and slaves suffered many legal disqualifications. Christians, Jews, Zoroastrians, as I have said, were tolerated, but consigned to a lower social position; and a Muslim apostate to any of their religions was subject to death. Polytheists, idolators, and freethinkers were, in theory, to be offered one choice—conversion to Islam or death.

Consciousness of the basic human need for freedom was not general and not strongly developed. It was not sufficiently strong, for instance, to produce rebels against societal restraint who might have fought such restraint openly in the name of individual freedom . . . Freedom, as an ideal, was not unknown. As a political force it lacked the support which only a central position within the political organism and system of thought could give it.[109]

As in India, formal disputations between representatives of different faiths were common, and the victory in Islam, too, may well have been won more often by the politically strong than by the dialectically acute faction. It was unwise to be stigmatized as too free a thinker and possibly fatal to so much as hint at blasphemous doctrines. Pious Muslims were often seriously opposed to philosophy and the other 'foreign sciences', even, sometimes, logic. All the same, pleas were made for broad tolerance, and there were Sufis who, like the more tolerant Indian mystics, accepted the essential identity of all sincere beliefs, whatever their origin. The favourite drama of religio-philosophical disputation was sometimes conducted fairly, it seems. An example is given by a tenth-century Muslim, who reports that he attended two philosophical assemblies in Baghdad:

At the first session there were present not only Muslims of all sects, but also agnostics, Parsees, materialists, atheists, Jews and Christians, in short, infidels of all kinds. Each of these sects had its own spokesman, who had to defend its views. As soon as one of these spokesmen entered, the audience stood up reverently, and no one sat down until the spokesman took his seat. . . . 'We are assembled to discuss matters,' one of the unbelievers declared. 'You know the conditions. . . . Each of us shall use exclusively arguments derived from human reason.' These words were universally acclaimed.[110]

The subject of medieval and later European tolerance, which is relatively familiar to us, can be abbreviated and confined to a few words on the tolerance of philosophy. For a time, medieval philosophy and theology contested for leadership. The condemnation of Aristotelian doctrines in 1277, which particularly rejected the claim that philosophy was superior to theology, clearly implied the rejection of the philosophy of Thomas Aquinas. Yet Thomas himself, whose technique of argument was so fair, had defended death as a punishment for heresy. 'Heresy', he had said, 'is a sin which merits not only excommunication but also death, for it is worse to corrupt the Faith which is the life and the soul than to issue counterfeit coins which minister to secular life. Since counterfeiters are justly killed by princes as enemies to the common good, so heretics also deserve the same punishment.'[111]

It is easy to recall the distinguished European philosophers who were condemned by authorities, with consequences ranging up to death.[112] Nicholas of Autrecourt, the sceptical fourteenth-century philosopher, had his writings burned in public and was expelled from his teaching position at the university. Bruno's death by burning is a well-remembered tragedy. Galileo's forced recantation aroused Descartes' caution; and Cartesianism was for some time banned from discussion in Holland. Spinoza published his *Tractatus Theologico-Politicus* anonymously and was afraid to publish his *Ethics* at all during his lifetime. Kant had to promise not to publish his *Religion within the Limits of Reason Alone*. These are notorious cases; but the pressure for conformity they reveal must have affected innumerable others. The pressure diminished in time, but even in the nineteenth and early twentieth centuries, universities in Germany, for example, accepted or excluded thinkers as local orthodoxy decreed. The freedom of Soviet philosophers, among others, is still drastically limited. However, considering everything, and judging in terms of the variety, contentiousness, and individuality of its thinkers, Europe undoubtedly became the most open of the philosophical civilizations.

The limits of Chinese tolerance are exhibited in its reaction to Buddhism, as well as in the reaction of one form of Chinese Buddhism to another. At the beginning, as has been explained, Buddhism was represented as a kind of Taoism. As its true nature became clear and as it became rich and powerful, it was attacked, and the long struggle between the Confucian bureaucracy and the Buddhist monastic establishments was opened. Buddhist monastic property, it was argued, was not taxed, the Buddhist clergy was not subjected to the standard corvée, Buddhist riches were unproductive, Buddhist monks did not serve in the army. Buddhism, it was argued, transferred loyalty from the Emperor to a religion of barbarian origin, unknown to the sages of China. Buddhism, it was said, was barbarous in preaching celibacy, a crime against the family. Barbarously, it caused the body to be mortified in life, and at death to be cremated, even though the body was a precious gift from one's ancestors. In general, it supplanted the authority of the elders of the family.[113]

The Buddhists naturally defended themselves. They claimed, plausibly or not, that Buddha had left his family to become a monk, not in order to repudiate, but in order to repay his parents' love. Confucianism, they insisted, taught filial piety, but Buddhism 'great filial piety', by which they meant, piety toward all living things.[114] The Buddhists also defended themselves in violent deeds. Between A.D. 402 and 517, peasants, inspired by Buddhist leaders, revolted against both the authority of the state and the established religion. The leader of such a revolt was often a monk who proclaimed himself the precursor or the incarnation of the messiah-Buddha, Maitreya, or the founder of the dynasty that would secure the Great Peace (*t'ai p'ing*).

In the seventh century, an emperor forbade parents to do obeisance to a son who had become a monk, and then, to complete the traditional Confucian dominance, decreed that monks and nuns must retain their status as children and subjects and pay homage to parents and rulers alike. He found it expedient to retract the latter decree, but half a century later, another emperor ordered that Buddhist and Taoist monks do obeisance to their parents. Yet these same emperors, for basically political reasons, supported the foundation of Buddhist temples, had Buddhist scriptures chanted at court, and heard lectures on Buddhism.[115]

Buddhists troubled by their own sectarian rivalry tried to reconcile the different versions of Buddhism current in China. In the sixth century, for example, a Buddhist monk, Chih-i, attempted to unite Hinayana with the domianant Mahayana Buddhism. He contended that the difference lay not in the scripture that was read, but in the reader's state of mind. A clear-minded person, he said, would read a Hinayana text and find a Mahayana truth in it, while a dull person would read Hinayana banalities into a Mahayana text. Like the Buddha himself, said the monk, a text taught each person just what he was capable of learning. Hinayana doctrine was for the limited or the ignorant, Mahayana, for the others. But, regardless of sectarian differences, there could be only One Vehicle. Chih-i also appealed to Chinese hopes by claiming that nirvana need not be postponed through an indefinite number of lives—it was possible to become a Buddha in one's present life.[116]

The doctrine flourished only as long as the Imperial Court supported it. As a result of a change in Imperial views, Hsüan-tsang's less conciliatory Buddhism flourished in the seventh century for a time and aroused great interest in its philosophical subtleties. Later in the same century, the Empress Wu, whose rule as a woman offended Chinese tradition, was proclaimed an incarnation of a future Buddha. She supported the school and philosophy of the monk-philosopher, Fa-tsang, who, in return, did what he could to support her. Fa-tsang, too, effected a Chinese compromise and again joined the different forms of Buddhism into One Vehicle promising universal salvation. His basic principle was that of the mutual interpenetration of all phenomena, for, he said, the empirical differences between phenomena, like those between ordinary men and Buddha himself, were only illusions; and if, he said, ostensibly unreal phenomena were as real as they were ostensibly unreal, why discriminate between them?

Despite his arguments against discrimination between

phenomena, Fa-tsang continued to discriminate between higher and lower forms of Buddhism. The doctrinal test he refused to abandon was supported, it seems, by a political test, acceptance at the Imperial Court. His faith in this political test is apparent in his ranking of Ch'an Buddhism. Because the Empress was friendly with some Ch'an monks, but not as friendly as with himself, he placed it in the next to the highest category. His own Buddhism occupied the highest, of course.[117]

Buddhism spread widely among both ordinary and educated people. Poets and painters came to converse with the Ch'an masters and to find retreats in Ch'an temples. Pervaded with a non-Chinese mentality, Buddhism extended the inward and outward horizons of the Chinese. Buddhist monks exercised many functions in daily life. They officiated at marriages and funerals and tended the sick, and they lent Chinese morality the simple human mercifulness that Confucianism, with its stress on family relationships and obligations, had denied it.

However, there was a long-standing and not infrequently bitter rivalry between the Buddhists and the Taoists, and when this rivalry came to a climax in palace politics—the palace eunuchs were mostly Buddhists—the Emperor issued a decree against Buddhism, the most severe and effective of its kind in Chinese history. The decree came at a time of general xenophobia, and was meant to destroy the political power of the Buddhist establishment and restore its assets, including the hoard of precious metals it had accumulated, to general circulation. The decree, which was made public in the year 845, proclaimed:

More than 4,600 monasteries are being destroyed throughout the empire; more than 260,000 monks and nuns are being returned to lay life and being subjected to the double tax [the bi-yearly land tax]; more than 40,000 temples and shrines are being destroyed; several tens of millions of *ch'ing* [a unit of about 15 acres] of fertile land and fine fields are being confiscated; 150,000 are being taken over to become payers of the double tax. Among the monks and nuns are both natives and foreigners. Since the latter make manifest foreign religions, we are returning more than 3,000 Nestorians and Zoroastrians to lay life, so that they will not adulterate the customs of China . . . We have driven away the lazy and idle fellows to a number of more than ten millions. We have done away with their gorgeous but useless buildings to a number not less than a myriad. Thenceforth, purity will guide the people, who will esteem Our effortless rule. Simplicity will be Our policy which will achieve the merits of a common culture. We shall have the people of the four quarters all submit to the Imperial way.[118]

As a result of the persecution that followed this decree, Buddhism went into a decline in China from which it never recovered. The old, vital tie with the distant centres of Buddhism had been cut off earlier, and now the immediate centres, the monasteries, were broken up and the Buddhist elite, the repositories of Buddhist tradition, were dispersed. Ch'an Buddhism, however, survived and even prospered for a while, perhaps because it was so simple, so well attuned to Taoistic attitudes, so close to the intuition the Chinese favoured; perhaps, also, because it depended less on the large metropolitan centres, or, conversely, because it was strongest in provincial centres that were remote from Imperial influence and even antagonistic to it; and perhaps because its monks worked and supported themselves. It made alliances with Pure Land Buddhism, which survived as the easy Buddhism of the populace. Finally, much of it was absorbed by Confucianism, which adopted the aesthetic, metaphysical, and not un-Buddhistic form of Neo-Confucianism. The victory of Confucianism was its partial surrender, and victor and vanquished joined, as so often, in a subtle compromise.

The Three Philosophies: Dogmas and Habits of Mind

When we turn from the subject of tolerance, which conditions philosophy, so to speak, from the outside, to the presuppositions of philosophy itself, we find that in each of the civilizations we are dealing with, philosophy assimilated certain dogmas and habits of mind. What is the difference between a dogma and a habit of mind? Perhaps no more, I take it, than that the dogma is consciously held and maintained in the face of opposition, while the habit of mind is so deeply ingrained that it is never recognized for what it is.

For Westerners, the most easily identifiable Indian dogma or habit of mind is the persistent belief in Karma and transmigration. 'Karma' means 'action,' or 'ritual action', or, in terms of the belief being referred to, 'action bearing its consequences in itself'. By extension, this last meaning becomes, 'the future or effect of one's actions'. The assumption was made that the universe was ruled by a natural moral law, which, for the many Indians who believed in it, connected the *is* of existence with the *ought* of morality. 'As it [the self] does,' one of the old Upanishads said, 'so it becomes; by doing good it becomes good, and by doing evil it becomes evil. . . .'[119]

Because Indians believed that every living thing had a particular organ of thought, they supposed, in explanation of the way that Karma worked, that one's actions affected the organ, and so affected the choice of the body to which the organ would attach itself in its next life. To explain how one's actions changed the organ of thought, they further supposed that the actions or the effects of the actions were precipitated as a fine material, which attached itself to the thought-organ. This moral-material residue then accompanied the thought-organ. It was imagined to follow it, I imagine, as the tail of a comet follows the comet. In short, one was believed to inherit one's fate, in a long circuit of rebirths, from oneself alone.

This whole doctrine was inacceptable to the Materialists (Carvakas), of whom more will soon be said, but was generally accepted by all the other schools. Even the Buddhists, who denied the metaphysical reality and the permanence of the self, accepted it. The possible endlessness of the circuit of rebirths emphasized the possible endlessness of the suffering it imposed, so that each philosophical school, again excluding the Materialists, offered some method of liberation (*moksha*) from it, whether by means of action, knowledge, purity, or faith. Considered in this perspective, each Indian philosophical school had as its basic purpose the teaching of the means of liberation in which it believed.

Parenthetically, it would be wrong to think that no rational defense was ever offered for the belief in transmigration. Indian philosophers argued, as Plato did, that life could only come from previous life. They also argued that because the self was single and indivisible, it could not be the outcome of the combined selves of its parents. Buddhists pointed out that human reactions, especially those of infants, could not be explained on the assumption that persons came totally into existence at birth and went totally out of it at death. They assumed that human reactions were learned from experience, but that the experience of a single lifetime was insufficient to teach us what we obviously knew (what the European rationalists considered to be innate knowledge). To give Indian examples, the infant's withdrawal of its hand from the fire, even preceding all experience of fire, and its ability to suck milk argue previous experience, which is to say, experience in a previous life. It is such experience that explains why different persons have different reactions, from birth on, to pleasure and pain, or, more generally, have different characters. Such Buddhist arguments, which depend on previous learning, do nothing to explain how learning first took place. Perhaps they contain an implicit infinite regress. Another Buddhist argument began with the assumption that our physical and mental states are not strictly correlative. That they are correlative at all, the argument went, is experienced only by each person in relation to himself. Each person, however, remains unconscious of his earliest life, and unconscious, therefore, of just how and when the correlation began; and he is unable to observe when it ends. Even in terms of our own observation of ourselves, we see, our preexistence and our survival after death remain possible. In addition, so went a Buddhist argument (once paralleled by Bergson at length), mental states *may* be caused by physical ones, but *some* mental states are not caused by them. The law of causation has no exceptions, so the mental states not caused by physical states must have been caused by mental ones. Mental states must therefore have preceded the physical states we identify with our present physical existence. Otherwise, some mental states would have been uncaused, an impossible assumption.

Each Indian school of philosophy had a characteristic set of doctrines describing the means for the acquisition of knowledge (*pramana*). It is not fair to consider these doctrines as either dogmas or habits of mind. But I mention them here because they were common, with variations, to all the schools and constituted a traditional foundation of their epistemologies. All the schools accepted direct perceptions as a valid basis of knowledge; all but the Materialists accepted inference as a valid basis; most accepted verbal testimony; some accepted analogy; and so on.[120]

The most apparent dogmas or mental habits of Chinese thinkers were those that expressed their belief in filiality and familiality, and, in natural conjunction with these, their pervasive, serious, and stylized respect for ancestors. It should be recalled that the followers of the philosopher Mo Tzu demanded universal love, in disregard of family relationships, and that they, together with the Taoist philosophers, opposed the ceremonious behaviour and expensive rites that the Confucians believed essential. But Confucianism overbore these objections, and morality became largely identified with ceremonious filiality and its extensions, according to which the ruler bore a father's responsibilities towards his subjects and exercised his prerogatives. It was the clash between the deep-seated belief in filiality and Buddhist doctrine and practice that made Buddhism such an intrusive, alien presence in the eyes of the more committed Confucians.

Another Chinese habit of mind, which, as I have explained, reflected social reality, made book learning and literary skill more important than other formal accomplishments. This habit, too, was resisted, at least in principle, by the Taoists and, later, by the Ch'an Buddhists. But the Taoists' contribution to Chinese habits of mind was not merely negative. The Taoists were very well attuned to typically Chinese cosmological assumptions. According to these assumptions, all nature was alive, animated by its cosmic breath, and kept in balance by the opposed, complementary forces of *yin* and *yang*, that is to say, cosmic passivity or femaleness, on the one hand, and cosmic activity or maleness, on the other. Sooner or later, Chinese thought equated the powers it believed to constitute the changing harmonies of the universe with the social harmonies it kept preaching. Among the Chinese, too, the *is* of existence was equated metaphysically with the *ought* of social welfare.

The dogmas and mental habits of the Muslims have already been touched on. They include the conviction that Arabic was the most beautiful and expressive of all languages, and that the early Arabs were the best of human models. The essential dogma and habit, for it was both, was their belief in their own indisputable superiority and in their right to regard others as either inferior but tolerable, if they had a Book, or fit only for conversion or death. Few Muslim thinkers wished or were able to break such habits of mind. By and large, Islamic philosophy was Islam expressed in a Neo-Platonic Aristotelianism, just as Christian philosophy was Christianity expressed in a Neo-Platonic or Neo-Platonic Aristotelian guise. Hindu philosophy had a perhaps more flexible relationship, which will be described in the next chapter, with its own scriptures; but its dogmatism, that of each school or sect superimposed on the common dogmatism, was no less marked.

What can be singled out as the obvious dogmas or mental habits of Europe, especially in contrast to India and China? What stands out as dogmatic or merely habitual in earlier Greek thought is the belief in the primacy of the city-state, with the corollary that human beings, whether as distributed in city states or divided between Greeks and barbarians, are by nature dis-united and naturally at war with one another. The respect of the Greeks for the athlete and warrior and their idealization of the human body influenced their philosophy and distinguished it from that of the Indians and Chinese. But the Greeks, like the Indians and Chinese, established the connection between *is* and *ought*. This connection, which was so important to Plato and Aristotle, was reaffirmed by the Neo-Platonists and the Stoics, and was transformed into almost sheerly religious dogma in the Middle Ages.

In medieval and later times, the requirement that all philosophizing be carried on with reference to Christian dogma brought distinctively European mental habits, influenced by Islamic ones, into being. The Christian view that God created man to rule over nature, or, at any rate, to strive towards his human uniqueness was expressed in the tendency, alien to India and China, to separate man from nature, and even to set him in opposition to it, instead of, as in India, to regard him as one of its manifestations, real or illusory, or instead of, as in China, to integrate him with it harmoniously. The European tendency to think of fixed, absolute metaphysical levels contrasted especially with the Chinese tendency to think of shifting equilibria. A typi-cal European thinker would search for single causes operating in linear sequences, whereas a typical Chinese thinker would look for reciprocal influences that alternately disturbed and restored homeostasis.

Like Judaism and Islam, Christianity assumed that God was nature's sovereign and therefore miraculously independent of it. The conditions for life and life after death were supposed to be set by him as if he were a great monarch issuing irresistible com-mands, while in India and China, surely among philosophers, the conditions for life and liberation tended to be regarded as laws of nature. That is, while the Indians and Chinese used every device they could think of, astrological, alchemical, ritual, artistic, or moral, to influence nature, they were more inclined to see everything as belonging together, either because everything was a manifestation of one or more forces, or because all the single things were thoroughly interdependent. To the extent that this contrast between West and East holds true, it may be said that Eastern thinkers believed more firmly in stable laws, which were easy to interpret or extend in a philosophical rather than a sheerly religious way. Maybe the very sharpness of the European contrast between God and nature, or miracle and natural law, made it easier to think about the difference and fix the conception of natural law more firmly in the end.

As the influence of Christianity waned, it began to be replaced by a different faith, that science and technology would progress indefinitely and liberate mankind from its ills. This faith was characteristically combined with another, that mankind would be liberated by new forms of political organization. The Pure Land of Europe was one of science, politics, or both.

The subject of dogmas and mental habits is close, of course, to that of orthodoxy and heterodoxy, which has already come up in the discussion of tolerance. It need not be repeated that orthodoxy in China was established in relation to the Confucian classics and to Confucian filial conduct, nor need it be repeated that European orthodoxy was established in relation to Christianity, to which nationalistic interests were added. But it is worth repeating, even before the extended discussion in the next chapter, that the sense of orthodoxy and heterodoxy in India was different from the sense we are familiar with. In India, orthodoxy was usually defined as faith in the Vedas, the sacred knowledge handed down in ancient hymn collections and ancient Upanishads. There was no Pope or similar authority (as there was not, I have said, in Islam) to decide on what counted as orthodoxy, so the issue was decided by each religious group for itself. The heretical religions or schools of thought were those that denied the truth of the Vedas. Two such heretical religions, Buddhism and Jainism, substituted scriptures of their own, while the Materialists, though they cherished their basic texts, poured scorn on all scriptures.

A word in particular on the Materialists, the Carvakas. Their doctrines seem to have been widespread at one time. Like Lucretius, they scorned religion in every form. 'Uncivilized ignorant fools,' they said, 'who imagine that spirit is something different from body, and repose the reward of action in a future state.' They asked, 'Who has seen the soul existing in a state separate from the body? Does not life result from the ultimate configuration of matter?' And they said, flatly, 'The three Vedas are a cheat.' To this they added, like the hedonists they were, 'The only end of man is enjoyment produced by sensible pleasures.'[121]

Opponents of the Carvakas tried to prove the existence of God by means of inference or induction, so the Carvakas played the role of sceptics and argued against 'induction', against, that is, the idea that experience could establish an invariable relation between two classes of events. It is beyond human powers, they argued, to establish that any universal generalization is invariably true. A single exception, which is always possible, is enough to prove the generalization false. It is therefore useless to try to prove an invariable relation either between two universal generalizations or between a universal and a particular. As to the relation between particulars, between, for example, particular fires and particular instances of smoke, the possible number of instances of either is infinite, so no particular number is ever enough to establish the reliability of the relation. Besides, there is no necessary element common to all the particular cases.[122]

It is interesting to note that the Śankaran opponents of the Carvakas agreed with them that no empirical generalization could be proved to be true. But their way of putting the doubt, and the moral thay attached to it, were quite different. They held that it was natural to believe anything that thought or experience seemed to teach, and that any universal proposition was and should be accepted as true as long as experience did not contradict it, meaning, as long as it was not falsified. But however strong the belief in the proposition, there was a rational possibility, they said, that some future experience would, in fact, falsify it, for no universal generalization was rationally necessary in itself. To them, rational arguments or hypotheses were always subject to possible counterarguments and disconfirming experiences. If any belief were necessary, it could not depend upon empirical experience or rational argument alone. To the Śankarans, the lesson was that genuine certainty could stem only from belief in inspired texts.[123] This theme will be discussed in the following chapter, on scriptures, revelation, and reason.

The Three Philosophies: Self Analysed, Society Moralized, and Nature Logicized

Indian philosophers excelled in exploring human thought and emotion. Their philosophical psychology, in which I include what we call 'epistemology', is partly arbitrary to us, but it is more detailed, critical, and profound than that of China or of the West until quite recent times. Each Indian school elaborated its own theory of the perception of space and motion, of time, of universals (if it took them to exist), of cognition (and reflexive cognition of cognition), and of self. They also theorized on indefinite perception, which they took to include doubtful, indeterminate, and conjectural perception. Their great interest in reality as against illusion led them to study dream and illusory perception with sharp attentiveness—or perhaps it was their interest in dreams and illusory perception that led them to study the nature of reality. They also described and tried to account for abnormal perception, the perception that accompanies disorders of sensation or intellection. Typically, they also believed in and tried to characterize 'supernormal' perception, exempt from all ordinary perceptual conditions.

Indian philosophers were also interested in analysing memory, imagination, thought, and language. Heirs of the oldest scientific grammar in existence, they constructed elaborate philosophies of grammar. Some of them thought that because grammar underlay meaning of every kind, it was a key to the metaphysical truth, if not that truth itself. Their interest in the self led them to make careful distinctions between experience of the body and experience of the self. Intrigued by consciousness, they enumerated its degrees and modes, and they inquired into the nature of volition and distinguished it from automatic or instinctive action. They inquired, too, into the nature of sexual, aesthetic, and religious emotion, at times with surprising penetration.[124]

In short, the Indians were explorers and categorizers of inner experience. After an initial period of exuberance, their exploration became painstaking. Sometimes they seem to have been possessed by a rage for categorization and logic or logic-chopping. They invented a formal logic, including a theory of syllogisms, which developed over a long period of time, from perhaps the second century A.D. to the seventeenth, though they never learned to express their logic in formal symbols. The logic they invented was without variables and was intensional, that is, did not deal with classes and propositions. Their interest in the effects of negation was old and keen. They devised effective technical procedures to help philosophers, of whatever epistemological or ontological views, to overcome the ambiguities of language. The masters of this logic, says a modern student, 'did not lay down conclusions first and justify them later with theory. They were seriously engaged in following reality wherever it might lead them.'[125]

In China, formal logic had an interesting start; but it did not develop. Taoists played in their imaginative way with such questions as, 'Does nothing precede something or vice versa?' Dialecticians spun out sophistries and enmeshed themselves and others in contradictions. Yet even the infusion, through Buddhism, of Indian philosophical reasoning, was not able to sustain the interest of philosophers in logic or epistemology, and their ontology was distinguished more by poetic pendantry, a quality which their example proves possible, than by analytic precision. They showed themselves able to analyse human aims, abilities, and personalities; but, like Aristotle and his followers, they were convinced that human beings were meant for society and became fully human only to the extent that they became fully engaged in it. They therefore preoccupied themselves mostly with social philosophy. They were all to some degree artists, however, and they also formulated and argued their aesthetic views. The fine distinctions they made in their relationships to their artistic predecessors were the aesthetic echoes of the Chinese concentration on filiality. For literature, especially poetry, for painting and, especially, calligraphy, they established canons of criticism and a sufficiently analytical vocabulary.

Compared with Indian philosophers, the Chinese, it is evident, were much less minutely analytical; but they had far more knowledge of history and respect for its facts. The Indian attitude was more abstractly metaphysical and consciously logical, the Chinese more concretely aesthetic and consciously historical.

The logic of the Chinese, which they exercised with an often stereotyped literary skill, was the kind of symmetrical concept-matching that has already been described and will be further exemplified.[126]

In Western philosophy, formal logic had its obvious beginning in Aristotle. Aristotle was also the first master of the particularly Western combination of sharp, original analysis and a sharp sense of empirical reality. Medieval philosophers made use of his analytical methods, but lacked, on the whole, his real if fitful respect for empirical reality. In the course of a few hundred years, their logic arrived at new subtleties, some of which are perhaps still being rediscovered. But although the subsequent European philosophers learned to reason minutely and exactly, they did so over a narrower range than the Indians. For a long time, the Europeans could match neither the far-ranging analytical conceptualization of the Indians nor the conscious aesthetic sensitivity of the Chinese.

The Three Philosophies: Three and One

It is not hard to summarize the very general likenesses between the three philosophical worlds of which we have been speaking. Consider, first, the following nine points:

1. All three worlds have their insularity, their pride, their conviction that anyone outside of their geographical or conceptual borders is a barbarian. Their insularity is their closure as conceptual worlds, each of them distinctive and relatively independent.

2. All three develop proto-sciences, by which is meant, cosmological theories of basic materials or forces, and basic kinds of cosmic organization. These proto-sciences may be valued in their own right by their inventors, but they are also valued, as a rule, for their supposed moral implications.

3. All three discover dialectical argument and logic, although these remain rudimentary in China. In India and Europe, they grow complex and formal.

4. All three arrive at the metaphysical doctrines that may be called, in European terminology, Realism, Idealism, and Phenomenology, the Chinese forms of these being largely borrowed from India. In all three there are moral-metaphysical doctrines that may be called, perhaps too laxly, Existentialism.

5. All three include basically critical philosophers, who oppose certain

dogmas or habits of mind, and who are, in consequence, sceptical, materialistic, or empirical.

6. All three give rise to ethical and social thought, although in India social thought, in the broad sense, is either ancillary to religious dogma or, for the most part, confined to a systematically 'Machiavellian' type. (I remind the reader, at this point, that social, ethical, and aesthetic thought are not taken up in the present book.)

7. All three give rise to aesthetic thought, each, of course, in relation to its own distinctive forms of art.

8. All three spend much effort in distinguishing between the relative and the absolute, which are taken to be respectively equivalent to the temporary and the permanent, the illusory and the true, and the valueless and the valuable. They all tend to identify the *is* of fact with the *ought* of morality. The Chinese, that is, Neo-Confucian, belief in a metaphysically real unifying principle is, to a degree, borrowed from Buddhism.

9. Finally, all three show the stubborn search for wisdom in every sense. Pessimists and cynics apart, they all teach what they take to be reasoned hopes, rational therapies, and final values and loyalties.

It is abundantly clear that these general likenesses between the three philosophical worlds do not preclude general differences, many of which have already been mentioned in one or another way. Judged by mutual comparison, each world has its evident strengths and weaknesses, a strength and a weakness being the possible obverses of one another. The sharpness and rationality of Indian analysis is balanced by its frequent superstitiousness, its school loyalties, its problem-solving by the mere multiplication of categories, its over-reliance on merely introspective evidence, and its near-neglect of political thought.* The human-

---

* The possibilities of seeing Indian thought as both rational and irrational can be neatly exemplified by D. D. Kosambi's *Culture and Civilisation of Ancient India in Historical Outline*. Kosambi writes (pp. 174–5):

'The "logic" advanced by the brahmins took care to avoid all reality . . . The absence of logic, contempt for mundane reality, the inability to work at manual and menial tasks, emphasis upon learning basic formulas by rote with the secret meaning to be expounded by a high *guru*, and respect for tradition (no matter how silly) backed by fictitious authority, had a devastating effect upon Indian science.'

In spite of this harsh verdict, Kosambi soon quotes (p. 177) Hsüan-tsang as saying that at Nalanda anyone particularly successful in logical disputation 'was mounted on an elephant and conducted (in procession) by a numerous suite to the gates of the abbey. If, on the contrary, one of the members breaks a rule in logic and adopts his words accordingly, they proceed to disfigure his face with red and white and cover his body with dust and dirt, and then carry him off to some deserted spot or dump him in a ditch.' [*Cont'd. p. 120*].

centredness of Confucianism is balanced by its sometimes tyrannical insistence upon social obligation and by its frequent reliance on dogma rather than experience. The scientific clarity of Western thought, its more profound and consistent tie to mathematics, and its fertility in suggesting social and political reforms, are balanced by its devotion to an often intellectually tyrannical religion or state, and by its separation, over long stretches of time, between abstract thought and considered empirical evidence.

Of course, what I say on the tie between Western philosophical thought and mathematics does nothing to clarify the possible equivalent tie in the other civilizations. Euclideanism was unique, but perhaps limiting in certain ways. Indian mathematics is said to have brought, 'not only a *deductive* process, building upon accepted axioms, postulates, and common notions, but an intuitive insight into the behaviour of numbers, and their arrangement into patterns and series, from which may be perceived *inductive* generalizations, in a word, algebra rather than geometry... It is to the philosophical mind of the Brahman mathematician engrossed in the mystique of number that we owe the origin of analytical methods. In this process of abstraction two particularly interesting features emerged, at the lower level of achievement the perfection of the decimal system, and at the higher the solution of certain indeterminate equations.

Speaking of Indian and Islamic mathematics, a mathematical historian says in praise, 'New ideas can come about only by the free and bold pursuit of heuristic and intuitive insights. The logical justification and corrective measures, should the latter be necessary, can be brought into play only when there is something to logicize. Hindu and Arab venturesomeness brought arithmetic and algebra to the fore once again and placed it almost on a par with geometry.'[127]

To sum up the philosophical superiority of each world in an over-simple judgment, India is superior in its careful introspectiveness and at least powerful in its linguistic analysis, dialectic,

---

Kosambi does not ask the difficult question if this Nalandan logic was valid (or only 'logic'), or whether it related to or avoided all reality. It was not, at any rate, 'the absence of logic' that he stigmatizes; not was it, I think, evidence of the superiority of Buddhist to Brahman logic.

and logic; China is superior in its insistence on a rational social life and in its long-cultivated aesthetic sensitivity; and the West, by which I now mean Western Europe, is superior in its balance between intellectual analysis and social reform and in its ability to assimilate the attitudes and results of exact science.

I am approaching the end of my chapter on the three philosophical civilizations, but, before the end, I want to compare the technological and scientific development of China and Europe a little more closely. China, to begin with, had many advantages over Europe: greater political cohesiveness, a more mature legal system, a superior educational system and, with it, a superior bureaucracy, a richer, more widespread culture of the book, a relatively advanced science, and a superior technology. Chinese craftsmen were superb. Well before the birth of Christ, they wove complex fabrics on complex looms. Chinese potters were ingenious, daring, and aesthectically sensitive, and capable, furthermore, of organizing the manufacture of their wares.[128] Chinese metal-workers, using coal as fuel and power-driven bellows and forges, manufactured iron for all its growing uses, in weapons, ships, buildings, industrial equipment, and elsewhere. To judge by appearances, China might have had an industrial revolution in the eleventh century.[129] The entrepreneurs were there. Confucian tradition, it is true, discriminated against merchants; but many of them, having made their fortunes, successfully evaded the law against conspicuous consumption, and, perhaps despite the law, got their sons into civil service positions that gave their families prestige and political influence. A poor but energetic and ambitious man could surely rise, and he or his sons could become assimilated to the ruling bureaucracy.[130]

If all this is true, why did Chinese technology and science eventually lag behind those of the West? For the Chinese iron industry of the eleventh century, the answer is given in terms of external factors, such as the Mongol invasions, and internal factors, summarized as traditional 'structural limitations'. The merchant could make a fortune and rise in society, but only on the terms that the bureaucracy laid down, for, unlike his European counterpart, he had no guaranteed freedoms. Whenever and however it pleased, the bureaucracy limited his business or replaced it by a government monopoly. Perhaps, then, his development, or the direction of his development, was limited in comparison with the European merchant. Prestige and power, it seems, continued to go mainly to those with a literary education. Therefore, in the long run, the empirical facts and prodedures the Chinese accumulated did not inspire many of them to become scientists in the later European sense. From the seventeenth century and on, rather down-to-earth Chinese scholars studied archeology and philology in a systematic, rational manner; but such sciences could not be as decisive for Chinese thought as mathematics had been for Western thought.[131]

How did the West compare? We can see the harbingers of Western science in Aristotle's biology, in Euclid's geometry, and in Hellenistic astronomy. For a while, these were partly lost to the Western consciousness; but, during the Middle Ages, they began to be recovered and sometimes advanced, thanks, in large measure, to the Islamic translators and scientists. During the Middle Ages there also began a decisive technological advance. Like Greek science, this advance could be seen to be decisive only in distant retrospect. The comparison with China serves to show that none of the individual factors usually singled out were in themselves decisive, but that there was something in their interrelationships that lent them mutual support and cumulative effect. The use of wind and water power became extensive. Metallurgy improved. With water-driven bellows a hotter and more continuous flame could be maintained and larger masses of metal smelted. The availability of larger masses of metal stimulated the building of larger furnaces and of power-driven hammers to reduce crude to wrought iron. In spite of difficult economic circumstances in the fourteenth and fifteenth centuries, the demand for iron continued to grow and metallurgy to flourish, for Europe needed farm implements, tools, anchors, nails, spears, swords, and armour, and, before long, cannons and machine parts, including gears. Wars that may have disturbed industrial development in general, stimulated the demand for weapons and so promoted the growth of the iron industry. A modern industrial economy, with all that it was later discovered to imply, was already beginning in the late Middle Ages.[132]

A word, now, of caution, to prevent hindsight from distorting the comparison between China and Europe. In its earlier history, during the Han Dynasty, which, with an interregnum, lasted from 206 B.C. to A.D. 220, China made many striking technological and scientific advances, and the prestige of scientists may well have been high. When a convocation of learned men was assembled in the year A.D. 4, those invited included experts

in the lost classics and ancient records, in astronomy and calendrical science, in mathematics and the acoustics of the standard musical tones, in philology and history, in magical or medical techniques, in the botany of woody plants and herbs, and in the five classics (including the) Confucian Analects, the Filial Piety Classic and the Literary Expositor. These doctors were given (as a special mark of honour) an authorization to add a second horse to each of their chariots. More than a thousand of them assembled at the capital.[133]

We do not know what happened at this assembly of scholars, though it is safe to assume that it included scientists. The scientific and technological passion of the Han period is personified in Chang Heng (A.D. 78–139). Chang Heng charted the movements of the stars with care, refined astronomical theories and instruments, and calculated the value of *pi* more accurately than ever before in China. It is possible that he invented a grid-system for cartography, and it is sure that he invented a sensitive seismograph.[134]

Born almost a thousand years later, in A.D. 1030, Shen Kua, a high government official, is another such outstanding example, 'perhaps the most interesting character in all Chinese scientific history.' Though occupied with official duties,

he never failed to note down all that was of scientific or technical interest. His *Men Ch'i Pi Than (Dream Pool Essays)*, the date of which is about 1086, is one of the first books to describe the magnetic compass. . . ; but it also contains much astronomy and mathematics, together with notices of fossils, the making of relief maps and other matters of cartographic interest, descriptions of metallurgical processes, and a high proportion of biological observations.[135]

One cannot read such examples without revising one's preconceptions about the scientific capacity of the Chinese during the ancient and medieval periods of European history. We know that during the T'ang Dynasty (A.D. 618–907), a small number of mathematicians were given government posts, though minor ones, while astrology and calendar-making were considered important functions, as, indeed, they remained. Astrologers, calendar-makers, mathematicians, doctors, and engineers could make minor bureaucratic careers in China. But this enumeration of government posts for scientists, as we may loosely call them all, cannot obscure the fact that the ruling spirit in China was less theoretical, in the scientific sense, than empirical, that there was little interest in the search for rigorous laws of nature, and that the examination system did not encourage technical specialization.[136]

Whatever the reasons, economic, political, social, or intellectual, we know of nothing in China, the Han assembly I have described possibly excepted, or in India, or in ancient Europe, to parallel the enthusiasm that ran through the whole of educated European humanity when the Royal Society was formed in the 1660s, or when the *Académie Royale des Sciences* was formed in Paris. This enthusiasm united artists, writers, scientists, and rulers, as well as ingenious mechanics, all of whom pursued invention no less because of its usefulness than because of its intellectual excitement. Where, outside of post-medieval Europe, could there have been men such as Robert Hooke, the secretary of the Royal Academy, or Christian Huyghens, both ambitious inventor-scientists, both of whom worked on the clock-mechanisms for precise astronomincal observation?[137] Even if some such men could be found in Alexandria, Benares, Ch'ang-an or Kaifeng (we have met two in China), outside of post-medieval Europe we do not (I think) find the sustained excitement in invention that secured the cooperation of rulers, rich men, theoretical scientists, and mechanics. This joint enthusiasm reflected a change of attitude toward the practical, a change that, in some not exactly defined way, accompanied expanding commerce and industry, a relative scarcity of labour, and the technological development that began, as I have noted, in the late Middle Ages.

It is unnecessary to continue and describe the scientific and philosophical revolution of the seventeenth century. It is sufficient to point out that it was then, in the seventeenth century, that the idea of a clockwork universe became embedded in science and philosophy and gave the assurance that the laws of nature could all be discovered and put into useful mathematical form.[138] The conception of such a universe gave European thought a unique advantage, for it extended its standards of exactness and gave it a new theoretical and practical power. Just as the technology of ships and guns had conferred on Europe the power to conquer the world materially, mathematics, physics, and the mechanical universe they made possible conferred on Europe the power to conquer the world intellectually.[139]

And yet, because a 'yet' there always is, even from the seventeenth century and on, the quality and depth of philosophic thought were not invariably to the advantage of the Europeans. The Europeans continued to search individually for their satisfaction or happiness and often continued to fail. We see this with especial clarity if we think of the philosophical influence of the great, unsystematic exceptions, the Pascals, Kierkegaards, and Nietzsches, and, more recently, of such thinkers as Camus and Sartre, and perhaps of Heidegger as well. In comparison with Pascal, Yoga and Ch'an Buddhism, though metaphysically doctrinaire, are psychologically and therefore humanly more profound, and in comparison with Kierkegaard, Nietzsche, Camus, and Sartre, better tempered, more consistent, and, I should judge, therapeutically more promising. To turn to aesthetics, the Chinese are often more sensitive and persuasive than the Europeans. For example, the aesthetic ideas of Paul Klee, which I admire, have a Chinese undertone and perhaps substance, but they are not clearly rooted in any tradition or clearly related to any practice but his own and, to some extent, Kandinsky's. In contrast, the aesthetic ideas of the Chinese constitute a tradition that represents the experience of countless individuals, whose differences it does not submerge, but relates. The Chinese ideas are therefore superior to Klee's in breadth of relevance and depth of resonance.

India, China, and the West—each has its philosophical strengths and weaknesses. Now, having compared the three, and having distributed praise and blame among them, I am struck by the misgiving that, like Klee, I speak only for myself, and that I have arrogated to myself the office of judge of all the worlds. But, having come so far, I will allow myself a few additional remarks before I end this chapter of general comparisons.

It appears to me that there have been some Western philosophies that lend themselves relatively well to total comparison with some Indian and Chinese philosophies. The Western are the Stoic, with its rational world-organism, and, above all, the Neo-Platonic. The structural resemblance between Neo-Platonic and Śankaran philosophy will be pointed out. When the comparison is made, it should not be forgotten how influential Neo-Platonic philosophy was in medieval Islam and Europe, and to what a degree it influenced later philosophers, including Spinoza, Leibniz, Fichte, Schelling, Hegel, Bergson, Whitehead, and, in an attenuated way, Sartre as well.

Apart from general structural likenesses of one entire philosophy with another, there are many partial resemblances, of particular philosophical ideas and mechanisms, some of which will be discussed in the following pages. The dissolution of philosophical wholes into parts is doubtless helpful to the exactness of the comparison. But although the philosophies and philosophers we are to consider can be studied with analytic exactness, and although this is the exactness that students of philosophy must, by nature, prefer, there remain elusive likenesses and differences that may be called, for want of a better word, aesthetic. Surely there is something aesthetically, psychologically, and philosophically European about Socrates, Plato, Aristotle, Hume, and Kant; and, just as surely, there is something Indian about Śankara, Vasubandhu, and Nagarjuna, and something Chinese about Chuang Tzu, Mencius, and Chu Hsi.

This observation, which is obvious but hard to develop exactly, accepts the expressive uniqueness of each tradition of thought, and so returns us to the related uniqueness of each particular language. The following words of George Steiner on different languages can be transposed to apply to different philosophical traditions:

> Different tongues give to the mechanism of 'alternity' a dynamic, transferable enactment. They realize needs of privacy and territoriality vital to our identity. To a greater or lesser degree, every language offers its own reading of life. To move between languages, to translate, even within restrictions of totality, is to experience the almost bewildering bias of the human spirit towards freedom.[140]

To make a deliberate choice between the three philosophical worlds is, finally, absurd. Whether or not we are attracted to the modes of life recommended in the worlds we are unfamiliar with, these worlds reveal the philosophical potentialities of human thought. To enter these worlds, barriers of dogma and strangeness must be crossed, but the crossing, once made, leads into an endlessly interesting landscape of ideas and nuances of ideas. It is natural to continue to live in the world in which one was born, but to exclude the others from thought is to will to remain intellectually insular. There are many reasons to remain insular, some of which may be good. Voltaire, whose restlessness was not cured by his own advice, advised that it was best to stay at home and cultivate one's garden. Staying home all the time may serve one's comfort, but it does not serve curiosity, humanity, nor, in the long run, the truth.

3

Scriptures, Revelation, and Reason

Shlomo Biderman

The problem of faith and reason, once so important to Western philosophy, has ceased to trouble the peace of mind of most Western philosophers. The comparison I am undertaking here is not intended to renew the problem as such, but to contribute toward the understanding of the effect of religious dogma on the development of philosophy. I therefore intend to compare different philosophical approaches to the validity of scriptures, and to comment on their success in dealing with contradictions between philosophical and scriptural statements. My interest here lies, not in the content of the contradictory statements, but in the principles by means of which contradiction itself was faced as a problem. To enable the discussion of the principles to be clear and brief, historical considerations will be largely ignored. Scriptures will be taken, neutrally, to be any collection of words accepted by a group of believers as unquestionably valid or as conveying a divine revelation. This characterization is meant to include both scriptures canonized after having been written down and scriptures in effect canonized in their oral form and written down at a later date. The discussion will be divided into three parts, followed by a supplement on China. The first part will survey attitudes toward the problem of reason and revelation in Christianity, with which I begin because of its familiarity; the second will survey analogous attitudes in Hinduism; and the third will compare Christian and Hindu attitudes and suggest such conclusions as emerge from the comparison. Islam will be represented, though only by Averroes. The supplement on China will deal with the authoritative Confucian books, which cannot rightly be called 'scriptures', but which exerted a strong, constant

influence on Chinese thought, philosophical and unphilosophical.

Christian Attitudes

The holiness of the Old Testament was established in Christianity
by the end of the first century A.D. The choice of the New Testament books to be declared holy, that is, canonized, was delayed
by debates among the Christians themselves, not to mention the
process by which they distinguished themselves from heretics.
The choice was completed by the fourth century. It should be
noted that a secondary kind of holiness was granted to other
writings, such as those of the Fathers of the Church.

The Christian concept of revelation is anchored, if I may
generalize, in historical reality. This is at least the position of
many twentieth-century Christian theologians, who argue that
revelation has been expressed in the succession of historical
events that began at the beginning of time itself, the moment of
the creation of the world from nothing. God's subsequent revelations in history have sometimes been direct, and sometimes by
means of intermediaries, the prophets, sages, and saints. The
climax of divine revelation, which extended the possibility of
salvation to each person, was the appearance on earth and in
history of Jesus Christ, the son of God. The function of scriptures
is therefore, as *The Gospel According to John* says, to record the
'signs' performed by Jesus, 'in order that you may hold the faith
that Jesus is the Christ, the Son of God, and that through this
faith you may possess eternal life by his name' (*John* 20/30, *The
New English Bible*).

This approach to scriptures, which is now dominant in Christian theology, is paralleled by a somewhat different one, which
takes the scriptures as not, primarily, an authoritative account of
the revelation of God in history, but as in themselves that revelation. The revelation is therefore transferred from the level of fact
and history to the level of words and meanings, in keeping with
the first sentences of *John*, 'When all things began, the Word
already was. The Word dwelt with God, and what God was, the
Word was.' According to those who used these sentences to
support their position, the fact that scriptures record historic
events does not diminish their nature as placeless, timeless,

fundamentally ahistorical truth. The events themselves may not be simply what they appear and are subject to varying interpretations, because their meaning as God's Word is not easily exhausted.

Both the historical and the ahistorical approaches have been widespread in the history of Christian theology, although, as I have said, the former has shown itself to be dominant. The difference between them has had important consequences for Christianity, but both share a basic belief that distinguishes them from the typical Hindu approaches that will be compared with them. The belief they share, in the very existence of God and in his nature as lawgiver and as validator of the scriptures, may appear too self-evident to mention; but what is self-evident in one culture is not necessarily so in another. In Christianity, on either of the two approaches that have been mentioned, belief in scriptures depends on belief in the existence of an omnipotent, onmipresent, onmiscient God, so that the denial of His existence amounts to a denial of the eternity and unquestionable truth of the scriptures.

This Christian conviction, making belief in scriptures depend on belief in an absolute creator-God, strengthened the threat posed by philosophy. The first Christian attempt to deal with the threat was simple and perhaps naïve. It was expressed in the proclamation that in every case of a contradiction between religious and philosophical truths, the latter should be disregarded and the former accepted without hesitation. Tertullian (A.D. 160–220), an early partisan of this simple view, writes of the difficulty in believing in the resurrection of Christ, 'The Son of God died; it is by all means to be believed, because it is absurd. And He was buried and rose again; the fact is certain because it is impossible.'[1] The phrase ascribed to Tertullian, though not found in his writings, *'credo quia absurdum'*, 'I believe because it is absurd', does not misrepresent him. God's words, it appears, make philosophizing unnecessary, and even make it plausible to believe that any attempt to philosophize is harmful. Tertullian is, in fact, antagonistic to philosophy as a whole, though he makes use of it, when expedient, to support Christian doctrine. Echoing Paul, he asks with rhetorical enthusiasm, 'What indeed has Athens to do with Jerusalem? What concord is there between the Academy and the Church?' His denial that there is any connection or concord is not based on dialectical considerations (which we find in the negations of the Buddhist philosopher, Nagarjuna), but on the denial of the applicability of dialectics. He is thus the faithful representative of the orthodox approach, which holds that the absolute truth is not to be found in abstractions, but in the practical goal of salvation.

About two hundred years later, in the fourth and early fifth centuries, Tertullian's view found an additional, wider expression in the thought of St. Augustine. Augustine's point of departure, pure religious faith, was not different from Tertullian's. Augustine's argument against philosophy was without doubt based upon the emotional, even mystical experience that he describes in his *Confessions*. Philosophy, so one can hear him arguing, is too cold, too intellectual, too ineffective, too arrogant, too essentially foolish.[2] Recognition of the truth and its realization are the sole province, he is sure, of faith, and they are based upon holy scriptures. He ascribes to philosophy only a secondary function, which follows on its acceptance of the faith, as an instrument to clarify the nature and intellectual representation of revelation. In his treatise on free will he writes:

> We cannot deny that believing and knowing are different things, and that in matters of great importance pertaining to divinity, we must first believe before we seek to know. Otherwise, the word of the prophet would be vain, where he says, 'Except ye believe ye shall not understand' (*Isaiah 7/9*). Our Lord himself, both in his words and by his deeds exhorted those whom he called to salvation first of all to believe.[3]

As this quotation shows, Augustine, unlike Tertullian, does not reject philosophy completely. Nevertheless, he sets clear limits to rational thought, and he appears to take genuine intellectual understanding as a state that cannot precede, but only follow faith. Understanding in his sense is more in the nature, I think, of intuitive than rational understanding.

Augustine's position was accepted as authoritative in the Christian Middle Ages, and theologians repeatedly emphasize the primary authority granted to revelation, as embodied in scriptures. They see philosophy as, at best, an instrument to aid theology. St. Anselm (1033–1109), whose method of reasoning tends to be more dialectical or Aristotelian than Augustine's, nevertheless echoes Augustine in all that touches on the issue of

revelation and reason. Anselm writes, 'I do not seek to understand so that I may believe; but I believe so that I may understand.
For I believe this also, that unless I believe, I shall not understand.'[4]

Yet Anselm makes a significant, non-Augustinian concession
to philosophy. The concession is most clearly made in *Cur Deus
Homo,* which is addressed both to Christians and to unbelievers,
by whom Anselm means Jews and sceptical or atheistic 'pagans',
all those who regard Christianity as contrary to reason. Anselm
hopes to persuade these unbelievers of the necessity of salvation,
and of its possibility by virtue of God's having become man,
having died, and having been resurrected. Anselm is quite aware
that he cannot persuade the unbeliever by simply affirming the
faith the unbeliever does not share, and he intends his argument
to proceed by 'necessary reason' alone. Temporarily, therefore,
Jesus must be excluded from the argument, though 'the impossibility that any man should be saved without him' is pointed out in
its course.[5] But *Cur Deus Homo* also expresses the position of the
believer, which Anselm represents in the person of a partner in
dialogue, whom he names Boso. Boso not only argues for the
priority of faith over reason, but adds, 'Even were I unable in any
way to understand what I believe, still nothing could shake my
constancy.'[6] Such belief without understanding ought not to
trouble the believer, because all human understanding is limited
by the limitations of human reason. 'We must understand',
Anselm says, 'that for all that a man can say or know still deeper
grounds of so great a truth lie concealed.'[7]

These last quotations from *Cur Deus Homo* may seem merely to
repeat that revelation is prior to reason; but Anselm's admission
that reason is the sole instrument by which unbelievers can be
convinced strikes me as significant. Can it be meant to be didactic
alone, or based alone on the nature of the person for whom he
intends his argument? It is hard to answer these questions une-
quivocally, but the distinction between arguments meant for
believers and unbelievers seems to me to bring with it some
weakening of the autonomy and ultimacy of theology. The distinction implies that in at least certain cases, theology is no longer
superior to philosophy, which becomes autonomous in relation
to unbelievers. A division between the tendencies and objectives
of theology and philosophy is at least hinted at. Undeveloped as

the hint may be, it is the harbinger of the more serious division suggested to Western Christian thought in the twelfth century by the Muslim philosopher, Ibn Rushd, better known in the West by his Latin name, Averroes, to whom I now turn.

The mention of a Muslim philosopher in the context of the Christian philosophy with which we are dealing is neither accidental nor arbitrary. The writings of Averroes (*c.* 1126–*c.* 1198) were not very influential on Muslim philosophy, but their importance for European philosophy, in both subject and method, is hard to exaggerate. Even now, his formulations, his style of argument, and his polemical methods remain fascinating examples of critical philosophizing. In all that bears on the relationship between theology and philosophy, it is worth recalling his essay 'On the Harmony of Religion and Philosophy'. As a rationalist he there holds that the laws of logic establish the truth or falsity of a statement; and if any statement has been proved to be logically valid, he continues, no power in the world, even if supernatural, can falsify it. But Averroes does not go on to deny the authority of scriptures. Instead, whenever a contradiction between reason and religion appears, he explains it as no more than apparent. He does this by assigning an allegorical meaning to the scriptural statement in question. Scriptures can therefore, he says, be understood in accord with many meanings, all of them intended. Persons whose imagination is stronger than their reason must suffice with blind faith and with open, literal meanings. Persons with a tendency toward dialectical thought (in the Aristotelian sense), casuistry, and sophistry, are suited to theology, which reveals probable, relative truths. Persons of the highest intellectual level, that is, philosophers, are not satisfied with any conclusions not established from a strictly logical standpoint.[8] They alone, according to Averroes, have the right to interpret scriptures allegorically, as they must interpret them whenever reason appears to conflict with scriptures.

Averroes therefore attacks the mystical al-Ghazali, who causes ordinary people confusion, he says, by giving the scriptures an allegorical interpretation in writings too accessible to the populace. 'Allegorical interpretations', he says, 'ought to be set down only in demonstrative books, because if they are in demonstrative books they are encountered by no one but men of the demonstrative class. But if they are set down in other than demonstrative books and one deals with them by poetical, rhetorical or dialectical methods, as Abu Hamid [al-Ghazali] does, then he commits an offence against the Law and against philosophy, even though the fellow intended nothing but good. For by this procedure he wanted to increase the number of learned men, but in fact he increased the number of the corrupted not of the learned!'[9]

Although Averroes exerted a strong influence on Christian philosophy, most of the philosophers inclined to agree with him seem to have found it too dangerous to express themselves openly. Instead, they took intentionally vague positions, one of which is the so-called 'double-truth' theory, which accepts the existence of two separate and distinct kinds of truth, of religion and of philosophy. This distinction made it possible to deal with the clash between the supposedly different kinds of truth by means of a forced compromise, which in some cases concealed heretical opinions. Yet the medieval European response to the distinction attributed to Averroes remained, for the most part, a religious one.[10] Its central expression is to be found in the attempt of St. Thomas Aquinas (1224–1274) to harmonize theology and philosophy. The result of his attempt, which resembles the earlier one of the Jewish philosopher, Maimonides, is the joining of Averroes' position with that of Augustine. On the assumption that philosophy and theology are different fields of discourse, he contends that philosophy deals with things as having a nature of their own, and theology with the same things as created by God and subject to him.[11] Philosophy is therefore a manner of relationship to the world that is, to begin with, independent of any external source, while theology is the science of revelation, the source of which is God's word as expressed in scriptures, and the basis of which is belief in the absolute truth of that word.

How, in Aquinas's opinion, can these two different ways of arriving at truth be reconciled? Showing his fine theological hand, Aquinas contends that the two, though distinguishable, are inseparable. His loyalty, like Augustine's, is at bottom theological, and his purpose is to unite philosophy and theology without damaging the latter's complete, eternal truth.[12] The basically theological character of his position is clear at the very beginning of his *Summa Theologiae* (as the *Summa Theologica* is more properly called), where he writes, 'It should be urged that human well-being called for schooling in what God has revealed, in addition to the philosophical researches pursued by human reasoning.'[13] To him faith in scriptures is the fundamental basis of any investigation whatsoever, even when it relates to fields that are within the grasp of our reason. The rational truth, he says, is the province of the very few, and even these few are subject to error in their reasoning. Therefore, in order to prevent error in the initial setting of the goal, the absolute truth of the scriptures must be accepted, without any connection with the discoveries and conclusions of the rational sciences.[14]

The priority of theology in Aquinas's thought can be illustrated by two examples from the *Summa Theologiae*. One of the first problems he dealt with in this book is the question whether Christian theology is a science. To this question he suggests two alternative answers, the first of which he will reject, and the second, accept. The first, unacceptable answer, is that theology is not a science. Every science begins in self-evident premises and principles, the answer goes (in imitation of Aristotle). Christian theology, however, begins in principles of faith that are not at all self-evident, and, unlike science, which deals with the general, deals with individual persons and events. In summary, 'Sacred doctrine is not a science.'

The second answer, which Aquinas finds acceptable, is that 'Christian theology should be pronounced to be a science.' The explanation is that only some sciences, like arithmetic and geometry, 'work from premises recognized in the innate light of intelligence', while others, like optics, start out 'from principles marked out by geometry and harmony from principles indicated by arithmetic'. Aquinas continues, 'In this second manner is Christian theology a science, for it flows from founts recognized in the light of a higher science, namely God's very own which he shares with the blessed. Hence as harmony credits its principles which are taken from arithmetic so Christian theology takes on faith its principles revealed by God.'[15]

Questionable as this last argument may seem, Aquinas believes it sufficient to create a harmony between reason and revelation. Having apparently learned from Averroes or Averroists or others that it is not enough simply to assert, with Augustine, that faith is always right, he feels impelled to prove that theology, a science in its own right, is not scientifically inferior to philosophy. In much the same vein, he answers the question whether Christian theology is more valuable than the other sciences. He again begins with an answer unacceptable to himself, which is that the other sciences appear more certain than Christian theology, the premises of which, the articles of faith, are open to doubt, while those of the other sciences are not. His second answer, which he accepts, is that theology is the queen of all the sciences, whether theoretical or practical. Sacred doctrine, he argues, is more certain that the theoretical sciences because it 'is held in the light of divine knowledge which cannot falter', and because it 'leads to heights the reason cannot climb'.[16] As for the practical sciences, the higher the aim the higher the science, so that sacred doctrine, which as a practical science aims at eternal happiness, teaches the end that governs the ends of all the practical sciences. 'Hence it is clear that from every standpoint sacred doctrine excels all other sciences.'[17]

As the most valuable of the sciences, theology is allowed, Aquinas says, to use the other, inferior sciences for its own purposes. That is, it has the right to borrow and use one or another part of their truths.[18] It is therefore right to use reason to prove theological truths rationally, though there are clearly theological truths, which can be known from scriptures alone. Reason, the expounder of philosophy, must therefore remain within its province, and not try to deal with problems such as belief in the Trinity, in the incarnation or the resurrection of Jesus, and the like.[19]

The attempt of Aquinas to reconcile reason and revelation can be summarized in the following three points:

1. The reconciliation is based first of all on a clear demarcation of philosophy from theology. In accord with Aristotle, philosophy is regarded as dependent on the light of reason alone. Theology, in contrast, is based on the authority of the scriptures alone.

2. The demarcation of philosophy from theology does not imply that the two are separate, for reason can never contradict the truths of revelation. Every apparent contradiction expresses the finiteness of human reason, which is apt to err.

3. There is a hierarchical distinction between philosophy and theology. Theology stands above philosophy both in theory and in practice.[20] Reason is therefore not only unable to contradict religious truths, but is subject to them.

I shall return to this attempt of Aquinas, as to the other Christian attitudes I have mentioned, in the third, comparative section of the present chapter.

Hindu Attitudes

The Hindu scriptures are divided into two groups. The first is called '*śruti*', a Sanskrit term meaning, literally, 'that which is heard'. The second group is called '*smriti*', meaning, literally, 'that which is remembered'. The *śruti*, 'heard' scriptures are considered to be infallible and to possess eternal, absolute authority, the *smriti*, 'remembered' ones, to be possibly fallible and to possess only secondary authority. *Śruti*, as its meaning testifies, originates in oral tradition. Its most ancient and sacred parts are the four Vedas, which are estimated to go back to 1200 B.C. or earlier. One of the Vedas is made up mostly of hymns in praise of the gods; a second, which contains the same hymns, records how they should be chanted; a third is made up of prayers to accompany the ritual of sacrifice; and a fourth has spells, magical incantations, and so on. The religion of the Vedas is predominantly polytheistic, but some of its later hymns imply or state other conceptions, which may be described, in Western terms, as henotheism (in which one god dominates the many), monotheism (in which, of course, only one god exists), and monism (in which the one god that exists is *im*personal).

To each of the Vedas there are attached other writings, also classified as *śutri*. It is enough merely to mention the Brahmanas, with their explanations of the hymns and rituals, and the Aranyakas or 'forest books', which are like the Brahmanas but tend towards mystical allegorizing. The Upanishads, however, must be characterized, even if only very briefly, because they are the greatest spiritual creation of the ancient Hindus and the source of much of the characteristic philosophical speculation of India.

Upanishad means 'sitting before', that is, 'sitting before the teacher'. A freer but more revealing translation might be, 'secret teaching'. As a group, the Upanishads are often called 'Vedanta', meaning, 'the end or completion of the Vedas', because they form the concluding part of the *śruti* scriptures. From a literary standpoint, the Upanishads are a series of treatises, some written in conventional verse ryhthms, and some in regular prose. In continuation of some of the late Vedic hymns and of the Aranyakas, they speculate on the source and purpose of the world. The earlier Upanishads, composed, perhaps, between 700 and 600 B.C., teach, among other doctrines, that Brahman, the absolute source of reality of the world, is identical with Atman, the impersonal inward self of man. The later Upanishads, in contrast, often teach a theistic world-outlook.

Of the *smriti* scriptures, only a few need be named here. They include ancient law books, the best known of which, *The Laws of Manu*, gives a kind of legal definition of the Hinduism of everyday life. They also include the Puranas, collections of myths and legends on the creation of the world, the genealogies of the gods, and much else. In contrast to the Vedas and Upanishads, the study of which was prohibited to the lowest social strata, the Puranas were meant for ordinary persons. Along with the Indian epics, the Puranas served, in fact if not in theory, as the scriptures of the untutored and the unholy. The two great Indian epics, the *Ramayana* and the *Mahabharata*, both classified as *smriti*, have been of incalculable importance to the believing Hindu. The *Mahabharata* goes so far as to say that everyone who reads or repeats it can regard himself as if he knew and understood the Vedas themselves.[21] One of the famous episodes of the *Mahabharata*, the *Bhagavad Gita*, is felt to be of such exalted holiness that some Hindus tend to classify it, not as *smriti*, but as *śruti*.

The last of the *smriti* scriptures to be referred to here are the basic texts, called *sutras*, of the six classic Hindu philosophies. A *sutra*, literally, 'a thread', can be defined as a string of aphorisms meant to serve as an authoritative summary of a doctrine. Philosophical sutras, like other *sutras*, were by nature fitted for memorizing and explication. It seems to me just that these mainstays of so many generations of philosophy students were assigned a degree, if only a secondary one, of holiness.

The subject of scriptures and holiness brings up that of orthodoxy. The nature of orthodoxy in India is not the same as in the West. When Hinduism excludes Buddhism, Jainism, and other, less important religious or irreligious groups, it is not because of any argument about God. From a usual Western standpoint, the Buddhists and Jains may be regarded as atheists;

but so may many perfectly good Hindus. In the Indian context, the heterodoxy of the Buddhists, Jains, and others, is neither more nor less that their denial of the validity of *śruti*. This denial, not the denial of God, strikes the Hindus as conclusive and damning, for, in contrast to Jews, Muslims, and Christians, they see no necessary connection between belief in the existence of God and in the validity of scriptures, the validity by which they establish who they are and with whom they may consort spiritually and physically.

Let me take a little time to clarify and support the contention I have just made. To begin with, let me put the contention in what may seem to be an extreme form: The more serious and personally involving the acceptance of scriptures by an Indian philosophical school, the less its tendency to believe in God, or, at the least, to see the existence of God as a precondition for the acceptance of scriptures. To give substance to this contention, which makes the relationship between acceptance of scriptures and acceptance or God a negative one, 'I shall survey the attitude toward belief in scriptures of three schools, the Mimamsa, Nyaya, and Vedanta, of the six classical schools of Indian philosophy.

I begin with Mimamsa, meaning 'inquiry' in Sanskrit, because it is considered the most religiously conservative of the philosophical schools, and because its attitudes contrast most sharply with the Western. Mimamsa, unlike the other schools of Hinduism, sees the Vedas and not the Upanishads as the primary scriptures. Its reason is that the Upanishads deal primarily with metaphysics, which is not relevant to the activities of daily life. The Vedas deal with these activities themselves and are therefore to be preferred. It must be understood, say the adherents of Mimamsa, that the purpose of scriptures is not to teach the human being how or what to think. More specifically, it is not to inform him how the cosmos came into being, to enlighten him historically or psychologically, to help him, as the other philosophical schools wish, to attain the presumed absolute truth, or, like them, to encourage his union with absolute reality. The scriptures are meant to command action—their authority lies solely in their power to do so.[22] 'The purpose of the Veda lying in the enjoining of actions', Mimamsa holds, the scriptures establish the rules by which one acts or refrains from acting.'[23] Indian thought categorizes actions as aimed at material wealth, at love or other emotional or aesthetic experience, or at the religious, moral order called *dharma*; but, according to Mimamsa, the pursuit of even wealth and love should conform to *dharma*, because *dharma* applies to all actions and is itself in practice defined by the Vedas.

As its name, 'Inquiry', indicates, Mimamsa considers the interpretation of scriptures to be its primary function. Interpretation should naturally be in the Vedic spirit, for, as the *Mimamsa Sutra* says, briefly but perhaps circularly, 'That which is based on the scriptures (is to be regarded as authoritative); because the scriptures are the basis of authority.'[24] Interpretation is essential because the scriptures contain no internal law by which the authoritative combinations of words and sentences can be fixed.[25] These are fixed in the light of the principle that the best interpretation is the one that best discloses the references of the text to human actions.[26] This process of scriptural interpretation in terms of actions is delicate and careful. It involves allegory, for it shows, for example, that a text that seems only to praise a god, in fact teaches what one should or should not do. As employed by Mimamsa, it rules out in advance any scriptural inconsistencies or contradictions.

What place can God have in this practical, scripture-centered religion? None at all, Mimamsa answers. It takes the position, recognized in Hinduism as orthodox, that the Vedas have no author, whether human, semi-divine, or divine. It holds that the authority of the scriptures is absolute just because they were not ever composed.[27] The reason given is simple if, to us, surprising: having an author would make the scriptures fallible, while, conversely, not having an external source or author would make them infallible. In keeping with Mimamsa doctrine, this argument can be stated in the form of a logical inference: Where there is no consequence, there is no cause—for example, smoke does not arise above a river, for its cause, fire, is not present in rivers. So, too, in the case of the scriptures. They cannot be subject to falsity because their falsity has no possible cause. The very possibility of falsity always depends on some person or other, human or divine, for every person is subject to desires, impulses, and intellectual limitations, which lead him at times to false conclusions. Therefore the Vedas, because they have no author or other external cause, cannot possibly be in error.[28] It is true, Mimamsa admits, that no positive proof of the validity of the Vedas can be given, for a positive proof must depend on something assumed to be prior or external to it. The proof of the validity of the scriptures is therefore purely negative.*

The upshot of this whole argument is that the authority of the Vedas is directly dependent on their *lack* of any author or cause (other, if causes can be so defined, than themselves). To admit that God was the author of the scriptures would obviously be fatal to the whole position of Mimamsa. Having no need of God to regulate human life, Mimamsa finds it easy, even without elaborate justification, to deny his existence. Like other metaphysical assumptions, the assumption that God exists is rejected as making no sense. This Godlessness resembles that of early Buddhism; but Buddhism is a religion of salvation, and Mimamsa a religion of obedience.**

As I have said, Mimamsa is more radical than any other Hindu school of philosophy in accepting the Vedas as the truth that must be literally obeyed. A quite different attitude can be found in the school of Nyaya, literally, 'Method'. Nyaya has been regarded by Westerners as the most modern and analytic of the Hindu philosophical schools, for it lays primary emphasis on logical, methodological, and linguistic problems. It is possible to see its thought as in many ways antedating the arguments of contemporary philosophy.

Although Nyaya justifies its Hindu orthodoxy by accepting the scriptures as such, it considers them infrequently, does not subject their contents to serious philosophizing, and cites them to strengthen its positions only very rarely. It is not clear, theologically or philosophically, why it needs the scriptures at all. It neither accepts them, as Mimamsa does, as the source of

* In direct continuation of this line of thought, later Mimamsa developed a negative theory of truth. According to this theory, it is not possible to prove the truth of any statement in a positive way. The criterion of truth is therefore the negative one of non-falsification, so that every statement continues to be regarded as valid as long as it has not been contradicted by another statement.

** Although Mimamsa rejects monotheism, that is, God with a capital letter, it requires at least some version of polytheism. The gods it accepts are not the creators or legislators of the cosmic order, *rita*, but, like man, are subject to it, and the rules of the Vedas apply to them just as they apply to mankind. They act, not freely, but in accord with a fixed causal principle, so that human ritual can obligate the gods to act for the benefit of human beings.

authoritative directives to action, nor derives any of its metaphysical assumptions from them. Its substantial independence of the scriptures is related to its rather vague conception of them as an archetype of 'verbal knowledge' or, in Sanskrit, *śabda*. A technical term, 'verbal knowledge' is understood to be a means of knowledge in addition to the other valid ones, such as perception and inference. Nyaya defines verbal knowledge as the assertion spoken by a trustworthy person, one who knows and speaks the truth.[29] Consequently, it sees the scriptures in the light of the possibility that valid information can be communicated, and it sets as the condition of their own utter validity that their source be always utterly reliable. In discussing the reliability of sources, it distinguishes between sacred and secular, and it says:

> There are two classes of sentences: those that belong to the *Veda* and those that belong to secular speech. Those that belong to the *Veda* are all statements of God and therefore authoritative. Of those that belong to secular speech, such as are produced by trustworthy persons are authoritative.[30]

Two points should be emphasized in relation to this passage. First, in direct contradiction to the views of Mimamsa and, it will be seen, of Vedanta, the scriptures get their authority directly from God. Secondly, scriptures make up only a part of verbal knowledge, the other part of which is secular and derived from ancient sages thought to be absolutely truthful in all they said. There is then no difference in principle between statements revealed to mankind by God and statements passed on to mankind by ancient sages. One of the important later exponents of Mimamsa, the philosopher Kumarila, also distinguishes between human and superhuman verbal testimony, the human being that given by trustworthy persons, the superhuman that given by the Vedas. This distinction is not present, to the best of my knowledge, in early Mimamsa. In any case, Nyaya accepts the testimony of trustworthy persons, that is, sages, as quite on a par with that of scriptures, while Kumarila, it seems clear, lays far more emphasis on and gives far greater credence to Vedic than to any human testimony.

The view that the scriptures are derived from God conflicts, as I have said, with the most widely accepted Indian tradition. There is no doubt that it weakens the position of the scriptures; for if the scriptures were revealed by God, it is at least difficult to regard them as eternal or beyond time. Certainly, Nyaya does not hesitate to deny them eternity in any form.[31] This denial helps Nyaya to develop its philosophy quite autonomously, to play down the issue of reason and revelation, and to relegate the scriptures to no more than a vague background. The attitude of this school to the contents of the scriptures often borders on indifference, and may not be very far from implicit rejection. The Nyaya habit of ignoring the scriptures subjected it to sharp attacks on the part of their opponents, who often charged it with heresy. The fact is, however, that Nyaya never explicitly renounced the scriptures and was therefore accounted one of the orthodox schools, in contrast to the Buddhists, Jains, and 'materialists'. It may be conjectured that the official orthodoxy of Nyaya is the result more of social adjustment than of philosophical persuasion.

Up till now, I have tried to bring evidence for the negative relationship between belief in God and in scriptures. Mimamsa, as we have seen, finds that one belief excludes the other, while Nyaya, which accepts God as the source of the scriptures, pays little attention to their contents. These two positions, of Mimamsa and Nyaya, may appear irreconcilably different. Nevertheless, they do have something in common, for both Mimamsa and Nyaya have no particular difficulty with the problem that so troubled Christian thinkers, the problem, I mean, of revelation and reason. It is, in effect, no problem to them, and they have no need to suggest solutions to it. In the comparative section of this chapter, I shall return to this point. At the moment, I should like to describe a third Hindu way of conceiving the relationship between the scriptures and God.

The third way I am referring to is that of the Vedanta. It will be recalled that the Upanishads were called 'Vedanta', 'the end of the Vedas', because they were the last part of the Vedas, in the broad sense of 'scriptures', to be composed. The name of the school of Vedanta testifies to the source of its inspiration, for its main purpose is to give a consistent, logical interpretation of Upanishadic thought. This school has been perhaps the most prolific of all the Hindu philosophical schools, and it is not possible to set out here all the variations of attitude toward scriptures that are to be found among its exponents. I therefore restrict myself to the attitude displayed by the Hindu philosopher Śankara (perhaps of the eighth century A.D.), the father of a major

subschool of Vedanta, and without doubt one of the most prominent, influential, and controversial of Hindu philosophers.

Śankara's position on the scriptures is intermediate between
that of Mimamsa and Nyaya. This intermediate position can be
put in the following three points:

1. In contrast to Nyaya, Śankara agrees with Mimamsa and holds that
the scriptures have no source external to themselves. Unlike Mimamsa,
he does not completely deny the existence of God, but God is not, in his
view, the source of the scriptures, which have their own, internally
guaranteed validity.[32]

2. Like Nyaya, Śankara regards the scriptures, along with perception
and inference, as a valid means of knowledge (*pramana*). But although,
he holds, the scriptures are to be classified among the valid sources of
knowledge, they are unique in that their knowledge is not of the perceptible, natural world, but of the imperceptible, supernatural world, the
existence of which would remain unknown to human beings if not for its
revelation by scriptures. He therefore contends that 'the scriptures are
meant for proving something that is not already known, for should they
restate something that is already known they would lose their validity'.[33]
This characterization of scriptures as a source of information clashes with
that of Mimamsa, which insists, it will be recalled, that the sole purpose
of the scriptures is to teach man which activities are permitted and which
forbidden.

3. In obvious contrast to the Nyaya, Śankara regards *śruti* in general
and the Upanishads in particular as of decisive religious importance. In
agreement with Mimamsa, he says that it is possible to find commandments in *śruti*, but, against Mimamsa, says that this is not their main
purpose, for the *dharma* found in the scriptures is meant only to prepare
human beings for their superlative goal. According to him, the basic
purpose of the Upanishads is to teach the absolute identity of Brahman
and Atman, the realization of which, he agrees with some Upanishads,
brings release from empirical existence and the suffering this existence
imposes. Salvation, Śankara emphasizes, cannot be gained by means
of perceptual or inferential knowledge, but only by means of the scriptures.[34]

The conception of scriptures as a means of knowledge forces
Śankara to pay attention to the possibility that a contradiction
between scriptural and other evidence may appear. He may,
therefore, seem to be in a position like that of the early Christian
thinkers, but this likeness between East and West is no more than
superficial, for it is based on the ambiguity of the concept of

philosophy. To Śankara, as to other Hindu philosophers, philosophy is for the most part concerned with epistemological matters, and the theory of knowledge he proposes deals with perceived reality as such, without any prior assumptions based on the origin or nature of this reality. He rejects the subjective idealism of the Buddhists, because this idealism, he says, imposes a metaphysical theory on perceived reality and so contradicts our basic common sense.[35] To use Western terminology, in Śankara's theory of knowledge the world is grasped as the totality of perceived facts and not as the totality of metaphysically interpreted things. His very definition of scriptural knowledge makes it impossible to apply such knowledge to facts—the scriptures cannot contradict the truth of a factual observation. From this view there is only a short step to the Śankaran conclusion: in every case in which information found in scriptures contradicts information arrived at after inquiry and with good reason, the scriptures are *not* to be regarded as authoritative. Śankara would reject the Old Testament report that the sun stood still at Joshua's command as a mere legend, or he would have given it a wholly allegorical interpretation. That is, Śankara would assume that the sun's motionless was in direct contradiction with evidence that there is no good reason to reject. He writes:

'You cannot prove that fire is cold, or that the sun does not give heat, even by citing a hundred examples [from scriptures], for the fact would already be known to be otherwise through other means of knowledge.'[36]

Śankara's radical separation between revelation and reason allows him to propose a harmony between them. Revelation and reason proceed, he thinks, on parallel paths, and as long as they do not stray from these paths, they cannot lead to contradictions. Philosophy is therefore quite autonomous within its realm, that of facts, while the possibility of salvation creates an autonomous realm, which may be considered, not without considerable ambiguity, I must add, the realm of values. If philosophy strays from its natural realm and tries to impose itself on metaphysical matters, it loses its persuasiveness and most likely falls into self-contradiction and meaninglessness. Likewise, if revelation strays from its natural realm, that of the supernatural, with respect to which its evidence is authoritative, and tries to invade the realm of facts, its conclusions cannot be accepted as valid unless they happen to coincide with those established by perception and reason.

Comparison

All I have so far written tends to show that the relations between revelation and reason are of doubtful philosophical importance. On the assumption that they are so, I will enter into them only insofar as they have led to various attempts to establish the proper boundaries of philosophy. It is hard to free oneself of the impression that the boundaries were actually set by the acceptance, sincere or merely expedient, of dogmas essentially foreign to philosophy, and that the price paid by philosophers for acceptance has always been heavy. I do not feel myself at all competent to judge whether this payment has been worthwhile socially, or whether the philosophers who made it have received in any way adequate compensation; but I can judge the heaviness of the price paid by philosophy itself. Comparison of East and West will teach not only the extent of the price, but the inevitability of its payment by a philosopher who so much as raises the problem of revelation and reason. What I am saying may betray some prejudice on my part, because the price may appear trivial in the eyes of a religious man not deeply aware of philosophical tradition. I must therefore be specific in saying that my own estimate is made from the standpoint of the philosopher alone. I should particularly like to use my comparison to sharpen and probe the ambivalence of the philosopher who is reluctant to sacrifice either reason on the altar of revelation or the opposite. It appears to me that the comparison will at least hint at the failure of the philosopher's ambivalence to lead any ultimately rational conclusion. The establishment of harmony between revelation and reason is a burden too heavy for the philosopher as such to bear. Whoever supposes that his failure has resulted from the specific conditions of one or another culture will find in the present comparison that the attempt and failure exact the same heavy price of the philosopher, whether he is a Hindu, a Muslim, a Christian, or, I suppose, a member of any other religion.

I begin the comparison with a discussion of the school of Mimamsa, not because of its venerable age, which exceeds that of the other schools of thought, Hindu or Christian, that I have mentioned, but because its solution of the problem of revelation and reason may not be objectionable to the contemporary Western philosopher. I do not mean, of course, that the Western philosopher may be tempted to become a Mimamsa, but only that many of the English-speaking philosophers of the present century are likely to have been quite willing to pay the kind of price demanded by Mimamsa, even apart from the comfort granted by acceptance into a religious community.

The standpoint of Mimamsa is unquestionably religious and unquestionably (in the relevant sense) atheistic. This combination suggests the inadequacy of the usual conceptions of religion and religious faith. The religion of Mimamsa has a colour all its own. It gives up the metaphysical or transcendental dimension almost completely. It has nothing of the emotional warmth of so much religious faith, nothing of the deep experience of the religious mystic, no explanation of the origin of the world, and not even an apocalyptic vision of another world for initiates to enter in place of the present world. Such warmth, experience, enlightenment, and hope are rejected by Mimamsa as meaningless or, at best, irrelevant. In their place Mimasa proposes what may be called 'religio-legal authority', in which it sees the whole of Hindu orthodoxy.

To Mimamsa, the position of philosophy is unambiguous. As they see it, philosophy does no more than help to interpet the scriptures, in keeping with the principle of action. This is certainly a minimizing and unusual delimitation of philosophy, but by confining it metaphysically, it frees it to deal with anything non-metaphysical that does not conflict with the commandments of the Vedas. The emptiness, to Mimamsa, of metaphysical speculation is compensated for by the ability, even the obligation, of philosophy to deal with epistemological problems. Because scriptures are presumed not to transmit information about the world, but only to regulate action, the philosopher is free to analyse words, concepts, and sentences, to examine the validity of arguments, and the like. The removal of metaphysics from the scope of philosophy is sufficient to prevent all conflict between theology, in the Mimamsa sense of scriptural interpretation, and philosophy, in the limited sense of theory of knowledge, philosophy of language, and logic. Philosophy and theology are then like two parallel lines that never meet, and the study of the one can never damage the other. In practice, Mimamsa prefers the study of scriptures to the study of philosophy in and for itself, but these two fields of study cannot, in principle, contradict one another.

The solution suggested by Mimamsa no doubt challenges the philosopher who favours metaphysics, but, I suppose, would not anger him. The position of Nyaya, on the contrary, might easily arouse his anger, for it can be taken to favour insincerity. Instead of dealing philosophically with the problem of revelation, Nyaya, it will be recalled, respects the scriptures theoretically but ignores them philosophically. The nerve of its solution is simple enough: acknowledge the yoke of the scriptures, show them respect, be ready in certain cases to ascribe informational value to them, but do not take what they say with excessive seriousness. This Nyaya solution is naturally never explicit, but it seems to me implicit in its actual philosophizing. The existence and even success of Nyaya within the confines of Hinduism is a testimony to religious toleration. The vehement attacks, including accusations of heresy, by philosophers of other persuasions on the Nyaya position remained verbal and never led, as they might have in Europe, to the torturer's rack.

The price paid by the school of Nyaya for its solution is, as it might appear to the external observer, social hypocrisy. It is not, in the direct sense, a philosophical price. The price demanded of Tertullian, Augustine, and, in part, Anselm is, on the contrary, a clearly philosophical one. Its payment enables these Christians to adopt a radical, religiously fortified standpoint. Tertullian, as has been said, rejects philosophy as unhelpful and sometimes even harmful, while Augustine sees faith as perfect and philosophy as no more than a help to the understanding of revelation.* Tertullian, Augustine, and Anselm simply remain faithful to the division made by saint Paul between the wisdom of God, expressed in revelation, and the wisdom of this world, expressed in philo-

---

* Wolfson has distinguished between the positions of Tertullian and Augustine, the first of which he calls 'the single-faith theory' and the second, 'the double-faith theory'. In making this distinction, Wolfson relies on the fact that Tertullian rejected philosophy completely, while Augustine, like Philo, allowed philosophy to serve theology. 'The Double Faith Theory in Clement, Saadia, Averroes and St. Aquinas', in H. A. Wolfson, *Studies in the History of Philosophy and Religion*, vol. 1, Harvard, Harvard University Press, 1973.

sophy.[37] 'For the wisdom of this world is folly with God,' says Paul in his first letter to the Corinthians (3/19).

It is evident that this Christian position, if consistently followed, would put an end to all serious philosophizing. To convince its partisans that they are wrong is almost impossible, at least for philosophers, because the rules of rational argument no longer oblige them. Like the partisans of Nyaya, though for different reasons, they have abandoned the attempt to make a compromise between faith and reason.

Is it possible to see a compromise in the thought of the philosopher, Averroes? The title of his book, *On the Harmony of Religion and Philosophy*, proclaims that harmony is his objective. As a rationalist, he stresses that philosophy is a science of the first importance, and the very first sentence of his book makes the impression of a desire to force reason on the scriptures. 'The purpose of this treatise', he writes, 'is to examine, from the standpoint of the study of Law [the Quran], whether the study of philosophy and logic is allowed by the Law, or prohibited, or commended—either by way of recommendation or as obligatory.'[38]

Averroes' answer is unequivocal. The scriptures, he says, neither attack nor prohibit the study of philosophy, but obligate it. Therefore anyone who tries to prevent a man of natural intelligence and religious conscience from studying philosophy breaks a specific scriptural commandment.[39] To counter the fear that the study of philosophy will injure religious faith, Averroes proposes the following simile:

A man who prevents a qualified person from studying books of philosophy, because some of the most vicious people may be thought to have gone astray through their study of them, is like a man who prevents a thirsty person from drinking cool, fresh water till he dies of thirst, because some people have choked to death on it. For death from water by choking is an accidental matter, but death by thirst is essential and necessary.[40]

To prove his contention that the study of philosophy is enjoined on qualified persons, Averroes quotes the Quran. Unfortunately, his quotations are unconvincing, and the impartial reader will have difficulty in finding others to show that the Quran requires the study of philosophy. In this instance, however, as in others, Averroes takes refuge in the hospitable arms of allegory, a method that he allows, as I have said, to philosophers alone. It is hard to be sure whether Averroes sincerely believes that the allegorical method gives a sound scriptural justification of philosophy, or whether he insincerely uses it for want of anything better. But it is sure that his argument is circular: by the allegorical interpretation of the Quran, we know that the Quran demands that philosophy be studied; but the permission to interpret the Quran allegorically is given only to someone who already knows philosophy. Does the philosopher begin by arrogating to himself the permission he has not yet teased out of the Quran, does he, having interpreted the Quranic allegorically, find that the permission to study philosophy has been given to him retroactively, or does he begin by depending, in Muslim fashion, on the testimony of a chain of witnesses going back, he has faith, to Muhammed or his companions? Such questions put Averroes' desired harmony in an absurd enough light. His need for the allegorical method pushes him on to the arbitrary, un-reasoned exegesis of scriptures. His example only strengthens the contention made by Spinoza in his polemic against allegorical interpretation of scriptures, that if it is assumed that the scrip-tures, for some reason unknown to us, have a meaning other than their evident one, the scriptures themselves are completely subverted—and so, I may add (if the assumption is for the sake of the harmony we have been discussing) is philosophy.[41]

There is no doubt that of all the positions I have mentioned, those of Aquinas and Śankara are most marked by ambivalence. But the character of their ambivalence is not the same. Aquinas's resides in initial theological assumptions, Śankara's in initial philosophical assumptions. To begin with Aquinas, the *Summa Theologiae* makes the impression of an attempt to develop a rational method, but of a failure to apply the method consis-tently, because of a bias in favour of religious faith. His bias is obvious, for example, in his willingness to consider Christian theology a science. In affirming it to be a science, he uses the same arguments by means of which, in his previous, negative argu-ment, he denied it was such. As I have said, he argues for the scientific nature of theology on the grounds that it depends 'on the light of a higher science, namely God's own.' It follows that to accept theology as a science, one must *first* believe in God, in

God's revelation, and in the scriptures that have passed this revelation on to us. The same faith that in Aquinas's first argument made theology a non-science now becomes the revelation of a higher, more-than-human science. The circularity of this reasoning is obvious, and is characteristic, as I will not try to demonstrate here, of his treatment of other, similar problems. By reasoning so, Aquinas empties the distinction between religion and philosophy of any clear content.

The surrender to faith of almost all medieval Islamic and Christian philosophy is very well expressed in the following words:

> Is it not characteristic of the sharing of concerns in medieval Islam and medieval Christianity that where St. Thomas Aquinas insists that we must investigate the method of scientific thinking before the sciences themselves, he bases himself on Aristotle but quotes in support Averroes referring to what the Commentator had to say on that self-same subject? And within the life of the spirit, both the Christian and the Muslim worlds, striving to reach the *revelabile* from the *revelatum*, had to leave intact (a dream less rarely realized than a modern would suspect) that sense of the superiority of simple faith, untaught faith, the *fides vetulae*, old women's faith, praised and preserved by Juwaini (d. 1085) and St. Thomas as the height of religious experience. The coincidence of order and mind that had satisfied the Greeks from Plato to Plotinus no longer sufficed.
>
> *Theologia* is subordinated to *fides, kalam* to *mushahada*. Logic builds the fortress, logic the machines to conquer it, but the prize it shelters is not reason but grace.[42]

Aquinas does, I admit, retain a distinctive, if narrow, field for philosophy, including whatever theology has not in fact referred to, in which philosophy is allowed to make its own decisions. But in sharp contrast to the autonomy granted philosophy by Mimamsa, the Aquinian autonomy seems more accidental than essential. According to Aquinas, theology does not in fact apply to some philosophical subjects, but his system gives no reason why theology should not contradict philosophy, and therefore gives philosophy no barrier beyond which it can function without being potentially overruled. Revelation is for him potentially all-inclusive, and its past concessions have not been concessions in principle. Aquinas thus returns in principle to the Augustinian position; but while Augustine rejects the possibility that reason can criticize theology and in this sense immunizes himself against rational criticism, Aquinas bares himself to such criticism, because he wants to enjoy the best of both worlds, those of both theology and philosophy. It seems that Aquinas has got himself into the predicament of the person described by Śankara, who cooks a chicken, eats half of it, and stores the rest of it to lay eggs for him.

It may now be inquired if Śankara, who inadvertently describes Aquinas's predicament, himself escapes it. It appears to me that the answer is simply negative. Like Aquinas, Śankara depends on prior assumptions that do now allow the establishment of clear mutual relations between revelation and reason. As I have already remarked, these prior assumptions of Śankara are not theological, but philosophical. Śankara's definition of scriptures as a means of knowledge and his acceptance of them as an integral part of any valid theory of knowledge highlight the problematic quality of his whole position. His intention in making the definition is clear. He wants to lend the information given by scriptures the same measure of validity granted to knowledge that comes by way of the senses or logic. In everything that concerns perceptual or logical knowledge, Śankara makes use of a clear criterion by means of which, he contends, the truth of any statement can be unambiguously tested. According to this criterion, which he holds in common with Mimamsa, any statement whatsoever is, to begin with, taken to be true, that is, requires no particular effort to validate it, and remains true as long as it has not been falsified by some other statement.

If this is the general criterion by which truth is tested, it should, it seems, apply to whatever is found in the scriptures, for the scriptures are included among the means of knowledge. This point is worth making with some care. Śankara, it will be recalled, does not allow the scriptures to contradict the testimony of the senses or of logic, and insists that in every case in which such contradiction is present, the testimony of the scriptures must be denied. The primary purpose of the scriptures, he maintains, is to give information on the supernatural or transcendental realm, and when scriptures restrict themselves to this purpose, one can take the statements to be found in them to be true because they have not been falsified.

At this point we have come to the heart of Śankara's ambivalence. His ambivalence is rooted in the question, why is it that the scriptures when transmitting 'metaphysical' information cannot be falsified? This question can be given two diametrically opposed answers. The first answer is, briefly, that the scriptures cannot be falsified because they contain metaphysical statements, and these are in principle unfalsifiable. The second answer bases the inability to falsify scriptures on their absolute, eternal authority. Let me explain these two answers and the unbridgeable gap between them. The first assumes that when we make, in the sense of the Positivists, a metaphysical statement, we go beyond the limits of what can be meaningfully said. Metaphysical statements, in this sense, are meaningless because they cannot be falsified, and it is therefore not possible to distinguish between a true and a false metaphysical statement. While a factual statement remains true as long as it is not falsified, a metaphysical statement, on Brahman, for example, is neither true nor false, for the very possibility of falsifying it does not exist.

By this answer, the first, the scriptures mark the border of human knowledge, which is the border of the possibility of truth and falsity. Śankara's definition of the scriptures as means of knowledge is then meant to indicate that humans are able to relate not only to what they know and can assign meaning to, but also to the transcendental realm that they in principle cannot know, and that human language is unable to express in any meaningful way. Everything said in the scriptures, whether briefly or at length, poetically or prosaically, implicitly or explicitly, does no more than express, in a way that must be paradoxical, that it is impossible to arrive at a positive, meaningful understanding of the transcendental.

As against this answer, there is the contradictory, second answer, which is far more dogmatic. According to this second answer, the scriptures attribute to themselves an eternal and absolute truth, which cannot be diminished by any factual statement. Eternality and absoluteness are necessary to one another. The reason is that the truth of factual statements is temporary, for they are always open to possible falsification by other factual statements; but scriptural statements cannot, by definition, be superseded by others, so that they must by regarded as eternal and authoritative.

The two possible answers I have outlined bring Śankara to a

crossroads. Before I continue with Śankara's own conclusions, I should like to ask which of the answers is theoretically more consistent with his philosophical position. I can at this point only state my choice. To give my reasons for it would require me to explicate the whole of Śankara's philosophy. My therefore unsupported though unhesitating choice is that the first answer is the more consistent. As I see Śankara's thought, it both accepts the identity between Brahman and Atman as a religious value and rejects this identity as philosophically meaningless. This answer, that the transcendental reality is, in human terms, meaningless, is common to a good deal of theology and is to be found in the celebrated passages of the Upanishads that say that reality is neither this, nor that, nor anything that can be clearly thought or said. But though present in the Upanishads, this negative approach to transcendent reality came to characterize, not orthodox Hinduism, but, in its most telling philosophical expression, the Buddhist philosopher, Nagarjuna, whose thought will be the subject of one of the subsequent chapters. It is no accident that Śankara was attacked by Hindu philosophers of other schools as a crypto-Buddhist. The accusation, to my mind, does have some basis.

Having chosen the answer most consistent with Śankara's philosophy, I owe the reader an account of which answer he himself in fact chose. To my own sorrow, I cannot determine which it was. So far as I have succeeded in interpreting Śankara, he himself never made the unambiguous choice between the two answers. For reasons which may well be social rather than philosophical, Śankara did not clearly choose the first answer, which appears the more compatible with his philosophy, but he also, it seems, was reluctant to make a clear choice of the second answer, which is so dogmatic that it would destroy the very basis of his philosophy. My opinion is that Śankara preferred to avoid the choice between the two alternatives, and his thought remains suspended between the acceptance of scriptures as expressing, in a negative sense, the meaninglessness of the transcendental realm, and between their acceptance as expressing in a positive, dogmatic manner the eternity, perfection, and infallibility of certain religious assumptions. Whatever the reasons for Śankara's ambivalence, there is no doubt that his attempt to harmonize revelation and reason is basically a failure.

We have been witnesses to the equal failure of Aquinas and Śankara. I have argued that the reasons for the failure of the one are theological, and of the other, philosophical. The difference in the reasons for the failure led to different consequences. Aquinas's attempt, I have said, was to include philosophy within the framework of theology. His failure was one of the causes of the increasing lack of stability of Western theology and, consequently, of the increasing secularization of Western philosophy and its increasing detachment from the problems of the Christian religion. Slowly, the problem of the status of the scriptures disappeared from the horizon of the Western philosopher. Now in the West, the questions concerning the validity and authority of the scriptures find their suitable place within theology, which is related to philosophy only by way of the history of thought. Western theology and philosophy have become polarized.[43]*

Śankara's failure, resulting from philosophical causes, had philosophical results. His attempt, the opposite of Aquinas's, was to include scriptures within a philosophical framework. The effect of his failure was the destruction of the philosophical framework as such. This destruction finds its expression in the development of the school of Vedanta after Śankara and, to a certain extent, in the development of all Indian philosophy after Śankara. To generalize somewhat crudely, it may be said that Indian thought after Śankara finds increasing interest in religion, while its interest in purely philosophical questions gradually slackens. The clearest exception is the school of Navya Nyaya, which renewed Nyaya doctrines. This school, which began in the thirteenth century, deals for the most part with questions of

---

* The polarization was expressed in 1928, in a series of three lectures by the noted French historian of philosophy, Émile Bréhier, under the title, 'Is There a Christian Philosophy?' His completely negative answer no doubt stemmed from the series of historic failures to create harmony between revelation and reason. Bréhier argued that it was possible to use the term 'Christian philosophy' in a purely historical sense, but that Christianity substituted for the Greek instrument of reason, the *logos*, the mysterious, supposedly infallible testimony of the scriptures. In doing so, Christianity created a fundamental difference between theology and philosophy, that is, authoritative faith and rationalism. Therefore, he said, the term 'Christian philosophy' united opposites that cannot really be joined and lacked a clear meaning. M. Nédoncelle, *Is There a Christian Philosophy?*, New York, Hawthorne Books, 1960, summarizes the debate between Bréhier, Gilson, and others.

formal logic, and its contribution to the traditional problems of Indian philosophy is slight. Such a development of technique, almost in and for itself, hardly diminishes the painful realization that Indian philosophy, once so vital and enormously rich, is being gradually emptied of life. One sees philosophy being replaced by various religious faiths and forms of mysticism. Philosophic method gives way to subjective intuition, and philosophic reasoning and logic to 'spirituality'. While the failure of Aquinas marks a point at which an autonomous European philosophy begins to live, that of Śankara, in my opinion, marks a point at which Indian philosophy begins to die.

My conclusion, that the attempts to create harmony between revelation and reason all failed, may appear too pessimistic. If, however, one accepts Spinoza's uncompromising distinction between theology and philosophy, it is not difficult to free oneself of the pessimism. One can also reconcile oneself to it, by recognizing that it could not have been avoided, for it has been no more than an expression of the human attempt to understand what is beyond understanding. To drive this truth home, I should like to recall the conversation in Kafka's *Trial* between Joseph K and the priest of the prison. When Joseph K tries to discover a clear, mutually acceptable meaning to the parable of the gate of the Law, the priest interrupts him and says:

'Don't misunderstand me. I am only showing you the various opinions concerning that point. You must not pay too much attention to them. The scriptures are unalterable and the comments often enough merely express the commentators' despair.'

Some Words on Authority and Reason in Chinese Philosophy[44] *(Ben-Ami Scharfstein)*

The description of Chinese society given in the previous chapter has no doubt left the impression that Chinese society was largely ruled by tradition and such of its living representatives as parents, elders generally, and the graduated ranks of scholar-officials. The question I should like to deal with, though only briefly and tentatively, is whether the authority of tradition ruled over philosophy, too, and, if it did, to what effect. My answer will limit itself primarily to Confucianism, because it was the official doctrine of China for long periods of time, because it was the predominant ideology of the scholar-officials, and because it exerted so deep an influence on the thought and character of the Chinese.

Confucianism became official during the early years of the Han Dynasty (207 B.C.—A.D. 220), when the state cult was conjoined to Confucianism and the state undertook to pay official honours to Confucius and his chief disciples. The dominance of the so-called New Text School of Confucianism resulted, not unironically, in the worship of Confucius, who had himself made no claim to authority beyond that embodied in decency and reasonableness. However, the New was gradually displaced by the Old Text School, which was, textual gullibility apart, more rationalistic or rational, and which regarded Confucius as a clearly human, though clearly extraordinary sage.

Whatever the dominant textual school, the Confucian books acquired the title *ching*, which is translated 'classic', and which generally implies regularity and authority. Five (or, for a time, six) Confucian books were recognized as classics: *The Book of Changes, The Book of History, The Book of Poetry, The Book of Rites,* and *The Spring and Summer Annals.* Although the number of Confucian classics was later raised to thirteen, these five continued to be distinguished as such. The classics were, of course, the substance of the curriculum in Chinese schools of all levels. With the help of these classics, students were taught such Confucian virtues as filial piety, brotherly love, goodness or benevolence, propriety, loyalty, and consideration (In Chinese, *hsiao, t'i, jen, li, chung,* and *shu*). This list of virtues, which , as moralists might suspect, is incomplete, will remain unexamined here; but it is plain that it emphasizes tradition, respect, and obedience, virtues that a contemporary Westerner is unlikely to associate with originality of thought.

As has been described, Confucianism found powerful and often successful rivals in Taoism and Buddhism. The reassertion or revival of Confucianism, against its rivals, against evil, or against both, signalled a longing for the past that was at least imagined to have been, in the Confucian sense, good, which is to say, sober, moral, rightly familial, and natively Chinese. One of the great revivers of Confucianism was the writer, Han Yü (A.D. 786–824), who uncompromisingly rejected Buddhism and Taoism as irrational and subversive of genuine values. Despite the official and unofficial hostility he faced, he insisted on Confucian orthodoxy, the terms of which he helped to formulate.

In later Chinese history, the mainstay of Confucian orthodoxy came to be the philosopher, Chu Hsi (A.D. 1130–1200), who was himself too independent intellectually to please the government of his time—the protester of one age, he was the measure of obedience of another. Chu Hsi claimed to have inherited the 'Way' of Confucius. The 'Way' was presumed to have been lost with the death of Confucius' disciple, Mencius, but recovered by means of the 'Learning of the Principle', '*Li-hsüeh*', which we in the West designate 'Neo-Confucianism'. Chu's claim made Mencius, who had refused to kowtow to authoritative books as such, the support of their exclusive authority. Chu laid particular stress, not on the Five Classics, but on the Four Books, the *Analects, Mencius, The Great Learning,* and *The Doctrine of the Mean,* all of which he edited, that is, divided into chapters, punctuated, and annotated. Taken alone, the Four Books allowed Chu to preach his own kind of Confucianism more effectively. He was also responsible for the final acceptance of a sort of Confucian credo, taken from the *Book of History.* Sixteen characters long in Chinese, the credo may be translated, 'Man's mind is prone to error, the Mind of the Way is subtle. Remain discerning and single-minded: Keep steadfastly to the Mean.'[45] This credo or formula, though generally accepted by Neo-Confucian philosophers, fixed very little doctrinally or philosophically.

It was natural for Confucian thinkers to express their philosophical differences in terms of different interpretations of the old Confucian texts they had studied. It is perhaps not excessive to say that all Chinese religious and philosophical authority came to be justified by way of interpretation of the Confucian Classics, and that most later Chinese philosophy utilized such interpretation as its medium. Influenced, it seems, by the Ch'an Buddhists, Neo-Confucians often recorded the talks or debates of their masters in 'records of conversations'. Much of their doctrine is also preserved in the form of the letters they wrote one another. Both in conversation and writing they make liberal use of phrases like 'rectifying the mind', 'making intentions sincere', and 'investigating things', and so remind us that philosophy in China too depended on a certain stereotyping of thought. Like the Chinese they are, these Neo-Confucians contradict the

Buddhists and argue that the perceptible world is the real one, and contradict both the Buddhists and Taoists and argue that family and social life are a supreme value. They resist any metaphysical pull away from the concerns of practical daily life.

The one fact that must be emphasized here is that the version of Neo Confucianism taught by Chu Hsi and his followers became official. Anyone who wanted to succeed in the civil-service examinations or to find favour in official eyes had to know and at least appear to agree, not only with Confucianism, but with Chu Hsi's particular interpretation of it. Chu Hsi was bred into the bones of innumerable Chinese scholars. Telling evidence of this can be found in a confession made by Chu Hsi's great sixteenth-century opponent, the general and philosopher, Wang Yang-ming. It appears to have been a deep internalization of Chu Hsi, and not expediency, or not merely expediency that led him to write:

> All my life Chu Hsi's doctrine has been a revelation to me, as though from the 'highest spiritual intelligence'. In my heart I could not bear to oppose him. Therefore it was because I could not help it that I did it. Those who know me say that my heart is grieved but those who do not know me say that I am after something. The fact is that in my own heart I cannot bear to contradict Master Chu but I cannot help contradicting him because the Tao is what it is and the Tao will not be fully evident if I do not correct him.[46]

The pressure exerted on Chinese thinkers to conform had an often transparently political motive, the desire of the government or, more particularly, of the Emperor, to rule at ease over a nation of conformists. The Emperor K'ang-hsi (1662–1722) ordered all the schoolchildren of China to recite regularly a select group of Confucian moral injunctions. His successor, Yung-cheng (1723–35) ordered that only Chu Hsi's interpretation of the Confucian canon be allowed. Yung-cheng's son and successor, Ch'ien-lung (1735–96), confirmed the order. Being informed that one Hsieh Chi-shih had written commentaries on the classics that disregarded Chu Hsi's interpretation, he decreed that Hsieh's writings be examined in detail and any place where he disregarded Chu Hsi's interpretation noted. 'I fear', the Emperor wrote in his decree, 'that men without knowledge will be unsettled' by the teaching of Hsieh's school, 'and that there will arise

variant modes of thought and behaviour. This would be dangerous both for the hearts and doctrines of mankind. I have not so far
made a crime out of the utterances of men, but this matter is of too
great significance.' The books in question, he decreed, must be
'utterly destroyed'. For emphasis he added, 'Let none be saved.'

This decree, dated November 3, 1741, aroused such protests
that, although the books and the woodblocks from which they
had been printed were burned, Hsieh himself was saved and
rehabilitated.[47] The next heresy hunt was postponed for more
than thirty years, when an edict was issued that all 'false, deceiving books' be handed over, 'in order that the land may be completely rid of them....'[48] Even the mildest hint of anything
against the Emperor or his dynasty, even the slightest disregard
of the ancient practice of elevating the emperor's name was
enough to condemn a book or author. The Emperor's index of
condemned books includes a number of commentaries on the
classics, making it appear that unorthodox Confucianism was
also to be consigned to the flames.[49] Some 2,320 books were listed
for total suppression, and 342 for partial suppression. Although
the inquisition soon fell into neglect, it had struck a substantial
blow against Chinese literature and against freedom of thought.

The literary inquisition I have described was too sweeping and
severe to be typical, but it does illustrate the typical desire of the
authorities to suppress disturbing thoughts. It strengthens the
impression that Chinese thought passed through an early creative period, but was later often subjected to heavy pressure to
conform to the prevailing orthodoxy. Such an impression is not
wrong; yet the conclusion should not be drawn that Chinese
thought was therefore simply conformist and servile. The truth is
that the pressure, which took many more forms than have been
recorded here, was perfectly obvious to the Chinese themselves,
and that the same Confucian tradition that represented conformity gave the more stubborn, independent, or honest Confucians
the impulse and justification not to conform if their consciences,
which were very acute, were offended.

Chinese philosophy, it has been noted, failed to develop in
certain directions, and much of later Chinese philosophy has,
from a modern Western standpoint, notable weaknesses. Yet,
speaking quite generally, I feel that pressure and persecution,
whatever their force at any particular moment of history, account

for much of the strength rather than the weakness of Chinese philosophy. Honesty and courage, expressed either openly or with cautious indirection, are quite as characteristic of it as the sacrifice of logical acuteness to poetic resonance. In other words, I do not think that such external pressure as was exerted succeeded in forcing Chinese philosophers into genuine conformity. Many of them were neither cowards nor fools.

It should be noted that the pressure for conformity in Chinese thought was not religious, nor was there any priesthood to exert it. Religious freedom, despite the persecutions I have reported, was usually far greater than in medieval or early modern Europe. Insofar as the pressure was political, it was basically the same as in any centralized regime. On some issues of interest to philosophers, there seems to have been no pressure at all. This is not to deny that the example of Confucius, the literature associated with him, and the orthodox and other interpretations given his teaching affected every Chinese thinker. I find it difficult, however, to be precise and to offer well-analysed examples of essential conformity or freedom among Chinese thinkers. The reason is that the subject has not drawn the same sustained attention as the problem of faith and reason in medieval Europe or Islam. Detailed research on the problem had hardly been done. My own too general words are an invitation to others to study and explain what I do not pretend to know.

4

Modes of Argument

Dan Daor

Seen from a distance, each philosophic civilization has its characteristic modes of argument. Each shows the preponderance of certain of the modes, follows certain sequences of philosophic moves, repeats certain stock examples, and, in general, shows the influence of a particular intensive indoctrination in approved forms of argument. It would be an instructive exercise to take a random group of arguments from the philosophers of each civilization, abstract the form of the arguments from the contents, and try to identify the civilizations in which they were respectively used. Later on in this chapter, one of the authors seems to imply that the identifications might often fail; but he has not in fact undertaken the exercise, and the reader is invited to try it in his place. If the reader becomes expert enough, he is invited to try to identify, not only the civilization, but also the period. Granted the self-consciousness of philosophers and the sophistication in argument they aim at, it is surprising that they have not tried more often or intensively to describe and evaluate the kinds of arguments they have actually made use of.[1]

By and large, the most self-conscious and highly formalized modes were those used in India, and the Indians therefore produced detailed handbooks on argumentation as such.[2] The Islamic and European medievals, of course, following Aristotle's lead, also formalized the process of argument.[3] Yet it is interesting, as will be pointed out, that much, perhaps most, of the reasoning in philosophy has followed intuitive rather than consciously formal patterns. However this may be, the comparison of the modes of argument used in the different civilizations is a subject of obvious interest, and a simple beginning is made here to a complex subject.

Indian Philosophical Reasoning: Tarka
(Shlomo Biderman)

It is perhaps difficult for those who have not studied Indian philosophy to free themselves of the prejudice that Indian philosophical argument is emotional or dogmatic rather than logical. This prejudice results from the belief, I assume, that Indian philosophy is primarily mystical and, for that reason, averse to the rigour that logic imposes. I hope that the following pages will show that Indian philosophical reasoning is as careful and logical as that of the West. There are certainly differences in emphasis and style, but not in intrinsic logicality.

The first point I should like to make is that the chief Indian modes of argument are essentially the same as the Western, but that the philosophical status of Indian argument is on the whole different from that of the West.[4] In some contrast to Western philosophy, Indian philosophy sees the precision of argument as a major criterion for deciding the validity of a philosophical system. I emphasize the word, 'some', because the difference is only one of degree. During what seems to me the most flourishing period of Indian philosophy, the first millennium A.D., the fate of every system depended on the logical consistency it could achieve. Unless it could achieve it basically, it was not recognized as having genuine philosophical interest. It was the demand for consistency that guided the complex, sometimes fascinating dialogue between the different philosophical schools. This dialogue proved to be inherent to Indian philosophy and must account for a good deal of at least its technical development. It was not a calm, neutral dialogue, but a duel of wits. Its aim was not compromise, but the satisfaction and advantage that follow from the exposure of one's philosophical opponent as incoherent. The success of each school was measured not only by the initial plausibility of its assumptions, but also by its ability to withstand contradiction. It is, therefore, difficult to avoid the impression that the Indians particularly emphasized the analytical, critical, and negative functions of philosophy.

The process of mutual criticism is called *tarka* in Sanskrit. *Tarka* includes many, sometimes complex, rules on which every philosophical debate was supposed to be based. Formal debates between thinkers appeared as early as the Upanishads, but the first text that applied rules explicitly to philosophical debate was the *Nyaya Sutra*, which is usually supposed to have been written during the second century A.D. For the sake of genuinely philosophical debate, it established not only rules, but nuances of rules. The *Nyaya Sutra* was followed by many other books for the regulation of debates. Often they are no more than cut-and-dried lists of fallacies and the like, which gives them something of the air and appearance of cookbooks.

The existence of rules or argument is self-evidently dependent on the willingness of debaters to accept them. Towards the beginning of the Buddhist text, *Milinda's Questions*, we find an entertaining example of an agreement to use reason, not force. The agreement, between King Milinda and the sage, Nagasena, whose conversation the text purports to record, is made in the following exchange:

'Revered Nagasena, will you converse with me?'
'I will converse with you, sire, will converse in the speech of the learned, but if you converse in the speech of kings I will not converse.'
'How, revered Nagasena, do the learned converse?'
'When the learned are conversing, sire, a turning over (of a subject) is made and an unravelling is made and a refutation is made and redress is made and a specific point is made against it, and the learned are not angry in consequence—it is thus, sire, that the learned converse.'
'And how do kings converse, revered sir?'
'When kings are conversing, sire, they approve of some matter and order a punishment for whoever disagrees with that matter, saying: "Inflict a punishment on him"—it is thus, sire, that kings converse.'
'I, revered sir, will converse in the speech of the learned, not in the speech of kings. Let the revered one converse unreservedly as he converses with a novice or lay-follower or with a monastery-attendant—let the revered one converse thus, let him not be afraid.'[5]

As has been noted in an earlier chapter, the recommendation to avoid anger was not in fact always adopted by even sophisticated debaters. It was evidently more an ideal restraint than a usual one. Yet Indian philosophical debate, as we have already seen, was conducted within a well-understood framework of rules. It can perhaps be best understood as a kind of formal game—it seems to have been no accident that chess was played in ancient India, and by kings as well as learned men. In the philosophic game, as in others, there are fixed rules, and their acceptance by the rivals is an essential condition for its playing; but incidents may easily arise in which the rivals dispute over the meaning or application of the rules. Similar tactical methods may serve different aims, or different methods the same aims. I say this because the similarity I shall show between Indian and European philosophical argument, and that will later be shown to extend in part to Chinese argument, ought not to cause us to forget that the tactics are employed in the service of broadly different strategies.

To go back to the analogy between philosophies and games, every player begins by placing his pieces on the board on which the game is to be played. By at least Indian (philosophic) standards, the number of pieces and their placement on the board depend on his desire or whim. The 'pieces' are his basic assumptions. After he presents his pieces (states his assumptions) and places them (states their logical connection), the game begins, with each player trying to force his opponent's pieces off the board (into absurdity). Although, as earlier described, an Indian debater may open by giving his own position positive support, in philosophical practice he seems always to be playing his opponent's position, that is, moving his opponent's pieces, not his own, which are assumptions his opponent cannot use to argue with, certainly not as a group. In the West, such a way of conducting philosophical argument has been characteristic principally of so-called sophists and of sceptics, but in India it has been characteristic of philosophers in general.

Islamic theologians, exponents of *kalam*, also often conducted their arguments negatively. 'In many cases the premises had no absolute or intrinsic value, but were taken from the adversary, good only for negative refutation, not for positive deduction ... In *jadal*, dialectics, one argues according to one's adversary.'[6] In India, likewise, this way of argument requires the destruction of the opponent's position by means of *reductio ad absurdum*. The *reductio ad absurdum*, Indian, Chinese, and European, will later be presented as a philosophical tactic, but its use is so dominant in India that it might be best to regard it there, not as a tactic, but as the grand strategy of debate.

To put the matter bluntly, a philosophical debate in India is not, as a rule, a clash of world-views, fundamental beliefs, or ideologies. The Indians are apparently sensitive to the danger that a debate will turn dogmatic and therefore be philosophically unconvincing and fruitless. To prevent the danger, a philosopher does not base his attack, technically speaking, on his own assumptions, but tries, instead, to expose the internal weaknesses in his rival's position. I should like to call this strategy 'minimal', because the attack it directs makes use only of assumptions the rival himself is willing to accept. Although I do not want to generalize too broadly, it seems to me that most of the arguments to be found in Indian philosophical literature are minimal arguments of this kind. The code of Indian philosophy requires that the enemy be downed by his own weapons.

Before I cite an example or two to clarify the structure of such minimal argument, I should like to say a brief word on the attitude of Indian philosophers toward inference. In Indian thought, inference is grasped primarily as one of the means of knowledge, or, in the Indian term, *pramanas*. Almost all the Indian philosophical schools accept inference as a valid means of knowledge, in addition to sensory perception which it is taken to complete. The distinction between the two, most Indian philosophers agree, is that sensory perception gives information on the environment here and now, while inference gives information on what is not directly grasped in sensory perception. To use a stock Indian example, I perceive that there is smoke on the hill, but I infer that the smoke is accompanied by fire and caused by it. This inference is of course derived from the assumption, used as if it were the major premise of a syllogism, that wherever there is smoke there is fire. The syllogism (or apparent syllogism) that results may appear to be the same as an Aristotelian one. However, while the structure of the Aristotelian syllogism is deductive, that of the Indian syllogism is inductive, for it emphasizes the dependence of what in the Aristotelian syllogism is the major premise on the existence of actual, empirical examples, examples which are added to the syllogism in order to ensure, from the Indian standpoint, that it is valid. From the Indian standpoint, a syllogism is incomplete without, in principle, two examples, which might be said to make the assumption of the major premise possible on inductive grounds. The premise itself is not put into words, but simply understood to be (inductively) true. In the case we are considering, the major premise, 'Wherever there is smoke there is fire', is true the Indian thinks, if and only if one example can be given to support the premise inductively and another to show that smoke is associated with fire rather than with other conditions—somewhat as Francis Bacon wishes to gather both positive and negative examples before concluding whether or not blood, light, or fire are always. that is, necessarily associated with heat.*

I forbear entering into the Indian theory of the syllogism—this chapter is devoted to modes of argument, not to logic as such. I have brought up the syllogism, the ancient model of deductive logic, only to indicate that its Indian equivalent has an empirical requirement. The empirical requirement makes the Indian 'syllogism' a means of knowledge. In contrast, *tarka*, the main subject here, is basically a game designed, not to add to knowledge, but to subject it to a negative test and to discard whatever proves vulnerable to its attacks.

To return to the structure of the minimal arguments I have been speaking of, I should like to give an example from a debate between the Buddhist philosopher Nagarjuna and an invented opponent. The argument under attack is Nagarjuna's contention that everything in the world lacks an 'intrinsic nature' (*svabhava*). 'Intrinsic nature' is taken to mean 'independent', 'uninfluenced by anything else', 'not relative to anything', that is, 'existing in its own right', and at least in this sense equivalent to the Aristotelian conception of substance. Nagarjuna's general position will be explained in a later chapter. He denies that the world has any independent being or intelligible nature; but here it is enough to attend to the *tarka*-nature of the debate in which he is engaged.

In the debate, Nagarjuna's opponent attacks Nagarjuna's statement, 'Everything in the world lacks intrinsic nature.' The question the opponent asks is the simple, obvious, and difficult one, whether Nagarjuna's statement itself has an intrinsic nature or not. The opponent says:

> If an intrinsic nature of things, whatever they may be, exists nowhere, your very statement must be devoid of an intrinsic nature. It is therefore not in a position to deny to intrinsic nature of the things . . . Now, if this sentence is endowed with an intrinsic nature, your former proposition is destroyed.[7]

* Sextus Empiricus uses the smoke-fire example and says, 'As we have often observed these to be connected with each other, as soon as we see the one— that is to say, smoke—we recall the other—that is to say, the unseen fire. He calls the smoke a 'commemorative sign".' *Sextus Empiricus*, vol. 2, *Against the*

Nagarjuna's opponent is clearly trying to find an exception to Nagarjuna's statement that *everything* lacks an intrinsic nature or independent existence. Not accidentally, the opponent hits on the statement itself and poses Nagarjuna a dilemma: if the statement lacks intrinsic nature it by definition also lacks intrinsic meaning and may hence be regarded as void of (independent) meaning. If, on the other hand, the statement is regarded as having its own intrinsic nature, it is in blatant contradiction with what it itself asserts and is hence itself void of meaning.

As the reader may rightly guess, Nagarjuna does not accept his opponent's argument. He agrees that the statement in which he has made his point has itself no independent existence—nothing in the world has it. But he argues that lack of independent existence does not deprive his statements of the ability to deny independent existence to other things, or rather, to all things, including itself. If the reader's logical instinct has been aroused, he may perhaps appease (or exacerbate) it with the more extended form of Nagarjuna's reply in a later section, 'Self-Refutation', of the present chapter. What, for the moment, is to be noticed is the opponent's use of negative reasoning or *tarka*. The opponent accepts Nagarjuna's statement for the sake of argument and tries to refute it using minimal means, that is, by trying to reduce it to absurdity. The opponent does not add any philosophical assumptions to those of Nagarjuna himself.

I should like to add another example of minimal argument. This one is taken from a debate between a Buddhist and a Hindu of the Nyaya school. The debate begins with the contention of the Buddhist that in everyday language it is legitimate to construct sentences in which the subject is non-existent. For example, one may legitimately say, 'The horns of the hare are not sharp,' or, to use a sentence famous in contemporary analytical philosophy, 'The present king of France is bald.' The Buddhist argues that the use of such language is legitimate because, like the others of their kind, they cannot be regarded as false. His Nyaya opponent argues, on the contrary, that the fact that the horns of the hare do not exist or, equivalently, the fact that there is no present king of

Logicians, trans. R. G. Bury, London, Heinemann, 1957, pp. 315–17 (sentences 151–2). This example was adopted, apparently from Sextus, and analysed by the Islamic theologians. J. van Ess, op. cit., pp. 26–7.

France makes the proposition false, as are all other conjunctions of the sort.*

Confronted with the Nyaya criticism... the Buddhist does not so easily give up.... He tries to point out that the position of the opponent, i.e., the Nyaya position, also involves a self-contradiction. By saying that an unreal entity... cannot be used as the subject of a proposition, the Nyaya actually mentions 'an unreal entity' in his speech-act.

That is, in order to refute the Buddhist use of the idea of a 'non-existent subject', the Nyaya argues:

'The hare's horn' cannot be used as the subject of a sentence because such a horn does not exist. Whoever uses it is in effect talking about nothing and therefore making no sense. The words, 'an unreal entity', are, like 'the hare's horns', literally non-existent and therefore empty and unintelligible.'[8]

Up until now, I have been giving examples of the use of minimal argument. It should not be forgotten, however, that there are cases in which a philosopher is unwilling, even for the sake of argument, to accept some assumption or assumptions of the position he is attacking. It is evident that minimal argument is then no longer helpful, and so is replaced by what might be called 'general argument'. 'General argument' is the kind in which the philosopher adds assumptions of his own to those made by his opponent. If we return to the analogy between philosophical debate and a game, it is clear that the use of 'general argument' implies a refusal to accept the rules, or at least all the rules of the game.

As an example of such 'general argument', we may take Śankara's criticism of the Buddhist Idealists. These Idealists regard the existence of external objects (objects in space and time) as a mere illusion, and they try to prove that such existence is solely in

* The reader who knows Bertrand Russell's article, 'On Denoting', will no doubt see the resemblance between Russell's position and that of the Nyaya. Like the Nyaya, Russell refused to assume 'that such phrases as "the present king of France", which do not denote a real individual, do, nevertheless, denote an individual of *some* kind, an unreal one'. This is essentially Meinong's view, which, Russell says, 'we have seen reason to reject because it conflicts with the law of contradiction. With our theory of denoting we are able to hold that there are no unreal individuals; so that the null-class is the class containing no members, not the class containing as members all unreal individuals.' B. Russell, *Essays in Analysis*, ed. D. Lackey, London, Allen and Unwin, 1973, pp. 117–18.

the consciousness of the perceiver. In his debate with them Śankara is not satisfied to reject Idealism on the grounds that it leads to logically absurd conclusions. He does attack it with a number of specific 'minimal arguments', but his central criticism is a general one: Idealism departs from conclusions that common sense teaches us directly. We learn from common sense, Śankara says, that 'in every act of perception we are conscious of some external thing corresponding to the idea, whether it be a post or a wall or a piece of cloth or a jar, and that of which we are conscious cannot but exist'. This argument is of the sort I have been calling general because Śankara does not accept the assumptions of the Idealist, as he might for the sake of argument, and does not try to show that Idealist assumptions lead to contradiction. Instead, he openly refuses to accept Idealist assumptions and implies that even if the Buddhist arguments are non-contradictory, that is, logically valid, their logical validity is not enough to make them acceptable. That is because, he claims, the Buddhist assumptions contradict everything that common sense conveys to us about the nature of our consciousness and of the world. Says Śankara in the course of his argument,

Why should we pay attention to the words of a man who, while conscious of an outward thing through its approximation to his senses, affirms that he is conscious of no outward thing, and that no such thing exists, any more than we listen to a man who while he is eating and experiencing the feeling of satisfaction avers that he does not eat and does not feel satisfied?[9]

The difference between minimal and general argument is clear. The minimal form is designed to expose the internal incoherencies of a philosophical standpoint, the general form, its external insufficiency. In minimal argument, the philosopher appears to say, 'If you want to erect such a structure on such a basis, you had better revise your engineering estimates, because they are wrong even in terms of your own basic principles.' In general argument, it is as if the philosopher says, 'No matter how sound your engineering estimates of the structure internally, you cannot build it, because its very basis is unsound.' If, as I think, the absence of mutually acceptable rules makes it much harder for opponents to engage in genuinely philosophical combat, the preponderance of minimal over general argument in India shows that Indian philosophers respected the condition that argument and counterargument be relevant to one another.

Chinese Analogy
(Dan Daor and Ben-Ami Scharfstein)

In China, unlike India, we find very little formal logic. Chinese philosophers had great interest in problems, such as the relation of language to the external world, that we think of as having to do with logic, but they seem never to have bothered much about formulating rules of inference. Syllogistic logic, considered by the previous generation of sinologues, along with so many others, the perfect expression of human reason, was never developed in China. In China, there are no *tarka*-like manuals specifying how a debate should be handled. Even the later Mohists, perhaps the most logic-minded of all Chinese philosophers, do not look as if they are trying to establish a theory of valid inference. Concentrating on the ways in which one may be misled by syntactic similarity into assuming logical similarity, they resemble, as will be explained, modern Anglo-American 'analytical' or linguistic philosophers rather than the logicians of India or Greece.[10] It is true that there were Chinese sophists, some of whose rather enigmatic paradoxes show an immediate resemblance to those of Zeno; but their paradoxes were never logically formalized.

The reason for the glaring omission of formal logic from what is otherwise a philosophical tradition as rich as those of India and the West may perhaps be found in the nature of classical Chinese. As the scholar J. Chmielewski has pointed out, valid intuitive reasoning was much easier in early Chinese than in Sanksrit or Greek:

> Chinese, with its practically uninflected monosyllabic words, undifferentiated by inherent grammatical quality, and having no morphologically delimited but logically misleading 'parts of speech', is much better equipped for spontaneous logical thinking than any of the Indo-European tongues . . . In fact, Chinese proves to be structurally much like the symbolic quasi-language of logic.[11]

As Chmielewski goes on to suggest, this very facility of Chinese may have been a handicap in the development of a systematic logic, because such logic was much less obviously needed. However that may be, the fact is that the Chinese philosophers, unlike the European and Indian, never developed formal logic. The question of whether this failure influenced the cogency of their reasoning is the subject of the following discussion of their use of analogy, as well as of the the later discussion of the universality of philosophical arguments.

The Chinese use of analogy in argument is rational, but its rationality may be easy to miss. The text of Mencius (fourth century B.C.) may serve as an example. Arthur Waley, no professional philosopher, but certainly an excellent translator, dismissed the philosophical acumen of Mencius with contempt.[12] That, however, was in 1939, since when D. C. Lau has clarified Mencius's use of analogy in a brilliant essay.[13]

Suppose that in the light of Lau's essay and in the words of his translation of Mencius, we recall the chapter in which Mencius has an argument with one Kao Tzu. Kao Tzu suggests a number of analogies, with all of which Mencius finds fault. Kao Tzu is, in effect, asserting and Mencius denying that animals and human beings are innately the same. That is, if Kao Tzu's analogies hold, human and animal nature are the same: just as humans and animals by nature share the need for food, they are both by nature non-moral. Mencius's position is, on the contrary, that human beings, unlike animals, are innately moral. Thus:

> Kao Tzu said, 'The inborn is what is meant by "nature".'
> 'Is that', said Mencius, 'the same as "white is what is meant by 'white'"?'
> 'Yes.'
> 'Is the whiteness of white feathers the same as the whiteness of white snow and the whiteness of white snow the same as the whiteness of white jade?'
> 'Yes.'
> 'In that case, is the nature of a hound the same as the nature of an ox and the nature of an ox the same as the nature of a man?'[14]

This is surely cryptic; but Lau's explanation of the 'no' implied at the end is simple and plausible. Mencius is arguing that a clearly specified term, such as 'whiteness', remains the same in many uses, but that an unclearly specified one, such as 'nature', leaves the analogies in which it participates empty and unpersuasive. With respect to the more particular point in question, Mencius argues that the fact that men and animals share certain traits does not justify the conclusion that their natures are the same and that both therefore share *all* essential traits.

This narrower point is still, of course, being argued, and might be put in the question, 'Is animal nature, however the ethologists or sociobiologists define it, an adequate or illuminating model for human nature?'[15] The more general point, on the criteria for the adequacy of analogies, also continues, of course, to need clarification. No one can deny the ubiquity, the usefulness, and the danger of arguing by analogy. Everyday, philosophical, and scientific reasoning all depend on it. Whether studied in itself or not, it has shown its great influence, not only in the Chinese, but in every other philosophical tradition as well.[16] If we think only of modern physics, the planetary model of the atom or the droplet model of the atomic nucleus rise immediately to mind; and if we think of brain research, the model of the computer. Some of these models may not fit the ancient Chinese imagination; but Lao Tzu may be said to have had a water-drop model of human nature. At any rate, the ancient Chinese not only reasoned a great deal by means of analogy, but, at least in their philosophers, understood the limitations of such reasoning. Mencius himself never made an explicit statement of the principle of analogy or of its testing. But in the *Hsiao Ch'ü* chapter of Mo Tzu, an obscure treatise on methods of argument, we find at least one technical term for argument by analogy. Mencius's method of comparing analogies is called 'parallel' and defined in the following words:

'Analogy is to put forth another thing in order to illuminate this thing. Parallel is to set two propositions side by side and show that they will both do.'[17] (This is reminiscent of, Abelard the European, saying of analogies, 'What occurs in the case of some proportional things happens in others.'[18])

Analogies must be tested, the *Hsiao Ch'ü* chapter says:

'Things may have similarities, but it does not follow that therefore they are completely similar. When propositions are parallel, there is a limit beyond which they cannot be pushed.'[19]

Chinese Analogists and Anglo-American Analysts

Analogical or other arguments were not usually used in China, any more than elsewhere, for the sake of mere speculation. They had some moral or political point, such as that words might be mere conventional tags, but that they had to be used precisely, in keeping with the realities of human life. It was said, by way of analogy, that a man who wanted a cow would not get it if he called it a horse.[20] More generally, it was said, 'If terms are used in their exact meanings the result is order; if terms lose their meanings the result is disorder. What causes terms to lose their meanings is sloppy discourse.'[21] Again and again we are cautioned that

what causes people to be badly misled is surely the fact that things resemble one another . . . In many cases things are so by analogy and yet not so in fact. Thus there is no end to lost states and executed people . . . Analogical categories definitely cannot be ascertained by hypothetical extension. A small square is analogous to a large square; a small horse is analogous to a large horse; but inferior intelligence is not analogous to superior intelligence.[22]

The words, 'lost states and executed people', show the political orientation of such talk. But taken in terms of the logical principle, that is, of the semantic caution involved, is this universe of discourse so different from that of the contemporary Anglo-American analysts, whose philosophy is said to have developed from the fundamental discovery that 'expressions may be grammatically similar and yet logically different'?[23] The illustration given is that the grammatical form of 'This is past' and 'This is red' is similar but logically very different. Doesn't this resemble what the Chinese philosophers have been saying just above? Ryle remarks, 'To talk of a person's mind is not to talk of a repository which is permitted to house objects that something called "the physical world" is forbidden to house.'[24] Dosen't this resemble the Chinese idea, exemplified above, that we confuse concepts with things? Isn't it like Mencius's 'The case of rightness is different from the case of whiteness'?[25] When Wittgenstein asks and answers 'yes' to the question, 'Now has "1" a different meaning when it stands for a measure and when it stands for a number?' isn't he asking and answering like the Mencius who objects that 'nature' may not mean 'nature'? When Wittgenstein asks insistently, 'What is the relation between name and thing named?—well, what *is* it?'[26] isn't he, like the Chinese, talking about the relation between words and things and isn't he engaged in his own version of what the Chinese called 'rectification of names'? And when Wittgenstein states, 'A main cause of philosophical disease—a one-sided diet: one nourishes one's thinking with only one kind of example,' would Mencius not agree?[27] Is A. C. Graham exaggerating when he says:

> The Mohist's target is a deductive fallacy, yet his way of attacking it is to expose false analogies... It is perhaps easier to understand now... since this kind of argument has become increasingly important in English philosophy during the last thirty years. The successors of Wittgenstein dislike fighting with the deductive weapons of their enemies, and prefer to undermine them by exposing false analogies very much in the manner of the Hsiao-chü.[28]

Given all these resemblances, the Chinese-British analogy may be extended. If the Austrian, Wittgenstein, could be imported to Cambridge, could not some Mohist, too, have been imported to Oxford's green and pleasant clime? Or maybe even Chuang Tzu, who is not merely a naïve and lyrical mystic. For Chuang Tzu uses the Mohist technical vocabulary and the Logician's own logical weapons to confute his logical opponents and establish his own humorously mystical relativism. He loves to play among paradoxes and lose himself in the implications of infinite regresses. If we know, he asks, how do we know that we know, and if there is a judge, who will judge that he is a judge? In his own way, he not only states, but glories in, the paradox of the liar, and intuitively foresees the related theorem of Goedel: all propositions are in the end rationally undecidable.[29] Through at least Chuang Tzu's reaction to them, the Chinese Logicians or Sophists, who seem to have played a merely abortive role in Chinese philosophy, have exercised a great and lasting influence on Chinese thought.

Although Chuang Tzu appears so relaxed and Wittgenstein so tense, the interest of both of them in the problem of certainty often brings them into the same universe of discourse and provides them with related modes of argument. Both of them are cagey about taking explicit positions, but Chuang Tzu is obviously more the sceptic. Thus Chuang Tzu says, 'Knowledge must wait for something before it is applicable, and that which it waits for is never certain,'[30] Refusing to take any definite stand, he refuses to agree that he knows something, or that he knows that he does not know something, or that he even knows that no one knows anything.[31] Wittgenstein, on the contrary, takes the

Mohist position and says, 'The game of doubting itself presupposes certainty.'[32] When he asks, Chuang-Tzu-like, 'If my memory deceived me *here* it can deceive me anywhere', he answers, Mo-Tzu-like, 'If I don't know *that*, how do I know my words mean what they believe they mean?'[33]

Chuang Tzu brings us to Buddhism, which was, as has been described, an importation, but which became indigenous, especially in the form of Ch'an Buddhism. The Buddhism that the Chinese came to know was based on centuries of debate, which among theologians and philosophers had gone into logical, epistemological, and metaphysical issues in great, sometimes excruciating detail.[34] Here was not merely logic, but logic rampant. The Buddhist philosopher Nagarjuna reacted somewhat as Chuang Tzu had done. That is, he used logic to refute itself, claiming, as well, that the use of logic to refute logic was not fatal to his argument, for, as has been said, he was only adopting his opponents' positions on their own terms and showing them that they were not, as they supposed, consistent. We cannot give an estimate here of Nagarjuna's success as a dialectician, but it is evident that he was a master of dialectical techniques (examples of which will soon be given). We make this point because it is his logical demolition of every dogmatic stand and every attempt to reach positive philosophical conclusions that furnishes the philosophical background of Ch'an Buddhism. Ch'an Buddhism thus assimilated the relatively intuitive dialectic of Chuang Tzu together with the compatible, more formal, detailed, and sophisticated dialectic of Nagarjuna. Not that every Ch'an Buddhist, even a Master, was a scholar of Nagaruna's thought, but, speaking historically, Ch'an Buddhism was not pre-logical but post-logical, or, perhaps better, it consciously avoided deduction and generalization in favour of 'complementarity' and particularity. Its avoidance of explicit logic was based, as its revelling in paradox shows, on an acute consciousness of logic and, we may assume, an implicit logic of its own.[35] In this respect it resembled the later, argument-shy, particularizing Wittgenstein.

The Universality of Philosophical Argument

Chinese analogy now somewhat explained and somewhat compared, I should like to take up the theme that, all things told, philosophical arguments do not follow any particular formalism or have, formally speaking, any philosophical particularity of their own. With certain evident exceptions, the way philosophers present their arguments is not much different from the way most people usually present theirs. Like everybody else, philosophers appeal to 'general' experience or describe their own, state the obvious or call attention to exceptions, or point out contradictions, question assumptions, draw analogies, quote authorities, and tell little stories. Take the following passage:

> That the preservation of a state depends mainly on the loyalty of its subjects, and on their excellence and steadfastness in executing commands, is taught very plainly by both reason and experience; but the means by which they should be led to preserve their loyalty and excellence consistently are more difficult to see. For all, rulers and ruled alike are men, i.e. are apt to slip from the hard path of duty into the pursuit of pleasure. In fact, those who know the utter fickleness of the people are driven almost to despair, for it is not guided by reason but solely by its passions: it has no self-restraint, and is easily corrupted by greed and luxury; every single man imagines that he has a monopoly of wisdom, and wants to direct everything to suit his own inclinations; he thinks things fair or unfair, right or wrong, only as he believes them conducive to his own gain or loss. . . . But there is no need to review the whole count. for everyone knows the wickedness which is often inspired in men by dislike of the status quo and desire for revolution. . . .[36]

This passage is fairly representative of a certain kind of philosophical writing anywhere, China, Europe, Islam, or India; but it might have been written by an old-fashioned statesman, an uncommonly lucid sociologist, or even a columnist in a respectable Sunday paper. There is nothing distinctly 'philosophical' about this melange of observations and assertions, implicit assumptions, conclusions unwarranted by logic, and common sense and bias, nothing *more geometrico* to tell us that it was written by the philosophers' philosopher, Benedict de Spinoza.

It is of course possible in principle that philosophy differs from other pursuits involving sustained reasoning, mathematics or criminal investigation, for example, merely by its subject matter (whatever that may be), which difference does not necessarily entail different modes of reasoning; but I do not think that this is in fact the case. Even if most philosophical writing looks like a lot of the unphilosophical, there are nevertheless certain ways of using common arguments which are peculiar to philosophy and a few arguments that can perhaps be found nowhere else.[37] It may be of some interest to single these out and see how they work in the three great philosophical traditions.

Now, comparing modes of argument is easier, in principle at least, than comparing concepts and ideas, as one does not have to bother much about context, historical, cultural, or linguistic. Dealing with structure rather than content of specific arguments, one need not have the erudition and sophistication which seem necessary if comparative philosophy is to become more interesting than the well-meant platitudes on perennial philosophy which it all too often is. The question of whether or not Saint-X talking about 'Nous' or 'the One' meant the same thing as Y-tzu talking about 'Li' or 'Tao', is enormously difficult to answer accurately; the more modest question, whether they use structurally similar arguments, seems less so. In addition to being more precise and more readily answerable, the latter question (and the more general, 'Did philosophers in India, China, and the West use similar modes of argument?') has another merit: having answered it we shall be in a better position to decide on the truth or falsity of generalizations like, 'Europeans and Asiaticks think differently', which still litter comparative studies. To take one example, Marcel Granet, in his widely read and in many ways excellent *La pensée chinoise,* claims that ancient China produced a sententious wisdom, not a philosophy—'La Chine ancienne, plutôt qu'une Philosophie a possédé une Sagesse.'[38] Had he troubled himself with the ways the Chinese sages argued when promoting their 'Sagesse' and compared them with the ways the Wise Men of the Occident argued their 'Philosophie', he might have been less happy with his catch-phrase.

Granted that comparative philosophy 'in the small' has obvious, if limited, merits, it is somewhat surprising that a comparison of modes of argument has not been attempted before. In fact, there are not so very many decent discussions of the structure of philosophical arguments in Europe alone.[39] It seems as if philosophers are less ready to analyze the way they themselves reason than they are that of other people. The following discussion is therefore by necessity rather sketchy. Starting with the most pervasive modes of argument in the European tradition, I then fished about trying to find their analogues in India and

China, limiting myself to clear-cut cases, the senses of which I could be reasonably sure I got right.

Valid Inferences

'In point of fact, it is astonishing how little formal logic is used, not only in everyday arguing, but even in the sophisticated inferences of higher mathematics.'[40] 'Or in philosophy', one would like to add, wondering why the historian of logic, Bochenski, who wrote the above, finds it at all astonishing. Most people, philosophers and scientists included, are more interested in saying something new than in spelling out the obvious, and while it is possible that the conclusion of a long chain of inferences is new (in the sense that most people hearing the premises would not expect it to follow), it seems hardly to be the case in most philosophical writings. Take the following example heard in a recent Spaghetti Western:

This is the cow we stole from Señor Gonzales.
This is a good cow,
Because everything we steal from Señor Gonzales is good.

If one is not already convinced of the truth of the conclusion one is not likely to accept that of the major premise; moreover, the former is more readily testable than the latter. If a good argument, as distinct from a valid one, is an argument the conclusion of which one is more likely to accept after hearing it expounded (in other words, a convincing or at least persuasive argument), then this is a pretty bad one.[41]

Valid inferences (of the short kind with unsurprising conclusions) are nevertheless found sometimes in philosophical writing, where they serve to clarify a position, spell our consequences, or point out where the real issue lies. A good example is furnished by Descartes:

It is clear that the cause must comprise as much as the effect
And I am a conscious being and have an idea of God within myself
So that whatever may be alleged to be my cause must also be acknowledged to be a conscious being and to possess the idea of all the perfections I attribute to God.[42]

It is true that the syllogistic exposition has not made Descartes' conclusion any more acceptable, but it has the great merit of clearly and briefly pointing to the Neo-Platonic source of a 'clear and distinct' idea.

A similar proof for the existence of God is given by the Indian philosopher, Śridhara (tenth century A.D.):

Anything that is an effect is preceded by [some] one having a cognition of it, as,
For instance, the jar. . . .
And the four great elementary substances are effects—
Hence they must be preceded by one having a knowledge of them[43]

After these examples of syllogisms, one used by a European and another by an Indian philosopher, it seems appropriate to add a bit to what has already been said about the Chinese lack of a theory of syllogisms. Attention to this lack, together with an inability to distinguish between talking logically and talking about logic, has led to some bizarre ideas about the nature of Chinese reasoning.[44] It has been said, for example, by Granet, that

the Chinese have no taste for the syllogism. Besides what is the value of syllogistic deduction for thinking that has refused to deprive Space and Time of their concrete character? How can one affirm that Socrates, being human, is mortal? . . . One can say, on the contrary, 'Confucius is dead, therefore I shall die; there is little hope that anybody deserves a lot in life that is greater than that of the greatest of sages.'[45]

Granet does not quote his source for this Chinese 'inference'. Maybe he has in mind a poem by the eighth-century poet and essayist, Liu Tsung-yuan, in which Liu says: 'And yet, why should I suffer/P'eng Tzu and Lao Tzu exist no more/Chuang Tzu and K'ung Tzu too are gone/Of those whom the ancients called "immortal saints"/not one is left today.' A fuller quotation would not make Granet's position any more tenable; and this is hardly the place to answer his magnificent nonsense. Very briefly, however, few people today would agree with what seems to be his position, that Newtonian concepts of space and time, and syllogistic logic, are synonymous with reason. The Chinese philosophers were able to reason as cogently as everybody else, meaning, that they used the same valid inferences. The fact that they did not develop formal logic did not stop them from spotting faulty arguments or from expounding perfectly valid ones. At times they even made use of syllogisms:

In all cases of serving another, one does so for one's own advantage;
Dying is not an advantage;
Therefore I did not die (in service).[46]

Mencius provides a slightly more complicated inference:

If one has it within, it necessarily assumes shape without.
I have never seen anybody who working at something has no results to show for it;
Hence there are no worthy men;
If there were I would necessarily have known it.[47]

Granting, as I think we ought to, that worthy men work to bring about good government, and that an improved government is not something that the speaker can possibly fail to notice, then it seems that the inference above is valid. Slightly expanded and partially translated into symbolic logic, this argument reads:

(y)–Ex(x works at y &–x produces signs of y)
(by instantiation)–Ex(x works at good government &–x produces signs of good government)
Ex(x works at good government)→Ex(x produces signs of good government)
(but) −Ex(x produces signs of good government)
(by modus tollens) −Ex(x works at good government)

Now this example does not show that the Chinese knew symbolic logic or that this is the way Mencius followed in his argument. Chmielewski's claim that classical Chinese is closer to the 'quasi-language of logic' is, I think, irrelevant to the question of how the Chinese in fact reasoned, although it might explain their failure to develop formal logic. All that this example suggests is that when we look closely at their arguments we shall find that the Chinese intuitively used the same modes of inference used by the Greek and Indian philosophers, and, I suspect, all rational human beings.

A final example, from India:

As a matter of fact we find that the existence of a perceptible object is always accompanied by a cognition of its shape or form;
In the case of the self we find there is no cognition of the shape of the self;
Hence, not finding its invariable concommitant, we cannot but reject the

existence of the self [or conclude that the self exists as an imperceptible object, a conclusion the proponent of this argument will have found absurd].[48]

The subject matter is different and the style is different, but both the Chinese 'sage' and the Indian metaphysician make use of the same 'law of thought', familiar to countless freshmen in philosophy, and apparently assumed by all rational human beings, $(A{\rightarrow}B)$ & $(-B){\rightarrow}(-A)$.

Proof by Elimination

Given a set of statements, one of which we know to be true, we can validly infer from the falsity of all the statements but one to the truth of the remaining statement; or, in the words of the immortal Sherlock Holmes, 'How often have I said to you that when you have eliminated the impossible, whatever remains, however improbable, must be the truth?' Thus, if a balloon factory produces blue, red, and yellow balloons only, and we happen to know that the Chinese embassy bought all the red ones for its New Year celebration, and that all the blue ones disintegrated because of a flaw in the dyeing process, then we can safely conclude that any balloons left in the factory are bound to be yellow.

Now philosophers, like mathematicians and police inspectors, have tried to prove all sorts of improbable truths by elimination. Here is a well-known example from Plato's *Phaedo*. The question at issue is whether we are born knowing 'the equal, the greater and smaller' and 'all things of that sort', or if we forget at birth all we knew before and, given the right stimulus, recollect it. Socrates asks his interlocutor, Simmias, whether it is plausible that people recollect what they once learned. Simmias answers, 'It must be so.' The conversation then proceeds:

'But when did our souls acquire this knowledge? Evidently not since our birth as human beings.'
'No, indeed.'
'Before that then?' . . .
'Unless possibly it was at the actual moment of birth that we acquired that knowledge, Socrates; there is that moment still left.'
'Yes, yes, my friend; but at what moment, may I ask, do we lose it? We

are not born with this knowledge; that we agreed a moment ago; do we then lose it the very moment we acquire it, or is there some other moment that you can suggest?'

'No indeed, Socrates; I see now that I was talking nonsense.'[49]

Now, both the activities of specifying the alternative statements, so that one has to be true, and of eliminating the 'impossible' are hardly as straightforward as this example might lead us to believe. In the normal, interesting case there are all sorts of presuppositions that take part. Thus, when a police inspector considers death to have been caused either by murder, suicide, or natural causes, he tacitly assumes that deaths are caused; and when he rules out suicide because the armless body was stabbed in the back, then telekinesis is presupposed to be impossible. Police inspectors, however, are seemingly quite happy working within a commonly accepted framework of presuppositions, so that in their case proof by elimination is a lot simpler in fact than in principle. Philosophers are less ready to work within a given framework, which explains why the Holmesian technique is so much less effective in philosophy. This is well illustrated by the following example taken from the Indian text of the fourth century A.D. that I have quoted before. Although the terminology may look strange, the structure of the argument seems to stand out clearly enough. The problem is to determine to what the consciousness can 'belong':

In the cognition of sound, etc., we infer a 'cognizer'.
This character cannot belong to the body, or to the sense-organs, or to the mind. . . .
Consciousness cannot belong to the body, as it is a material product . . . and no consciousness is found in dead bodies.
Nor can consciousness belong to the sense organs, because these are mere instruments, and also because we have no remembrances of objects even after the sense-organ has been destroyed. . . .
Nor can it belong to the mind; because if the mind be regarded as functioning independently to the organs, then we would have perception and remembrance simultaneously presenting themselves. . . .
And thus the only thing to which consciousness could belong is the self which thus is cognized by this consciousness.[50]

This beautiful argument is rather convincing in a sort of commonsense way, but it is useless, as later Indian philosophers pointed out, against people who do not accept the existence of a 'cognizer' over and above 'cognitions', or against anyone who is not prepared to assume, as does the author of the argument, a mind-matter dichotomy. Moreover, the arguer seems to have in mind a notion of individual 'selves', so that the whole argument may be regarded as irrelevant by someone who believes in one cosmic 'Self' or suchlike.

For a Chinese example of proof-by-elimination, we turn again to Mencius. In a famous short passage he argues for the inherent goodness of human nature:

Suppose a man were, all of a sudden, to see a young child on the verge of falling into a well.
He would certainly be moved to compassion,
Not because he wanted to get into the good graces of the parents,
Nor because he wished to win the praise of his fellow villagers or friends,
Nor yet because he disliked the cry of the child.[51]

This 'thought experiment', although not perhaps explicit enough for modern philosophical tastes, has a certain analytical ring to it, and for all of its conciseness, is a pretty good one. Assuming that the hypothetical man is indeed moved to try and save the child, and not push it into the well (as would have been natural if the third alternative were the case), then inserting the condition, 'all of a sudden', is effective in eliminating the first two putative explanations. The man of course is 'everyman', not a learned Confucian, which rules out the possibility that his hypothetical behaviour is a conditioned reflex, the outcome of moral brainwashing at an early age. Mencius does not claim that the man will actually go and save the child, only that he is initially moved to do so. He does not say that men are 'good', only that they have what he terms, 'a beginning of goodness' in them, a beginning which he then considers a necessary attribute of 'being human'.

Proof by Elimination:Reductio ad Absurdum

If arguing by elimination, as in the previous examples, is common to reasoning in general, a more radical kind of elimination seems more distinctly philosophical. The more radical kind occurs when, having compiled our list of alternative statements (a list believed to be exhaustive) and having eliminated the impossible, we are left with no statements but with a certain feeling of paradox. An argument of this sort is meant to refute the assumptions underlying the compilation of the list of alternatives, and is thus similar to a *reductio* demonstration, like those in high school geometry. There is a difference, however, in that the underlying assumptions in the philosophical case are commonly held to be true, are warranted by our experience, or are of the kind that no sensible person can seriously doubt. Zeno's four arguments against motion, taken together, are a good example: space and time are either continuous or discrete, but motion is 'logically' incompatible with either alternative, so that our initial assumption that motion 'exists' is refuted.

The Idealist Buddhist philosopher, Vasubandhu, who lived during the fourth century A.D., uses a *reductio* argument in order to refute the assumption that there are external objects:

If there really are external bases of sense cognition . . .
Then such an outer realm must either be one, as in the assertion . . . that there is form having parts;
Or it must be . . . many real atoms acting separately as objects;
Or it must be . . . many real atoms which in agglomeration and combination act together as objects.
But the external object cannot be one, because we cannot grasp the substance of the whole apart from its parts.
Also it is not many, because we cannot apprehend the atoms separately.
Again logically, they do not in agglomeration and combination make objects, because the theory of single real atoms is not proved.[52]

Like Berkeley's Idealism, that of Vasubandhu was seriously intended—later on in this book a comparison of the two is attempted. I am less sure of the seriousness of Gorgias's claim that nothing exists. The structure of his argument is however similar: Whatever exists has to be either the existent or the non-existent; the non-existent is easily shown not to exist, and then the existent is shown not to exist either. In Gorgias's own words:

If it [the existent] exists, it is either one or many. . . .
If it is one, it is either a discrete quantity or a continuum or a magnitude or a body. . . .
But if it be a discrete quantity it will be divided, and if it be a continuum it will be cut in sections;
And similarly, if it be conceived as a magnitude it will not be indivisible,

while if it is a body it will be threefold, for it will possess length and
breadth and depth.
But it is absurd to say that the existent is none of these;
Therefore the existent is not one.
Yet neither is it many...
For the many is the sum of the ones,
And hence if the one is destroyed the many are also destroyed with it.[53]

One might perhaps accept this as a good argument and conclude that there must have been something queer about the
notion of 'existence' and the way it functioned in traditional
European philosophy. This, however, does not seem to have
been Gorgias's intention.

The third example of a philosophical reduction is more limited
in scope, as the assumption it is meant to refute is not as warmly
cherished as the one about the existence of the external world. It
is *a reductio* nevertheless and has a certain mathematical charm.
Coming from the third century B.C. Mohist school, it is designed
to meet the charge that it is impossible to love all men without
knowing how many there are. The charge goes:

If the south has a limit it can be exhausted;
If it has not it cannot.

If whether it has a limit or not cannot be known, then whether it can be
exhausted or not, whether men fill it or not cannot be known;
Whether men can be exhausted or not cannot be known either, and the
claim that men can all be loved is false.

The answer to the charge goes:

If men do not fill the limitless, then they have a limit, and to exhaust
that which has a limit is no problem.
If they do fill the limitless, then the limitless is exhausted, and to exhaust
the limitless is (thus) no problem.[54]

There is, I think, no doubt about the philosophical character of
the examples I have just given. If nothing else, they are odd
enough to be dubbed 'philosophy' by the layman. Their oddity,
however, derives from the oddity of their subject matter than
anything about the structure of the argument. Proof by elimination is a commonplace in criminal and scientific investigations,
and most people are familiar with *reductio* from their study of
geometry. The following argument, or rather cluster of arguments, is much less familiar.

Infinite Regress, etc.

It is perhaps an exaggeration, although not a gross one, that the history of philosophy is a series of sceptical crises and attempts at resolving them. Kant following Hume is the stock example in European philosophy. Hsün Tzu following Chuang Tzu in China and Vasubandhu following Nagarjuna in Indian Buddhism are perhaps no less instructive. In this constant war between dogma and doubt it is not always clear who the winner is, but, like the Republicans in the Spanish Civil War (according to Tom Lehrer), the sceptics seem to have all the better arguments. A list of these, attributed to Agrippa, is found in the well-known *Outlines of Pyrrhonism* by the Hellenistic writer, Sextus Empiricus. Designed to achieve a suspension of judgment (*epoche*) and thereby peace of mind (*ataraxia*), this list of five *tropoi* or modes is the closest to a list of the major dialectical moves ever made by philosophers:

The later sceptics handed down Five Modes leading to suspension [of judgment]; namely these: the first based on discrepancy, the second on regress *ad infinitum*, the third on relativity, the fourth on hypothesis, the fifth on circular reasoning. That based on discrepancy leads us to find that with regard to the object presented there has arisen both amongst ordinary people and amongst the philosophers an interminable conflict because of which we are unable either to choose a thing or reject it, and so fall back on suspension. The mode based on regress *ad infinitum* is that whereby we assert that the thing adduced as a proof of the matter proposed needs a further proof, and this again another, and so on *ad infinitum*, so that the consequence is suspension as we possess no starting-point for our argument. The mode based upon relativity . . . is that whereby the object has such or such an appearance in relation to the subject judging and to the concomitant percepts, but as to its real nature we suspend judgment. We have the mode based on hypothesis when the Dogmatists, being forced to recede *ad infinitum*, take as their starting point something which they do not establish by argument but claim to assume as granted simply and without demonstration. The mode of circular reasoning is the form used when the proof itself which ought to establish the matter of inquiry requires confirmation derived from the matter; in this case being unable to assume either in order to establish the other, we suspend judgment about both.[55]

These five *tropoi*, which are meant, as is made plain by this long quotation, to be ways of achieving *epoche*, may be taken rather as 'modes of argument'. They break naturally into two groups, the first and third forming one group, and the rest another. The first and third modes point out that all our judgments involve a point of view and are therefore hopelessly subjective. They were used to great effect by Montaigne in his celebrated *Apologie de Raimond Sebond*, and seem to be at the base of current dogma in anthropology and related disciplines. As these ideas are clear and well enough known, I will give just two examples. Both are taken from the *Chuang Tzu*. The first illustrates 'discrepancy', the second explicates 'relativity':

Lady Mao and Lady Li were beautiful in the eyes of men, but when the fish saw them they plunged into the deep, when the birds saw them they flew high, when the deer saw them they broke into a run. Which of these four knows what is truly beautiful in the world?

Suppose I argue with you; you win the argument and I don't. Does it follow that you are right and I am wrong? If I win the argument and you don't, does it mean that I am right and you are wrong? Is one of us right and the other wrong? Are we both right? Or both wrong? If you and I cannot know it, the others are bound to be even more in the dark. Whom shall I call on to decide the matter? Is someone who agrees with you to decide? But since he already agrees with you, how can he decide the matter? Is someone who agrees with me to decide? But since he already agrees with me, how can he decide the matter? Is someone who differs with both of us to decide? But since he already differs with both, how can he decide the matter? Is someone who agrees with both to decide? But since he already agrees with both, how can he decide the matter? Thus, neither you nor the other can decide the matter. Shall we then wait for yet another man?[56]

The modes in the second group on Agrippa's list (the second, fourth, and fifth *tropoi*) are closely related moves in an attempt to refute all dogmas, and are of a more 'technical' nature. Like the 'elimination' and 'reductio', and unlike specific arguments (the 'two-world argument', or arguments to prove God's existence). they do not depend on the vagaries of a particular language or culture, and they can thus be used in a variety of dialectical situations.[57] Moreover, unlike the 'reduction', they seem to be rarely found outside of what is commonly regarded as philosophical writing. For both these reasons, they are ideally suited to the kind of comparative study attempted here.

The beauty of the sceptical strategy lies in the simplicity of its component arguments and in the way they all fit together: If your opponent claims that P, you ask him to justify his claim. He supplies P'. Asked to justify that, he supplies P", and so on. If his P's are all different from one another, he is open to the charge of infinite regress. If he claims that after a finite number of answers one arrives at a P'····' which is somehow self-evident and stands in no need for further justification, he is guilty of 'Hypothesis'. If two of his P's are the same for different indices, his argument is circular. Hume's proof that a principle of induction is untenable is the best-known European example of the successful use of the infinite-regress argument. I give three further examples, one each from India, Islam, and China. The Indian example is taken from a fourteenth-century summary of the doctrine of the Car-vaka, that is, the Materialistic or Sceptical school. To begin in the middle of the argument:

> Nor can inference be the means of the knowledge of the universal proposition, since in the case of this inference we should also need another inference to establish it, and so on, and hence would arise the fallacy of an *ad infinitum* retrogression.[58]

Such arguments, as I have been stressing, are natural to scep-tics. But they can be used by others, as witness an example from al-Ashari, the tenth-century Islamic theologian. In this example, al-Ashari, who is trying to prove that the Quran is uncreated, uses an infinite-regression argument in the service of proof by elimination, and for the sake of dogma:

> We hold that because God has said: 'When we will a thing our only utterance is that we say to it "Be!", and it is' (16/40/42). So if the Quran had been created, God would have said to it 'Be!' But the Quran is His speech, and it is impossible that His speech be spoken to. For this would necessitate a second speech, and we would have to say of this second speech and its relation to a third speech what we say of the first and its relation to a second speech. But this would necessitate speeches without end—which is false. And if this be false, it is false that the Quran is created.[59]

The Chinese example comes from Kuo Hsiang's (third century

A.D.) commentary to the *Chuang Tzu*. The text to be commented on reads:

Am I so because there is something on which I depend? Is what I depend on so because it too depends on something else?

The commentary reads:

If we look for that on which it depends and investigate that which it follows then there is no end to the looking for and investigating, so that finally we get to what has nothing to depend on, and the princple of uncaused transformation is made clear.[60]

To avoid an infinite regress, Kuo Hsiang has to assume something, i.e., that 'things are what they are of themselves' (whatever that means); and, indeed, most people will readily admit that in reasoning of any sort one has to start with some assumptions. The importance of the infinite-regress and circular-reasoning arguments, I think, is that they can be effective in making us see more clearly what these assumptions are; in short, that they lead us to 'Hypothesis'. This is neatly illustrated in the *Vigrahavyavartani* of the second-century Buddhist philosopher, Nagarjuna, whose dialectical prowess has already been mentioned a number of times. Nagarjuna's hypothetical opponent has been forced into answering a charge of 'Hypothesis' by an infinite-regress argument, namely, 'If the pramanas (means of knowledge) are established through other pramanas, then thére is an infinite series.' He is now charged with inconsistency and perhaps incoherence:

Now, if you think: those pramanas are established without pramanas; the objects to be cognized, however, are established through the pramanas, then your position that objects are established through pramanas is abandoned. There is, moreover, a discordance, namely that some objects are established through pramanas while others are not. And you should state the special reason why some objects are established through pramanas, while some others are not. But you have not stated that.[61]

Having to admit that one is in fact assuming all kinds of things is hardly damaging in itself. One can, and one often enough does, assume that some things are immediately 'given', and so require no justification. It is only because the charge of 'Hypothesis' is coupled with Agrippa's remaining two modes,

'Discrepancy' and 'Relativity', that it becomes such a deadly weapon. Philosophers may be prepared to admit thay they make assumptions which to them are self-evidently true; but they are less ready to swallow the fact that other people, equally 'rational', do not find them so.

Self-Refutation

What is the poor dogmatist to do? He may of course stick to his basic assumptions, declaring them to be true by dint of his superior intuition or the grace of God or what not. Sticking to assumptions so is hardly satisfactory to a philosopher, as it takes his argument outside the domain of rational discourse to which all philosophers are at least nominally committed.

The dogmatist may also answer the sceptic with a 'tu-quoque', i.e., 'and-the-same-to-you' argument: the sceptic is in no better position, as he too has to make an unfounded assumption, even if it is only that 'all judgments are subjective'. I am not sure that 'tu-quoque' arguments are necessarily bad arguments. Some at least may have the merit of advancing the debate. For example, if A makes the accusation that 'the Brazilian government is systematically exterminating the Indians' and B answers that A is in no position to say this, as 'the Brazilian government has denied the accusation and A has never been to Brazil', then for A to say that 'B has never been to Brazil either' is a good move. The two can then go on and discuss whether the Brazilian government can be trusted, etc. The discussion has been well served by this particular 'tu quoque'. A dogmatist's 'tu quoque' seems to be less useful. He is merely playing into the hands of the sceptic, who may gladly admit that his own assertion is just as subjective as the dogmatist's; but this does not further the debate one bit.

A more promising attack would be for the dogmatist to claim that the sceptic's position is self-refuting. Broadly speaking, this claim may not mean very much. It has, for example, been taken to mean the following: 'The sceptic's position is untenable because, while claiming that no knowledge is possible, he behaves in all sorts of ways which indicate that he does in fact believe certain things to be known, and his position is thus self-refuting.' But this way of interpreting self-refutation, though it may be effective in practice, and though it may affect our readiness to believe what the sceptic says, is not of any great theoretical interest

This brings us to the more interesting interpretation of the self-refutation charge: To claim that 'no knowledge is possible' is, say, self-contradictory because, on the one hand, this statement entails its own truth, and, on the other, it is itself a bit of knowledge and therefore implies that some knowledge at least is possible. In the same way, 'All philosophical statements are false', being itself a philosophical statement, is self-refuting.

There seem to be three ready answers to the charge, and the great sceptics—Nagarjuna, Sextus Empiricus, and Chuang Tzu—make use of a combination of all three. The answers are: (1) The sceptic does not have to make any statement. (2) The universal statements made by the sceptic are of a different kind from those which he attacks. (3) The charge holds, but then 'son las cosas de vida', and it only goes to show that one ought not to talk of what one should not talk.

The first way out can best be illustrated by a quotation from Sextus's *Outlines of Pyrrhonism*:

> Whereas the dogmatizer posits the things about which he is said to be dogmatizing as really existent, the sceptic does not posit his formulae in any such absolute sense; for he conceives that, just as the formula, 'All things are false' asserts the falsity of itself as well as of everything else, as does the formula, 'Nothing is true', so also the formula, 'No more' asserts that itself, like all the rest, is 'No more (this than that)'. . . . And, most important of all, in his enunciation of these formulae he states what appears to himself and announces his own impression in an undogmatic way, without making any positive assertion regarding the external realities.[62]

Thus, according to Sextus, the Pyrrhonian sceptic is not open to the charge of self-refutation. Unlike the 'Academic' sceptic, who makes the one assertion, 'We know nothing', he never asserts anything. The Pyrrhonian sceptic does not refrain from speaking, but his utterances are not statements, in the sense that they do not entail their own truth. Uttering 'The sun is shining', or 'Two and two make four', the sceptic does not intend his utterances to mean, 'It is true that the sun is shining', or, 'The statement "two and two make four" is a true statement.' The sceptic says of his fraternity, 'We do not positively affirm that the fact is as we state it, but simply record each fact like a chronicler, as it appears to us at the moment.'

This does not appear to me satisfactory, as it makes rational discourse impossible. Sextus has more to say; but it seems to me better to go on by quoting Nagarjuna, whose basic attitude is the same, but who is a more subtle philosopher. The following quotation is taken from the text and commentary of the *Vigrahavyavartani (Averting the Arguments)*, both by Nagarjuna. First comes the objection, which we have heard before, in somewhat different words:

> If all things are void, your statement ('all things are void') is void, being included in all things. A negation by a void statement is a logical impossibility. If, on the other hand, the negation (the claim that all things are void) is valid, then your statement is not void . . . and your proposition is contradicted by its own example . . . If your statement is not void, there arises the following discordance: some things are void while others are not void. You have, however, not stated the special reason for this discordance. In these circumstances, your statement that all things are void is not valid.

Nagarjuna's reply to this objection is:

> The voidness of my statement is established because of its being devoid of an intrinsic nature. And just as this statement is void . . . so are all things void. . . . But things like a cart, a pot, a cloth, etc., though devoid of an intrinsic nature because they are dependently originated, are occupied with their respective functions. . . . Similarly this statement of mine, theough devoid of an intrinsic nature because it is dependently originated, is engaged in the task of establishing the being-devoid-of-an-intrinsic-nature of the things . . . In these circumstances, your statement that . . . being void, it cannot negate the intrinsic nature of all things, is not valid.
>
> Since my statement is dependently originated . . . it is void. There is therefore no discordance, and your demand that a special reason be given for it is not valid.[63]

It seems that we can get the main points of this long, if much abridged and somewhat paraphrased, discussion even without getting into what 'intrinsic nature', 'void', and 'dependent origination' actually mean. The hypothetical objector seems to be saying that if one maintains that P ('all things are void') then either P itself is a thing, in which case it is void, and therefore cannot serve to state that P; or P itself is not a thing, in which case one has to show why not, a demonstration that Nagarjuna has not made. As it stands, therefore, P is untenable.

In his reply, Nagarjuna avoids the second horn of the dilemma by stating clearly that he does not claim special status for P. Taken as a statement, P is as void as everything else. All the same, he denies that from the voidness of P it follows that P is incapable of demonstrating what it appears to be stating, namely, that all things (including statements) are void. To his mind, the first horn of the dilemma is as imaginary as the hare's horns in the well-known Indian syllogism. What matters is not the fact that P states the voidness of all statements, but P's role as an aid in directing the mind toward a realization of the voidness of all things. Having heard it uttered, one is reminded of the reasoning that led Nagarjuna to say that 'all things are void' ('Whether in the causes, in the conditions, in the combinations of the causes and conditions, or in a different thing, nowhere does there exist an intrinsic nature of the things. . . .'). What P does is to refer to the process of reasoning. P is a shorthand formula reminding us of this process. The same reasoning that leads the objector to say that P is void, is effective in demonstrating the voidness of all things.

Assuming that this interpretation is correct, and that we ought to consider P as a reminder of the argument that led Nagarjuna to state that P, and not as a particular statement, we are still left with the question of the ontological status of the argument itself. Is it different from all others and therefore immune to the charge of voidness? Is it somehow not a thing? Does Nagarjuna opt for the second of the three ready answers mentioned above, and resort to a theory of types in order to grant validity to the argument of which P is a reminder? Nagarjuna himself does not think so, as is made clear by his example of the cart, pot, cloth, etc. The fact that all these things are void does not stop them from fulfilling the functions for which they are made. In a shadow world, one shadow can kill off another without being any less a shadow. Nagarjuna goes on to say, 'Suppose that an artificially created man prevents another (from doing anything). . . . The magic man who is prevented is void, and he who prevents is also void. In a like manner, a negation of the intrinsic nature of all things is possible even though this statement is void.' That is, you don't have to be right in order to win an argument *fairly*.

The shift from P to the argument of which P is a reminder is therefore not a shift from a void statement to a set of non-void 'metastatements'. This easy way out of self-refutation is not taken by Nagarjuna. Nor is it taken by Sextus or Chuang Tzu. The virtue of the shift lies somewhere else. It is a shift away from total scepticism, called 'Academic' by Sextus, and refuted by the charge of self-refutation—refuted successfully, if one is committed to a moderate rationalism, as I think all three are. The shift is to a piecemeal, 'Pyrrhonic' scepticism, 'Scepticism in the small' as against 'scepticism in the large'. A sceptic may claim that 'given any metaphysical statement, my move is to demonstrate its falsity by arguments my opponent considers good', or he may claim that 'all metaphysical statements are false'. The second claim is self-refuting; the first is not. The argument of which P is a reminder is not less void than P itself, but it is acceptable to Nagarjuna's hypothetical opponent.

Chuang Tzu, like his fellow-sceptics, the Indian and the Greek, is sometimes engaged in 'scepticism in the small', as, for example, when he refutes Hui Shih's claim that 'all things are one'; and he, like them, realizes that his scepticism, interpreted 'Academically', is self-refuting. Less verbose than the other two, he resignedly opts for the third answer listed above, and says, 'Now, as far as I am concerned, I have referred to something, but still do not know whether in referring I really referred to something or did not refer to anything.'[64]

Part II
Particular Comparisons

'Cogito Ergo Sum': Descartes, Augustine, and Śankara

Ben-Ami Scharfstein

Descartes and Augustine[1]

The formula, 'Cogito ergo sum', may well be the most famous in the whole of modern philosophy. It sticks to the memory. Not only does it have an immediate persuasiveness of its own, but Descartes, whose influence has been so decisive for modern thought, used it as a kind of Archimedean point on which he could rest his philosophical fulcrum and move the world, that is, establish a firm basis, not only for his system, but for philosophy and science in general. The formula is therefore an attractive choice for a first extended exercise in particular comparison, which should also serve as an introduction to Śankara's implicit system. Although the comparison cannot be extended as far as I should like—it could easily become a book in itself—I mean to do my best to be clear and avoid secondary points that need long explanations of their own.

I begin by recalling the familiar occasion, so effectively dramatized by Descartes, when he tried to doubt everything, but failed to be able to doubt that he doubted. This failure cannot have disappointed him seriously, for he was, all things considered, a believing and intellectually ambitious man, and he gave his failure, which was his success, the positive form, 'Cogito, ergo sum', 'Je pense, donc je suis', which is, of course, 'I think, therefore I am'.

This is the point at which, to be careful, we should turn to the words of Descartes himself:

I resolve to assume that everything that ever entered into my mind was no more true than the illusions of my dreams. But immediately afterwards I noticed that whilst I thus wished to think all things false, it was absolutely essential that the 'I' who thought this should be somewhat, and remarking that this truth *I think, therefore I am'* was so certain and assured that all the most extravagant suppositions brought forward by the sceptics were incapable of shaking it, I came to the conclusion that I could receive it without scruple as the first principle of the philosophy for which I was seeking.[2]

For the sake of the care that comparison demands, it seems best to recall, in Descartes' own words, three other occasions on which he repeated his argument, each time in some significant variation. The occasions I mean are the appearances, in this order, of the *Meditations on First Philosophy*, the *Principles of Philosophy*, and the posthumous dialogue, *The Search After Truth*.

In the *Meditations*, Descartes significantly omits the word, 'therefore'. He arrives at the argument, as we remember, after raising the possibility that some powerful evil genius may be engaged in deceiving him, and he says:

Then without doubt I exist also if he decieved me, and let him deceive me as much as he will, he can never cause me to be nothing so long as I think that I am something. So that after having reflected well and carefully examined all things, we must come to the definite conclusion that this proposition: I am, I exist, is necessarily true each time that I pronounce it, or that I mentally conceive it.[3]

In the *Principles of Philosophy*, Descartes speaks of 'a contradiction in conceiving' and restores the word, 'therefore':

While we thus reject all that of which we can possibly doubt, and feign that it is false, it is easy to suppose that there is no God, nor heaven, nor bodies, and that we possess neither hands nor feet, nor indeed any body; but we cannot in the same way conceive that we doubt these things are not; for there is a contradiction in conceiving that what thinks does not at the same time as it thinks, exist. And hence this conclusion *I think, therefore I am*, is the first and most certain of all that occurs to one who philosophises in an orderly way.[4]

In *The Search After Truth*, Descartes adds the formula, 'I doubt therefore I am', which he considers equivalent to 'I think therefore I am'. He says, this time rather expansively:

I do not think that anyone ever existed who is stupid enough to have required to learn what existence is before being able to conclude and affirm that he is; the same holds true of thought and doubt. Indeed I add that one learns those things in no other way than by one's self and that nothing else persuades us of them except our experience and this knowledge and internal testimony that each one finds within himself when he examines things. In vain shall we define what white is in order to make it comprehensible to him who sees absolutely nothing, while in order to know it, it is only requisite to open one's eyes and see the white; in the same way in order to know what doubt is, or thought, it is only requisite to doubt and think. That teaches us all that we can know of it, and explains more respecting it than even the most exact definitions.[5]

It is perhaps surprising that in Descartes' own writings, the Latin formula, 'Cogito ergo sum', does not appear. The Latin translation of the *Discourse* says, 'Ego cogito, ergo sum, sive existo', while the Latin of the *Meditations* is, 'Ego cogito, ergo sum'. In both Latin formulas, there is an emphasis, which fits Descartes' whole exposition, on the *I*, the dramatic implication being that this is an argument to be used by the very person who has been trying, unsuccesfully, to doubt his own existence. In view of what has earlier been said on the verb *to be*, it is interesting to note that in the first of the Latin formulas, the verb *sum* is apparently not enough to convey the necessary stress on existence, so a second, less equivocal verb, *existo*, is added to strengthen it.[6]

Descartes' temporary omission of the 'therefore' from his argument was the result of his fear that he would be vulnerable to the charge that the argument was nothing more than the conclusion of the syllogism: 'All that thinks exists. I think. Therefore I exist.' It would clearly be awkward if the first of all reliable truths were only the conclusion of a syllogism. Questioned on this point, Descartes answered:

When we become aware that we are thinking beings, this is a primitive act of knowledge derived from no syllogistic reasoning. He who says, '*I think, hence I am, or exist*', does not deduce existence from thought by a syllogism, but, by a simple act of mental vision, recognizes it as if it were a thing known *per se*. This is evident from the fact that if it were syllogistically deduced, the major premise, *that everything that thinks is, or exists*, would have to be known previously; but yet that has rather been learned from the experience of the individual—that unless he exists he cannot learn. For our mind is so constituted by nature that general propositions are formed out of knowledge of particulars.[7]

To anyone not accustomed to the vagaries of intellectual history, it may appear odd that so simple and natural an idea, that a person is not reasonably capable of denying his own existence, should have been assumed to be so new, and, as a novelty, should have aroused such extensive debate. Long before, the Greek sceptics had apparently been ready to accept it. Even earlier, Aristotle had put something sufficiently like it, though as a more or less self-evident hypothesis, preceded by the word, 'if'. With the omission of this hypothetical beginning, Aristotle's words are:

> He who sees perceives that he sees, and he who hears, that he hears, and he who walks, that he walks, and in the case of all other activities there is something which perceives that we are active, so that we perceive that we perceive, and if we think, that we think; and if to perceive that we perceive or think is to perceive that we exist (for existence was defined as perceiving or thinking). . . .[8]

I leave this complex sentence unfinished—for my purposes, the evidence is sufficient. For some reason, however, the principle involved was never particularly identified with Aristotle, but, instead, with St. Augustine, who used it repeatedly and with great emphasis. Descartes was told of three different Augustinian texts that seemed to anticipate his argument. For example, in the *City of God*, Augustine writes, with his rather un-Cartesian dialectical verve:

> I am most certain that I am, and that I know and delight in this. In respect of these truths, I am not at all afraid of the arguments of the Academicians who say, What if you are deceived? For if I am deceived, I am. For he who is not, cannot be deceived; and if I am deceived, by this same token I am. And since I am if I am deceived, how am I deceived in believing that I am? For it is certain that I am if I am deceived. Since, therefore, I, the person, should be, even if I were deceived, certainly I am not deceived in this knowledge that I am. And, consequently, neither am I deceived in knowing that I know. For, as I know that I am, I know also this, that I know.[9]

In *On the Trinity*, Augustine insists that the sceptical, Academic philosophy is 'wretchedly insane by doubting all things', and he counters this insanity by arguing:

In regard to this, indeed, we are absolutely without any fear lest perchance we are being deceived by some resemblance of the truth; since it is certain, that he who is deceived, yet lives... The knowledge by which we know that we live is the most inward of all knowledge, of which even the Academic cannot insinuate: Perhaps you are asleep, and do not know it, and you see things in your sleep. For who does not know that what people see in dreams is precisely like what they see when awake? But he that is certain of the knowledge of his own life, does not therein say, I know I am awake, but, I know that I am alive; therefore, whether he be asleep or awake, he is alive. Nor can he be deceived in that knowledge by dreams; since it belongs to a living man both to sleep and to see in sleep.[10]

It should be noted that in the background of Augustine's argument, there lies the conviction, inherited from the Neo-Platonists, that God, who is the 'intelligible light', lends us the illumination by which we see or participate in the eternal truth.[11]

When Descartes took the trouble to look up one of these Augustinian texts, he remarked, in effect, that there really was a substantial similarity with his own argument, and that he was glad to have the saint's backing; but that his own argument was different because differently used. In other words, Descartes was making the same kind of contextual plea that has often been made in order to question the basis of comparative philosophy: the meaning and therefore the identity of an argument depend on the uses to which it is put. (This plea is clearly a twin to that of the linguists, discussed in an earlier chapter, who insist that a word in one language is different from the 'same' word in another.)

Descartes writes in a letter:

I am obliged to you for drawing my attention to the passage of St. Augustine relevant to *I am thinking, therefore I exist* [the reference is to the *Discourse*]. I went today to the library of this town [Leyden] to read it, and I find that he really does use it to prove the certainty of our existence. He goes on to show that there is a certain likeness of the Trinity in us, in that we exist, we know that we exist, and we love the existence and knowledge we have. I, on the other hand, use the argument to show that this I which is thinking is an immaterial substance with no bodily element. These are two very different things. In itself it is such a simple and natural thing to infer that one exists from the fact that one is doubting that it could have occurred to any writer. But I am very glad to find myself in agreement with St. Augustine, if only to hush the little minds who have tried to find fault with the principle.[12]

It is obvious enough that Descartes makes an un-Augustinian use of the argument. Descartes is not interested in it to prove anything about the Trinity. He uses it, instead, as a first truth from which to begin his philosophy, a philosophy that establishes the fundamental bifurcation of reality into thinking substance and corporeal substance, the latter the subject of a mechanistic physics. But it is equally obvious that Augustine and, with him, the Augustinian tradition, regard the argument as establishing an irrefutable truth, sufficient to prove the falsity of extreme scepticism. In this, Augustine is the same as Descartes. Furthermore, as in the case of Descartes, the argument serves Augustine to prove that the soul is a thinking, spiritual substance—not air, not such and such a body or assemblage of bodies, not anything external that the senses grasp, but an immediately experienced, internal self-identity, a true presence that lives, remembers, knows, and wills; and that knows, with the most direct knowledge, that it lives, remembers, knows, and wills. Finally, like Descartes, Augustine bases a proof of God's existence on the self-evident certainty of the arguer's existence. His conception of God and of God's relation to the individual human being is certainly much like Descartes'. The conclusion must be that Descartes' metaphysics is characterized by Augustinian traits.

Descartes' very conception of intuition has an Augustinian, Neo-Platonic background. Descartes writes:

By *intuition* I understand, not the fluctuating testimony of the senses, nor the misleading judgment that proceeds from the blundering constructions of imagination, but the conception which an unclouded and attentive mind gives us so readily and distinctly that we are wholly freed from doubt about that which we understand. Or, what comes to the same thing, *intuition* is the undoubting conception of an unclouded and attentive mind, and springs from the light of reason alone; it is more certain than deduction itself, in that it is simpler, though deduction, as we have noted above, cannot by us be erroneously concluded. Thus each individual can mentally have intuition of the fact that he exists, and that he thinks; that the triangle is bounded by three lines only, the sphere by a single superficies, and so on.[13]

Descartes uses the term, *intuition*, in its etymological sense of 'seeing'. We see intellectually, he says, 'by means of a certain inborn light, and without the aid of any corporeal image'. He speaks, too, of 'the pure light of reason' and 'mental vision'.[14]

Having explored Descartes' 'Cogito, ergo sum' as far as practicable here, and having considered its direct or indirect Augustinian background, I shall try to characterize his argument in a somewhat analytical way. It is not, to the modern way of thinking, a formally logical argument. While Descartes does speak of 'a contradiction in conceiving', he refuses to regard his statement as syllogistic. He prefers to regard it as known 'by a simple act of mental vision'. It is humanly impossible, he is sure, to think otherwise. This self-evidence is renewed each time he pronounces or even conceives the idea, which is known to each person by virtue of his experience and 'internal testimony'. Any self-experience gives, or, rather, constitutes this testimony. Speaking dramatically, as Descartes does, anyone who confronts himself and pronounces the words, aloud or silently, 'I do not exist', knows that they are false because he, who is said not to exist, is there confronting himself, the person who is experimenting with the claim. Because this confrontation takes place within the same consciousness, which needs next to no time to see that the reality contradicts the claim, the claim is rejected as it is being made, which is to say, it cannot be assigned any experiential content. The words in which it is made may therefore be considered false, empty, self-contradictory, or meaningless. The very attempt to doubt one's existence renews the evidence for it.

Śankara[15]

'Cogito ergo sum', whether Cartesian or Augustinian, has at least apparent analogues in India. Indian philosophers, traditionally drawn to introspection, thought in a systematic and often subtle way about the nature of self-perception. Their opinions were so numerous and different that they might seem, at first glance, to have exhausted the possible variations on the theme. Some Indian philosophers, using a mode of analysis that we identify with Hume, denied that a coherent self existed, and yet, strangely to our eyes, they contended that self-perception was possible, in the sense that perception, even though without a genuine perceiver, was able to perceive itself. Others held that the self could not be known by immediate self-perception or intuition, but only a process of inference. There were those, too, who stressed that self-knowledge was of a unique kind, not the usual knowledge, which is of an object by a subject, but the knowledge of a subject by itself. There was also a widespread belief in extraordinary, 'Yogic' perception, which Westerners might consider magical and Indians simply 'supernormal'.[16]

So many views of self-perception were held in India that an attempt to discuss even a representative selection would be too burdensome here. For this reason, a single philosopher, Śankara, will be chosen to compare with Descartes and Augustine. Śankara (conventionally c. 788–c. 820) matches Descartes in reputation as a philosopher, in ability to renew philosophy, and in a problematic relationship with orthodox scriptural religion.[17] Other Indian philosophers might provide a closer parallel to Descartes' *cogito*, but, as the sequel will show, I am aiming beyond the *cogito* itself.

It is not difficult to find passages in Śankara's writings that recall the self-perception I have been discussing. One brief passage of this kind reads, 'Every one is conscious of the existence of (his) Self, and never thinks, "I am not".'[18] Another, equally brief passage reads, 'The existence of the witnessing Self is self-proved and cannot therefore be denied.'[19] A third, more extensive passage distinguishes between 'adventitious' knowledge, gained by means of sense or reason, and 'self-established knowledge, the Self's own self-knowledge, gained without either senses or reason':

> Just because it is the Self, it is impossible for us to entertain the idea even of its being capable of refutation. For the (knowledge of) Self is not, in any person's case, adventitous, not established through the so-called right means of knowledge; it is rather self-established. The Self does indeed employ perception and the other right means of knowledge for the purpose of establishing previously non-established objects of knowledge . . . But the Self, as being the abode of the energy that acts through the means of right knowledge, is itself established previously to that energy. Any adventitious thing, indeed, may be refuted, but not that which is the essential nature (of him who attempts the refutation); for it is the essential nature of him who refutes. The heat of a fire is not refuted by the fire itself.[20]

In a dialogue reasonably attributed to Śankara, and without doubt reflecting his manner of thinking, there is a Cartesian conversation between a teacher and his pupil. The pupil raises an objection, the same as that raised against Descartes' view that a person is essentially a thing that thinks, doubts, affirms, denies, wills, refuses, and imagines and feels. The pupil asks, if the self is identical with consciousness, how does it happen that consciousness is interrupted although the Self is supposed to be continuous? 'Did I not point out,' he says, 'that (the Self) does depart (from me) when I said that in the state of deep sleep I do not see?' The teacher answers, 'That is not right, for it is contradictory.' To the pupil's question, 'How is it a contradiction?' he answers, 'Although you are seeing, you say, "I do not see". This is contradictory.'[21] The accent in the teacher's answer is, of course, on the *I*.

It would be hard not to be struck by the likeness between these and the preceding words of Descartes. Luckily, however, the translations I have been quoting are awkward or strange enough to remind us that the likeness may be deceptive. Phrases like 'the so-called right means of knowledge' and 'the abode of energy' hint at concepts perhaps different from the European. Even the capitalization of the word, 'Self', should arouse caution.

For the sake, then, of caution, it might be wise to stop and examine what Śankara means by this word, 'Self'. Perhaps he and Descartes are speaking of two different things. The Sanskrit word that Śankara usually uses is *atman*. *Atman* is likely to be related etymologically to the German *Atem*, meaning 'breath', and *atmen*, meaning 'to breathe'. It resembles the Greek *psyche* and the Latin *spirit* in identifying a person's vital principle with his breath. Ordinarily, *atman* is used in Sanskrit just as *self* is used in English, and it carried no necessary metaphysical implications. But in Śankara, who inherits major conceptions from the Upanishads, *atman* usually means *self* in the sense of a cosmic, and not merely an individual self. It is therefore appropriate to capitalize the word in English whether as Self or as *Atman*. Śankara's text and perhaps his argument grow ambiguous when it is not clear in which sense, the limited or the cosmic, he is using the term.[22]

Apparently this is not a quite Cartesian kind of self, and an explanation is in order. To Śankara, *Atman* is pure intelligence, thought, or consciousness. As such, he believes, it is identical with the ultimate metaphysical reality, *Brahman*, which, in the final analysis, is the being of the whole universe. As absolute intelligence, *Atman* is the illumination that makes things clear everywhere. Yet *Atman*, although it is intelligence itself, cannot be known in the sense in which to be known is to be grasped as an object of thought by a subject of thought. Nothing can, in the ordinary sense, be known or described unless it shows differentiation or change. The mind needs to grasp its subject by something in it or of it, so to speak; the subject must stand out from its background or vary from its previous self. But *Atman* in itself is through and through the same unchanging reality. To know itself or, which is the same thing, to be known by an intelligent creature, *Atman* would have to divide itself into knower and known, subject and object. As indivisible, *Atman* cannot therefore be known in any usual way. Perhaps, however, it can be known, as subject to itself, by some extraordinary, immediate, non-divisive consciousness.

The cosmic, 'self-luminous' principle of reality, *Atman*, begins to be known, in the usual sense, when its cosmic power of illusion causes the single reality to become apparently differentiated. Then *Atman* becomes visible as Intellect or Intelligence, which even well-educated persons confuse with their ultimate Selves. Like an emerald dropped for testing into milk, Says Śankara, the Shining Self imparts its lustre to everything, especially to the Intellect, which, in its translucency, assumes all colours, shapes, and meanings.[23]

The intellect is that which is illumined, and the light of the Self is that which illumines, like light; and it is well-known that we cannot distinguish the two. It is because light is pure that it assumes the likeness of that which it illumines. When it illumines something coloured, it assumes the likeness of that colour . . . Therefore through the similarity of the intellect, the Self assumes the likeness of everything. Hence it will be described later on as 'Identified with everything'. Therefore it cannot be taken apart from everything else, like a stalk of grass from its sheath, and shown in its self-effulgent form.[24*]

* The transparency of intellect that leads Śankara to describe it as 'Identified with everything' is strangely like the 'nothingness' that Sartre attributes to consciousness in *Being and Nothingness*. I am tempted to prolong this comment, but forbear.

The unknowability of the Śankaran Self is interestingly like the Jungian self. Jung writes, with an explicit Kantian reference, which I omit:

'It is easy enough to say "self", but what exactly have we said? That remains

Now we can return to the Śankaran 'Cogito ergo sum'. Now the light is more obviously metaphysical and Indian. As in Descartes, the argument still has its appeal to the most ordinary and ubiquitous human intuition; but it turns out to be impossible to deny, in terms of Śankara's metaphysics, because it is impossible to deny Self in its cosmic sense, and this is because Self is the totality of all intelligence and consciousness. If there were no Self, there would be nothing at all, at least nothing that could know, be known, or be argued over. What, then, is the relation between the Self and self? The cosmic Self witnesses its own existence in the individual, because the individual self is, so to speak, a limitation of the great Self, distinguished from it 'in the same way as a drop of water from the mass of water'. To use another image, which has, to the Indian philosopher, a different resonance, the individual self is distinguished from the great Self as a reflection in a mirror from that which the mirror reflects.

Beyond the Cogito

Before the comparison with Descartes is continued, a word must be added on the nature of *Brahman*, the ultimate metaphysical reality that Śankara, drawing on tradition, supposed identical with *Atman*, the Self. Like *Atman*, certainly, it is not subject to change, diversity, or plurality. Human beings may grasp it as, at once, being, consciousness, and bliss; yet the value of such concepts, says Śankara, is primarily negative, for they help to set off Brahman from everything lesser. Such concepts, he holds, are denials of their opposites, denials, that is, that Brahman is non-being, unconsciousness or misery. Rather than attempting to say what Brahman may be, we should perhaps characterize it only by

shrouded in "Metaphysical" darkness. I may define "self" as the totality of the conscious and unconscious psyche, but this totality transcends our vision; it is a veritable *lapis invisibilitatis* . . . We should not be the least surprised if the empirical manifestations of unconscious content bear all the marks of something illimitable, something not determined by space and time.' C. G. Jung, *Psychology and Alchemy*, Princeton, Princeton University Press, 1953, par. 256.

Jung's 'unconscious' as part of the 'metaphysical' self is perhaps like the Atman that 'even well-educated persons', according to Śankara, 'confuse with their ultimate Selves'. I cannot go on with this comparison, which is complicated, but I should like to hint at its nature by calling Jung, if the name is philosophically possible, a sceptical Neo-Platonist.

repeated negations, for it is, in the words of the Upanishads, 'Not this, nor this'.

Like any philosopher who assumes that reality is an unchanging absolute, Śankara must try to understand the relation of the absolute to the at least seemingly changing, plural world. Śankara tries by conceptualizing a metaphysical hierarchy, as if the interposition of its graded stages makes it easier to understand the transition to change and plurality. The first hierarchical distinction that Śankara makes is between Brahman without and Brahman with qualities. Brahman with qualities, which is, of course, lower than unqualified Brahman, possesses the power by which the further, the mutable and therefore illusory members of the hierarchy are produced, in due order, out of itself. Sometimes Śankara uses the customary language of Hindu theology and speaks of 'the Lord', who may well be synonymous with the lower, qualified Brahman. The Lord, he says, recalls the words of the scriptures and, in keeping with them, produces the world of constant forms and transitory individuals.[25] The world that appears, says Śankara, is compounded of constancy and change. Its constancy, of structure and function, is maintained by the constant sameness of each 'genus'. To use a different concept, the world of appearances is maintained by each 'name-and-form'. This is so because each individual thing or person is determined, and therefore known, by its 'name', which is its word-known inwardness, and by its 'form', which is its shape-known outwardness.

The world of appearances, Śankara believes, is that of the successive evolution of individual existences that have been individuated by name-and-form. 'There are many distinct kinds of genus', he says, which, 'through a series of intermediate steps . . . are included in a supreme genus, Pure Intelligence.'[26] Each successive member of the hierarchy of existences, each life or soul—for everything has its modicum of life—shows successively less of the nature of Brahman, less, in other words, of knowledge, power, and bliss. As the hierarchy is descended, sense organs and bodies become necessary, because these are the signs or conditions of natural limitation. Absolute knowledge or life, on the other hand, is without darkness, without parts, and without organs:

'Because cognition inheres in Brahman, as shining as the

sun, as an eternal law of nature, it requires no organs to this end.'[27]

Now, having considered the concept of Brahman, too, as lying behind Śankara's argument for the existence of the self (or Self), we may again compare his and Descartes' arguments on self-knowledge as proving self-existence. On the most simple, human level, the Descartes and the Śankara who are each unable to doubt his own existence resemble one another, and are reacting as would almost anyone when faced by extreme scepticism. Their proof, such as it is, may be thought of as an exercise in the semantics of self-reference, or in the use and meaning of the personal pronoun, or, a little more pretentiously, in existential (rather than logical) self-contradiction, or, quite unpretentiously, as a direct psychological response. While the Cartesian-Śankaran argument was contested both in Europe and India, it seems fair to say that it was often regarded, in both places, as convincing.

There is a further similarity. Both Descartes and Śankara hope to build on the plausibility of their argument, the former to secure belief in God as the basis of his, Descartes' self, and the latter to secure belief in *Atman* as the basis of the individual self. This leap from the immediately known, psychologically speaking, to that which is assumed to be metaphysically prior and metaphysically ultimate is made by both Descartes and Śankara, and in both it is questionable.[28]

At this point, the comparison between Descartes and Śankara might well be concluded. If we are convinced by the letter in which Descartes claims that his argument differs from Augustine's because his use of it is different, it is easy to extend his claim and conclude that the difference between his and Śankara's metaphysics makes their arguments for self-existence different. The likeness, though unmistakeable, might then be looked on as philosophically trivial and even misleading.

Yet the comparison should not end here. Descartes, it is true, wants to go on and develop his physics and mechanistic physiology; but his philosophy retains some strong and evident Augustinian traits. It is, of course, possible that his 'Cogito' is based on a conscious or unconscious memory of a text of Augustine or one of his followers. Apart from this possibility, however, he, like Augustine, uses the 'Cogito' to demonstrate that he, as a soul, is purely spiritual; and, like Augustine, he finds that his human limitations argue the existence of an unlimited being, God, from whom his knowledge and very existence are derived. These are such obviously Augustinian traits that it seems plausible to say that Descartes' argument appears in Europe in a partly Augustinian context. Therefore, just as we have examined the context of Śankara's version of the argument, we may briefly examine that of Augustine.

Metaphysically, Augustine was a Neo-Platonist who made adjustments in his Neo-Platonism for the sake of his Christianity.[29] For one thing, he had to include a Christian God. But the changes he made, important as they may have been for Christian thought, need not detain us here, and we may complete the comparison with Śankara after sketching the relevant features of Plotinus's not very systematic system.[30]

At the head of the system is the One, which Plotinus takes to be identical with the Good. Existence as such, he says, demands unity, so that everything that exists does so because it 'participates' in unity; and the grade of its existence is equivalent to the completeness of its unity.[31] To put Plotinus's justification briefly: everything that exists is either one or many; but every plurality is made up of unities, so the one is the cause of the many and, as cause, superior to it. It is evident that Plotinus, like Descartes after him, thinks it self-evident that a cause is always more perfect and powerful than its effects, to which it is, as it must be, metaphysically superior. As for goodness, it is necessary to existence, because everything, in order to exist, must maintain its unity, that is, aspire to unity as a goal, and that which is aspired to is, by definition, the good (or the Good).

Because the One cannot be divided into subject and predicate, nothing, strictly speaking, can be predicated of it, and it therefore cannot, strictly speaking, be thought of, nor can it, strictly speaking, even think of itself, nor does it, strictly speaking, even exist. Strictly speaking, it can best be related to by means of negation, which at least makes clear our inability to grasp its absoluteness.[32] Yet perhaps it itself is aware of itself by some unique self-apprehension. At least, if it does not, strictly speaking, know anything, it is not ignorant of anything either.

The One spontaneously shines or radiates, without in any way diminishing its infinity. It remains unmoved, as the sun remains unmoved while its light rises from it and encircles it. In the sense of this analogy, it radiates forth Intelligence, which is unity-in-plurality. Intelligence is such unity because, comprehending plurality in itself, it remains the one in the many, just as every mathematical theorem, and therefore the whole of mathematics, is contained in every mathematical theorem.[33] Intelligence requires and is constituted by Forms or Ideas, which are not static patterns, but which, by their own force, the intuitive force of Intelligence, shine or radiate forth their existence, and, with the help of ideal Matter, give rise to the world. It is notable that Plotinus, unlike Plato, believes that individuals, too, have their Forms.

The hierarchy continues to develop. By means of its spontaneous radiation, Intelligence comes to be Soul, which is both unity and plurality—plurality understood as the failure of unity to be evident.[34] Provided with Forms and ideal Matter and radiating its force of life, it comes to be the World Soul. This, the World Soul, actually produces the sensible world, in a hierarchy of diminishing unity, power, and goodness. For the matter that pluralizes is 'truly not being'.[35] Rather, it is 'a sort of fleeting frivolity; hence the things which seem to come to be in it are frivolities, nothing but phantoms in a phantom, like something in a mirror which really exists in one place but is reflected in another; it seems to be filled, and holds nothing; it is all seeming. . . .'[36]

The lower beings on the scale of existence need bodies. To help themselves to survive and to recall what, as Intelligence, they once knew and still unconsciously know, they also need sense organs. Unfortunately, bodies and sense organs are hindrances to higher understanding.[37] When the soul returns to intuitive contemplation, it no longer needs its lower faculties, and the distinction between subject and object vanishes, or nearly does. Inspired by a final caution, Plotinus often says or implies that souls, although contained in the One and not really different from it, remain individual. Souls may, so to speak, see the light, or touch reality, or blend with reality, but the One remains transcendent.

Now that the metaphysical schemes of Śankara and Plotinus have both been sketched, they may be compared. To begin with the terms used, there is not a single one in Śankara's metaphysics that has a really exact counterpart, taken as a sheer abstraction, in

Plotinus's metaphysics. When examined in detail and in linguistic and metaphysical context, the terms that appear equivalent will all, I think, show significant differences. For those who would like to pursue the comparison, some of the more important Sanskrit and Greek terms are transliterated in the following paragraphs; but it should be remembered that neither Śankara nor Plotinus are explicit system-builders, that is, their systems are not expounded by them as such, but must be teased out of their writings, and they both use terms they may have inherited from disparate sources or chosen for their poetic resonance, without indicating the exact relations between them.[38]

Despite their terminological differences, which I have suggested rather than expounded, it is obvious that the two systems have a strong structural likeness. The Sanskrit Brahman, which is *Atman*, and the Greek One (*hen*), which is the Good (*agathon*), stand at the head of their respective hierarchies, equally absolute and indescribable, though often described in particular superlatives or their negations. Brahman, which is Atman, is self-luminous (*svayamprakaśa*) and, though itself unchanging, mysteriously creative; while the One or Good, though itself unchanging, mysteriously creates by means of its shining forth (*eklampsis*).

Both Brahman and the One may, so to speak, experience themselves as their own subjects, the first by an intuitive, non-divisive consciousness (*anubhuti*), the second by an altogether direct, non-divisive self-apprehension (*epibole*). In the process of its illusory descent toward increasing plurality, Brahman becomes, or, rather, appears to be Brahman-With-Qualities (*saguna brahman*) or the Lord (*iśvara*); while the One descends, or appears to descend, toward increasing plurality, into Intelligence or Intellect (*nous*) and Soul (*psyche*). Soul, in turn, radiates the whole hierarchy of souls, beginning with the World Soul (*psyche tou pantos*) and ending with the soul of plants.

From the standpoint of the Hindu cosmic Self (*atman*), the equivalent of the Greek stage of Intelligence, especially World Soul, is the like-named Intelligence or Intellect (*buddhi*). On this level, Hindu or Greek, an at least nascent plurality becomes visible and the visible process of creation begins. The Hindu creative power (*śakti*) is immanent in (or perhaps makes use of) the constant Form (*niyata-akriti*), or the Genus or Universal (*samanya*), or

Name-and-Form (*namarupa*) in order to bring individual beings into apparent, hierarchically arranged existence. The Greek creative Power (*dynamis*) is immanent in the Forms and is expressed in the union of Matter (*hyle*) and Form (*eidos* or *morphe*) in all individual beings in their apparent, hierarchically arranged existence. Finally both the Hindu and the Greek philosophers believe in the reincarnation of souls, the soul of a man passing from his human body into perhaps that of an animal or a plant.

So the One reality, Hindu or Greek, assumes its great multiple disguise, with its apparently separate selves trying, consciously or not, to win their ways back to their own blissfully undifferentiated being or, in positively negative words, non-non being.

The comparison that has just been made has been inadequate on both its sides, the Hindu and the Greek. It will not be elaborated, because it is sufficient for its purpose, which is to point out the complications that are met with in the act of comparison and the points at which, rightly or wrongly, one may be tempted to abandon it. Even if the comparison had been more exact or prolonged, it is likely that the same kinds of differences in conceptual materials would have emerged, together with the same kind of structural similarity. At the metaphysical top there is the mystic, more-than-self-conscious unity, that which men, said Augustine, conceive of as eternity, light, and beatitude. This unity is assumed, imagined, or 'proved' to be the only reality; and then, strangely, reality, like a Hindu magician or a Greek manipulator of lights and mirrors, gives rise to a simultaneously real and unreal world out of which we are bidden to find our way back to the real that is real alone; for the great Self of reality-in-itself and the small self of each individual person are identical or nearly so.

There have been scholars who have assumed that Neo-Platonism was influenced by the same Upanishadic thought that Śankara comments and elaborates on. This meeting between Indian and Greek was historically possible. The Greek terms in Indian astronomical treatises show an intellectual influence of the one culture on the other. It is known that India and the Greco-Roman world were engaged in trade, and there seem to have been Indians in Alexandria, where Plotinus lived until his thirty-ninth year. Plotinus is said to have become 'eager to make acquaintance with the Persian philosophical discipline and that prevailing among the Indians'.[39] But although Greek influence on Neo-Platonism is possible, we lack any direct evidence for it. Even if there had been borrowing, it would have given evidence of the existence of native Greek needs or impulses of a kind that made a Neo-Platonic or Neo-Upanishadic thought-structure plausible.*

Before I conclude my structural comparison, I should add that it neglects the strong interest of both Plotinus and Śankara in self-consciousness. A knowledgeable scholar has claimed that Plotinus was among the first thinkers in the European tradition to show a clear grasp of self-consciousness, in the sense that is, of the ego's awareness of its own activity. Plotinus's notion of self-consciousness may not coincide precisely with any Indian one, but his 'secret inner man engaged in noesis' (*Enneads* 4/8/8 and 5/1/12) is interestingly reminiscent of the inner 'witness' (*sakśin*) that plays a traditional and important role in Indian conceptions of human self-consciousness.[40]

If I were trying to make the foregoing comparison philosophically more complete and sociologically more realistic, I should have to compare the texts of the Bible and the Church Fathers, on which Augustine relied, with those of the Upanishads, on which Śankara relied. I should have to consider the philosophers—

---

* It has been claimed, by J. M. Rist, that the philosophy of Plotinus cannot have been based on the Upanishads, because Plotinus believes that the One is in all individuals, but that the individuals are not identical with the One. This distinction, Rist says, is quite absent from the Upanishadic doctrine of the identity of Atman and Brahman. 'If the doctrines are unlike,' he sums up, 'derivation or significant influence can be forgotten.' But the very distinction to which Plotinus holds was a crux in developed Indian philosophy, for there are many Upanishadic texts in which the individual soul is taken to be different from Brahman. The Indian theologian-philosopher Ramanuja (whose traditional dates are A.D. 1017–1137) insisted on the difference, and was therefore often able to give less forced interpretations of Upanishadic texts than Śankara. On this point, compare J. M. Rist, *Plotinus: The Road to Reality*, pp. 225–30, with the *Vedanta Sutras of Badarayana with the Commentary by Śankara*, translated by G. Thibaut, vol. 1, pp. lxxxvi–ci.

Rist's apparent reluctance to look at the Upanishads themselves recalls what another scholar, the classicist, Hermann Fränkel, once said of a criticism of an attempt to compare Heraclitus with the Upanishads:

'See how the Greek scholar fears the Upanishads. He does not merely think they are dangerous, he is really surprised to find that interest in them can coexist with sound interpretation'. M. L. West, *Early Greek Philosophy and the Orient*, London, Oxford University Press, 1971, p. 201.

Plato, Aristotle, the Stoics, and, of course, Plotinus—who influenced Augustine, with those—Gaudapada and others—who influenced Śankara. I should have to consider the differences between Christ and Iśvara or, more likely, Śiva. I should, furthermore, have to consider against whom and for whom both of these energetic, reforming philosophers were working—clearly doctrinal matters apart, Augustine attacked sexual licentiousness, and Śankara, religious branding of the body, explicitly sexual worship of Śakti, and human sacrifice. Much else, I am sure, would also have to be considered, though I cannot now think just what.

But even if a complete comparison has not been attempted, something of the difficulties and possible rewards of the comparison have been exposed, I hope. See the house that the simple 'Cogito' has built! We began with the natural though dramatically employed idea of self-evidence and the desire to base philosophical systems on it. At first, it seemed clear that Descartes' 'Cogito', meant to establish his dualism and further his science, belonged functionally to seventeenth-century Europe. Descartes' thinking self appeared, on reflection, so different from Śankara's self that the initial likeness between self and Self might easily have been taken to be trivial. But the idea of self-evidence has a history, and we were led from Descartes to Augustine, whose presence in the Cartesian philosophy became apparent, and from Augustine to Plotinus. The comparison between Śankara and Plotinus, which now suggested itself, showed a range of similar but associatively different concepts united into wholes with a distinctly similar structure. Whether there was any direct influence to account for the similarity we were not able to tell. It seemed plausible, however, that the similarity depended on the similar psychological, philosophical, or social ends that the two philosophies served. There the comparison (somewhat to my relief) ended.

6

Between Fatalism and Causality: Al-Ash'ari and Spinoza

Ilai Alon

Some Introductory Remarks

If this book were not as serious as it is, I should change the non-committal 'Al-Ash'ari and Spinoza' of my title to, 'An Illegitimate Comparison, to Be Taken with a Grain of Salt, Between Al-Ash'ari and Spinoza'. The reader will soon appreciate why I take my comparison to be both problematic and worthwhile; but I want to concentrate not on the contextual differences that make an exact comparison so difficult, but on the clarity that may be gained by the very attempt to compare. Broadly speaking, my subject is the stereotype, so prevalent in the West, that the Islamic faith is by nature fatalistic. To examine this stereotype, and, as I now see, to point out its limitations, I shall compare various Islamic views with those, more familiar in the West, of Spinoza on causality, on the freedom of the human will, on the freedom of the will and action of God, and on other, related issues. Let me emphasize that the comparison is not meant to suggest that al-Ash'ari exerted any real, that is, historical influence on Spinoza, or that his position or Spinoza's are really opposed or really identical. I pair al-Ash'ari with Spinoza for what might be termed methodological convenience. My hope is that the direct comparison of Islamic thinkers, notably al'Ash'ari, with Spinoza will cast a strong light on the problem of fatalism and causality as it exists, in all its centrality, in the whole of Islamic thought.

Before the comparison is actually begun, it should be noted

that many of the Islamic views have survived only in reports the accuracy and objectivity of which are open to serious question. The reports are often those made by their opponents; and survival in even such reports is likely to be more satisfactory than in so-called 'heresiography', which describes and catalogues the many heresies the rise of which Muhammed is traditionally said to have prophesied. Not only are heresiographies arranged in terms of the persons rather than the arguments of the 'heretics', but they are, as a rule, far too concise to give an adequate exposition of the arguments. I am afraid, furthermore, that the expositions made by modern scholars are not always freer of bias than the earlier, Islamic ones. I mean that questions of causuality, determinism, and the like seem particularly apt to invite the intrusion of personal convictions.[1] Because scholars are generally too subtle to express their biases openly, they do so instead in their answers to such questions as the degree of indebtedness or originality of Islamic thought, their answers implying their judgments on the 'culpability' or 'innocence' of Islam with regard to determinism.

The comparison that follows will be based, on its Islamic side, on theologians rather than philosophers, philosophers, that is, in the Islamic sense of the word, which has been explained in an earlier chapter. I hope the philosophical reader will not be deterred by the name 'theologian'. The Islamic distinction between theologians and philosophers, natural though it is in its context, cannot oblige the reader who attends more to thinkers' arguments than to their professional titles. Islamic theologians and philosophers both often deal with common topics, for example, matter and form, good and evil, and creation and causality, both rely basically on Greek logic, and both have faith in Islam as their basic background. Moreover, in later stages of even Islamic thought, the term 'philosopher' comes to mean 'anyone interested in questions of philosophy', and not 'a thinker belonging to the Aristotelian school'. The Aristotelian, or Aristotelian-Neo-Platonic position is, in any case, quite familiar in European philosophy, so that the Islamic 'theological' one is likely to interest, not only by its frequent sharpness, but by its relative strangeness and piquancy.

To these reasons for resting one side of the following comparison on Islamic theology, and to the intrinsic importance to Islam of the questions involved, it may be added, to justify the other side of the comparison, that Spinoza, thanks to his interest in separating theology from philosophy, resembles the Muslim al-Ashari in having a foot in both.

On the Historical Legitimacy of the Comparison

I have said that I intend to avoid the problem of the historical relationship between Islamic and Spinozistic thought. I owe it to the reader, however, to summarize scholarly opinion on the subject. First of all, it is clear that there is a chain of ideas, starting in Presocratic philosophy, that extends into Syriac translations of Greek philosophy, into Arabic translations, usually from the Syriac, into Latin translations from the Arabic, and then, it is argued, into the philosophy of Spinoza and other moderns. The scholar H. A. Wolfson makes the idea of this chain, and especially of the philosophies of Aristotle, Philo, and Spinoza as its critical links, the theme of his series of studies, some published and others only projected, of the history of philosophic systems.[2] In an article close to the topic that is engaging us, Wolfson tries to prove that the Muslim theologian al-Ghazzali (d. 1111) was known to the fourteenth-century Latin thinkers.[3] Other scholars, as well, have tried to establish the historical connection of Islamic ideas of causality and determinism with both earlier and later European ones.[4] As the curious reader will discover, scholars differ on the relative importance of Aristotelian, Stoic, and Neo-Platonic influence, not to speak of that of Indian or Christian thought.[5]

There are, however, other, less directly historical grounds on which to compare Spinoza with Muslim theologians. Spinoza'a ideas sometimes resemble those of the Stoics (included under the Muslim nickname, *'Dahriyyun*), to which at least the mainstreams of Muslim orthodoxy were strongly opposed. One might therefore treat Spinoza and the Stoa as if they belonged to the same camp, which has its established place in Muslim theological polemics.

Although the two persons to be compared, al-Ash'ari and Spinoza, are chronologically, geographically, and philosophically remote from one another, they share some not inconsiderable resemblances of person and situation. Both exhibit the intellectual courage of thinkers who become bitter opponents of the points-of-view to which they were initially educated. Both, because of their historical backgrounds, begin with the difficulty in relating philosophy to theology. Both live at a time when humanistic and rationalistic ideas are popular, though circumspectly expressed, and both react to them, although with opposite views. Both fall back on basically the same sources, namely, Aristotle, Alexander of Aphrodisias, and Christianity and Judaism, though, here again, each draws his own conclusions.[6] Finally, this is not the first comparison of the sort, for Wolfson has compared Spinoza with Maimonides, who refers to the Ash'ariyyah, the exponents of al-Ashari's doctrines.[7]

Two Lives, Two Views

Abu al-Hasan al-Ash'ari, the descendant of an influential theologian-politician, was born in Basra in 873/4. He studied there under al-Juba'i, a teacher of the Mu'tazilah school, a school, as will be explained, of rationalistic theology. At the age of forty, al-Ash'ari abandoned his master and joined the very orthodox school of Ahmad ibn Hanbal, becoming, in time, one of the most important of Mulsim theologians. He was pious and ascetic. 'I never saw a Shaikh,' an admirer wrote, 'more restrained concerning the things of this or more active about the things of the next world.'[8] In his numerous writings, of which the best known are *Views of the Muslims*, *Clarifications of the Roots of Religion*, and the *Book of Gleams*, al-Ash'ari expounds both his own views and those of other thinkers and sects, some of which will be dealt with later.[9]

Al-Ash'ari should be judged in relation to the spirit of his time, which was largely determined by the Mu'tazilah. This school, which began as a form of orthodoxy attempting to support Islamic dogmas by means of rational argument, soon found itself unable to accept the literality of the anthropomorphic expressions in the Quran, and generally unable to accept traditional ideas that it found to be contradictory to reason. Soon the Mu'tazilah became the rationalists of Islam, so much so that they were accused of preferring the conclusions of the human intellect when these contradicted the scriptures. They believed, it should be noted, in a kind of atomism. Al-Ash'ari attempted to create a viable

orthodox compromise between their rationalism and the opposite extreme of literalism. 'The Mu'tazilah held their heads high,'
a source tells us, 'till God sent al-Ash'ari and he made them
withdraw into sesame shells.'[10]

The Mu'tazilah adhered to five basic principles: (1) the justice
of Allah; (2) the unity of Allah; (3) the duty to do right and abstain
from wrong; (4) the position intermediate between complete
atheism and unquestioning belief; and (5) the inevitability of
divine reward and punishment. Each of these principles could,
and indeed did, provoke controversy, which culminated somewhat before the prime of al-Ash'ari, who took it upon himself to
set Islam to rights.

Spinoza, surely, needs less introduction. Born in Amsterdam
in 1632, he was excommunicated by its Jewish community, as is
well known, when he was twenty-four. His revolt against
orthodoxy, which he found intellectually inacceptable, made his
position very nearly the opposite of al-Ash'ari's. The contrast
between him and al-Ash'ari is quite interesting. Al-Ash'ari's
main problem seems to have been that of man's place and activity
in relation to Allah, a problem to which he responded by means
of a dynamic approach, in the sense that he assigned an essential
role to time both in divine creation and in human activity. His
method of writing, by direct question and answer, and by exposition and refutation of other views, was similarly dynamic. In
contrast, Spinoza constructed a static system, designed,
perhaps, to answer the question, 'How is the world built?' in
which temporal creation was ruled out, and in which ethics had
less to do with with improvement of the world than with submission to it.

Let me continue with the contrast, and sharpen it. Al-Ash'ari
and Spinoza were equally in search of certainty, but took, as has
become obvious, opposite paths, al-Ash'ari becoming disappointed with intellect and turning to belief, Spinoza becoming
disappointed with belief and the revelation on which it was
based, and turning to intellect. Likewise, the attitudes of the two
towards systemization were opposed. Whereas al-Ash'ari, who
seemed not to want to satisfy purely intellectual curiosity and
even to play the intellect down, found the concept of an embracing system of thought alien to himself, and was willing to accom-
modate lacunae of thought, which he filled in with scriptural

evidence, Spinoza was preoccupied with the need to construct an embracing system, with no recourse to divine or other supernatural explanations. Writing, it may be said, for the sake of Allah, al-Ash'ari could dispense with any attempt at argument-proof systematization, while Spinoza, writing for the sake of humans and defending himself against them and against fluctuating and negative emotions, found that a system made geometrically impregnable was necessary to himself and to anyone else who wanted the natural blessedness he felt he had achieved. Using his deductive method, he started from a latent system, which he made explicit, and which he could use to deal with particular cases, while al-Ash'ari dealt with every case separately, in relation to Allah, whom he understood to be attentive to individuals and individual acts. Both thinkers regarded the conclusions they arrived at as eternal and as teaching the farsighted how to act. In a direct sense, however, al-Ash'ari's conclusions went further, for they were meant to dictate a Muslim's religious beliefs and precise daily acts, all of which, Allah willing, were taken to have paradise or hell as their eternal consequences. Such was hardly true of the pure system of Spinoza, so adamantly closed to future reward, punishment, and bodily survival, and so sterile, I imagine, to those who needed more than it could promise.

Causality and Theology

The idea of causality preoccupies both al-Ash'ari and Spinoza. It preoccupies al-Ash'ari as the subject of a long, bitter debate, originating, some scholars hold, in the Quran's contradictory expressions on human free will, or, others hold, in the theology of peoples conquered by the Muslims; but, whatever its source, the conflict, as he sees, endangers the unity of Islam. As for Spinoza, causality preoccupies him because, as he understands it, it allows him to deny miracles and free will, divine or human, and yet to believe that the 'wise man' can release himself from bondage to emotion and gain 'freedom of mind or blessedness'.[11]

In considering causality, the pious al'Ash'ari begins with Quranic statements on God as cause, that is, on Allah's omnipotence and omniscience. The Quranic statements on which he depends are such as, 'Mighty is Allah and all-knowing', 'Allah has power over all things', and, 'He has knowledge of all things.'[12] These statements are naturally echoed in theology, in, for example, the al-Ash'ari-like creed that attributes 'life, power, knowledge' to Allah's essence. Perhaps equally naturally, the statements are given a confining interpretation by Mu'tazilites, who argue that Allah's power and knowledge are finite.[13]

As I have said, Al-Ash'ari opposes both the rationalistic, Mu'tazilah extreme, which deprives Allah of the power and knowledge he considers essential to him, and the literalist extreme, according to which Allah's power and knowledge are analogous to those of human beings. If Allah were like his creatures, writes al-Ash'ari, arguing in terms of the either-or of logic, 'He would be like them in all respects or in some one respect. So if He were like them in all respects, He would be temporally produced, as they are, in all repects. And if he were like them in some one respect, He would be temporally produced in that respect in which He was like them. But it is impossible for the temporally produced to have preexisted eternally.'[14] Allah's knowledge is therefore divorced from human knowledge, not only by its infinite extent, but by its eternality—humans draw their information from temporal experience, which cannot serve to indicate the future, while Allah's knowledge, all-embracing and unchangeable, is necessarily immune to time, that is, change.

Al-Ash'ari's position is extended by later theologians, exponents of atomism who maintain that Allah is not only omnipotent, but is the only truly potent, existing being.[15] A belief in the true existence of any other agent, explains al-Ghazali, would imply polytheism.[16] In later theology, God, his power identified with his wisdom, is said to be restricted by nothing.[17] This lack of restriction, however much it gratified traditional theology, and however well it fitted in with the belief in miracles, proved troublesome and invited restrictions of one sort or another. Thus the Mu'tazilite al-Nazzam (d. 846) claims that God does not act unjustly or deceitfully because he does not have the power to do so, and al-'Allaf denies God the power to endow the dead with sight or knowledge.[18] Pushing theological logic to its extreme, an authority declares that the only thing impossible to God is to create another God equal to himself. Ibn Hazm (d. 1064), who deals systematically with the question, concludes that some impossibilities, such as the transformation of one kind of animate being into another, are impossible only in relation to humans, and some, such as a man sitting and standing at the same time, are impossible, thanks to Allah's unfathomable wisdom, in this, but not in another world; but that the essence of Allah should undergo a change, in contradiction to the divine unity, is absolutely impossible.[19] To this enumeration of impossibilities by Ibn Hazm, we may add the later one made by al-Ghazali, who generalizes that violations of the law of contradiction are absolutely impossible, as are, he says, transformations from one genus into another, of 'blackness', for example, into 'power'.[20]

How would Spinoza fit into the Islamic discussion of impossibilities? Easily enough, especially in the guise of a Mu'tazilite. In his *Thoughts on Metaphysics,* he points out that there are 'chimeras', merely verbal entities, such as a square circle, the contradictory nature of which precludes their existence, and in the *Ethics,* he says, similarly, 'The nature of the thing itself shows the reason why a square circle does not exist, the reason being that a square circle involves a contradiction.' The general principle involved is, he agrees, that a thing is impossible if its essence involves a contradiction.[21] Descartes is likely to be the immediate source of Spinoza's conception of a self-contradictory being, but the remote source is, perhaps, Ibn Sina (Avicenna, d. 1037), who, though a philosopher by Muslim definition, was familiar with the reasoning of the exponents of *kalam.*[22]

God as Cause

For Spinoza, God is a cause, but not a temporal or creative one. He bases his view on the inconceivability of an infinite regression of the causal principle. Like medieval philosophers, who make much of this inconceivability, he comes to the conclusion that there must be a final cause, which he calls, God, but which he does not regard as the creator, that is, the temporal cause of the world.[23] While some Mu'tazilites resemble Spinoza in rejecting the idea of God as the creator of the world in (or together with) time, orthodox Muslim thinkers, including al-Ash'ari, proclaim that belief in temporal creation is essential to Islam, for Allah is the creator *ex nihilo,* the ultimate cause, in relation to which all other causes are secondary, or perhaps, as al-Ash'ari maintains, not true causes at all.[24]

In spite of their respective denial and affirmation of creation in time, Spinoza and the orthodox Muslim theologians are alike in emphasizing that God must continue to give the universe what might be termed his ontological support. In his early and perhaps not fully authentic work, the *Short Treatise on God, Man and His Well-being*, Spinoza adopts the Neo-Platonic argument that the same activity is required of God to maintain things in existence as to create them, for otherwise things would not be able to subsist even for a moment.[25] Likewise, in the *Ethics*, after stating that God 'has from Himself an absolutely infinite power of existence,' and that 'the essence of things produced by God does not involve existence', he concludes,

Hence it follows that God is not only the cause of the commencement of the existence of things, but also of their continuance in existence, or, in other words (to use scholastic phraseology), God is the *causa essendi rerum* . . . The essence of existing things cannot be the cause of their existence nor of their duration, but God only is the cause, to whose nature alone existence pertains.[26]

To orthodox Muslims, the conception of a God who is solely a creator and who, after creation, abstains from intervening in the world's affairs can only be an affront to Allah, because, as a representative creed says, Allah 'has been from eternity and will be to eternity with His names and qualities, those which belong to His essence as well as those which belong to His action.' To his essence, the creed goes on, there belong the qualities of life, power, knowledge, hearing, sight, and will, and to his actions, the qualities of creating, sustaining, producing, renewing, making, and so on.[27] Spinoza's comment on such a list would be, it appears, that only power belongs to God's essence, power granting him the ability to sustain the existence of other, or apparently other things, and granting him life in the Spinozistic sense of the power by which things persevere in their own existence. Knowledge and will are only modes of God, he would say, and will, having its cause in thought, is determined, not free.[28] God's hearing and sight he would, of course, reject as anthropomorphic, and the quality of creating, in the absolute Muslim sense, as metaphysically impossible.

Unlike Spinoza, Muslim thinkers are committed to belief in creation, though some of them, as will be seen, understand it in an unusual sense. Before I report some of the positions they take on the issue, I should like to turn a moment to predestination, to which their tradition, *hadith*, also commits them. I turn to it because their conceptions of its nature affect the stands they take on the issue of creation and, more broadly, causality.

The Muslim teaching of predestination is expressed, for example, in the *hadith*, 'God wrote down the decrees regarding the created world fifty thousand years before He created the heavens and the earth, while His throne was on the water.' The theologians, of course, interpret the fifty thousand years of this *hadith* as a metaphor for eternity, but, in any case, the writing is said to have been done with a pre-existent pen on a safely preserved tablet (preserved, the commentators say, against alteration). In the words of another *hadith*,

The first thing Allah created was the pen. He said to it, 'Write'. It asked, 'Lord what shall I write?' He answered, 'Write the destinies of all things until the advent of the Hour.' My son, I heard the Prophet of Allah say, 'Whoso dieth with a belief differing from this, he belongeth not to me.[29]*

There are enough traditions to give rise to the view that they express a pre-Islamic fatalism at odds, often, with the Quran itself.[30]

The belief in Allah's intimate preordination of everything is contravened in Islam by Mu'tazilites and philosophers who presume that the tie to him can be less than constant. With the inspiration, perhaps, of Plato's *Timaeus*, whose God implants a rational soul in the world he has created, and then—who knows?—leaves to itself this joint work of reason and 'errant' necessity, these Muslims envisage a world in which the substances, all created by Allah, are independent of him and act only in accord with their own inherent natures.[31]

It can be imagined how much this independence threatens the

---

* The Quran describes its revelations as taken from 'a hidden book' or 'preserved tablet' (85/22, 56/79). The idea of a pre-existent, uncreated, eternal Quran resembles the earlier Jewish one of a pre-existent Torah (Jewish scriptures), created, it was supposed, before the creation of the world. An analogous Christian belief presumed an uncreated, pre-existent Christ. It will be recalled that *śruti*, 'what is heard', was taken by Hindus to reveal superlative, timeless truth.

For the present chapter, the idea of the heavenly tablet as the uncreated Quran is less important than that of the tablet as a record of Allah's timeless decisions, which rule all time, including the future. See the article *'Lawh mahfuz'* in the *Encyclopedia of Islam*, and H. A. Wolfson, *The Philosophy of the Kalam*, chap. 3.

orthodox view of things, and how willingly theological and philosophical compromisers set to work to bring the extremes together. To soften the contrast, they envisage a less stridently independent world, its laws created by God and its proceedings under his supervision. Such is the view taken by the Mu'tazilite al-Nazzam.[32] The Aristotelian-Neo-Platonic philosophers, such as al-Farabi (d. 950) and Ibn Sina (d. 1037), assume that the world is created in the sense of eternally emanating from God. Ibn Rushd (Averroes, d. 1198), who is too purely Aristotelian to accept the theory of emanation, nevertheless believes in God's atemporal, eternal creation of the world. He argues that the Quranic verbs implying its creation do not necessarily mean that it was created at a particular time, and he protects his orthodoxy by suggesting that when Muslims repeat that the world is not eternal, they mean, rightly understood, that it is not self-sufficient. The self-sufficiency of nature is limited, he says, because its functioning depends ultimately upon Allah, who is capable of changing its laws at will.[33]

Even in its softened form, however, the idea of a separate nature, equipped with laws of its own, proved an affront to the orthodox. In their eyes, secondary causes interposed between Allah and his creation derogate from Allah's status as the sole cause of everything. But the orthodox, though outraged, were subject to some philosophical constraints, and to destroy the plausibility of a separate nature, they had to overcome two major difficulties. The first, relating to natural phenomena, was to explain the stability of the succession of causes and effects, and the second, relating to ethics, was to explain the sense of freedom that people experience.

The orthodox solution of these two difficulties is primarily by means of a thoroughgoing atomism, which adherents of *kalam* adopted and developed in the course of the ninth century. The best account of the theory is given by Maimonides (d. 1204), according to whom it rests on the following twelve premises: (1) Every body in the world is composed of tiny, indivisible, identical particles, substances that God is constantly creating and can annihilate. (2) These atoms exist within a void. (3) Time is composed of instants, temporal units too short to be divisible. (4) Accidents exist—accidents in the Aristotelian sense of non-essential attributes. (5) Accidents are inseparable from atoms. (6)

Accidents remain in existence for only a single unit of time. (7) Accidents may be either positive or negative—motion, knowledge, and life, for example, are positive accidents, and rest, ignorance, and death are negative ones. (8) Nothing exists but atoms and accidents, the atoms differing from one another only in their accidents. 'Natural forms', such as animality, humanity, and rationality, are no less accidents than are whiteness or sweetness. (9) Accidents exist only in substances, that is, atoms, and never in other accidents. (10) Everything that is imaginable is also possible. 'This is the main proposition of kalam.' It excludes whatever involves logical contradiction. (11) The existence of any infinite whatever is impossible. (12) The evidence of the senses is uncertain and therefore insufficient to demonstrate the truth.[34]

This atomic theory allowed the orthodox to establish or re-establish the unlimited priority of Allah, and, so to speak, to disestablish nature as anything in itself. It established that Allah alone is a creator; that his creation is constant; that nothing comes into being or perishes except by means of his creation (perishing is a created accident); and that causal and temporal relations manifest, not natural law, the existence of which is only an illusion, but Allah's habits, which he can change at will.

In keeping with this position, any appearance of causal relationship is explained away by its analysis into atomic constituents between which there is no necessary connection. Thus, to give an Islamic example, the movement of a pen in the hand of a scribe requires, first, the human will to move the pen, second the human power to move it, third, the movement of the hand, and, fourth, the actual movement of the pen. Each of these stages is a series of accidents, each accident created by Allah at the moment of its manifestation, sequential in time, but unrelated by causality. The closeness of this analysis to that of Malebranche and even Hume is itself not, I think, an accident.

Al-Ash'ari shares only some of the atomists' views. Anchored in the anti- or transrational principle of 'without (asking) why' (*bila kaifa*), which requires the unquestioning acceptance of all the Quran says about Allah, he is freed of the burden of proof or rational explanation. Perhaps inconsistently, he does try to explain somewhat. Everything is created by means of Allah's order, 'Become!' Al-Ash'ari says, and so before an event actually takes place, no human being can initiate a process to cause that

event. Human beings, he believes, have no initiatives or possibilities of their own, for everything is in Allah's hands and is the
product of his omnipotence, omniscience, and other perfections.
That leaves the problem of miracles. To al-Ghazali, a miracle is
a phenomenon that contradicts the laws of nature, its cause being
God's will to achieve some aim, such as to persuade unbelievers
to accept the prophecy made by a certain individual. This conception of a miracle as an intended breach of natural law cannot
satisfy al-Ash'ari and his followers, any more than it satisfied
Mu'ammar before them, because it allows nature a certain independence. To the Asharites, a miracle is no more than a breach of
Allah's habit, and it is as reasonable and legitimate as the ordinary course of events.[35] But for Spinoza, as the reader may recall,
a miracle, assuming it has really taken place, is simply a
phenomenon the explanation of which is unknown. Out of
ignorance, Spinoza says, people believe that the 'bending' of the
laws of nature proves that God exists, though his existence is
best proved by the order and permanence of these laws. To Spinoza, a miracle contradicts the natural order caused by God, and
so he who believes in it is, in fact, discrediting God.[36] Later, in the
Ethics, Spinoza becomes still more open, and insists, as all students of philosophy know, that God and nature are identical.

Human Freedom and Divine Omnipotence

In Islamic as in European thought, the discussion of causality
merges with that of free will. The background, as I have already
said, includes a pre-Islamic Arab fatalism, as well as Christian
theology, in particular that of John of Damascus.[37] The Quran
itself contains some statements that must be taken to affirm free
will, and others that clearly imply its denial. The affirmation is
evident, for example, in the exhortation, 'Let him who will,
believe it, and him who will, deny it', while the denial is evident,
for example, in, 'He whom Allah guides is rightly guided; but he
whom He misleads shall find no friend to guide him.'[38]
    The issue of free will appears to have first become explicit in
Islamic theology as the issue of divine justice. The Mu'tazilah
were bold enough to prefer God's justice to his omnipotence,
with which they found it to clash. His justice, they urged, must
allow freedom of choice, for it is intolerable if God punishes

someone who is not genuinely responsible for his acts. But if free will is assumed, there are troublesome questions to be asked about God's power and foreknowledge. Other questions arise; for example, whether it is right of God to inflict harm on creatures, that is, children and animals, that cannot be considered responsible. The Mu'tazilah answered such questions in the light of freedom and justice; the orthodox theologians, in the light of the deterministic statements of the Quran and the more consistently deterministic ones of *hadith*.

No ingenuity was spared in the attempt to reconcile the belief in free will with that in Allah's omnipotence and omniscience. Thus the suggestion was made that Allah wills a person to perform a pious act at just the moment that the person decides to perform it, so that the act's free choice and determination are simultaneous. But what, then, can be said of impious acts? Can these, too, it was asked, be willed by Allah, and if willed by him, is the person who commits them rightly punished? Is Allah, it was asked, the creator of good deeds alone, or bad as well as good? And does Allah know literally everything? The questions were numerous and, given the essential beliefs of Islam, difficult.

The Mu'tazilah, though they put justice first and held man to be free to choose, added that he is predestined to a degree, because God supplies him with the lawful bread to which he is entitled. Later, the Mu'tazilah were engaged in controversy over the question of whether the power to act must be created in a human before that human performs a given act, or whether he can act in consonance with God's will alone, without the special creation in him of the power to do so. The Mu'tazilite al-Nazzam argued that in order to enable the human to make a real choice, the power created in him should be applicable to both of the alternatives he faces.[39] Others, also interested in enlarging the scope of human freedom—from an orthodox standpoint, at God's expense—maintained that not only a human's act, but everything that results from it should be ascribed to his responsibility.[40]

Perhaps the most original and certainly the most characteristic Islamic answer to such questions is in terms of the doctrine called 'acquisition'. It is said to have been invented by the eighth-century theologian Dirar, who is said to have been expelled from among the Mu'tazilah for his belief in it.[41] Elaborated by al-Juba'i

(d. 933) and al-Ash'ari, the doctrine asserts that, while Allah creates deeds, man 'acquires' them by his own will and action. The advantage of the doctrine to Muslims is that it maintains divine omnipotence and an at least moderate determinism, but does not deny the feeling of human freedom of will and action. In al-Ash'ari's interpretation, the human power to act is created by Allah for the sake of a particular action alone, and not for its alternative, meaning that man cannot choose what to do with the power given to him. Al-Ash'ari even adopts the pre-Islamic idea, echoed in *hadith*, that whatever one has done could not have been done otherwise. It seems, nevertheless, that the customary picture of him as an arch-determinist is exaggerated, because, as a recent analysis has shown, he in fact tries to find a position between the extreme determinism of the strictly orthodox and the freedom of the Mu'tazilites.[42] According to this analysis, al-Ash'ari changes the Mu'tazilite stress on man's creation of his acts to stress on Allah's total creation. That is, Allah's total creation includes the creation of man's power to act, which al-Ash'ari therefore calls 'an acquired act' (*fi'l muktasab*), implying that man, not Allah, is the immediate cause of his own acts.[43] Yet, always cautious on this issue, al-Ash'ari accepts neither the concept of an independent human nature nor that of a true causal order, but contends that the power to carry out an act is created in a person at the very moment of the act's performance. Struggling to make a difficult compromise, al-Ash'ari asserts that Allah is the only efficient, that is, direct, cause of any act or event, but that, all the same, there is human causality.[44] In other words, although a secondary cause can never be *sufficient* for the total realization of an act, it is *necessary*, for Allah creates causality in human beings, but not the results of this causality. God's power, which pre-exists all events and actions, is thus expressed at the moment of action by the power he just then creates in man. To the question of whether Allah is unjust in creating the human power to do injustice, al-Ash'ari answers negatively, on the grounds that Allah creates the unjust act as the possession of another, not of himself.[45] I find it sad to comment that this refined but forced compromise of al-Ash'ari does not solve his basic problem, for though it leaves Allah as the sole creator, it deprives him of his providence, his unlimited supervision over the world's events.

All the contestants in the debate I have been reporting agree that if a Muslim acts in accord with Allah's will, Allah is committed to reward him, as he is commited to punish the unbeliever. In their devotion to this commitment, the Mu'tazilah, as I have reported, grant considerable freedom to man and considerably restrict the freedom of Allah, for they insist that Allah, no less than man, must submit to the requirements of intellect and justice. The orthodox reaction to this insistence, the principle of without (asking) why', means that Allah is committed to no one and nothing outside himself, and that justice, defined as whatever Allah does, lies outside the scope of human judgment.

Despite their differences, the Mu'tazilah and the orthodox Muslim theologians agree that humanity enjoys a special status in the world. In contrast, Spinoza, to whom I return for a moment, emphasizes God's commitment, so to speak, to the whole of nature, for, in his philosophy, men cannot justly claim any special divine favour, nor can God grant it to them. If God had any moral responsibility, Spinoza reasons, it would imply that the condition of the world could be bettered, and this would in turn imply that the world as it exists is not perfect. This implication Spinoza cannot accept. Yet, to speak too briefly and imprecisely, the whole comparison I have attempted shows Spinoza to have in some ways been a kind of modern, sophisticated Mu'tazilite, who could easily fit into the Islamic theological controversies of the eighth, ninth, and tenth centuries.

Some Final Questions and Comments

Is Islam fatalistic? I suppose that if this question were put to a modern Westernized Muslim, the answer would be negative, and, indeed, the mainstreams of Islam do not accept the idea of fate, a non-theistic power that issues simply arbitrary decrees. Except for brief episodes in the history of Islamic thought, the basic Islamic view was that Allah predestines what happens, but that, however his actions appear to human beings, he is not unjust. In spite of cultural pressure in the direction of determinism, great efforts were made to arrive at a view that would somehow preserve human freedom of will and action. These efforts, which were, and could only be, I suppose, partially successful, came to their most characteristic conclusions in the sort of compromise offered by al-Ash'ari and, after him, al-

Ghazali. The truth is that even Spinoza, here regarded as a continuation of a certain Islamic and medieval European line of thought, did not arrive at a radical solution of the problem. Sharing the Islamic ascription to God of such attributes as omnipotence and omniscience, he resembles al-Ash'ari in that he, too, finds a mean between extremes, in his case the extremes of a neutral, atheistic science and a dogmatic religion supported by presumed miracles.

Two Islamic theories seem to have attracted the most appreciation. The first is that of acquisition, which, as explained, takes Allah to be the sole creator of every thing and act, yet, by the human acquisition of the power he creates, puts the burden of moral responsibility on humans. The second theory is the atomism that takes creation to be continuous, frees Allah from obligation to any person or thing, and yet allows for the regular development of events.

Why, of all the problems the Muslims dealt with philosophically, did that of predestination and free will arise, as seems probable, first? The reason may be that it reflected a dilemma already embodied in the words of the Quran. Whatever the reason, the authoritative character of Islam, its very strict monotheism (as contrasted with the Trinitarian monotheism of Christianity), and the complete submission of the Muslim to Allah, seem to have formed a background that made the meeting between Islam and Eastern Christianity so intellectually fruitful. Granted all the intellectual history I have and have not commented on, it might almost be argued that predestination was a question to which Islam was by nature predestined.

7

Two Metaphysical Concepts: *Li* and *Idea*

Dan Daor

On the Prehistory of Universals
(Ben-Ami Scharfstein)

As its title shows, this chapter is devoted to a comparison of one of the most basic Chinese metaphysical concepts with an equally basic Greek one. The comparison, which bears, of course, on the issue of Nominalism and Realism, is made difficult by subtle differences, perhaps best considered aesthetic, between Chinese and Greek philosophical perception. Many things can be said about it approximately, but what can be said exactly? It is the very difficulty of the comparison and the rather surprising contrast that emerges from it that make it rewarding.

Metaphysical concepts do not, I think, spring forth full-born, but have a kind of infancy, of which at least a preliminary word should be said. To broaden the perspective in which the Chinese-Greek comparison is seen, a hint should also be given of the ways in which Indians argued the issue of Nominalism and Realism.

It is obvious that philosophy, in the technical sense, has been nourished by pre-philosophical reasoning, reasoning saturated with imagination and sustained by magical and religious needs. Concepts that may reasonably be called metaphysical therefore appeared long before philosophy, in its technical sense, came into existence, and continued, and still continue, to form in extra-philosophical matrixes of all sorts.

Let me give a number of examples of metaphysical concepts that played the part, so to speak, of universals, though endowed (as Plato's and especially Plotinus's remained endowed) with magical force. Surely, the belief held in ancient Egypt, Mesopotamia, and India, not to speak of Africa and elsewhere, that a magical force resides in the names of gods, people, and things, was a proto-philosophical one, for these names were magical essences that could be used to create or destroy whoever or whatever bore them. Furthermore, names, words, and incantations were often assumed, as such, to have creative force, to be used, it might be, by gods engaged in the act of creation.[1]

Surely, too, there was something of the sense and force of a Platonic universal in the Sumerian concept of the cosmic rules, or, in perhaps more fitting, administrative language, powers of office that ensured, the Sumerians believed, the orderly operation of the universe. These rules or powers (each, in Sumerian, a *me*) included lordship, godship, shepherdship, kingship, truth, prostitution, art, music, heroship, goodness, justice, judgment, and much else. Each cosmic and cultural phenomenon seems to have been assigned its fitting rule or power. As a Sumerian myth makes clear, the rules or powers could be presented, stolen, and restored by the gods, for these rules had, in our language, an ontological substantiality of their own.[2]

Such incipient Platonism is also discoverable in the tendency of each culture to reify the principle of order in both the universe and society. Thus the Egyptians tended to reify the principle of *ma'at*; the Indians the principle of *rita*; the Iranians the principle of *asha*; the Chinese the principles of *li* (in one of its senses), of *hsing* (as the nature of things and men), or even of Heaven; and the Greeks the principles of *nomos* and *dike*.

A more picturesque incipient Platonism is discoverable in some of the concepts held by tribal cultures. Let me give, as an instance, the belief of American Indians (specifically, the Iroquois and Algonquin) that whatever existed on earth had an 'elder brother', which or whom we might consider to be a living prototype or archetype. Such archetypes were believed to exist for, among others, the deer, the bear, the beaver, the wind, the light of day, and the sun. In the Algonquin version, which recalls Eskimo and Siberian variants, the soul of an animal that felt itself disrespectfully treated complained to its prototype or 'master', who caused the animals whose power was concentrated in himself to disappear from the usual hunting grounds.[3] Not very differently, the Navahos believed that some natural phenomena were taken possession of by 'one who lies within it'. Such an 'inner form', they thought, was 'a being independent of the object which it happens to occupy. . . . The personalized "inner forms" of animals, plants, and inanimate natural phenomena are addressed in prayers and mentioned in myths and ceremonies'.[4]

From the incipient Platonism of ancient and tribal cultures, I turn to India.

On Indian Nominalism and Realism[5]
(Ben-Ami Scharfstein)

In India, as in the West, not only were metaphysical concepts cultivated, but their status became a problem in itself. The Indians asked, with acumen and pertinacity, whether or not abstract concepts could be considered to exist in some sense, and how, in any case, the relation between such concepts and the whole, ordinary objects of experience might be understood. The issue, which we term that of Nominalism and Realism, was pursued in India with no less intensiveness than in the European Middle Ages, and, it must be said, with greater variety, for the medieval European debate began from more or less Platonic or Aristotelian assumptions, while the Indian philosophers were able to draw on metaphysical assumptions of a much wider range.

Nominalism in India was a characteristically, though not exclusively, Buddhist position. The basic reason is easy to grasp. Buddhist tradition taught that men suffer because they assume that they are true physical, psychological, or metaphysical unities, and not, as they must learn, merely collections of materials and experiences, which are scattered at death. Such a teaching led the Buddhists to oppose belief in the metaphysical existence of any complex or collection having what we should call organic unity, and therefore also to oppose the belief in the 'existence' of universals. One prominent school of Buddhist philosophers, led by Dignaga, argued that the only real elements in perceptual experience were the unique, momentary, inexpressible sensations on which it was founded. It followed that any more complex experience or idea must have been artificially constructed by imagination or intellect.

The Buddhists were involved in persistent debate with the

most Realistic of Indian philosophers, those of the school of
Nyaya (or Nyaya-Vaiśesika) and of the subschool of Mimamsa
that agreed with them. Although the Nyaya were Realists, none
of their relevant concepts are identical with Platonic or Aristotelian ones, for each of the Indian and Greek concepts must be
understood in the context of the whole philosophy of which it is a
part. Nevertheless, there is something in the moderation of the
Nyaya position that makes it comparable with that of Aristotle.

I shall not try to expound the details of the Nyaya position,
some of which are distinctly arcane, nor to be accurate in the
sense of expounding a particular text or commentator. But I can
say, nevertheless, that the Nyaya, like Aristotle, were Realists in
both of the usual philosophic senses. That is, they believed in the
real existence of the objects revealed by sensory perception, and
they believed in the real, ontologically separate existence of universals or generic properties, which they named either *samanya*
(generality) or *jati*, the predominant term in later periods.

Let me explain, even if only very briefly. The Nyaya believed
that perception does not fundamentally mislead us and, accordingly, that the ordinary objects of our perception are, as a rule,
just as they appear to be. Perception, they said, reveals not only
that the objects are real, but that each of them is both particular
and universal (or general). The particularity and generality of
objects are both necessary to them, for their particularity is perceived by us as the fact of their separateness and individuality,
and their generality as the fact of their identity with others of their
kind. Some general traits, the Nyaya held, are accidental, temporary, or 'imposed'; but a true generic property is eternal, meaning, unaffected by whatever occurs to the particulars in which it
manifests itself. Despite its eternality, however, it can manifest
itself only in particulars, to which it is bound by the 'real' relation
of inherence. In analogy with material bodies, said the Nyaya,
generic properties are impenetrable to one another, but lower
properties, those the extension of which is narrower, can 'nest' in
higher ones and form a hierarchy that culminates in the generic
property of 'being'.

In comparing the Nyaya with the Aristotelian position, it is
well to keep in mind not only the difference between the Nyaya
generic property and the Aristotelian notion of form, but also the
Aristotelian connection between form and the actualizing of

potentiality, the latter an idea absent from the Nyaya armoury of metaphysical concepts.

As explained in a previous chapter, the position of Śankara, including his doctrine of generic properties, is comparable to that of the Neo-Platonists, though this likeness is considerably weakened in most of his followers. Perhaps, though I cannot go into the Indian debate, the reader will find himself sympathetic to the position of the Mimamsa philosopher Kumarila and of some of the Jain philosophers, who held that everything is in a sense general and in a sense particular, for both generality and particularity are indivisible aspects of everything, so that, in Indian terminology, the general and particular are related by identity-in-difference.

The comparison of the Chinese and Western concepts of the general or universal is more difficult to put precisely than that of the Indian and Western, for the Chinese depend less, as has been said, on abstract characterization and more on semantic resonance. As might be expected, a comparison of the Chinese concept, *Li* and the Greek, primarily Platonic concept, *Idea*, shows both similarities and differences. The Greek concept is aimed at explaining the constancy of things, while the Chinese is primarily aimed, as will be seen, at explaining the ability of things to remain individual and separate.

(Han Fei Tzu's) Li and (Plato's) Idea

Li is a concept crucial to very much of Chinese philosophy. One of the few incontestably technical terms in a tradition relatively free of jargon, it is second in importance only to the ubiquitous and elusive *Tao*. Appearing rather late on the philosophical scene, it had a long and varied history in Neo-Taoist and Buddhist philosophies, until it became the key term in Neo-Confucianism, which the Chinese themselves call 'Li Hsueh' or 'Li Learning'.

One can claim almost, but not quite as much for the term *Idea* in Western philosophy. It, too, had a long and varied history, and it, too, at one time enjoyed the position of the most important term in an undoubtedly important philosophical system; but whereas *Li* remained supreme for centuries, *Idea* never regained the glory it possessed in Plato's philosophy, or perhaps, to be cautious, in Plato's philosophy at one stage of its development.[6]

This difference in historical importance is of course not enough in itself to rule out a comparison of the two terms. It seems to me, on the contrary, that if we were to make a detailed comparison of the career of *Li* in China and of *Idea* in the West, we should learn a good deal about the ways in which the two traditions handled central metaphysical concepts, and we should no doubt bring into sharper focus differences likely to be somewhat blurred in a comparative investigation of more limited scope. I cannot, unfortunately, undertake the detailed comparison here—I should need far more knowledge and space than are at my command. Instead, I shall concentrate on a certain passage in the *Han Fei Tzu*, a work of the third century B.C., attempt to clarify the term *Li* in the passage, and then compare this *Li* with the term *Idea* (or *Form*) in Plato's *Phaedo, Republic*, and *Timaeus*.[7]

My choice of the passage I have mentioned needs explanation. It occurs in the chapter called 'Chieh Lao' 'Explaining the *Lao Tzu*'. Although there are at least two English translations of it, the one by W. K. Liao, in the *Complete Works of Han Fei Tzu*, and the other by W.-t. Chan, in his widely used *Source Book in Chinese Philosophy*, and although Chan, like Fung Yu-lan before him, pointed out its importance for the study of *Li*, it seems to have attracted little attention, and, to the best of my knowledge, there is no study of it in any Western language.[8] Yet this passage remained for several centuries the only real attempt to give an exposition of *Li*, a fact that is unlikely to be obvious to a Western reader of either translation.

The 'Chieh Lao' chapter is attributed to the Legalist philosopher, Han Fei, who shaped the ideology of the first Emperor of China, Ch'in Shih Huang Ti, and is found, as the previous paragraph makes evident, in the book bearing his name. It may not, in fact, have been written by Han Fei, but by someone who lived a short while after him; but it is, in any case, the first of many attempts to make clear the short and eminently obscure *Lao Tzu*. The passage on *Li* seems to be related in particular to chapters one and fourteen of the *Lao Tzu*, and is intended to explicate the concept of *Tao* or *Way*. The term *Li* itself, though not present in the *Lao Tzu* or in the authentic chapters of the other great classic of Taoism, the *Chuang Tzu*, was perhaps first used in a systematic manner by a Taoist school, trying to make sense of

Tao, some time at the end of the third century B.C. or the beginning of the second.

The following is a translation of the passage, complete except
for a few uninstructive examples:[9]

The Way is what the myriad things regard as 'so', what the myriad *Li*s
combine into. The *Li*s are the markings of the completed things; the Way
is what makes the myriad things complete. Therefore it says, 'The way is
what orders (*Li*s) them'. Having *Li*s, the things cannot crowd out one
another, and so the *Li*s regulate the things. Each of the myriad things has
a different *Li*, and in each having a different *Li*, the Way is exhausted. It
combines the *Li*s of the myriad things, and so it cannot but be transformed; as it cannot but be transformed, it has no constant hold; it has no
constant hold, and so the breath of (both) death and life is endowed by it,
the myriad wisdoms fill their cups from it, the myriad affairs wane and
wax by it. Through it heaven is high and earth is a storehouse, the sun
and moon extend their light, the five constants (wood, fire, metal, water,
and earth) keep their positions constant, the stars stay in their orbits, and
the seasons replace one another . . . The Way is wise with Yao and Shun
and mad along with Chieh Yu; it perishes with Chou and Chieh and
flourishes with Tang and Wu. You think it near—it travels to the four
corners of the world! You think it far—it is always by my side! You think
it dark—its light is dazzling! You think it bright—its thingness is obscure!
Its achievement forms heaven and earth; its harmony transforms the
thunder. Things in the world depend on it for their completion.

The *Li*s are what distinguish the square from the round, the short from
the long, the coarse from the fine, and the fragile from the hard. Therefore, it is only after *Li*s are determined that the Way can be attained.
Therefore, among the determined *Li*s there are survival and extinction,
death and life, flourishing and decline. Now, (a state of affairs such) that
things now survive and now become extinct, sometimes die and sometimes live, at first flourish and later decline, cannot be called 'constant'.
Only that which was born when heaven and earth were pulled apart,
and which will not die nor decline till heaven and earth melt away, can be
called 'constant'. But that which is constant suffers no change, has no
determined *Li*, and resides in a constant place.[10] It cannot therefore be
regarded as the Way. The sage observes its profound emptiness, makes
use of its ubiquity. Forced to call it a name, he says, 'Way', after which
alone it can be discussed. Therefore it (the *Lao Tzu*) says, 'A way which
can be regarded as the Way is not a constant way.'[11]

The curious metaphysical picture of the world embodied in this
passage has no familiar landmarks for a Western reader. It contains no substances and attributes, no minds and bodies, no

atoms and forces. It seems to be made up of three kinds of entities: a large number of *things and affairs,* as many *Li*s, and, apparently a *Tao. Things* include everything that can be perceived—heaven, earth, ghosts, the madness of Chieh Yu, the fall of the house of Chou, and Shun's filiality, not to speak of the things on Alice's Walrus's list. Although we find, besides the word *things (wu),* the word *affairs (shih),* there seems to be no philosophical interest in this distinction. Everything there is and everything that happens can be said to be either a *wu* or a *shih.* Perhaps *events,* understood as including stones no less than revolutions, may serve best as a general name for all the entities of the first kind.

Li is translated by both Liao and Chan as *principles;* but this translation hardly helps us to understand what *Li*s are, and of the five senses of *principle* given in the *Concise Oxford Dictionary,* none means anything like *Li.* How are we to understand it? As the one new term it is defined in the passage in relation to both *things* and *Way,* terms familiar from the *Lao Tzu.* The *Li*s are said in the passage to be 'the markings (or lines, *wen*) of the things' and to regulate the things and make sure that the things are kept distinct. The *Li*s seem to answer at least one metaphysical question, somewhat similar to that posed by Plato, 'Why is a thing what it is?' A thing is white, or round, or filial, because it has the *Li* of whiteness, or roundness, or filiality. Moreover, the *Li*s serve to individuate the things, thus answering another metaphysical question, natural to a Taoist, who viewed the world as in constant flux, 'Why doesn't everything become everything else?' The *Lao Tzu* itself, warning that 'as a thing, the Way is shadowy and indistinct', makes the answer obscure; but the *Han Fei* passage dispels much of the abstruse magic surrounding the concept of *Tao,* the *Way,* by describing it in terms of the concept of *Li.* The passage's description of the *Tao-Li* relationship is, in fact, dual. According to the one, more or less metaphysical description, the Way combines all the *Li*s of all of the different things, for it is 'what the myriad *Li*s combine into', while according to the other, more or less epistemological description, the *Li*s are a precondition for attaining the Tao, the understanding of the Tao being taken to depend on the prior determination of the *Li*s. The second description does not imply the first. In any case, no transcendental leap is assumed between the comprehension of the *Li*s and the attainment of the Tao. The notion of such a leap might make better sense of the *Lao Tzu*, and is indeed adopted for its interpretation by the great third-century commentator, Wang Pi; but the *Han Fei* interpretation, it seems clear, is a reductionist one, according to which the *Way* is neither more nor less than the combination of all the *Li*s. Yet, like the *Lao Tzu*, the author of this interpretation makes great claims for the Way, whose 'achievement', he says, 'forms heaven and earth', and adds, 'the myriad affairs wane and wax by it', and so on.

Such claims for the Way impel one to try to give an account of how this profoundly empty, ubiquitous, essentially nameless non-thing is responsible for everything that happens. In what sense can it be said that 'the Way is what makes the myriad things complete'? The answer lies, I think, in the first sentence, 'The Way is what the myriad things regard as "so" ', or, phrased somewhat differently, 'The Way is the "so-ness" of all things', meaning that it is the way things are, that the world, which is made up of a myriad of different 'things' or events, is held together by the one metaphysical 'fact' that 'everything is what it is'. When we refer to 'the Way' we do no more, therefore, than point to this presumed fact. This is a different conception of Tao, which deprives it not only of its magic, but also of its constancy. That is, whether we call the Tao 'constant' or not seems to depend on whether we think of it as a transcendental being granting the *Li*s power to regulate and individuate all 'things' and guaranteeing that 'everything is what it is', or whether we think of it, in accord with the reductionist *Han Fei* passage, as no more than a shorthand reminder of this basic tautology.

What I have just said brings me to the one controversial section of my translation. Both Chan and Liao take this section to lead to the *Lao Tzu*'s famous first line in its usual interpretation, which is, 'A way that can be spoken of is not the constant Way', and so to indicate that the Tao is ineffable and transcendental. It seems to me, however, that a more natural reading of the *Han Fei* passage, though not necessarily of the *Lao Tzu*, makes this interpretation unlikely. The reason is that the passage takes the trouble to define 'constant' as that which does not change, does not shift its place, and is uniform throughout, and it makes it clear that a state of affairs in which 'things now survive and now become extinct . . . cannot be called "constant" '; and yet this is the state of affairs that is the very 'so-ness of things', the Way itself.

How do the *Han Fei* conceptions I have described compare with the Platonic Ideas? There seems, first of all, to be a difference in what might be called metaphysically numerical relationships. The phenomena whose existence call for Platonic Ideas or Forms are as numerous and varied as the 'things' that constitute the *Han Fei*'s ontology. Thus we have 'the Beautiful' and 'the Just', 'the Equal' and 'the Even', the Idea of Man and the Idea of Bed. But whereas the *Han Fei* says explicitly that there are as many *Li*s as there are 'things', in Plato's metaphysics, there are, at least on the face of it, many fewer Forms. The mapping from 'things' to *Li*s is one to one, while that from phenomena to Forms is many to one. In the world of the *Han Fei*, to each horse-event there corresponds a unique *Li*, specifying its size and colour, as well as its birth, life, and death. In Plato's world, to the many phenomenal horses, there corresponds the one Ideal Horse, of which they all are poor replicas. (Indeed, this kind of 'philosophical economy', whether or not it works philosophically, must have been a powerful motive for conceiving the theory of Forms.[12]) Yet we should remember that the relationship of phenomena to Forms is not simply many to one, because the counterpart in the world of Ideas to a running white horse is not one, but three Forms, 'Horseness', 'Whiteness', and 'Motion'. To Plato, a particular horse is white because of 'Horseness' and 'Whiteness', the Forms of which it is said to 'share in' or 'resemble'. If, at a certain moment, it is running, it is doing so presumably because the Form of Motion has approached and that of Rest withdrawn; as, Plato says, snow, 'on the approach of the hot will either withdraw or perish'.[13]

Plato's Forms are simple, that is, incomposite and unchanging, invisible, and not located in either space or time.[14] The *Li*s, too, do not change, and so may be considered not to be located in time, and they are, I should assume, invisible. Moreover, they have a constant place, which probably means that they are not located in space, for if they were, they could be shifted from place to place, which seems nonsensical. Unlike Forms, however, the *Li*s are not simple, but composite, as they have to be in order to account for the different characteristics of events. Their nature may perhaps be clarified by comparing them with chromosomes as conceived in modern biology. On this analogy, each 'thing' or event has a sequence of *Li*s that specifies all its properties as well as its history. On the same analogy, the Platonic Forms would each be like a separate gene, but each determining the present being of the 'thing' rather than its changing history.

Faced with the same world of phenomena, which are ever-changing and yet display certain regularities, the Taoist metaphysician and Plato ask themselves different questions. Plato seems to be struck by the fact that many things in the world look alike, and conceives of the Forms to account for this resemblance. The Taoist seems to be impressed more by the separateness that things display and their relative permanence, and he conceives of his *Li*s as principles accounting for both individuation and change. Whereas Plato abstracts from his resemblance-classes a set of Forms forever petrified in the timeless world of Ideas, the Taoist envisages a complicated network of *Li*s on which events are strung like beads. Whereas change is banished from Plato's real world and relegated to the shadow-world of the cave, in the Taoist's world change is captured and 'spatialized' by the *Li*-lines running through space-time. Plato needs his other, Idea-world because his basic metaphor is of objects illumined by the sun and casting thin, misleading shadows of themselves, or of an artisan copying out an image he has in his mind. He sees shapes, and his key verb is therefore 'to imitate'. In contrast, the Taoist does not need another world of any kind, because his basic metaphor is that of the criscross paths that give a paddy-field its structure, or the veins that pattern a piece of jade. He sees lines, and his key verb is therefore 'to run through'.

For all its stress on change, the *Li*-world is fundamentally as lifeless as the world of Ideas or as a Minkowski diagram of space-time, for the *Li*s, which give the world its structure, are immutable. The *Li*-world comes to life only because of the Tao, of which it is said, 'The breath of death and life is endowed by it, the myriad wisdoms fill their cups from it, the myriad affairs wane and wax by it.' In Plato's scheme of things, at least as he describes it in the *Republic*, the Form of the Good seems to be needed for much the same reason, to animate an otherwise rather dead world; for the Good is not only 'the brightest of all realities', but 'is inferred to be responsible for everything right and good, producing in the visible realm light and the source of light, and being, in the intelligible realm itself, the controlling source of reality and intelligence.'[15] Though the Good is 'beyond reality', it has been kind enough not to have remained there, in isolation with the objects of knowledge, but to have 'begotten' the sun 'in its own likeness', showing fecundity much like that of the Tao of the *Lao Tzu*.

I have mentioned only some of the similarities and differences between Plato's metaphysical picture and that of the unknown Taoist whose text I have been drawing on; others can be discovered by a careful reading of the texts. As in most metaphysical exercises, these two philosophers appear to begin by reasoning out the general features of the world, and, again as in most of them, they end up with platitudes about the ineffable. To my mind, such rather similar beginnings and conclusions are relatively uninteresting. The good metaphysician becomes interesting somewhere in the middle, where reason is aided by intuition, metaphor, and myth, where the greatest variety of metaphysical formulations is to be found, and where metaphysics combines analytical skill and poetic imagination.

8

'Dream-World' Philosophers: Berkeley and Vasubandhu

Yoel Hoffmann

To Introduce Vasubandhu
(Ben-Ami Scharfstein)

Students of European philosophy all have some sense of who Berkeley was, at least as a thinker. The charming style in which he proposed what, to most readers, seemed and perhaps still seems outrageous has been enough to make him memorable. Beyond the charm and the outrageousness, he was a deeply cultured, public-spirited man, whose philosophic Idealism was meant to save the world he knew from materialism, atheism, and inhumanity. Berkeley is, then, a recognizable figure, and one more influential in European philosophy, it turns out, than a superficial glance might show. In contrast, Vasubandhu, I must suppose, is unknown to the reader, and it seems only right to introduce this study with a few words on him, though these will leave his person enigmatic and his system unexplained as such.

Vasubandhu and his elder brother, Asanga, are great figures of a school of Mahayana Buddhism called Yogacara or, less frequently, Vijnanavada. The name, Yogacara, meaning, 'yoga practice', emphasizes the kind of practice the school encouraged, while the name, Vijnanavada, meaning, 'consciousness doctrine', emphasized its metaphysical position. The school began to develop during the second century A.D., and reached a period of high creativity by the fourth, the time, it appears most likely, when Vasubandhu and Asanga flourished. Its popularity in

China is attested by its four surviving translations, the most notable of which is that by Hsüan-tsang. Perhaps too abstract and unyielding for Chinese taste, it did not hold its ground in China for very long, though it won adherents in Tibet, in Korea, and in Japan, where it became known as the Hosso School.

Vasubandhu himself remains a riddle to scholars. To account for the difference in the writings attributed to him, he has even been divided into two authors, each one a Vasubandhu, living a century apart. The comparison that occupies the present chapter is based on a work plausibly attributed to the Vasubandhu who was Asanga's brother, and who was born, the ancient *Life of Vasubandhu* says, in what is now Peshawar, in present-day Pakistan. The title of the work, abbreviated in Sanskrit as *Vimśatika*, may be fully translated, *The Treatise in Twenty Stanzas on Representation Only*. Containing not only the twenty stanzas of the title, but also Vasubandhu's own commentary on them, the work is an Indian-style demolition of the views of other schools, those of 'the outsiders' who teach the existence of an external world, independent of consciousness. *The Treatise in Thirty Stanzas on Representation Only*, abbreviated *Trimśika* in Sanskrit, summarizes Vasubandhu's full position, which remains suspended curiously, from a modern Western standpoint, between what one is at least tempted to call Subjective and Objective (or Absolute) Idealism.

Vasubandhu has the traditional reputation of a quick-minded polemicist, one who had 'quick and sudden flashes of ideas' in controversy, whereas his brother, Asanga, 'required some time to give a good answer'.[1] The *Life of Vasubandhu* I have mentioned, written by a Buddhist monk in the sixth century, tells how Asanga converted Vasubandhu from Hinayana to Mahayana Buddhism. No one can vouch for the accuracy of the story, but it is a well-known episode in Buddhist tradition, and so I allow myself to repeat that Asanga was afraid that his gifted younger brother might compose a work that would devastate the Mahayana position, so that, to have the chance to change his brother's mind, he lured him to him. As the story goes, Asanga sent word to Vasubandhu that he was seriously ill; and when Vasubandhu came to see him, he explained that Vasubandhu's attacks on the Mahayana had given him a serious heart disease. 'For this evil action,' Asanga said, 'you will be sure to sink for ever into a miserable life. I am now grieved and troubled for your sake and to such an extent that my life will not last long.'

Surprised and alarmed, Vasubandhu requested his brother to expound the Mahayana to him, and he quickly discovered that the Mahayana was the more complete and correct teaching. Conscience-striken and afraid of punishment, he approached his brother and said, 'I do not know by what means I can be pardoned for my former evil action. I did harm speaking ill of the Mahayana by means of my tongue. I will now cut it out in order to atone for the crime.' His brother answered, 'Even if you cut out your tongue a thousand times, you cannot wipe out your crime. If you really want to wipe it out, you must find some other means.' To Vasubandhu's request for a suggestion, Asanga answered, 'Your tongue was able to speak very skilfully and efficiently against the Mahayana, and thus discredit it. If you want to wipe out your offence you must now expound the Mahayana equally skilfully and efficiently.'[2]

Presumably, the Vimśatika, which enters into the immediately following comparison, was one of the results of this brotherly exhortation.

The World as 'Dream Stuff'

Suppose, to begin with, we compare a passage from Berkeley's *Dialogues Between Hylas and Philonous* with Stanzas I and II of Vasubandhu's *Vimśatika*. Both passages first raise the argument of a proponent of 'matter', who claims that the world exists independently of the perceiving mind. Berkeley and Vasubandhu both try to refute this view by means of the argument that there is no fundamental difference between the so-called 'real world' and the phenomena of dreaming. The passage from Berkeley's *Dialogues* is as follows:

Hylas. I profess I know not what to think, but still there are some scruples remain with me. Is it not certain I see things at a distance? Do we not perceive the stars and moon, for example, to be a great way off? Is not this, I say, manifest to the senses?

Philonous. Do you not in a dream too perceive those or the like objects?

Hylas. I do.

Philonous. And have they not the same appearance of being distant?

Hylas. They have.

Philonous. But you do not thence conclude the appartions in a dream to be without the mind?

Hylas. By no means.

Philonous. You ought not therefore to conclude that sensible objects are without the mind, from their appearance or manner wherein they are perceived.[3]

I quote Vasubandhu's two stanzas in prose form, with the removal of their translator's square brackets, which mark words added to complete the sense. The first stanza puts the argument of the hypothetical opponent, who claims that if ideas never corresponded to real, that is, external objects, the objects represented would not be localized as they are in space and time, would not appear, as if objectively external, in the streams of consciousness of different individuals, and would not exert physical (or physical-seeming) effects. The opponent says:

'If representations [ideas] are without real objects, then their spatial and temporal determination, the indetermination of the perceiving stream of consciousness, and their action, must be unfounded.'

Vasubandhu answers:

'Place and time are determined as in a dream. . . .'

He explains that there is, in fact, spatial and temporal localization in dreams:

'That is, as in a dream although there are no real objects yet it is in a certain place that such things as a village, a garden, a man, or a woman are seen, not in all places; and in this place it is at a certain time that this village, garden, etc., are seen, not at all times.'[4]

The Idealistic claim that the world is 'mind stuff' goes against the common, deeply ingrained intuition of the 'externality' of the perceived world. In its most extreme and logically most coherent form, solipsim, the Idealistic argument would sound to most people like the philosophy of a lunatic. Though the argument of the Realist may not be logically superior, most of us, explicitly or implicitly, accept the 'solidity' and 'externality' of the perceived world, and even if we do not like it, resign ourselves to it. The Idealist, however, seems to suffer from an abhorrence of 'solidity', as though he could not bear the thought that 'impenetrable' and 'dead' matter should be the stuff of the world. For him, the 'dream quality' of the world seems to be not the conclusion of philosophical analysis, but an existential premise.

As may be seen from the quoted texts, there is a substantial similarity between the argumentation of the eighteenth-century British philosopher and the fourth-century Indian one. Berkeley and Vasubandhu are generally considered the representatives of Idealistic philosophy in their respective philosophical traditions. It is relatively easy to point out the general similarities of the two philosophers. However, a more subtle comparison, of variations in method of exposition, of style, and of other details, may give insight into the differences between the philosophical traditions of Christian Europe and Buddhist India.

Arguments Against the Concept of Spatiality

In *An Essay Towards a New Theory of Vision*, Berkeley contends that distance or 'outness' is not directly perceived. The immediate object of vision, he says, is two-dimensional, whereas the third dimension of 'depth' is provided through the sensations we have when we adjust our eyes, and through the senses of touch and motion. In other words, we do not directly *see* visual depth. The three-dimensional visual field, space, is an abstract concept constructed from the disparate sensations of sight, touch, and motion:

> *Distance* or outness is neither immediately of itself perceived by sight, nor yet apprehended or judged of by lines and angles, or anything that hath a necessary connection with it: but it is only suggested to our thoughts, by certain visible ideas and sensations attending vision, which in their own nature have no manner of similitude or relation, either with distance or things placed at a distance.[5]

The Newtonian concepts of absolute space, absolute motion, and absolute time are all discredited by Berkeley as abstract ideas. The idea of space, he claims, is derived from the sensation of motion:

> When I excite a motion in some part of my body, if it be free or without resistance, I say there is *space*: but if I find a resistance, then I say there is *body*: and in proportion as the resistance to motion is lesser or greater, I say the space is more or less *pure*.[6]

Berkeley excludes the concept of power from that of motion. Power, he says, is the attribute of 'spirits', but the sensible qualities that compose the so-called 'bodies' of the external world are 'passive' ('non-spiritual') existences, and they cannot, therefore, originate their own movement. He grants that 'motion' can be defined as the change of position of two bodies in relation to one another, but as the 'bodies' themselves are nothing different from the form in which they are perceived ('ideas'), the concept of 'motion of bodies' derives from the succession of ideas in our mind. He says in his private notes, 'Certainly we should not see Motion if there was no diversity of Colours. Motion is an abstract Idea i.e. there is no such Idea that Can be conceived by itself.'[7]

Newton's notion of absolute time flowing uniformly is rejected for the same reason, namely, that there can be no temporal existence separate from and independent of the actual succession of ideas in the perceiving mind. 'Whenever I attempt to frame a simple idea of *time*,' says Berkeley, 'abstracted from the succession of ideas in my mind, which flows uniformly, and is participated by all beings, I am lost and embrangled in inextricable difficulties. I have no notion of it at all.'[8]

In the cryptic notes of his *Philosophical Commentaries* (or *Commonplace Book*), Berkeley hints at another argument against the materialist concept of material space. In a spirit not unlike that of Vasubandhu's main argument, soon to be summarized, he writes, 'Each particle of matter if extended must be infinitly extended. or have an infinite series of extension. Our idea we call extension neither way capable of infinity. i.e. neither infinitely small or great' (sic)[9]

Berkeley is ready to accept the concept of a 'unit' as long as the 'unit' is perceivable, for as far as the perceivable data ('ideas') are concerned, it is possible to measure the limits of perception of the various sensation-fields and determine minimal or maximal units. But if, like Newton and Locke, one assumes imperceptible material units and defines them in terms of shape, size, and weight, in terms, that is, of 'primary qualities', one is bound to fall into logical absurdities concerning infinitesmals.

Vasubandhu's argument (*Vimśatika*, stanzas X–XIV) against an outer world of sense objects revolves around the impossibility of the concept of 'atom'. The logic of this general argument runs so:

1. An outer world of sense objects cannot be assumed unless we assume the existence of atoms.
2. The assumption of the existence of atoms is logically absurd.
3. An outer world of sense objects cannot be assumed.

Vasubandhu argues that if an outer world exists, it is either a basic plurality, by which he means, constituted of atoms, or a basic unity. For the sake of the present exposition, I start with the second possibility, that the outer world is a basic, i.e., absolute unity. Vasubandhu denies this possibility, of course. His argument is surprising, because in making it he seems to burst into an open door: nobody in his right mind would claim (Parmenides to the contrary) that the outer, spatial world was an indivisible unity. Vasubandhu's main argument is therefore directed against the usual notion that the spatial world is constituted of three-dimensional atomic particles. But for the sake, I assume, of logical neatness, he does not want to leave unrefuted the logical alternative of an indivisibly spatial world, and he says (Stanza XIV):

'Assuming unity, there must be no walking progressively, no simultaneous grasping and not grasping, and no plural, disconnected conditions; moreover no scarcely perceptible, tiny things.'

If the spatial world were a unity, says Vasubandhu in this stanza, a statement that is true of one 'part' of it should hold true for all the rest of it. For instance, if the spatial world is absolutely one and altogether indivisible, it cannot be maintained that walking in it is possible, or assumed that a foot covers one part of it and not, simultaneously, another. For to say that the *same* indivisible unity is partly covered and partly not covered is logically contradictory. If we try, impossibly, to imagine the act of walking in a one-unit space, we have to assume that *all* space is covered at once by the foot or that *no* space is covered, for it is impossible for the contradictories, covered and not covered, to be true at once of the same unity. Similarly, we cannot say that some one thing, some 'part' of the spatial world, is grasped and another not—either *all* or *none* of it is grasped at once.

In his commentary (the translation of which I change somewhat) Vasubandhu explains:

A single place, also, ought not to contain disconnected things such as elephants, horses, etc. For where the one is contained, the other must then be contained. Since all occupy the one undivided place, how can we say that one is distinguished from another?

We cannot, Vasubandhu claims, distinguish between the parts of a unitary world in terms of 'this' or 'that' or 'here' or 'there'. In short, the concept of a unitary spatial world allows nothing but the unity itself to be posited of the world and cannot be assumed if we wish to account for the world we actually perceive.

If the spatial world cannot be thought of as one unit, it must necessarily be composed of separate units. But the idea of a minimal unity of material extension, an atom, is also logically absurd, claims Vasubandhu, and thus all the schools that base their views of the world on the concept of 'atom' must be rejected. 'That realm', he says (Stanza X), 'is neither one thing, nor is it many atoms; again, it is not an agglomeration, etc., because the atom is not proved.'

In his commentary on the beginning of the stanza, Vasuban-dhu explains that 'the external object cannot logically be one, because we cannot grasp the substance of the whole apart from the parts'. He is referring here to the Hindu atomists of the Vaiśesika school, who assume that the universal is ontologically distinct from the separate components of 'things'. His refutation of the Vaiśesika theory requires no new argument, for it goes against the Buddhist 'non-substance' view. The general argu-ment of Buddhism against the existence of universals is therefore as effective for him against the Vaiśesika as against others. That is, if the Vaiśesika claims that the 'hand' is something different from the five fingers and palm, or the 'forest' different from the separate trees, the Buddhist would answer that a 'thing' is no more than its component parts, and that any concept beyond this is a mere mental fabrication.

After the Vaiśesika, the stanza refers to the atomic theories of two Buddhist schools, that of the Sarvastivadins and of the Sau-trantikas. The Sarvastivadins assume that an object is composed of many atoms between which there is empty space, whereas the Sautrantikas assume close contiguity between the atoms. As far as Vasubandhu's refutation is concerned, there is no difference whether the atoms are separated or close, for his argument denies the concept itself of the atom. Whatever the position of atoms or the relations between them, a theory dealing with atoms cannot be true, because its fundamental premise, the existence of an atomic unit, is absurd. 'One atom', says Vasubandhu (Stanza XL) 'joined with six others must consist of six parts. If it is in the same place as six, the aggregate must be one atom.'

The logic of this argument goes: If the atoms joining an atom on six presumed sides are in different places, the atom in the middle must have six areas or parts, one to join each facing atom; but something that consists of six parts cannot be an atom, which is defined as a partless, indivisible unity. On the other hand, if the atoms joining each other are partless, they cannot be said to be in different places, for there is nothing to prevent them from occupying the same place, and if they occupy the same place, the seven atoms are necessarily no bigger than the one atom and, in effect, identical with it.

The logical device behind Vasubandhu's argument is his equation of the infinitesmally (he might say, infinitely) small with zero, nothing. An accumulation of no-things (partless atoms) leads, of course, to nothing. Such argument is strikingly similar to that of Zeno's paradoxes, and it leads to the same problems concerning space, time, and motion. I shall not enter here into the still disputed logical problems involved in these paradoxes. For our purpose, it suffices to point out that both Berkeley and Vasubandhu reject the concept of the so-called 'external', that is, materially extended world. In the following section, I propose to deal with the positive premise of the two systems, the conception of the world as 'mind stuff'.

Levels of Reality

The rejection on philosophical grounds of a materially extended world does not, of course, annul our environment. We are still surrounded by mountains, fields, houses, humans; we still move, talk, eat, and drink. This environment, however, claims Berkeley, is not the 'stupid, thoughtless *somewhat*' it is too often considered to be.[10] It is a more refined, mental stuff, which he terms 'ideas':

I say it is granted on all hands (and what happens in dreams, phrensies, and the like, puts it beyond dispute) that it is possible we might be affected with all the ideas we have now, though no bodies existed without [outside], resembling them. Hence it is evident that the supposition of external bodies is not necessary for the producing of our ideas. . . .[11]

I shall discuss the logical problem involved in the 'mind-stuff' theory in the last section of this chapter. Here I want to deal with the distinction in the two systems between 'ideas' of the so-called external world and dream images.

The claim that reality has the quality of a dream does not necessarily put reality on the same level as a dream. The analogy of the dream is used in Berkeley's and Vasubandhu's philosophy to reject the concept of 'matter' as the substance of the 'outer' world. To both of them, the reality of the waking world and the 'reality' of the dream world are the same in that they are *non-material*; but both philosophers admit that the two worlds are different in degree of coherence and intensity. The following are a few of Berkeley's statements on the distinction between reality and dream:

Ideas of Sense are the Real things or Archetypes. Ideas of Imagination, Dreams etc., are copies, images of these.[12]

The ideas imprinted on the sense by the Author of Nature are called *real things*: and those excited in the imagination, being less regular, vivid and constant, are more properly termed *ideas*, or *images of things*, which they copy and represent.[13]

The ideas of sense are more strong, lively, and distinct than those of the imagination; they have likewise a steadiness, order, and coherence, and are not excited at random, as those which are the effects of human wills often are, but in a regular train or series. . . .[14]

The ideas formed by the imagination are faint and indistinct; they have besides an entire dependence on the will. But the ideas perceived by sense, that is, real things, are more vivid and clear; and, being imprinted on the mind by a spirit distinct from us, have not the like dependence on our will. There is therefore no danger of confounding these with the foregoing: and there is as little of confounding them with the visions of a dream, which are dim, irregular and confused.[15]

In the writings of the Yogacara, we find a distinction between three aspects (*lakksana*) of 'intrinsic nature' or 'own being' (*svabhava*). The first, and least 'real', aspect is the 'imagined' (*parikalpita*), which included the phenomena of fantasies, illusions, and dreams. The second, more real, aspect is the 'interdependent' (*paratantra*). It is more real than the first, though ultimately 'non-real', because it is more coherent, that is, evolves in a regular, coherent way, in accord with the laws of 'dependent origination'. The distinction between these two aspects is not unlike the one Berkeley draws between 'ideas of sense' and 'ideas of imagination'.

In the *Vimśatica*, the theory of levels of reality is not explicitly mentioned. In order, no doubt, to lend force to his refutation of his 'externalist' opponent, Vasubandhu stresses the similarities between the 'real' and the dream world. He says (Stanza II), as will be recalled, 'Place and time are determined as in a dream,' and he adds, 'As in dreams there is function in the loss of semen.' Later (Stanza XV) he emphasizes, in the same vein, 'Immediate awareness is the same as in dreams etc.'

Vasubandhu's hypothetical opponent resists. He makes the claim that dream images are private and, unlike real objects, are not perceived by many individuals in common. To this Vasubandhu replies (Stanza II) that 'the ghosts together behold the same river of pus'. His meaning is that the souls condemned to purgatory all see the same visions, though these do not represent any real (external or material) object. He further replies that dreams may have 'real' effects, for example, seminal emission without actual sexual intercourse. The quality of awareness, he also insists, has the same directness and immediacy in dreams as in the state of wakefulness.

It must be said that all these replies of Vasubandhu are exaggerated. He himself is forced to this admission when his opponent argues that if a dream were as 'real' as wakefulness, a man could be held responsible for the crimes he dreamed. To this, Vasubandhu says (Stanza XVII), 'The mind by sleep is weakened: dream and waking retributions are not the same.' Dreaming, admits Vasubandhu, is, after all, a weaker reality than wakefulness.

The 'Self' and the 'Other'

Had Berkeley and Vasubandhu been consistent, they should have ended up as solipsists. However, for reasons to be discussed later, they did not deny the existence of the 'other', and so created a basic contradiction in their own systems. Berkeley's famous definition of existence, 'to perceive or be perceived', declares active perceiving spirits and passive sensible ideas to be the sole constituents of reality. It may be granted, with Berkeley, that we have direct, intuitive knowledge of the 'self' as an 'active perceiving spirit'; but his system does not provide for any means of recognizing the 'other'. The 'proof' he provides for the existence of the 'other' is by means of analogy: We know ourselves as active spirits connected with a bodily form, and although we cannot have *direct* knowledge of other active spirits—not being 'ideas', they are unperceivable—when we perceive bodies like our own and hear words similar to ours originating in these bodies, we may conclude that in these bodies, too, there dwells a spirit.

Berkeley's proof of the existence of God sounds similar. The similarity, however, is misleading, for while his proof of God's existence is correct from a purely logical point of view, that of the existence of the 'other' is not really deductive. An abbreviation of both proofs should help make this clear. His proof for God's existence is:

1. If there are 'ideas', there must exist a spirit that creates them.
2. There are the 'ideas' we call nature . . .
3. There exists a powerful spirit that creates them.

Berkeley's proof for the existence of the 'other' is:

1. We recognize our own self (spirit) to be combined with a body.
2. We perceive other bodies. . .
3. There are other spirits connected with these bodies.

Because the principle of the origination of ideas in spirits is a premiss of Berkeley's thought, his proof of God's existence can take a genuinely deductive form. The proof of the existence of the 'other,' however, can be presented as at most inductive.

The clarity of thought and the shrewdness which characterize Berkeley's arguments on the supposed primary and secondary qualities of matter are completely lacking in his dealings with the problem of the 'self' and the 'other'. Berkeley claims that natural bodies are creations of the divine spirit and are moved according to its will. It follows that our bodies, being parts of nature, can be perceived, like any other bodies (complexes of ideas), but cannot be *moved* by them. Berkeley prefers to disregard this obvious conclusion, and, supposedly for reasons of religious morality, attributes to human spirits the power to cause motion in 'ideas' created and regulated by God. This is the power by which we make voluntary motions of our own bodies and effect changes in other bodies.

Berkeley hardly deals with the problem of human communication. Believing in 'Laws of Nature', he assumes, as I have said, that most ideas or sensations perceived by us are caused by the will of an all-powerful spirit, who arranges the ideas so admirably in order to give us 'a sort of foresight, which enables us to regulate our actions for the benefit of life.' It is the same spirit, God, 'who *upholding all things by the Word of his Power*, maintains that intercourse between spirits, whereby they are able to perceive the existence of each other', and helps them to maintain their intercourse by providing each individual spirit with ideas sufficiently similar with those of every other.[16]

In the *Viṁśatika* we find a discussion of the same difficulties in knowing the 'other' and participating in a common world. Vasubandhu's basic view is that events appearing in the stream of consciousness are determined by the process of Karma, and, as there is no objective world, our experience is constituted by the 'representations' of our own minds, the representations evoked by the conditioning power of the Karmic evolution of each of us. 'The apparent object', says Vasubandhu (Stanza XVI), 'is a representation. It is from this that memory arises.' In other words, to remember some *thing* does not mean to remember an external object, but to remember a previous idea of one's personal stream of consciousness. In the ultimate sense, he claims (Stanza XX), ordinary humans and other non-Buddhas have no knowledge at all, either of their own minds or of the minds of others, for the world perceived while in the Karmic process remains illusory, divided in terms of the subject and object of knowledge. Only the knowledge of a Buddha can reach 'the ineffable object'.

However, Vasubandhu does not rest satisfied with this mystical statement and tries to deal with the difficulties arising from his Idealistic standpoint in more rational terms. We experience a 'common' world, he says, not because we all perceive the same external objects, but because of the arousal in us of similar images by a similar Karmic process. If ten people 'perceive' the same landscape, it is not because there are indeed mountains and rivers 'out there', but because the life-process of the ten has developed similarly. To put the Yogacara doctrine in too compressed a way, the past deeds of the people have left in the 'store-consciousness' of each of them similar 'seeds' or 'latent impressions', which reach their fruition (appear in consciousness) at the same time and result in the same cognitions in the minds of each. To be fair to Vasubandhu, it should be added that the absurd results of such an explanation would not have embarrassed him. He would have wholeheartedly agreed, I suppose, that an enlightened person, one who has freed himself from Karmic causality, might indeed 'see' something else—most probably no-thing—where others see mountains and rivers.

But, still, how can we say, argues the opponent, that we all function in the same world, meet one another, and use language to communicate with each other, as you, Vasubandhu, do when you are talking to me, if, as you claim, there are no external things? To this Vasubandhu answers (Stanza XVII), 'By the power of reciprocal influence the two representations become determined.' He explains, 'That is to say, because a distinct representation in one stream of consciousness occasions the arising of a distinct representation in another stream of consciousness, each becomes determined, but not by external objects.'

Two streams of consciousness, Vasubandhu is saying, may mutually affect one another in such a way that images, which we wrongly attribute to the external world, appear in both streams. That is, you, to whom I am addressing myself now, are not in reality 'out there' in material space, for it is impossible that I should communicate with something that is outside my mind. There is nothing but two streams of consciousness, mine and yours ('where?' one is tempted to ask) affecting one another. As a result of this mutual influence, suitable cognitions in both consciousness-streams appear and enable communication. To use a simpler metaphor, I dream you at the same time that you dream me, and in this way we are able to communicate with each other.

The opponent, who is Vasubandhu arguing with himself, does not seem convinced, and asks, 'If only representations exist, and there is no body nor speech etc. how are sheep etc. killed by anybody?' In other words, how can you say that anything *happens* at all? To this Vasubandhu only repeats (Stanza XVIII) what he has said before, 'Because of transformation in another's representation, the act of killing and injury occurs; just as the mental power of a demon etc. causes another to lose his memory.' The act of killing, explains Vasubandhu, takes place in the consciousness of the killer, and as a result of the process there, the consciousness of the victim is affected in such a way that its life forces are annihilated. To satisfy the opponent, Vasubandhu adds illustrations from Buddhist folklore to prove how powerful the mental forces of demons, saints, and other such beings are, and what terrible effects they may cause. The reliance on beliefs in magic in this answer is evident enough. Through such illustrations Vasubandhu endeavors to prove that no physical contact has to occur in order to effect changes in the world. If I possess the special mental power, says Vasubandhu, I can use it against the opponent who appears in my 'dream' and cause his annihilation, the whole process being a purely mental one.

The Absolute

Both Berkeley's writings and Vasubandhu's *Vimśatika* (and *Trimśika*) start with the arguments for the Idealistic principle of 'mind only' in a quasi-logical-philosophical mood and end up with the concepts of God and Buddha. It seems, however, that the end is in the beginning, and that Berkeley's God and Vasubandhu's Omniscient Buddha are premisses rather than conclusions. The whole train of Idealistic argumentation in both systems is intended, I believe, to create a world view compatible, in the one case, with Christian morality, and, in the other, with Buddhist meditation. I intend to deal with the cultural motivations of the philosophers in the next section. In this one, I want to compare the concept of God in Berkeley's philosophy with that of Buddha in Vasubandhu's and to define the function of these two concepts within the respective systems of the two philosophers.

If we put aside the general theological motivation of Berkeley and evaluate his philosophy on a purely philosophical basis, we may say that God is brought into the system to save it from solipsism. Berkeley has to give an account, within the terms of his Idealism, of the continued existence of things outside of human perception:

When I deny sensible things an existence out of the mind, I do not mean my mind in particular, but all minds. Now it is plain that they have an existence exterior to my mind, since I find them by experience to be independent of it. There is therefore some other mind wherein they exist, during the intervals between the times of my perceiving them: as likewise they did before my birth, and would do after my supposed annihilation.[17]

This 'other mind' is the infinite mind of God, eternally (or since creation, perhaps) producing the ideas we call 'the natural world'

in the minds of humans and sustaining these ideas when no one
(or no one else) is perceiving them.

The concept of God provides Berkeley not only with a substitute for 'matter', but with an explanation for force and causality.
We all admit, he says, that the ideas we produce in dream and
imagination derive their cause and moving power from the
human spirit that creates them. In the same way, God provides
the cause and power that moves and regulates the infinitely
greater and more magnificent 'dream' we call 'the world of
nature'. The force of gravity, he writes, 'depends entirely on the
Will of the *governing spirit*, who causes certain bodies to cleave
together, or tend towards each other, according to various laws,
whilst he keeps others at a fixed distance. . .'[18] Analogously, he
writes, 'One idea is not the cause of another, one power is not the
cause of another. The cause of all natural things is onely God.'[19]

Such a concept of God, although it provides an answer, so to
speak, to the problem of the continued existence of the non-
perceived, creates a new problem. Man perceives 'ideas' through
his sense organs, but God cannot be said to have sense organs. It
would be a serious imperfection in God if he felt the heat of the
August sun as we do, or saw the Atlantic Ocean as it appears
from the height of 2,000 feet rather than from all possible heights
and depths. Berkeley is thus forced to admit that 'God knows or
hath ideas; but His ideas are not convey'd to Him by sense, as
ours are.'[20] He is forced, too, to admit that 'God May comprehend
all Ideas even the Ideas wch are painfull & unpleasant without
being in any degree pained thereby.'[21] From this it follows that
what we humans perceive are only copies or representations of
the things and not their original form, as they exist in the mind of
God. Such a conclusion is diametrically opposed to Berkeley's
difinition of Being as *percipii*, and creates one more internal contradiction in his system.

Berkeley's conception of God may be contradictory, but he
makes his views quite clear to the reader. It is, however, not at all
clear what Vasubandhu means by the 'knowledge of Buddha'. In
the *Vimśatika* (XX) Vasubandhu claims that, as our mind is
'covered over and darkened by ignorance', we cannot know it 'as
the ineffable object reached by the pure knowledge of a Buddha'.
In the *Trimśika* (XXX) he describes 'perfect wisdom' as 'the realm
of passionlessness purity, which is beyond description, is good,

and is eternal, where one is in the state of emancipation, peace and joy'. From the last stanza of the *Vimśatika* we learn that even if we realize the truth of 'mind only', we still have not attained knowledge of the true essence of things. Only the Buddha knows things as they 'really' are.

I have already mentioned the Yogacara theory of the three aspects or kinds of 'own-being'. The first and second aspects (*parikalpita* and *paratantra*) refer to things as they appear in normal experience, whereas in the third, the 'absolute' or 'perfected' view (*parinspanna*), the thought penetrates, as it were, into the very essence of things, and everything appears in its 'suchness', free of the discriminations that characterize normal experience. This characterization is derived, I believe, from meditational experience, in particular the meditation on the four formless states, and aims at a definition of what is considered the highest state of meditative insight.

In later Yogacara, we find doctrinal disputes on the nature of Nirvana. Nirvana is described by all sects as a state of pure illumination from which all the conceptual and formal functions of normal consciousness, such as discrimination, naming, and judgment, have been removed. The dispute revolved around the question of whether this is a state of complete 'emptiness', an imageless state, or a state in which the myriad images of the world still appear, but in their absolute, original purity—nameless and contentless. The first view refers, I think, to the state of 'no perception and no non-perception', a deep trance in which the activity of the senses is almost completely subdued, whereas the second view is not unlike the Berkelean ideal, a clear view of the evolving images of nature unobstructed by the impurities of human concepts and categories. It is hard to say which of the two views was held by Vasubandhu.

Psychological and Cultural Origins of the 'Dream-World' Philosophy

While reading the arguments of the 'mind' philosophers, we are inclined to feel that they present a new and revolutionary ontological principle. But once the emotion they have aroused settles and we are left to look around again, we see the same mountains, trees, persons, as solid as ever, as 'other' as ever—'out there'. Then we may realize that the effect of the 'dream-world' philosophy is not due to any new principle, but mainly to the magic power of words. What *is*, after all, the object 'out there'? In a non-philosophical frame of mind, we just call it by a name, 'book' or 'tree', and that's all. It is no doubt out there in its solidity and otherness whether we perceive it or not. Neither Berkeley nor Vasubandhu claim that the tree in my garden is the same as the tree in my dream. All they say is that the tree in the garden is itself a 'dreamlike' tree. Does that mean that the tree is not as solid as I thought it was? Perhaps so. After all, if I do not touch it very often, it may seem quite unsolid, and it may even 'disappear' if I shut my eyes. But if I relate to the tree in an active way, touch it, talk to others about it, I simply refer to the tree out there, solid and green, for all to see. If asked what the tree *is*, I should say, or, rather, we should say, that it is a tree, and if asked what it *really* is, I or you should probably say again that it is a tree, because by 'tree' we mean that trunk and those branches and leaves which look big when we stand close and small when viewed from a distance, green by daylight and grey at dusk. If we have to, we may say, 'It is matter', by 'matter' meaning the solid stuff that is 'out there'; but if somebody wishes to call the solid stuff out there, 'mind', we should not object as long as he refers to the same thing. The choice of words is, after all, a matter of convention and attitude. John may be 'John' to his friends, 'Johnny' to his mother, and 'Dearest' to his lover, but whatever you call him, he is still the same fellow.

The matter is different in the case of the solipsist, whom I admit to be a rare or hypothetical character, who claims that *his* is the only mind, and that everything is within his mind. We cannot convince *him* that John and the tree are out there for us also to see, for we too are, as far as the solipsist is concerned, within his mind. It is therefore best to leave the solipsist to himself, for there is nothing he lacks. Berkeley and Vasubandhu, happily enough, admit the existence of other human beings. They only claim that these are souls (Berkeley) or streams of consciousness (Vasubandhu). Now if one admits that *two* of anything exist, we are entitled to ask, 'Where?', for either we are dealing with a dream or with the space in which we all exist and move. If we are merely appearing in the philosopher's 'dream', he is not entitled to admit our real existence. However, if we are not his dream-creatures, on what grounds can he argue that we *are*, but not in objective space? Once you admit the plurality of real objects, you have to admit their existence in objective space, understood as whatever allows *ex*ternal relations.

The arguments of Vasubandhu against the concept of the atom, and those of Berkeley against the concepts of absolute space and time cannot provide a refutation of external existence. Perhaps Vasubandhu is right when he claims that our notion of atomic particles is self-contradictory, and Berkeley may have hit on a true point in his criticism of the Newtonian notion of absolute space and time. The concepts they criticized have indeed been abandoned in quantum mechanics and in relativity theory. But in rejecting the concept of objective space altogether and substituting the concept of mind for it, they effected a change of nothing but terminology, for in their systems the objective world is there as ever, but it turns from a three-dimensional, spatial one into a non-dimensional community of 'spirits' or 'streams of consciousness'.

Through sensory contact we become aware of the relation between our bodies and external objects. For instance, the sensation of something as 'solid' is in direct proportion to the resistance we *feel* when pressing it. In the act of pressing an object, we may concentrate on the object, directing our attention to its 'hardness'; but it is also possible to direct our attention to the organ, i.e., the hand, and define the sensation as 'painful pressure'. As far as the sensation itself is concerned, we may, if we wish, define it as 'in the mind,' that is, psychological. In the same way, we may say that, in a strict sense, sight images are not 'out there' but 'in the mind'. These forms of speech, however, do not correspond with the actual nature of our experience. In experience, we clearly distinguish between the *exploratory* act of stretching out our hand and touching the object (feeling 'pressure' in the hand), and the *findings* of the exploratory act—the object itself, its 'hardness'. In the same way, we distinguish between the exploratory act of seeing and the object of sight: our language clearly reveals the distinction between things as they *appear* and things as they *are*. Thus when we watch a tower from the distance, it appears small, but we know that from a short distance it would appear big, and this is included in what we mean by 'the tower,' namely, its appearing small from far and big from close by. The relations between the various appearances of an object are absolute, that is, they hold true for any human with the same sense organs. Other creatures, with different sense organs, would of course have different sensations of the same object; but if we know the structure of these sense organs, we can within limits predict the sensations they would have if they came in contact with a particular object. We distinguish the various possible 'appearances' of an object, e.g., a tower, from its objective mode of being, and describe its actual features in attributes denoting its size, shape, colour, etc., according to the conventional standards of common-sense or scientific language. The same is true of the concept of time. Things may seem to happen 'quicker' or 'slower', but we use our watches, we may reach consensus on the *common* time.

Berkeley's and Vasubandhu's philosophical argumentation reveals a quality of self-centredness. Both disregard the objective pole of the act of perception, the *thing* perceived, and interpret perception only in terms of the inner experience, narrowly interpreted, of the perceiving subject. The question that remains is, what drove these two philosophers to oppose the normal, deeply ingrained conviction of the existence of the external world? Bishop Berkeley was motivated mainly, it seems, by his Christian background. In his private notes we find the remark, 'N.B. To use utmost Caution not to give the least Handle of offence to the Church or Church-men.'[22] It was his earnest belief that his system provided the orthodox Christian with a new philosophy, with the help of which he could defend the principles of the Christian faith against the materialistic trends of the age. In his own words, first from his notes:

The great danger of making extension exist without the mind. in yt [in that] if it does it must be acknowledg'd infinite immutable etc. wch will be to make either God extended (wch I think dangerous) or an eternal, immutable, infinite, increate being beside God.[23]

That impious and profane persons should readily fall in with those systems which favour their inclinations, by deriding immaterial substance, and supposing the soul to be divisible and subject to corruption as the body; which exclude all freedom, intelligence, and design from the formation of things, and instead thereof make a self-existent, stupid, unthinking substance the root and origin of all beings.[24]

Vasubandhu's philosophical motivation, too, is best understood against his extra-philosophical, that is, Buddhist background. The mental states that occur as the result of meditative practice are really of 'Idealistic' nature. It is the declared aim of meditational practice to direct the attention away from the objective pole of the act of perception to its subjective effects, to analyse the perceived object into its various sensory components, and finally to make it disappear altogether from the 'mirror of consciousness'.

In this connection, it would possibly be helpful to recall meditative states of 'concentration' and 'mindfulness'. Our usual state of mind is characterized by its lack of fixed 'concentration.' This is so because normal perception constantly requires the function of comparison and contrast, identification, and synthesis. It is only through such basic forms of our thought that we are able to refer conceptually to experience. We are therefore in a state of incessant 'movement of mind' from object to object, identifying, naming, comparing, and contrasting. The meditative technique of 'concentration' and 'mindfulness' requires a constant fixation of the senses on one object, a flower, sand-ring, or the like. In the first stages of this meditation, the thing commonly perceived as a solid object disintegrates into a flux of flickering and sparkling particles, and disappears completely from consciousness as a 'thing'. The meditator is then said to have achieved the stage of 'mindfulness of emptiness'.

A similar level of absorption may also be achieved through the meditation on the 'four formless states'. The meditator sometimes uses a *kasina*-object, for example, a flower, light, or geometrical figure drawn on sand, as an object of meditation. In the first stages of this meditation, the awareness of a definite, separate unit weakens, and the object seems to dissolve into momentary impressions of form and colour. In the Buddhist commentaries on this type of meditation, it is said that the meditator 'purifies' the object from its coarse physical form in normal perception into its faint 'abstract' images, and then extends the object, as it were, over infinite space, this by meditative attention to 'space, space, infinite space'.[25] By the act of extension to infinity, consciousness is said to have reached a state in which any limitation or differentiation is negated. But space, though infinite, is not 'pure' enough. In the following stage, the meditator reflects, 'consciousness, consciousness', and pure consciousness in its infinity becomes its own object. This 'internalization' of consciousness, explain the sources, reveals the 'emptiness' of consciousness. Dwelling in the 'infinite emptiness of consciousness', the meditator is said to have reached the ultimate limit of purity, the state of 'neither perception nor non-perception'.

Such a state of absorption is, I believe, what Vasubandhu means when he talks of awakening from the 'dream of reality'. He says (Stanza XVI), 'Before we have awakened we cannot know that what is seen in the dream does not exist,' and comments, 'After this [awakening from the 'dream of reality' into enlightenment], the purified knowledge of the world which is obtained takes precedence; according to the truth it is clearly understood that those objects are unreal.'

In spite of the striking similarities in the basic philosophical principles of the two Idealists, the differences in their faiths were enough to make them, as a whole, clearly different thinkers. In Berkeley's thought we find a clear distinction between the three pillars of Christian faith, man, nature, and God. Strange as Berkeley's Idealistic terminology may sound, it does 'not give the least offence' to Christian dogma. God remains and is glorified as the divine creator and ruler of the universe, as He 'in whom we live, and move, and have our being'. Man, that is to say, spirit, is put in the world of nature, that is, of the 'ideas' of God, to pursue the path of righteousness and redeem his soul for eternity.

Whereas Berkeley shows an enthusiastic attitude to nature, Vasubandhu believes, it seems to me, that in the absolute sense, in the 'pure knowledge of Buddha', all the appearances of nature are revealed in the aspect of 'emptiness'. Whereas in Berkeley's system the concept of a 'person' is firmly founded, in Vasubandhu's it is only of a temporary and relative nature, a stream of interrelated cognitions that will ultimately dissolve into 'pure consciousness'. In Berkeley's philosophy, the power of causality is attributed mainly to God, whereas in Vasubandhu's it inheres in the Karmic process, and its course of development depends on the 'personal stream'. It may be concluded, on the whole, that whereas Berkeley thinks in accordance with Christian principles of divine providence and salvation through morality, Vasubandhu's philosophy reveals the Buddhist pattern of thought—atheism, monism, and salvation through 'self-purification'.

9

The Possibility of Knowledge: Kant and Nagarjuna

Yoel Hoffmann

An old man was about to die. His family was gathered around his bed. Suddenly he broke into laughter and said, 'Would *I* laugh, if I passed into the hereafter and there, too, there was nothing.'

Philosophical Crisis and Response

Philosophy sometimes has crises of its own making. sometimes, for example, after comfortable metaphysical absolutes of one or another sort have been established, not without considerable intellectual effort, an analytical philosophy appears and threatens to disintegrate them. Such a disintegrative crisis was caused in the West by Hume's philosophy of sense-impressions, and in India and adjacent countries by the Hinayana philosophy of *dharmas*, the minimal, infinitesmally brief, self-existent states (or factors, elements, or events) whose flow was taken to constitute the universe.*

Hume's scepticism, as he loosely called his view, went against deeply rooted conceptions of the Western mind. It attacked the basic assumptions of mechanistic science and exposed the epistemological arbitrariness of religious and moral dogmas. The philosophy of *dharmas*, with its ontological gap between the stream of impure, conditioned *dharmas* and the pure, unconditioned one of Nirvana, went against the deeply rooted Indian

---

* *Dharma* often means 'sacred law' or the like, but it is used here in a particular technical sense of Buddhist philosophy. The Buddhists analysed everything that existed into ultimate factors or elements, flashing briefly in and out of existence, of matter, mind, and 'forces'. A scholar has summarized some of the connotations of the term, *dharma*, as follows:

intuition of an absolutely unified, that is, non-dual universe. It was in reaction to these disintegrative world views that Kant in Europe and Nagarjuna in India created their philosophies.

Western man views his world with two faces, the one turned toward empirical reality, the other towards a separate realm of morality and religion. With the one face, he discovers a nature manifesting constant change; with the other he envisions a supernatural reality of static perfection. In his mythology, the constantly changing natural order is said to be the creation of the perfect eternal reality. Man, according to this mythology, participates in the two orders of reality, his bodily part dying and rotting like autumn leaves, his spiritual essence being lifted into eternity and bliss. This split-person myth appears throughout Western history in various forms, economic, literary, religious, and philosophical. In philosophy it expresses itself in a constant wavering between the concepts of Being and Becoming, the Rational and the Empirical. Clinging to its dualistic myth, the Western mind has been reluctant to allow the prevailing balance between the two aspects of its vision of reality to be disrupted. The Being-extremism of Parmenides and the Becoming-extremism of Heraclitus were restored to balance by Plato's compromise between them. In the same way, Kant found the compromise between seventeenth-century Continental Rationalism and eighteenth-century British Empiricism. Kant's philosophy is thus essentially an expression of the Western mind, which strives to know the natural order as positively as it can, but seeks its raison-d'être elsewhere, in the supernatural order. To reach the compromise,

1. Every element is a separate entity or force.
2. There is an inherence of one element in another, hence no substance apart from its qualities, no matter beyond the separate sense-data, and no soul beyond the separate mental data.
3. Elements have no duration, every moment represents a separate element; thought is evanescent, there are no moving bodies, but consecutive appearances, flashings, of new elements in new places.
4. The elements cooperate with one another.
5. This cooperating activity is controlled by the laws of causation.
6. The world-process is thus a process of cooperation between seventy-two kinds of subtle, evanescent elements, and such is the nature of *dharmas* that they proceed from causes and steer towards extinction.

See Th. Stcherbatsky, *The central Conception of Buddhism*, London, Royal Asiatic Society, 1923, pp. 73–75.

Kant had to find a systematic way to restore the validity of concepts such as 'substance' and 'causality,' which he took to be necessary for all thought, including natural science, and to postulate an order that, unlike the natural one, justified moral and religious hopes.

Nagarjuna's philosophical motive, it seems, was quite different. The Hinayana theory of *dharmas*, as I have said, undermined the Brahmanical intuition of a unified, non-dual reality. In Nagarjuna's eyes, this theory seemed superior to a commonsense view, but no better than the Brahmanical philosophy it came to replace. His aim was basically to restore, in a systematic, logical form, the view of unity and non-duality already suggestively expressed in Brahmanical and early Buddhist literature.

Both Kant and Nagarjuna exhibit highly sophisticated, critical minds. Their arguments are quite complicated and open to various interpretations. I believe, however, that an attempt to compare their thought is worthwhile, mainly because they created their philosophies as a negative reaction to the similarly disintegrated world views of Hume and Hinayana Buddhism. In my comparison, I shall contend that Kant's system is an endeavour to restore some form of common sense to science and to give a philosophical justification for morality and religion. Nagarjuna's thought, in contrast, will be seen to be much more radical, for he denies philosophical and commonsense views alike, rejecting all human categories of thought and language as contradictory and therefore invalid.

Kant

Let me begin my consideration of Kant with some words on the philosopher whom Kant called, 'the celebrated David Hume', and whom he described as 'one of those geographers of human reason who have imagined they have sufficiently disposed' of questions concerning the *a priori* 'by setting them outside the horizon of human reason'.[1] Hume's philosophy is not without its difficulties and ambiguities, but it is perfectly clear that he tries to rid thought of its metaphysical entities and concepts, and to demonstrate that everything we know depends on 'perceptions', which he divides into 'impressions', which are primary, and 'ideas', which are derived from impressions. He does not pretend to know the origin of the impressions, whose ultimate cause, he says, is 'perfectly inexplicable by human reason'.[2] With a touch of acidity, he observes that the rest of mankind (some metaphysicians excepted), 'are nothing but a bundle or collection of different perceptions, which succeed each other with an inconceivable rapidity'.[3] Considering the great differences between Hume and the Hinayana Buddhists, it is astonishing how generally close his description of the human mind is to theirs. He writes:

> The true idea of the human mind, is to consider it as a system of different perceptions or different existences, which are link'd together by the relation of cause and effect, and mutually produce, destroy, influence, and modify each other. Our impressions give rise to their correspondent ideas; and these ideas in their turn produce other impressions. One thought chaces another, and draws after it a third, by which it is expell'd in its turn.[4]

Kant cannot accept this, so to speak, dispersion of reality into sense-perceptions. As he repeats forcefully, it is an error of Hume to give them priority, for the very reference to them implies their unity as objects of thought, and implies, correlatively, the unity of the consciousness that thinks them as its object. Kant writes, 'It is only because I ascribe all perceptions to one consciousness (original apperception) that I can say of all perceptions that I am conscious of them.'[5] Concepts such as 'self', 'substance', and 'causality', are not derived from sense-perceptions, but, because they are conditions of experience *per se*, must be inherent in consciousness. Any human mind, to be one, requires spatial and temporal 'intuitions' or perceptions, organized by means of the systematically related categories of thought. Only this dual sensory influx, complex organization, and imposed unity can yield the structured, intelligible world we in fact perceive.

Thanks, therefore, to the *a priori* capacities of the mind, it is an objective world that we perceive; but Kant agrees with Hume that what lies beyond this world, which can be no more than 'phenomenal', is beyond rational knowledge. He acknowledges that we are able to form the pure, abstract ideas of 'the absolute (unconditioned) *unity* of the *thinking subject*', meaning, the self or soul; of 'the absolute *unity* of *the series of conditions of appearance*', meaning, the world or cosmos; and of '*the absolute unity of conditions of all objects in general'*, meaning, God.[6] But, Kant explains, all these ideas, unempirical applications of the categories of thought, are void of sensory 'intuition', merely speculative or metaphysical, and so void of genuine knowledge. Such 'transcendental ideas', such a conception of soul, world, or God, can neither be proved nor disproved, Kant holds. They lead, in relation to the soul, to paralogisms (formally fallacious syllogisms); in relation to the ultimate nature of the world, to antinomies (inevitable contradictions between cosmological theses and antitheses); and in relation to God, to the transcendental ideal of necessary, unconditioned being, for which only invalid proofs can be offered. If, for example, we apply the category of causality, which is so necessary to the understanding of the phenomenal world, to the metaphysical 'ideal' of the world as a whole, we are led to conclude that the world must be finite in time and space, but cannot be. We conclude that it must be finite in time because an infinite series of events cannot, by definition, have been completed; and we conclude that it must be finite in space because if it were not, the successive enumeration of its parts, by which we should know it as a whole, would require an infinite time to have elapsed. On the other hand, we conclude that the world must be infinite in time because to be finite, it must have been preceded by empty time, but empty time, by definition, has no distinguishing condition to explain how anything can arise; and we conclude that the world must be infinite in space because, to be finite, it must be related to an empty space beyond it, but empty space beyond the world cannot, by definition, be an object of intuition, so that relation to it would be relation to nothing, which is impossible. Therefore, all arguments considered, time and space can be neither finite nor infinite, and the world as a whole cannot be thought.

This dilemma has interesting consequences, because it cannot simply be dropped. That is, reason, even though it learns caution, cannot help relating itself to its boundary and to that which lies outside the boundary. We cannot extend our empirical, scientific knowledge without the desire to attain systematic unity, and so we relate experience to that which is beyond it, that is, to the ideal of the mind as a simple substance having personal identity, of the world as an endless and yet complete series of appearances, and of God as the all-sufficient ground of appearances—apperances must be appearances *of* something. Therefore, all our intellectual needs considered, we can neither accept nor deny that which is beyond us.

This uncomfortably indeterminate state, in which we need to know what we cannot, sharpens the problem of morality for Kant. Convinced that morality cannot be based on empirical experience, which is determined by natural laws alone, or on self-interest, he argues that it requires us to venture beyond our cognitive capacities and assume what we cannot prove, namely, that our wills are free, that we are rewarded and punished in a future life, and that, consequently, the soul is immortal and God exists. Our access to these trans-empirical, hypothesized realities is by means, Kant says, of a faculty of 'rational faith' or 'practical reason'. In his *Critique of Practical Reason*, he tries to convince us that freedom, reward and punishment, God, and an immortal soul, though not objects of knowledge, are necessary postulates of 'rational faith', without which morality would be void of any rational ground. A stricter attention to his epistemology should perhaps lead him to conclude that morality really is void of any such ground. It seems, however, that Kant feels that it would be intolerably painful for humans to exist without belief. 'I inevitably believe,' he declares, 'in the existence of God and in a future life, and I am certain that nothing can shake this belief, since my moral principles would thereby be themselves overthrown, and I cannot disclaim them without becoming abhorrent in my own eyes.'[7]

This confession, I think, reveals the mood behind Kant's insistence on some substitute for the traditional concepts of God and soul. He makes the substitution by means of the concept of 'the thing in itself'. He seems to believe that we ought to possess a notion of reality as it is in itself, and not as it appears in our consciousness. Though the idea of a teleological order is perceptually unverifiable, and though the proof of the existence of such an order is, he says, impossible, he thinks that we have grounds to hope and to 'rationally' believe that, beyond its appearance as a chain of causally connected events, the world embodies a meaningful moral purpose. He claims that the distinction between what only appears and what really exists is based upon our conviction that the phenomenal self, the 'appearing I', is not identical with the noumenal self, the 'real I', and that just as the ultimate 'I' ought to be different from the superficial one, so the 'in itself' ought to be different from appearances.

Some critics of Kant have preferred to discount his concept of a thing in itself as logically absurd. But even if it is granted that Kant's own epistemology requires us to interpret this concept as merely the symbol of the inconceivability of any ultimate knowledge, it is essential to interpret the concept positively in order to understand his moral system. Moreover, if we disregard the distinction in Kant's system between the outer aspect of reality, the phenomenon, and its inner aspect, the noumenon, we cannot fully recognize Kant as the representative of European Christian culture that he is.

Kant grants that we cannot *know* the rational structure of noumenal reality, but holds with respect to at least the 'noumenal self', that although we cannot know rationally what it is, we know *that* it is. In the same way, while we do not possess any rational *knowledge* of the world-in-itself, we 'rationally believe' that, behind its spatio-temporal-causal appearances, the world embodies the logos of the perfect being, God, to which our noumenal self, the soul, makes rational moral responses.

In referring to the soul, Kant uses not only the term, 'noumenal self', but also 'transcendental ego', and 'moral self'. A detailed analysis of the functions of these terms in his system is beyond the scope of this chapter, but it would reveal, I think, a considerable number of incoherencies. Generally speaking, however, the term, 'noumenal self', appears to serve as an inclusive term for the inner aspect of our reality, whereas the two other terms refer respectively to the epistemological and moral functions of the 'noumenal self'. Thus, 'transcendental ego' is used mainly to refer to the ordering of the data of perception according to the forms of space and time and the categories of thought, while the term 'moral self' is used mainly to account for the concept of freedom, an essential assumption of morality. Moral principles, claims Kant, ought to express the pattern of a universally binding law of reason, and it is the function of the 'moral self' as free will to act in accord with this law. To Kant, a moral act reveals the presence of a higher self, which is able to detach itself from natural causality and self-interest and respond to the rational imperatives of the moral law.

Nagarjuna

In Western terms, the Hindu Brahman-Atman philosophy represents a kind of Rationalism centering around the concept of absolute being or reality, whereas the Hinayana Buddhist philosophy represents a kind of Empiricism stressing change or becoming. Nagarjuna (second or third centuries A.D.) rejects these two extremes, as well as the more commonsense synthesis according to which reality is substance in the process of change. To put it in philosophical language, Nagarjuna's declared philosophical motive is to disclose the conditions that govern the knowledge of reality, and to distinguish such knowledge from empirical knowledge, a motive not very different from that behind metaphysical systems in general.

Nagarjuna and his followers assert that Hinayana thought does not go far enough when it analyses the 'objects' of everyday life into *dharmas*. They grant that it is more beneficial to enlightenment to interpret experience as a succession of interrelated momentary states than to interpret it, in the ordinary way, as that of objects having attributes and agents performing actions. They hold, however, that the concept of *dharmas* should, in the end, also be subjected to destructive criticism, and the 'emptiness' or insubstantiality of the *dharmas* realized.

It cannot be denied that one of the 'marks' (essential attributes) of the *dharmas* in Hinayana thought is that of 'non-self', insubstantiality. But the Hinayanist tends to regard the *dharmas*, especially in relation to meditative techniques, as the elements of ultimate reality. The Madhyamika (Middle Doctrine) school of Nagarjuna regards that tendency as a form of 'attachment' to worldly conditioned things, because, this school says, the *dharmas*, too, are illusory in nature.

For the concept of *dharmas*, Nagarjuna substitutes that of 'emptiness' (*śunya*), according to which the 'real' is neither Atman (Being), nor Anatman (Non-being or Becoming), nor a synthesis of both (Being in change), nor neither of these. The suggestion that the attempt to comprehend reality through reason is futile can already be found in the utterances attributed to Buddha. In a famous early passage (*Majjhima-nikaya, sutta* 63), Buddha rejects all metaphysical alternatives: that the world is eternal, or that the world is not eternal; that the world is finite (in space), or that the world is infinite; that the soul and body are identical, or that the soul is one thing and the body another; and that the Tathagata (Buddha, or, here, the saint exempted from rebirth) exists after death, or that the Tathagata does not exist after death, or that the Tathagata both exists and does not exist after death, or that the Tathagata neither exists nor does not exist after death. All these alternative views are regarded as futile, because not leading to emancipation. A similar, strong rejection of all possible metaphysical views is made in the chief canonical work of the Madhyamika school, the *Prajna-Paramita (Perfection of Wisdom) Sutra.* According to this rejection, every view suffers from the same logical flaw as its opposite—not because the correct view has still to be thought out, but because philosophical reasoning, when applied to reality, is inherently contradictory. In rejecting philosophical reasoning, which postulates various concepts in order to explain the 'structure' of reality, Nagarjuna does not imply, so far as I have discovered, any rejection of formal logic. On the contrary, he uses formal logic as a tool to expose contradictions in the thought of the various philosophical schools of his time.

The central Buddhist theory of 'dependent origination' or 'dependent co-production' is used by the Abhidharma schools to deny the concept of a permanent Atman (soul-substance), and to establish in its place the reality of separate momentary elements of existence.

Let me pause a moment and explain the term and the name I have just used. 'Dependent origination' or 'dependent co-production' are two of many translations of the Sanskrit term *pratityasamutpada, paticcasamuppada* in Pali. It can be more simply though, of course, loosely translated, 'causation'. A contemporary Buddhist scholar who translates it so claims that Buddhism gives us the first clearcut Indian theory of causation, one which, in early Buddhism, is neither subjective nor a category imposed by the mind on phenomena. In this theory, causation 'is said to have the characteristics of objectivity, necessity, invariability and conditionality. . . Whenever A is present B is present. Whenever A is absent, B is absent'. The 'effort of the individual', however, is said to make a difference.[8]

A contextually Buddhistic explanation of the concept is given by Buddhaghosa (early fifth century A.D.), the great commentator. He explains that the concept 'dependent' (*paticca*) is aimed against those who believe that there is no cause, or that the cause is a primordial essence, atoms, time, or the like, or a god, world-soul, or the like. The concept 'origination' (*samuppada*), the second element of the compound *paticcasamuppada*, is aimed, Bhuddhaghosa says, against those who believe that the soul is annihilated, that there is no use in charity, that there is no other world, and so on.[9]

As for the name I have used, *Abhidharma* or (in Pali) *Abhidhamma* means 'supplementary dharma' or 'special dharma', *dharma* here meaning 'doctrine'. The name is the title of the third of the three collections of Buddhist canonical books, and also designates the scholastic, analytical method used in this collection. While the less technical Buddhist literature speaks of 'individuals', 'persons', 'I', 'self', and so on, the Abhidhamma 'treats of realities, i.e. of psychical and physical phenomena, which alone may rightly be called realities, though only of momentary duration, arising and passing away every moment. . . The whole Abhidhamma has to do only with the description, analysis, and elucidation of such phenomena.'[10]

The Madhyamika system interprets 'dependent origination', not as a temporal sequence of *dharmas*, but as the principle of the *essential interdependence* of everything that thought can conceptualize and language name. This principle of the essential dependence of everything on everything else rules out logically the concept of a real *ens*, a real entity or thing, because to form a correct concept of it, one has to attribute to it, by common Indian reasoning, an unconditioned, unchanging essence. But according to the principle of 'dependent origination' as understood by the Hinayana Buddhists, this attribution cannot possibly be made, for their philosophy demands that both 'substantiality' and 'momentary existence', which contradict one another, be ascribed to each *dharma*, that is, to each infinitesmal elementary state, which I may be pardoned (the ambiguities of language being what they are) for calling a 'thing'.

Neither common sense nor science may be bothered by at least apparent logical discrepancies in their basic concepts as long as these concepts are useful within their communicative systems. Common sense may easily accept the notion of a substance that changes, just as science may accept the complementarity of waves and particles. But a philosophy that aims at a unified view of reality must ordinarily reject self-contradictory concepts. Thus, in Nagarjuna's view, the theory of reality as an incessant stream of *dharmas* that originate, continue for the briefest moment, and then cease to exist, is self-contradictory. Origination, continuance, and cessation cannot possibly occur at the same time, he says, for they are defined as different states, nor can they possibly occur at different times, for they would then, though states of the same momentary entity, be decisively separated from one another. In other words, if a *dharma* is to be a self-identical *thing*, it cannot be said to undergo change, and if it is not a thing, it is self-contradictory to speak of some one thing as changing. In Nagarjuna's words, 'The extinction of a real existence is not true to fact, since it is not true to fact that existent and inexistent occur in a unity.'[11]

The idea behind these words is that a true elementary event, a *dharma*, is by definition indivisible, so that the idea of its change, as by extinction, is self-contradictory, because it implies the simultaneous attribution to the event of both existence and nonexistence. The assumption that the *dharma* exists for only the briefest moment does not free its concept of self-contradiction, for however brief the time, argues Nagarjuna, it can be divided into the three sub-units of arising, abiding, and ceasing. He therefore concludes that if a *dharma* cannot be conceived as permanent, it cannot be conceived as momentary, for to be in existence, whether momentarily or permanently, is to be subject to the same logical conditions.

Nagarjuna's definition of an 'existent' is used by him to attack all possible descriptions of reality, so before entering further into his dialectic, I should like to explain his conception of an 'existent'. An 'existent', he emphasizes, must possess 'own-being', that is, be related only to itself. Otherwise, its relation to something other than itself, implying, in the broad sense, a dependence on the other, would mean that it contained 'other-being' But the principle of 'dependent origination' requires all *dharmas* to be conditioned, and therefore, in contradiction to the Hinayana view, no separate *dharma* can be considered an 'entity' in itself. This is what is implied by the Madhyamika phrase, 'emptiness of all *dharmas*', which means that any *dharma*, considered in itself, is not substantial, has no essence, is no thing at all.

Because Nagarjuna's definiton of 'entity' does not allow the entity to be modified, it excludes any recourse to a relational category such as 'substance-attribute' or 'agent-action'. For the same reason, the theory of a self with changing attributes is untenable. That is, the self, as Buddhists hold, must be identical with its momentary states, and these momentary states, to be considered the states *of* someone, cannot be void of self, that is, of essence of a particular kind; but they are void. The difficulty extends to all possible alternatives. That is, a true entity cannot be referred to as (1) a self (changeless essence); or as (2) non-self (essenceless change); or as (3) both self and non-self; or as (4) neither self nor non-self. Alternative (1) is contradicted by the principle of 'conditioned co-production'. Alternative (2) is contradicted by the definition of an entity. Alternatives (3) and (4) are contradicted by the rules of logic, which forbid a third term in addition to what is affirmed and negated, forbid a synthesis of what is affirmed and negated, and forbid a denial of what is both affirmed and negated. In Nagarjuna's words, 'If the nature is inexistent, to what will otherwiseness belong? If the nature is existent, to what will otherwiseness belong?'[12]

In these words Nagarjuna argues that if an entity is unreal (has no 'own-being' or essence), no change can be attributed to *it*, for it cannot be said that there is any *thing* to change. But if, on the other hand, an entity is real (has 'own-being'), it cannot change, because change implies 'otherness' in its 'own-being' and thus contradicts the *ownness* of 'own-being'. Generally, because 'dependent co-production' establishes a model of endless change, no elemental entity can be assumed to exist, and, strictly speaking, it cannot even be said that there is change, for there is no *thing* to change.

Nagarjuna's denial of Being on the grounds of the principle of 'dependent origination' leaves us with a changing somewhat, to which, paradoxically enough, we cannot refer with the help of universals, for these imply the notion of essence, and so cannot refer to it truly at all. To put this conclusion in syllogistic form:

(1) There can be no thing (entity) that is not absolutely identical with itself, as established by the definition of 'entity.'
(2) No thing is absolutely identical with itself, as established by the principle of 'dependent co-production'.
(3) There is no thing (or nothing).

Nagarjuna warns against the hypostatization of the term, 'emptiness'. To say that there is nothing does not mean that an entity named 'nothing' or 'void' exists. 'Emptiness' refers, not to a metaphysical entity, but to our logical, and hence lingusitic, inability to refer to reality. It means, not that 'an *x* that is empty is', but that 'it cannot be said (any saying is empty) that *x* (any thing) is'.

Let me elaborate somewhat. To make a statement concerning any thing we have to apply both of the (contradictory) concepts of identity (*something* changes) and difference (something *changes*). If these two terms had identical meanings, no meaningful statement could be made, because no function whatsoever can be described by just one term. But if they are different, that is, have different meanings, they cannot refer to any entity, because 'entities' in a relation of dependence cannot be considered entities in the proper sense, which excludes 'other-being'. Furthermore, if we attempt to either synthesize identity and difference or reject them both, we encounter purely logical absurdity. It therefore follows that no *true* statement can be made at all. A statement in the form of, 'X is a table', is self-contradictory, because for X to be a true *ens*, it must necessarily also be a 'non-table'. This is so because 'dependent co-production' establishes that the X that is a 'non-table' cannot be unrelated to the X that is a table. Thus X, if it is to be a real *thing*, has to be both 'table' and 'non-table'. In other words, for X to be *something*, it has to be *everything*; but as it cannot be said of *any* thing that it is a *thing*, *every* thing is *no* thing.

All other forms of statement are contradictory for the same reason. If a statement such as, 'The table is made of wood' (there is an *x* that is a table and made of wood) is to be meaningful (i.e., refer to reality), *x* has to be considered an entity in Nagarjuna's absolutist definition of the term; and so it has to be both a table and a non-table, and both made of wood and non-wood. It follows, by simple generalization, that no terms which we use can refer to true entities, and because non-entities are 'empty' (are no things), words denoting non-entities necessarily refer to nothing.

Through such *reductio ad absurdum* (*prasanya*) argument, Nagarjuna reduces all possible alternative views to absurdity, exposing them as untrue, illusory representations of reality. By his logic, the concepts of Being, Becoming, and Being that changes, which represent, respectively, the Brahmanical, Hinayana, and commonsense viewpoints, are all reduced to absurdity.

The same reductio ad absurdum argument is applied by Nagarjuna to such conceptual pairs as 'cause-effect' and 'agent-action'. He argues that the concept of causality is not possible according to the Brahmanical Atman-Brahman view, because nothing *new*, that is, no genuine effect, can result from a perfect, changeless being. The concept of causality as understood by the Hinayana is illogical, he says, because the theory of *dharmas* allows no connection between cause and effect. And the attempted synthesis of the contradictory views, that there is substance, but that it changes, is contradictory because it assumes both identity and difference in the same entity. As Nagarjuna says, 'If the cause is empty of effect, how can it produce the effect? If the cause is not empty of effect, how can it produce the effect? For oneness of cause and effect is never a fact, and otherness of cause and effect is never a fact.'[13] As for the assumed relations between the concepts of 'agent' and 'action', the activity (of moving) can be conceived neither as identical with the agent (the mover) nor as different from him. If identical, no such distinction (between agent and action) can be made; if different, the mover and the activity of moving could exist without one another, which is absurd.

The correlative concepts of 'cause-effect' and 'agent-action' provide Nagarjuna with a way of refuting thought constructions that refer to both the objective and the subjective aspects of experience. For example, to refute the concept of a personal self, he argues, 'That I existed in past time is not a fact, because he who was in former time is not identical with this one.'[14] He adds, to complete the refutation, 'Neither is it a fact that I did not exist in past time, for this one is not other than the one who existed in former lives.'[15]

Nagarjuna here argues that the Atman as *ens* is an unsatisfactory concept because it does not account for change, whereas the Anatman concept is unsatisfactory because it does not provide any unifying basis for changes in one's self. He adds, as usual, that a synthesis of both views and a rejection of both are absurd, for they contain the logically contradictory terms of unity and difference ('is and is not', and 'neither is nor is not').

Once all the categories of thought have been exposed as contradictory, everything one might wish to refer to by means of
thought or language is found to be 'empty'. This holds true for
any reality of any degree or presumed kind, for Nagarjuna's logic
allows for no distinction between 'phenomenon' and 'noumenon'. He regards the Hinayana distinction between conditioned
and unconditioned *dharmas* (the latter usually space and Nirvana)
as invalid. The conception, so profoundly native to Buddhism, of
a transition from a state of bondage and suffering to a state of
liberation and bliss, is exposed as contradictory with the same
dialectical tools, because it is based upon the absurd assumption
of an essence or substance that changes. Nagarjuna says, 'If
own-being existed, cultivation of the path would not be a fact; if
the path is cultivated, then your 'own-being' does not occur.'[16]
Furthermore, 'When suffering, arising and cessation do not
occur, what path is supposed to be attained through the cessation
of suffering?'[17] And furthermore, 'Where there is no imposition
of nirvana and no repudiation of samsara, what samsara and
what nirvana are conceived?'[18]

In a system of religious philosophy, such statements might
seem strange, at least at first sight. One is tempted to wonder if
Nagarjuna, a philosopher of the Nirvana-religion, does not go
too far in his negativism. But misinterpretations of the 'identity of
Samsara and Nirvana', a phrase equivalent to the 'identity of the
pheneomenon and the noumenon', are apt to occur only if we
assume that what cannot be referred to through thought-
categories and linguistic symbols does not exist. Nagarjuna does
not mean that. True, verbal constructions, according to him, are
'empty', no entity they seem to refer to can possibly exist, and the
concepts of Samsara and Nirvana are therefore 'void' of meaning.
This by no means prevents Nagarjuna from granting that the
concepts may be used metaphorically, as a pedagogical device, as
Buddha used them for those wanting in wisdom. But the gist of
the matter is not there. Most people do not easily distinguish
between statements referring to reality and statements, or,
rather, meta-statements referring to language; and they may
therefore be inclined to interpret Nagarjuna's philosophy as
claiming that reality is empty, whereas what he tries to convey is
the 'emptiness' of thought and language, their inability to touch
on reality. The true referent of language, he contends, is not

reality in itself, but the fabric constructed by means of our categories of thought. Nagarjuna's dialectic is meant to prove that this fabric is irrevocably contradictory and cannot refer to any real *thing*. This 'self-reference' of language and thought, by which the common mind evolves, is Nagarjuna's concept of the 'phenomenon'. For him, the 'phenomenon' is nothing but the self-enclosed system of thought-constructions we refer to in language, an illusory, self-contradictory fabric the unenlightened call 'reality'. For him, therefore, liberation consists of the negative act of abandoning thought-games and their symbolic representations in language-games.

The intuition that underlies Nagarjuna's philosophy is very hard to identify. He shields it, as he thinks reality is shielded, from exposure in words. As in Vasubandhu's case, I am tempted to try to understand him by way of the experience of meditation. He suggests, paradoxically, that in order to reach the ontological, it is necessary to abolish the epistemological. 'When the sphere of thought has ceased,' he says, 'the nameable ceases; Dharma-nature is like nirvana, unarising and unceasing.'[19] But even when the nameable ceases, experience does not, and Nagarjuna certainly has an experiential goal.

Kant-Nagarjuna and Hegel-Nagarjuna

As I have said earlier, the philosophical problems faced by Nagarjuna and Kant are generally similar. The two agree in rejecting the philosophy of Being, with its static, eternal reality, and in rejecting the philosophy of Becoming, with its reality of incessant change. Both are convinced that the unrestricted use of such categories of thought as 'entity' or 'substance', 'soul', and 'causality', lead to insoluble contradictions. Both claim that the uncritical application of such categories to reality creates dogmatic, illusion-fostering metaphysics. They agree that this is so because our categories of thought are not representations of reality, but are projected on reality by our minds.

For Kant, the forms of perception, space and time, and the categories of thought are *a priori* in a strictly logical sense, that is, they are necessary conditions of any experience of the phenomenal. For Nagarjuna, conceptual constructions (*vikalpas*) are prior to experience in a psychological rather than logical sense.

They are not inherent categories of the mind as such, but only of the 'ignorant' mind. That categories of thought are imposed upon reality is already recognized by the earlier, Abhidharma literature. According to the Hinayana, categories such as 'object' and 'self' can actually be eliminated by devotional and meditative practices. To Hinayana, the removal of such imposed forms reveals the real momentary elements, the *dharmas*, which resemble, as I have said, Hume's 'perceptions'. Kant and Nagarjuna are dissatisfied with, respectively, the doctrine of perceptions and the doctrine of *dharmas*, because they feel that these can enter experience only if grasped by means of the thought-category of 'objects', which has no correspondence with reality in itself.

However, what most troubles Kant in the Humean theory of perceptions is different from what Nagarjuna finds most wanting in the Hinayana theory of *dharmas*. Whereas Kant feels that Hume's analysis negates too much of what is commonly regarded as valid knowledge, Nagarjuna feels that the Hinayana critique of what is regarded as valid knowledge is not radical enough. Thus Kant, wishing to reunite the dismembered Humean world, argues that our categories of thought yield the only form possible to us of objective phenomenal knowledge. His epistemology may therefore be termed descriptive, for he assumes that phenomenal reality appears in consciousness as largely unchangeable, necessary knowledge, the formal aspect of which he analyses and distinguishes from the material aspect.

Nagarjuna, far from taking any form of knowledge for granted, makes a logical analysis of essential categories of thought and concludes that none of them can possible refer to reality, for they are all discovered to be confused and contradictory. This basic difference in approach between Kant and Nagarjuna is related to their different views of the function of language. Both Kant and Nagarjuna regard metaphysical statements as meaningless in terms of ultimate knowledge, but only Nagarjuna, and not Kant, would regard an empirical statement as meaningless. Kant grants that we do not know reality as it is in itself, but he contends that appearances are objective in the sense that their form is necessary to human consciousness and in the sense that they provide a common object of cognition for all human minds. It almost seems as if Kant thinks that phenomena are to noumena as a translation in a certain language is to the original in another. However, to apply the metaphor of translation to Kant's epistemology is, in a way, misleading, for a translation from language to language must convey the meaning of the translated text, its essence, whereas in Kant, the original, noumenal text and the phenomenal, translated text have ineradicably different meanings. This relationship between noumenal and phenomenal, which Kant sees as cognitively so obscure, threatens his whole philosophy, because if the phenomenal world we know is totally different from the noumenal, the 'knowledge' grasped or (to distinguish) hypothesized by our reason must be illusory. It is true that different scientific concepts, such as those of particles and waves, can be applied to the same object of research. But this is possible only if there is some logical correspondence between the theories, for if, for example, the Euclidean mathematics of Newtonian theory were not translatable into the non-Euclidean mathematics of Einsteinian theory, it is difficult to see how the two theories could be referring to the same world. Likewise, although the concepts of modern science sometimes appear very distant from those that common sense derives from ordinary perception, it should, in principle, be possible to translate the concepts of the one sort into those of the other. Otherwise, we should be driven to the conclusion that they apply to different realities. I am therefore inclined to believe that the difficulties, whatever they are, in finding systematic correspondences between scientific and everyday concepts are of a technical nature alone. Therefore, if Kant's philosophy is to be interpreted reasonably, the phenomenal world must correspond, even if in an unknowable way, to the noumenal world. Kant's paralogisms, antinomies, and invalid proofs for God's existence only show, if they themselves are accurately formulated, that the categories of thought cannot be applied to non-phenomenal conceptions such as 'soul', 'total universe', or 'God'. He can only assume, but not demonstrate, that phenomena *must* be different from noumena; and if, for the sake of his philosophy, they must be assumed to be totally different, it is only his philosophy that suffers.

Nagarjuna's theory of knowledge expresses a much more radical point of view. Nagarjuna claims that our categories of thought and the representation-language that incorporates them correspond to *nothing*. He does not set out with the epistemological question, 'What is the structure of knowledge?' but with the ontological one, 'What is an *ens*?' From the definition of an *ens* as an absolute, self-sufficient unity, he proceeds to an analysis of categories of thought that purport to represent the *ens*, that is, reality, and tries to prove dialectically that thought cannot refer to any such reality, any *thing*. In his view, language is confined to a social, pragmatic use. Language, he thinks, is effective only in the sense that a group of equally 'unenlightened' people choose to abide by the rules of the same 'language-game'. Such a 'language game' may turn out to contain logical contradictions; but a language that means to represent reality is *required* to be logically coherent. Nagarjuna's logical requirements for a reality-representing language are, however, very radical. He rules out as contradictory, and therefore as 'not true to fact', any terms that bear any kind of relation to other terms. Under his conditions, no 'language-game' whatsoever can be 'true to fact', for what he actually demands of 'correct' language is that is be able to refer to reality in one isolated term. But any statement reveals some pattern of relations, underlying which are basic concepts of relation like 'substance-attribute', 'cause-effect', and 'agent-action'. Nagarjuna's analysis of such concepts shows that they all include what he considers to be the logically contradictory assumption of both identity and difference.

Although my main subject is the comparison of Kant with Nagarjuna, I should like to point out a superficial, and yet interesting, similarity between the dialectic of Hegel and of Nagarjuna. Hegel begins and Nagarjuna at least plays with the assumption of an absolute, absolutely unified reality, and both therefore reject as ultimately untrue any language that cannot refer to this absolute unity. But whereas in Nagarjuna's philosophy it is logically impossible for both unity and difference to pertain to the same *ens*, in Hegel's philosophy it is the very tension between unity and difference that constitutes the structure of reality. To emphasize this, let me recall the four alternative metaphysical views that Nagarjuna rejects. They are (1) the substance or Atman-view, which he rejects as incompatible with change; (2) the Becoming- or *dharma*-view, which he rejects because change is impossible without a subtance to undergo change; (3) the synthesis of (1) and (2), which he rejects as self-contradictory;

and (4) rejection of both (1) and (2), which he also rejects as self-contradictory.

Hegel's philosophy is based upon the assumption that the synthesis of Being and Becoming, alternative (3), is, in fact, possible, and, in fact, necessary. He admits that Being and Becoming are contradictory in terms of traditional logic, but he reconciles them, as he says, dialectically, by limiting the applicability of the 'law of the excluded middle'. If language is to depict reality, it is not only possible, but necessary, Hegel believes, for contradictions to be reconciled in a hierarchy of syntheses. The logical tension between unity and difference, which creates an unbridgeable dichotomy in Nagarjuna's dialectic, in Hegel's dialectic creates the fundamental structure of thought, and, because thought is identical with reality, of reality. According to both Nagarjuna and Hegel, any ordinary predicate taken as a qualifier of reality is self-contradictory. Nagarjuna therefore concludes that *no* predicate can qualify reality. Hegel, however, concludes that while predicates in isolation cannot refer correctly to reality, a logical system of *all* possible predicates does. Thus while for Nagarjuna every possible statement is absolutely false ('empty'), for Hegel every statement is relatively true. In Hegel's philosophy, to refer quite correctly to a, so to speak, separate 'entity', a table, for example, one has to take into account the whole universe. Such a position might be plausible as a mystical insight into the incorporation of everything within the whole; but Hegel does not rest satisfied with the mere assumption of the relational affinity of everything in the universe. He actually believes in the power of reason to reconcile 'self-alienated thought', in which things are viewed in their separateness, with the 'absolute Spirit', reality as a unified whole. Even, however, if we accept his basic belief in a unified system of all relations, his belief that it is possible to expose the development of the universe as an absolute in which everything separate is 'logically' incorporated gives too much credit, it seems to me, to the human mind. When Hegel actually tries such an exposition, he forcibly squeezes various data to make them fit his dialectical pattern. In Russell's ironic remark, one cannot understand Hegel's account of the development of the universe unless one assumes that 'the universe was gradually learning Hegel's philosophy'.

Hegel's philosophy is, of course, related to Kant's. Hegel

attempts to unify Kant's world within an embracing logical synthesis. In Kant's philosophy, man is hopelessly split between the empirical, which is knowable but morally useless, and the transcendent, which is morally significant but unknowable. Hegel's synthesis bridges the logical and epistemological gap between causal and teleological order, and between a phenomenal and a free self. Although I cannot now explain why, it appears to me that in Hegel's philosophy the concepts of the world and of man lose their meaning. The same, I admit, can be said, and with fewer qualms, of Nagarjuna's way of reasoning. Nagarjuna's complete rejection of any attempted reference by thought and language to reality leaves us with no more than the ('empty') concept of 'emptiness'. Personally, however, I feel that Nagarjuna's thought suggests a valuable insight.

The difference in insight between Hegel's and Nagarjuna's philosophical absolutism is related to the problem of time. Normal perception is spatial and temporal. Psychologically speaking, our concept of space is largely derived from the sense of motion and the feeling of the solidity of the objects of perception, while our concept of time is derived from the awareness of the constant change of events. Psychologically, it is possible for some people, the relatively quiescent ones, I should assume, to reduce the awareness of space, and some, especially in periods of mental stress, may regard the objects of perception, including people, as unsolid. That is to say, those with a certain temperament or in a certain frame of mind, in which the sense of solidity is reduced, may be naturally inclined toward Idealism. Although time-awareness is also subject to considerable differences, I think that it resists abolition more strongly. It is just when the sense of the perceived world's solidity is reduced that thought and imagination are likely to flourish and the awareness of at least inward time to increase.

In a system of what may be called Rational Idealism, the awareness of the flow of (mental) events in time creates a conflict. On the one hand, there are the abstract concepts, mathematical, logical, or metaphysical, that are regarded as having an independent, time-immune reality, while, on the other hand, the contents of sense-perception, memory, and imagination can only be regarded as existent in time, because they are contingent and signify nothing universal, independent of the thinking mind. It is this very tension between the contingent-private ('temporal') and the rational-universal ('non-temporal') aspects of thought that underlies Hegel's philosophy. Driven by the urge to create a non-contingent world picture, Hegel gives priority to the rational aspect of thought; but he does not forget the contingent aspects, which belong to the troublesome 'alienation of the Absolute Spirit from itself.'

Hegel and Nagarjuna. The many moons reflected in the lake are actually the reflection of one moon, distorted by the waves. Once the water becomes calm, the one moon. . . This suggestive Eastern metaphor drives home both the Hegelian and the Buddhist intuition. However, the means to calm the surface of the water, that is, the disordered movement of the mind, are very different. Hegel seems to believe that we can pursue the way of unification without losing the consciousness of the separatedness—the constant dialectical movement from the separate to the unified should never lose sight of the separate. For such a process of unification, the concept of change, that is, the awareness of time is necessary. But Hegel, understanding temporal development in his own way, insists that what we ordinarily see as contingent and arbitrary can be dialectically understood as a process embodying ever-growing rational and moral significance. Of course, all temporal processes are encompassed by 'logical' and therefore atemporal relationships.

Like Hegel, Nagarjuna also rejects the temporal causal view, but, unlike him, does not substitute any rational pattern for it. Instead of grasping separatedness in terms of unity, as Hegel advocates, Nagarjuna refers, perhaps, to a meditative state, or to the effect of such a state, in which, paradoxically, separatedness may exist as before, but is not taken as such: one seems to have lost, or, rather, overcome the awareness of events in time. Not that one ceases to react to phenomena, but that one acts as though the moment of action is eternity.

Nagarjuna's insight, I think, should have been clarified in less intuitive terms. But I must admit that I do not find the right words to define it. But perhaps finding them is missing it. What Nagarjuna helps us to do, and Kant and Hegel do not, is to forget about philosophy and still rest satisfied.

Notes

The bibliographical notes contain a number of brief, more specialized bibliographies. Books listed in the general bibliography are referred to in abbreviated form. Likewise, books listed in chapter-section bibliographies are referred to in abbreviated form in the references of the same or immediately succeeding chapter-sections.

Introduction

1. For a general survey of the relations of Europe with the rest of the world in the eighteenth century, see M. Devèze, *L'Europe et le monde à la fin du xviiie siècle*, Paris, Albin Michel, 1970. On French eighteenth-century reactions to China, see Etiemble, *Connaissons-nous la Chine?*, Paris, Gallimard, 1964. P. Marshall, ed., *The British Discovery of Hinduism in the Eighteenth Century*, London, Cambridge University Press, 1970, is an anthology of British reactions to Indian culture. To this may be added N.C. Chaudhuri, *Scholar Extraordinary: The Life of Professor the Rt. Hon. Friedrich Max Müller, P. C.*, London, Chatto & Windus, 1974, an insightful biography of the nineteenth-century pioneer of Indian studies.

2. India's influence on German thinkers is described in H. von Glasenapp, *Das Indienbild deutscher Denker*, Stuttgart, Koehler Verlag, 1960; S. Sommerfeld, *Indienschau und Indiendeutung romantischer Philosophen*, Zurich, Rascher Verlag, 1943; and H. von Glasenapp, *Kant und die Religionen des Ostens*, Kitzingen am Main, Holzner Verlag (Beihefte zum Jahrbuch der Albertus-Universität, Königsberg), 1954.

3. The attitude of Europeans toward the East has tended to vary between contempt and romantic wonder. On the contempt,

see V. G. Kiernan, *The Lords of Human Kind: European Attitudes to the Outside World in the Imperial Age*, Harmondsworth, Penguin Books, 1972. For attitudes towards China, not necessarily contemptuous, see R. Dawson, *The Chinese Chameleon: An Analysis of European Conceptions of Chinese Civilization*, London, Oxford University Press, 1967; or the same author's chapter on the subject in *The Legacy of China*. European reactions to India are described in R. Schwab, *La renaissance orientale*, Paris, Payot, 1950; and in G. R. Rawlinson, 'India in European Literature and Thought', in *The Legacy of India*, an essay which, supplemented by F. Wilhelm, is reprinted in Basham, *A Cultural History of India*.

1. *Cultures, Contexts, and Comparisons*

1. J. T. Fraser, ed., *The Voices of Time*, New York, Braziller, 1966, is an interesting general anthology. Part I contains articles on the idea of time in philosophy, including Christian, Indian, Japanese, and Chinese thought. Part II contains articles on time in language and literature, music, children's perception, psychiatry, and subjective experience generally. On time in experimental psychology, see P. Fraisse, *The Psychology of Time*, London, Eyre & Spottiswoode, 1964; and R. E. Ornstein, *On the Experience of Time*, Harmondsworth, Penguin Books, 1969. On time especially in physics: G. J. Whitrow, *The Philosophy of Time*, London, Nelson, 1961. On time as philosophers, old and new, construe it: R. M. Gale, ed., *The Philosophy of Time*, London, Macmillan, 1968. Subtle explorations in time as revealed in European literature from Montaigne to Proust: G. Poulet, *Studies in Human Time*, Baltimore, Johns Hopkins Press, 1956. Time in relation to art, to Patristic Christianity, to Islamic and Indian thought, and to the *Book of Changes*: J. Campbell, ed., *Man and Time*, New York, Pantheon, 1958. Time in relation to different cultures: L. Gardet et al., *Cultures and Time*, Paris, Unesco Press, 1976.

2. K. Oatley, 'Clock Mechanisms of Sleep,' *New Scientist*, May 15, 1975.

3. On language, grammar, and time, see G. Steiner, *After Babel: Aspects of Language and Translation*, New York, Oxford University Press, 1975, pp. 130–61. Steiner gives further references.

4. 'Time-Reckoning' and 'Clocks' in N. G. L. Hammond and

H. H. Scullard, eds., *The Oxford Classical Dictionary*, 2nd ed., London, Oxford University Press, 1970. H. Bengtson, *Einführung in die alte Geschichte*, 3rd ed., Munich, 1959, pp. 25–26. On the temporal vagueness of sixteenth-century Europe: L Lefèvre, *Le problème de l'incroyance au xvie siècle*, Paris, Albin Michel, 1947, pp. 420 ff.; R. Mandrou, *Introduction à la France moderne (1500–1640)*, 2nd ed., Paris, Albin Michel, pp. 99–101. On medieval clocks: L. White, *Medieval Technology and Social Change*, London, Oxford University Press, 1962, pp. 119–29; C. Cipolla, *European Culture and Overseas Expansion*, Harmondsworth, Penguin Books, 1970.

5. C. Geertz, *The Interpretation of Culture*, New York Basic Books, 1973, pp. 391–92.

6. E. E. Evans-Pritchard, *The Nuer*, London, Oxford University Press, 1940, pp. 94–104; pp. 102, 103 quoted.

7. A. I. Hallowell, *Culture and Experience*, University of Pennsylvania Press, 1955. For an Eskimo calendar-vocabulary see N. A. Chance, *The Eskimo of North Alaska*, New York, Holt, Rinehart & Winston, 1966, pp. 35–6.

8. *Language, Thought and Reality: Selected Writings of Benjamin Lee Whorf*, Cambridge (Mass.), M.I.T. Press, 1956. H. Hoijer, ed., *Language in Culture*, Chicago, Chicago University Press, 1954.

9. E.g., R. L. Gregory, in R. L. Gregory and E. H. Gombrich, *Illusion in Nature and Art*, London, Duckworth, 1973, pp. 60–9. On language and cognition: A. Schaff, *Language and Cognition*, New York, McGraw-Hill, 1973, pp. 51–77; D. E. Cooper, *Philosophy and the Nature of Language*, London, Longman, 1973, chap. 5; R. Jacobson, *Main Trends in the Science of Language*, London, Allen & Unwin, 1973, chap. 2.

10. On China: Granet, *La pensée chinoise*, Paris, Albin Michel, 1934, pp. 88–89. On India: H. Nakamura, *Ways of Thinking of Eastern Peoples*, pp. 73–86. On Semitic and Greek time-sense and grammar: T. Boman, *Hebrew Thought Compared with Greek*, London, SCM Press, 1960; refuted by J. Barr, *The Semantics of Biblical Language*, London, Oxford University Press, 1961. My references to Indian, Chinese, and Muslim time-senses refer to the respective articles of R. Panikkar, C. Larre, and L. Gardet, all in L. Gardet, ed., *Cultures and Time*.

11. See, in general, R. H. Robins, *A Short History of Linguistics*, London, Longmans, 1967. For a brief history of the two views, see J. M. Penn, *Linguistic Relativity versus Innate Ideas*. Penn says

that the first suggestion of the influence of language on thought is in Plato's *Cratylus* (435b), but that its first clear statement is in Hamaan and Herder. Penn's citations show that both Whorf and his teacher, Sapir, sometimes stated their view in an implausibly extreme form and sometimes in a more qualified, plausible one.

12. P. Alexandre, *An Introduction to Languages and Language in Africa*, London, Heinemann, 1972, p. 25.

13. *Language, Thought, and Reality: Selected Writings of Benjamin Lee Whorf*, pp. 213–15.

14. S. Ullman, *The Principles of Semantics*, 2nd ed., Oxford, Blackwell, 1957, pp. 60ff. (word-autonomy and context); 96ff. (emotive function of language). Ullman suggests the relative autonomy of words in German. The idea that German retains more of an old autonomy is attributed to Franz Nikolaus Fink (1899), and that it displays a fear of the concrete to Viggo Bröndal (1936).

15. Ullman, op. cit., pp. 152ff. G. A. Miller and P. N. Johnson-Laird, *Language and Perception*, Cambridge (Mass.), Harvard University Press, 1976, pp. 237–40.

16. E. Durkheim and M. Mauss, *Primitive Classification*, London, Cohen & West, 1963 (French original, 1903). Miller and Johnson-Laird, op. cit., pp. 375–410.

17. Miller and Johnson-Laird, op. cit., pp. 333–60. B. B. Lloyd, *Perception and Cognition*, Harmondsworth, Penguin Books, 1972, chap. 23. The snow and egret feathers are from G. Steiner, *The Penguin Book of Modern Verse Translation* (renamed *Poem into Poem*), Harmondsworth, Penguin Books, 1966, p. 23.

18. Chinese and Indian philosophers will be characterized in the next chapter. On the associations of the German *wissen*, see Ullman, op. cit. pp. 165ff.

19. *The Shorter Oxford English Dictionary*, 1973, and C. T. Onions, ed., *The Oxford Dictionary of English Etymology*, 1966.

20. J. L. Ackrill, 'Plato and the Copula: *Sophist* 251–59'; G. E. L. Owen, 'Plato on Not-Being'; both in *Plato: A Collection of Critical Essays*, ed. G. Vlastos, vol. 1, Garden City, Doubleday (Anchor Books), 1971. 'Editor's Introduction', in *Plato's Sophist: A Commentary by R. S. Bluck*, ed. G. C. Neal, Manchester, Manchester University Press, 1975.

21. The thesis that Aristotle's categories were derived from the

construction of the Greek sentence was first apparently elaborated by A. Trendelenberg, in his *Geschichte der Kategorienlehre*, vol. 1, Berlin, 1846. Hermann Bonitz criticized Trendelenberg and began a sharp controversy among scholars.

22. The curious beginner might look at a simple, readable introduction such as R. Newnham, *About Chinese*, Harmondsworth, Penguin Books, 1971. B. Karlgren, *Sound and Symbol in Chinese*, rev. ed., Hong Kong University Press and Oxford University Press, 1962, is a brief, readable introduction to the history and nature of the Chinese language. Rather out of date, it is, nevertheless, worth the beginner's while. P. Kratochvil, *The Chinese Language*, London, Hutchinson, 1968, is an up-to-date but difficult introduction.

23. A. C. Graham, 'The Logic of the Mohist Hsiao-ch'ü', *Toung Pao*, vol. 51, p. 47.

24. Ibid., pp. 48–49.

25. "Being' in Classical Chinese', in J. W. M. Verhaar, ed., *The Verb 'Be' and Its Synonyms*, vol. 1, Dordrecht, Reidel Pub. Co., 1967.

26. A. C. Graham, ' "Being' in Classical Chinese', pp. 35–6.

27. Ibid., pp. 16–17.

28. C. D. Hanson, 'Ancient Chinese Theories of Language', *Journal of Chinese Philosophy*, vol. 2, no. 3, June, 1975. The reference to a Taoist is specifically to Ho Yen, as quoted in the Chang Chan commentary to *Lieh Tzu*, chap. 4.

29. A. C. Graham, *Two Chinese Philosophers*, London, Lund Humphries, 1958, p. 41.

30. *The Confucian Analects*, trans. J. Legge, 13/3/5–6.

31. S. F. Barker, 'Number', in P. Edwards, ed., *The Encyclopaedia of Philosophy*, New York, Macmillan, 1967.

32. I. Thomas, *Selections Illustrating the History of Greek Mathematics*, vol. 1, London, Heinemann (Loeb Library), p. 67 (Euclid, *Elements*, 7). H. G. Apostle, *Aristotle's Philosophy of Mathematics*, Chicago, University of Chicago Press, 1952, pp. 83, 84, 89–90. Aristotle, *Topica* 108b 26–30. J. Klein, *Greek Mathematical Thought and the Origins of Algebra*, Cambridge (Mass.), MIT Press, 1968.

33. M. Kline, *Mathematical Thought from Ancient to Modern Times*, New York, Oxford University Press, 1972, pp. 251–4, 542.

34. J. von Uexküll, 'A Stroll Through the World of Animals

and Men', in C. H. Schiller, ed., *Instinctive Behavior*, New York, International Universities Press, 1957.

35. O. W. Sacks, *Awakenings*, Harmondsworth, Penguin Books, 1976, p. 83.

36. B. B. Lloyd, *Perception and Cognition: A Cross-Cultural Perspective*, Harmondsworth, Penguin Books, 1972, p. 79.

37. B. Berlin and P. Kay, *Basic Color Terms: Their Universality and Evolution*, Berkeley/Los Angeles, University of California Press, 1969; as summarized in Miller and Johnson-Laird, *Language and Perception*, pp. 346–50.

38. K. W. J. Corcoran, *Pattern Recognition*, Harmondsworth, Penguin Books, 1971.

39. Y. Okamota, *The Namban Art of Japan*, New York/Tokyo, Weatherhill/Heibonsha. In general, M. Sullivan, *The Meeting of Eastern and Western Art*, London, Thames & Hudson, 1973. On Japanese prints and Western Art, C. F. Ives, *The Great Wave*, New York, Metropolitan Museum of Art, 1974; and B. Dorival, 'Ukiyo-e and European Painting', in C. F. Yamada, ed., *Dialogue in Art: Japan and the West*, Tokyo, Kodansha, 1976.

40. On the problem of translation, which is relevant to this whole section, see G. Steiner, *After Babel: Aspects of Language Translation*, London, Oxford University Press, 1975, especially chap. 2, 'Language and Gnosis'. See also R. Jacobson, 'On Linguistic Aspects of Translation', in R. A. Brower, ed., *On Translation*, Cambridge (Mass,), Harvard University Press, 1959.

On the Roman assimilation of Greek Culture see A. Wardman, *Rome's Debt to Greece*, London, Paul Elek, 1976. On the Roman attitude to the Greek language, see pp. 41–50.

41. *Lucretius*, ed. C. Bailey, 3 vols., London, Oxford University Press, vol. 1, pp. 51–52 (on Epicurus's care in the use of words), 138–40 (on Lucretius's use of Greek words and invention of words), 183 (book 1, lines 136–45, quoted); vol. 2, pp. 622–3.

42. Apart from Wardman, op. cit., I have consulted P. Grimal, *La civilisation romaine*, Arthaud, 1960, pp. 175–6; and R. Bloch and J. Cousin, *Rome et son destin*, Paris, Armand Colin, 1960, pp. 137–9.

43. S. Pines, 'Philosophy', in P. M. Holt, A. K. S. Lambton and B. Lewis, eds., *The Cambridge History of Islam*, vol. 2, p. 781. On translation into Arabic see also De Lacy O'Leary, *How Greek Science Passed to the Arabs*, London, Routledge & Kegan Paul, 1949, pp. 164–70; R. Arnaldez and L. Massignon, in *Histoire*

générales des sciences, vol. 1, pp. 439–43, 449–51; F. E. Peters, *Aristotle and the Arabs*, New York, New York University Press, 1968, pp. 58–69; and F. Rosenthal, *The Classical Heritage in Islam*, London, Routledge & Kegan Paul, 1975, pp. 15–23.

On translation into Hebrew see C. Singer, 'The Jewish Factor in Medieval Thought', in E. R. Bevan and C. Singer, ed., *The Legacy of Israel*, pp. 202–45; H. Wolfson, *Crescas' Critique of Aristotle*, Cambridge (Mass.). Harvard University Press, p. 7 (on the translators' success); S. Baron, *A Social and Economic History of the Jews*, 2nd ed., New York, Columbia University Press, 1958, vol. 8, p. 316, note 31 (for bibliography).

44. F. Rosenthal, *Knowledge Triumphant*, pp. 196–203.

45. F. Rosenthal, *The Classical Heritage in Islam*, p. 17 (from as-Safadi, A. D. 1305).

46. S. Pines, op. cit., p. 781.

47. For translation into Latin: E. Gilson, *History of Christian Philosophy in the Middle Ages*, New York, Random House, 1955, pp. 235ff., 652ff.; F. von Steenberghen, *Aristotle in the West*, Louvain, Nauwelaerts, 1955, chap. 5; R. R. Bolgar, *The Classical Heritage*, Cambridge, Cambridge University Press, 1952, pp. 149ff., 229; F. E. Peters, *Aristotle and the Arabs*, pp. 221–37; and F. Gabrielli, 'The Transmission of Learning and Literary Influences to Western Europe', *The Cambridge History of Islam*, fol. 2, pp. 852–63.

48. L. Febvre, *L'incroyance au xvie siècle*, Paris, Albin Michel, 1942, pp. 385–400.

49. Greek influence: R. Walzer, 'On the Legacy of the Classics in the Islamic World', in *Greek into Arabic*, Oxford, Bruno Cassirer, 1962; F. Rosenthal, *The Classical Heritage in Islam*. Translation: For bibliography consult J. D. Pearson, *Index Islamicus*, Cambridge, Cambridge University Press, 1958—, sec. 4–2 ('Transmission of Greek and Latin Science to the Arabs'). Philosophy: F. Rosenthal, op. cit., pp. 75–161, which includes what is here called 'popular philosophy' in 'philosophy'. Popular philosophy in Greek and Arabic: A. Müller, 'Über einige arabische Sentenzensammlungen', *Zeitschrift der deutschen Morgenländischen Gesellschaft* 31 (1877) pp. 506–28; F. Rosenthal, 'Sayings of the Ancients from Ibn Duraid's *Kitab al-Mujtana*', *Orientalia* 27 (1958), pp. 29–54, 150–83; A. Halkin, 'Classical and Arabic Material in Ibn Aqnin's 'Hygiene of the Soul', *Proceedings*

of the American Academy for Jewish Research 14 (1944), pp. 25–147.

50. F. Rosenthal, op. cit.; G. Bergsträsser, *Hunain ibn Ishaq und seine Schule*, Leiden, Brill, 1913; A. Badawi, *La transmission de la philosophie grecque au monde arabe*, Paris, Vrin, 1960.

51. F. Rosenthal, op. cit., pp. 17–23.

52. C. Bürgel, 'Some New Material Pertaining to Plato's 'Phaedo', in the *Commemoration Volume of Al-Biruni*, Teheran, 1976; F. Rosenthal, 'On the Knowledge of Plato's Philosophy in the Islamic World', *Islamic Culture* 14 (1940), pp. 387–422; R. Walzer, 'Platonism in Islamic Philosophy', in his *Greek into Arabic*. For translations of Aristotle see F. E. Peters, *Aristotles Orientalis*, Leiden, Brill, 1968.

53. For Plato's *Republic* see *Averroes' Commentary on Plato's 'Republic'*, ed. and trans. E. I. J. Rosenthal, Cambridge, Cambridge University Press, 1956; reprinted with corrections, 1969. For Galen, see P. Kraus and R. Walzer, *Galenic Compendium Timaei Platonis (Plato Arabus, I)*, London, 1951.

54. O. Bardenhewer, *Die pseudo-aristotelische Schrift über das reine Gute, bekannt under den Namen Liber de Causis*, Freiburg, 1882. F. Rosenthal, 'Al-Shaykh al-Yunani and the Arabic Plotinus Sources,' *Orientalia* (1952–3, 1955).

55. The less known gnomonologies have been edited by L. Sternbach, K. Wachsmuth, and others.

56. According to the Quran, messengers were sent by Allah to the various nations. See, e.g., Quran 11/60.

57. Socrates has appeared in many guises. There is a 'Hellenistic' Socrates and a 'Christian' one. For the latter see, e.g., Justin Martyr, *First Apology*, 46; and T. Daman, *Socrates et Jesus*, Paris, 1944. For the Socrates of the eighteenth century Germans see B. Böhm, *Sokrates im achtzehnten Jahrhundert: Studium zum Werdegang des modernen Persönlichkeitsbewusstseins*, Leipzig, 1929; Neumünster, 1966. For Socrates and the English church see, e.g., J. Priestly, *Socrates and Jesus Compared*, London 1745, which reports a usual rejection of the comparison.

58. See al-Razi, *Al-Sirah al-Falasafiyyah*, ed. and trans. into French by P. Kraus, in *Orientalia* N.S. 4 (1935), pp. 300–334.

59. See, e.g., *Gamal al-Kin al-Hilli, Anwar al-Malakut ti Sharh al-Yaqut*, Teheran, 338 A.H., p. 28/13, who mentions Socrates as

one of the philosophers who had, in contrast with Islam, maintained that the world was eternal.

60. See the Arabic story in Ibn Abi al-Hadid, *Commentary on Nahj al-Balagha*, Beirut, 1964, 4, p. 264/4.

61. There are a number of Arabic versions of this story, e.g., al-Kindi, 'Ma naqalahu al-Kindi min altaz suqrat,' in M. Fakhri, 'Al-Kindi wa-suqrat', in *Al-Abhath* (1969), pp. 23–30. In Greek literature this anecdote is inter alia in Ovid, *Ars Amatoria*, 1/99.

62. D. Snellgrove and H. Richardson, *A Cultural History of Tibet*, London, Weidenfeld & Nicholson, pp. 74–76 (76 quoted), 118ff. 160–72. C. Bell, *The Religion of Tibet*, London, Oxford University Press, 1931, pp. 43, 46. M. Maspero, rev. by P. Demiéville, 'Langues de l'Asie du Sud-Est', in A. Meillet and M. Cohen, *Les langues du monde*, Paris, CNRS, 1952, pp. 542–47.

63. H. Maspero, *Mélanges posthumes*, vol. 1, pp. 65–83, 195–211; vol. 2, pp. 185–211. A. F. Wright, *Buddhism in Chinese History*, pp. 35–38. A. F. Wright, 'The Chinese Language and Foreign Ideas', in A. F. Wright, ed., *Studies in Chinese Thought*, Chicago, University of Chicago Press, 1953. E. Zürcher, *The Buddhist Conquest of China*, 2 vols., rev. reprint, Leiden, Brill, 1972, pp. 11ff., 47, 69, 103, 202–203. K.K.S. Ch'en, *Buddhism in China*, pp. 43ff., 50, 53, chap. 13 (esp. 369–72, 'Problems in Translations'). R. H. Robinson, *Early Madhyamika in India and China*, Madison, University of Wisconsin Press, 1967. J. W. de Jong, *Buddha's Word in China*, Canberra, Australian National University, 1968.

64. De Jong, op. cit., p. 10.

65. A. F. Wright, 'The Chinese Language and Foreign Ideas', p. 287.

66. Ch'en, op. cit., pp. 367–8.

67. *L'enseignement de Vimalakirti*, trans. E. Lamotte, Louvain Publications Universitaires/Institut Orientaliste, 1962, p. 9.

68. R. H. Robinson, *Early Madhyamika in India and China*, Madison, University of Wisconsin Press, 1967, pp. 88, 157–7.

69. F. Wilhelm, 'The German Response to Indian Culture', *Journal of the American Oriental Society* 4 (Sept.-Dec., 1961).

2. *Three Philosophical Cvilizations: A Preliminary Comparison*

1. For a discussion of world population statistics in history, see

F. Braudel, *Civilisation matérielle et capitalisme (xve-xviiie siècles)*, vol. 1, Paris, Armand Colin, 1967, chap. 1.

2. M. Lombard, *The Golden Age of Islam*, Amsterdam/New York, North-Holland/American Elseivier, 1975, esp. pp. 97–8.

3. For Christian traits in Islam: L. Gardet and M. A. Anawati, *Introduction à la théologie musulmane*, Paris, Vrin, 1948, esp. pp. 191–247. For parallels between the Bible and the Quran: C. C. Torrey, The Jewish Foundation of Islam, New York, 1933. For *Hadith:* I. Goldziher, 'The Hadith and the New Testament', in his *Muslim Studies*, vol. 1, London, Allen & Unwin.

4. E. g., P. H. Davidson, 'John Philoponus as a Source of Mediaeval Islamic and Jewish Proofs of Existence', *Journal of the American Oriental Society* 89 (1968) pp. 357–91.

5. A. Ahmad, *Studies in Islamic Culture in the Indian Environment*, London, Oxford University Press, 1964, pp. 74–76 (quotation p. 76, from Tara Chand).

6. Al-Razi: M. Fakhry, *A History of Islamic Philosophy*, pp. 46–7. The partisan of Indian influence is M. Horten. See his *Die Philosophie des Islam*, Munich, Ernst Reinhardt Verlag, 1924. For the view that Islamic atomism is derived from India, see his study, 'Die philosophischen Systeme der spekulativen Theologen im Islam', *Renaissance und Philosophie*, Heft 3, Bonn, 1910. On this problem, see also S. Pines, *Beiträge zur islamischen Atomenlehre*, Berlin, 1936, pp. 102–23.

7. *Al-Kindi's Metaphysics*, trans. A. L. Ivry, Albany, State University of New York Press, 1974, p. 58.

8. F. Rosenthal, *The Classical Heritage in Islam*, pp. 39 (Sa'id al Andalusi), 43 (Moshe ben Ezra). For a sketch of the relationship between Greek and Islamic philosophy, see 'The Diffusion of Aristotelianism' and 'Philosophical Movements in Islam', in F. E. Peters, *Aristotle and the Arabs*.

9. F. Rosenthal, *Knowledge Triumphant*, p. 337. On the influence of Muslim on Christian medieval philosophy, see Peters, op. cit., pp. 221–37; and, in general, W. M. Watt, *The Influence of Islam on Medieval Europe*, Edinburgh, Edinburgh University Press, 1972.

10. See, for this section, the books listed in the general bibliography under the title, 'India: General Background'. In addition, see the following: *The Cambridge History of India*, vol. 1, esp. chaps. 8, 9 (for early India); and, for the same period, R. Gopal,

India of Vedic Kalpasutras, Delhi, National Publishing House, 1959. J. Auboyer, *Daily Life in Ancient India from 200 BC to AD 700*, London, Weidenfeld & Nicolson, 1965. Abbe J. A. Dubois and H. K. Beauchamp, *Hindu Manners, Customs and Ceremonies*, 3rd ed., London, Oxford University Press, 1906, a relatively complete description of Indian life toward the beginning of the nineteenth century; decidedly Christian, but also the shrewd, unsentimental observations of a man who dressed and lived like a Hindu for over thirty years. L. S. A. O'Malley, *Popular Hinduism*, Cambridge, Cambridge University Press, 1935, a simple, reliable description of the beliefs and practices of simple Hindus. N. S. Chaudhuri, *A Passage to India*, London, 1960, in which a veteran Indian Anglophile tells how he first saw England at the age of fifty-seven and was moved to contrast it with India. S. C. Dube, *Indian Village*, Ithaca, Cornell University Press, 1955, the report of a collective investigation of the village of Shamirpet. A. R. Beals, *Gopalur, A South Indian Village*, New York, Holt, Rinehart & Winston, 1964, a level-headed study of a village only ninety miles from Shamirpet; the village, described as in 1959–1960, sounds relatively well-off and happy. G. M. Carstairs, *The Twice-Born: A Study of a Community of High-Caste Hindus*, Bloomington, Indiana University Press, 1958, a psychiatric study that neither the author, despite his cautions, nor the reader can help generalizing to India at large. D. G. Mandelbaum, *Society in India*, 2 vols., Berkeley, University of California Press, 1970, an anthropologist's clear and comprehensive explorations of Indian social structure.

11. *Cambridge History of India*, vol. 1, chaps. 1, 2. *Oxford History of India*, 3rd ed., ed. P. Spear, London, Oxford University Press, 1958, pp. 1–4. Renou and Filliozat, *L'Inde classique*, vol. 1, paras. 1–50. S. A. Tyler, *India: An Anthropological Perspective*, p. 13 (anthropological variety). Dubois and Beauchamp, *Hindu Manners*, pp. 316–25 (appearance, clothing), 332–35 (ornaments). A. L. Basham, *The Wonder that Was India*, pp. 212–15 (clothes and ornaments).

12. Generalizations on Indian History: *Oxford History of India*, pp. 5–6. H. L. Basham, 'The Indian Subcontinent in Historical Perspective', *Saeculum* 10 (1959), pp. 196–207. W. von Pochhammer, 'Zur Darstellung der Indischen Geschichte', *Saeculum* 12 (1961), pp. 291–305.

13. R. Gopal, *India of Vedic Kalpasutras*, pp. 145–47.

14. N. S. Chaudhuri, *A Passage to India*, pp. 29–30.

15. A. L. Basham, *The Wonder that Was India*, p. 445 (from Dandin).

16. B. A. Saletore, *Ancient Indian Thought and Institutions*, London, Asia Publishing House, p. 524 (from Kalhana's *Rajatarangini*).

17. J. Auboyer, *Daily Life in Ancient India*, p. 69.

18. Chaudhuri, op. cit., p. 132.

19. S. C. Dube, *Indian Village*, p. 92. On peasant hardship, J. A. Dubois and H. K. Beauchamp, *Hindu Manners*, pp. 82–4; L. S. A. O'Malley, *Popular Hinduism*, p. 50.

20. Holy men: Dubois and Beauchamp, op. cit., pp. 108–111, 123–38, 160–541. O'Malley, chap. 7. J. Gonda, *Der jüngere Hinduismus*, pp. 288–92. G. S. Ghurye, *Indian Sadhus*, 2nd ed., Bombay, Popular Prakashan, 1964.

21. O'Malley, op. cit., pp. 124–8. Gonda, op. cit., pp. 278–279.

22. O'Malley, p. 38. Home rites: O'Malley, pp. 105–111; Gonda, pp. 261–5.

23. Dubois and Beauchamp, p. 550.

24. Fire and water: ibid., pp. 241–2, 255, 549–55.

25. Dubois and Beauchamp, pp. 14–80. O'Malley, pp. 74–79, 220–22. *Oxford History of India*, pp. 61–70. *Cambridge History of India*, vol. 1, pp. 53–6. R. P. Masani, 'Caste and the Structure of Caste', in *The Legacy of India*. L. Renou, *Sanskrit et culture*, Paris, Payot, 1950 (review of P. V. Kane, *History of Dharmaśastra*). J. H. Hutton, *Caste in India*, Cambridge, Cambridge University Press, 1946. D. G. Mandelbaum, *Society in India*, vol. 1, chaps. 1, 2. R. Lannoy, *The Speaking Tree*, part 3. L. Dumont, *Homo Hierarchichus*, London, Weidenfeld & Nicolson, 1970. Ram Gopal, *India of Vedic Kalpasutras*, pp. 118–127.

26. Dubois and Beauchamp, p. 38.

27. S. S. Anant, *The Changing Concept of Caste in India*, Delhi, Vikas Publications, 1972. L. I. Rudolph and S. H. Rudolph, *The Modernity of Tradition*, Chicago, University of Chicago Press, 1967.

28. S. C. Dube, *Indian Village*. Further on Indian village life: A. R. Beals, *Gopalur*; D. G. Mandelbaum, *Society in India*, vol. 1, chaps. 3–5; R. Lannoy, *The Speaking Tree*, part 2.

29. G. M. Carstairs, *The Twice-Born*.

30. R. Lannoy, *The Speaking Tree*, pp. 106, 107.

31. For a similar description of Indian family life in general, R. Lannoy, op. cit., pp. 85–131, and S. A. Tyler, *India: An Anthropological Perspective*, pp. 134ff. On the difficulties and rewards of cross-cultural comparisons of the kind indulged in here, see B. B. Whiting and J. A. M. Whiting, *Children of Six Cultures: A Psychocultural Analysis*, Cambridge (Mass.), Harvard University Press, 1975.

32. W. D. O'Flaherty, *Asceticism and Eroticism in the Mythology of Siva*, London, Oxford University Press, 1973, pp. 141–2, 318 (quoted).

33. S. Dasgupta, *A History of Indian Philosophy*, vol. 5, pp. 1–4 (on 'horrid practices', etc.).

34. R. K. Mookerji, *Ancient Indian Education*, London, Macmillan, 1947, which is relatively detailed, adulatory towards tradition, and makes rather free use of the sources. P. Deussen, *The Philosophy of the Upanishads*, pp. 367–73. R. Gopal, *India of Vedic Kalpasutras*, chaps. 14 (on educational rituals), 15 (on the system of education). J. Gonda, *Change and Continuity in Indian Religion*, The Hague, Mouton, 1965, chaps 8 ('The Guru'), 9 ('Brahmacarya'); detailed scholarly studies.

35. Gopal, op. cit., p. 298. for uniforms, etc., see pp. 290–5.

36 Ibid., p. 326 (according to Apastamba).

37. Tattiriya Upanishad 1/9, as in *The Thirteen Principal Upanishads*, trans. R. E. Hume, London, Oxford University Press, p. 280.

38. D. Ingalls, 'The Brahman Tradition', in M. Singer, ed., *Traditional India: Structure and Change*, Philadelphia, American Folklore Society, 1959, p. 7.

39. J. N. Farquhar, *An Outline of the Religious Literature of India*, pp. 174–75. G. S. Ghurye, *India Sadhus*, pp. 90–96 (p. 96 quoted).

40. For general background, the UNESCO *History of Mankind*, vol. 3, chap. 7 ('Learning and Education'). R. K. Mookerji, op. cit., esp. chap. 9; the accounts of the Chinese pilgrims are summarized extensively by Mookerji and a description of Nalanda and other educational institutions is given in some detail. See the same author's *The Culture and Art of India*, London, Allen & Unwin, 1959, pp. 163ff. and chap. 10 ('Life and Learning at the Buddhist Universities'). S. Dutt, *Buddhist Monks and Monasteries of*

India, London, Allen & Unwin, 1962.

41. Mookerji, *Ancient Indian Education*, pp. 260–61.

42. Ingalls, 'The Brahman Tradition,' p. 5.

43. *Tibet Is My Country: The Autobiography of Thubten Norbu*, as told to H. Harrer, New York, Dutton, 1961, pp. 121–2.

44. T. J. Norbu and C. Turnbull, *Tibet: Its History, Religion and People*, Harmondsworth, Penguin Books, 1972, p. 293; see further, pp. 260–7, 292–4, 306–12. For other brief descriptions of philosophic-religious education in Tibet, see R. A. Gard, ed., *Buddhism*, New York, Washington Square Press, 1963, pp. 183–90, and C. Trungpa, *Born in Tibet*, Harmondsworth, Penguin Books, 1971, pp. 91–9, 114, 121–22.

45. E. A. Solomon, *Indian Dialectics: Methods of Philosophical Discussion*, vol. 1, Ahmedabad, B. J. Institute of Learning and Research, Gujarat Vidya Sabha, 1976, pp. 15–16.

46. Ibid., chap. 1 ('Types of Debate *(Katha)*').

47. Ibid., pp. 346–8 (p. 347 quoted).

48. Ingalls, p. 11. I have taken the story from D. H. H. Ingalls, *Materials for the Study of Nayya-Nyaya Logic*, Cambridge, (Mass.), Harvard University Press, 1951, pp. 13–15, and S. C. Vidyahusana, *A History of Indian Logic*, Delhi, Motilal Banarsidass, 1971 (originally, 1921), pp. 463–64.

The quality of Raghunatha's thought may be judged by a translation made by K. H. Potter of *A Demonstration of the True Nature of the Things to Which Words Refer*, or, in its more nearly Sanskrit form, *The Padarthatattvanirupanam of Raghunatha Siromani*, distributed for the Harvard-Yenching Institute by the Harvard University Press, 1957.

49. Shaman Hwui Li, *The Life of Hiuen-Tsiang*, trans. S. Beal, new ed., London, Kegan Paul, Trench & Trübner, 1911, pp. 177, 178–79.

50. Hiuen Tsang, *Si-Yu-Ku, Buddhist Records of the Western World*, trans. S. Beal, vol. 2, London, Luzac, 1884, pp. 170–71 (as quoted by Dutt, op. cit., p. 332).

51. *The Life of Hiuen-Tsiang*, p. 112.

52. *Buddhist Records*, vol. 2, p. 170 (as in Dutt, p. 332).

53 Ibid., pp. 176ff. (quoted from I-Tsing).

54. K. K. S. Ch'en, *The Chinese Transformation of Buddhism*, p. 273.

55. Trungpa, op. cit., p. 122.

56. Renou and Filliozat, *L'Inde classique*, vol. 1, paras. 1150–6 (on the ends of life).

57. O. Lewis, *Village Life in Northern India*, Urbana, University of Illinois Press, 1958, pp. 252–4 (on traditional but this-worldly peasants).

58. E.g., J. A. B. Van Buitenen, *Tales of Ancient India*, Chicago, University of Chicago Press, 1959.

59. M. Biardeau, *Clefs pour pensée hindoue*, Paris, Seghers, 1972, pp. 173–210.

60. The reference is to Th. Stcherbatsky.

61. O'Malley, *Popular Hinduism*, chap. 8. Dubois & Beauchamp, *Hindu Manners*, pp. 119–21. P. Hacker, 'Religiöse Toleranz und Intoleranz im Hinduismus', *Saeculum* 8 (1957), pp. 167–79; perhaps unique in the breadth with which the question of Indian tolerance is treated.

62. *The Laws of Manu* 12/95–96, trans. G. Bühler, Oxford, 1886; reprinted New York, Dover, 1969, p. 505.

63. Ibid. 4/30, p. 133.

64. Ibid. 4/61, p. 138.

65. Ibid. 9/225, p. 381.

66. G. S. Ghurye, *Indian Sadhus*, chap. 6. S. Dasgupta, *A History of Indian Philosophy*, vol. 5, p. 54.

67. Dasgupta, op. cit., p. 3.

68. *Śribhyasa of Ramanuja*, ed. and trans. R. D. Karmarkar, vol. 1, Poona, University of Poona, pp. xiv–xv. Gasgupta, op. cit., vol. 3, p. 101.

69. Dasgupta, op. cit., vol. 5, p. 45.

70. O'Malley, op. cit., p. 232.

71. *Alberuni's India*, trans. E. D. Sachau, vol. 1 (of 2 vols. in 1), Delhi (reprint), S. Chand & Co., 1964, pp. 22–23.

72. A. Ahmad, *Studies in Islamic Culture in the Indian Environment*, London, Oxford University Press, 1964, pp. 82–85.

73. Ibid., p. 134.

74. Ibid., pp. 87–88.

75. Ibid., pp. 92–95.

76. E. C. Dimock, *The Place of the Hidden Moon*, Chicago, University of Chicago Press, 1966, p. 184.

77. Ibid., chap. 3

78. L. D. Barnett, *The Heart of India*, London, John Murray (Wisdom of the East), pp. 100, 101, 102.

79. For the cultural geography of China and adjacent lands, see A. Kolb, *East Asia*, London, Methuen, 1971. For a discussion of food supply, famines, and epidemics from a world standpoint, see F. Braudel, *Civilisation matérielle et capitalisme (xve-xviiie siècles)*, vol. 1, Paris, Armand Colin, 1967, chap 3. Among the books listed in the 'General Bibliography: China', B. Wiethoff, *Introduction to Chinese History* is especially relevant. Although I have not mentioned the subject of peasant revolts, it is highly important. See J. Chesnaux, *Peasant Revolts in China 1840–1949*, London, Thames & Hudson, 1973. For Europe there is an embarrassment and confusion of riches. In general, see C. M. Cipolla, *Before the Industrial Revolution: European Society and Economy, 1100–1700*, London Methuen, 1976. The register of misfortunes is kept for the poor in J.-L Gogelin, *Les misérable dans l'Occident médieval*, Paris, Seuil, 1976. For the Middle Ages I have also used: C. M. Cipolla, ed., *The Fontana Economic History of Europe*, vol. 1, London, Collins/Fontana, 1972; J. H. Mundy, *Europe in the High Middle Ages, 1150–1309*, London, Longman, 1973; and M. M. Postan, *The Medieval Economy and Society*, London, Weidenfeld & Nicolson, 1972. For France, in a later period, see R. Mandrou, *Introduction à la France moderne (1500–1640)*, 2nd ed., Paris, Albin Michel, 1975; and P. Goubert, *The Ancient Régime: French Society 1600–1750*, New York, Harper & Row, 1974. The data concerning Islam are summarized in E. Ashtor, *A Social and Economic History of the Near East in the Middle Ages*, London, Collins, 1976; if I am not mistaken, a book unique of its kind.

80. Kung-chuan Hsiao, *Rural China: Imperial Control in the Nineteenth Century*, Seattle, University of Washington Press, 1960, pp. 13, 378.

81. G. Wiet, V. Elisseeff and P. Wolff, *The Great Medieval Civilizations*, vol. 1, p. 290.

82. F. Brandel, *Civilisation matérielle et capitalisme*, chap. 1, esp. p. 63.

83. R. Mandrou, *Introduction à la France moderne*, p. 46. P. Goubert, *The Ancient Régime*, p. 107.

84. Rudolph Glaber, on a famine of 1032–34, as quoted in V. H. H. Green, *Medieval Civilization in Western Europe*, London, Edward Arnold, 1971, p. 25.

85. Cipolla, *Before the Industrial Revolution*, p. 151.

86. Braudel, op. cit., pp. 55–56.

87. E. Ashtor, *A Social and Economic History of the Near East*, p. 86. Eleventh-century plagues are noted on p. 170.

88. Ibid., pp. 67–68 (quoted), 159, 169.

89. R. Levy, *The Social Structure of Islam*, Cambridge, Cambridge University Press, 1957, chap. 1 ('The Grades of Society in Islam'). F. Rosenthal, *The Muslim Concept of Freedom*, Leiden, Brill, 1960. B. Lewis, *Race and Color in Islam*, New York, Harper & Row, 1971.

90. There is a brief summary of Chinese social structure and relations in B.-A. Scharfstein, *The Mind of China*, chap. 1, and a more detailed and scholarly one in T'ung-tsu Ch'ü, *Law and Society in Traditional China*, rev. ed., La Haye, Mouton, 1965.

91. On Chinese family life, see: M. C. Yang, *A Chinese Village*, New York, Columbia University Press, 1945, and F. L. K. Hsu, *Under the Ancestor's Shadow*, New York, Columbia University Press, 1948. A. H. Smith's older *Village Life in China*, New York, 1899, takes a disparaging yet observant view.

92. P. Ariès, *L'enfant et la vie familiale sous l'ancien régime*, Paris, Plon, 1960; abbreviated edition, Paris, Seuil, 1975 (collection Points); in English translation, *Centuries of Childhood*, London, Jonathan Cape, 1972. P. Laslett, ed., *Household and Family in Past Time*, Cambridge, Cambridge University Press, 1972. P. Laslett, 'Philippe Ariès et 'La Famille'', *Encounter* (March, 1976). J. H. Mundy, *Europe in the High Middle Ages*, pp. 270–4. L. Genicot, *Le xiiie siècle européen*, Paris, Presses Universitaires, 1968, pp. 61–70, 320–2. S. G. Checkland, *The Rise of Industrial Society in England 1815–1885*, London, Longman, 1964, pp. 318–22, 291–4.

93. Braudel, op. cit., chap. 8. Kolb, *East Asia*, pp. 159–62. E. Balasz, *Chinese Civilization and Bureaucracy*, New Haven, Yale University Press, pp. 71–106. M. Loewe, *Imperial China*, chap. 8. W. Eberhard, *A History of China*, pp. 52–54. P. Wheatley, *The Pivot of the Four Quarters: A Preliminary Enquiry into the Origins and Character of the Ancient Chinese City*, Chicago, Aldine Publishing Co., 1971; on cities in the earliest periods of Chinese History. I have not seen G. W. Skinner, ed., *The City in Late Imperial China*, Stanford, Stanford University Press, 1977.

I. M. Lapidus, *Muslim Cities in the Later Middle Ages*, Cambridge (Mass.), Harvard University Press, 1967. C. Cahen, 'Economy, Society, Institutions', *Cambridge History of Islam*, vol. 2, pp. 52–53. Ashtor, *A Social and Economic History of the Near East*, p. 114.

F. Rörig, *The Medieval Town*, Berkeley/Los Angeles, University of California Press, 1969. L. le Goff, 'The Town as an Agent of Civilization', *Fontana Economic History of Europe*, vol. 1. Mundy, *Europe in the High Middle Ages*, pp. 239–41, 413–59.

94. Scharfstein, *The Mind of China*, pp. 15–22.

95. Introductory for China: Scharfstein, op. cit., pp. 12–22. On elementary education in recent times: Smith, *Village Life in China*, chap. 9; Yang, *A Chinese Village*, pp. 143–8. Especially for higher education: H. S. Galt, *A History of Chinese Educational Institutions*, vol. 1, London, Probsthain, 1951.

96. Smith, op. cit., p. 109.

97. Galt, op. cit, p. 352.

98. 'Muslim Philosophical Institutions', in F. E. Peters, *Aristotle and the Arabs*, New York, New York University Press, 1965, pp. 72–8. 'Institutions of Higher Learning', in S. H. Nasr, *Science and Civilization in Islam*, Cambridge (Mass.), Harvard University Press, 1968. S. Pines, *Cambridge History of Islam*, vol. 2, pp. 84–85.

99. Nasr, op. cit., p. 73.

100. Pines, op. cit., p. 84.

101. A. J. Arberry, *Reason and Revelation in Islam*, London, Allen & Unwin, 1957, pp. 37–38.

102. *The Life of Ibn Sina*, ed. and trans. W. E. Gohlman, Albany, State University of New York Press, 1974, pp. 27–31.

103. *The Faith and Practice of al-Ghazali*, trans. W. M. Watt, London, Allen & Unwin, 1953, p. 20.

104. G. Leff. *Paris and Oxford Universities in the Thirteenth and Fourteenth Centuries*, New York, Wiley, 1968.

105. Ibid., pp. 3ff.

106. Ibid., chap. 3. J. le Goff, *Les intellectuels au moyen age*, Paris, Seuil, 1957. Mundy, *Europe in the High Middle Ages*, chap. 13.

107. A. Momigliano, 'Freedom of Speech in Antiquity', in *Dictionary of the History of Ideas*, ed. P. P. Wiener, New York, Scribner's, 1973. G. Glotz, *The Greek City*, New York, Knopf, 1929. M. P. Nilsson, *Greek Piety*, London, Oxford University Press, 1948. E. R. Dodds, *The Greeks and the Irrational*, Berkeley/Los Angeles, University of California Press, chap. 6, esp. pp. 189–95. W. K. C. Guthrie, *The Fifth-Century Enlightenment*, Cambridge, Cambridge University Press, 1964, chap. 9. R. Hackforth,

The Composition of Plato's Apology, Cambridge, Cambridge University Press, chap. 4.

108. R. Levy, *The Social Structure of Islam*, chaps. 1 (on social equality), 2 (on the status of women). G. E. von Grunebaum, *Medieval Islam*, 2nd ed., Chicago, Chicago University Press, 1953, chap. 6. B. Lewis, *Race and Color in Islam; Islam*, vol. 2, sect. 6 (sources on 'Race, Religion, and Condition of Servitude'); 'The Faith and the Faithful', In *The World of Islam*, esp. pp. 27–31. F. Rosenthal, *The Muslim Concept of Freedom*. S. W. Baron, *A Social and Religious History of the Jews*, 2nd ed., vol. 5, New York, Columbia University Press, 1957, chap. 24 ('Socioreligious Controversies').

109. Rosenthal, op. cit., p. 122.

110. Baron, op. cit., p. 83.

111. *Summa Theologiae* 2/2, qu. 11, art. 2; as quoted in R. W. Southern, *Western Society and the Church*, Harmondsworth, Penguin Books, 1970, p. 17. On heresy see Mundy, *Europe in the High Middle Ages*, chap. 14.

112. See, e.g., J. M. Robertson, *A Short History of Free Thought*, New York, 1957. J. B. Russell, *Dissent and Reform in the Early Middle Ages*, Berkeley/Los Angeles, New York, Wiley, 1971. H. Kamen, *The Rise of Tolerance*, Weidenfeld & Nicolson, 1967. R. H. Popkin, *The History of Scepticism from Erasmus to Descartes*, rev. ed., Assen (Netherlands), Van Gorcum, 1960 chap. 6. P. Hazard, *The European Mind*, New Haven, Yale University Press, 1953, chap. 4. J. S. Spink, *French Free-Thought from Gassendi to Voltaire*, London, Athlone Press, 1960.

113. A. F. Wright, *Buddhism in Chinese History*. K. K. S. Ch'en, *Buddhism in China; The Chinese Transformation of Buddhism*. R. R. Robinson, *The Buddhist Religion*, chap. 4. E. Zürcher, *The Buddhist Conquest of China*, rev. ed., vol. 1, Leiden, Brill, 1971, chap. 5. P. Demieville, 'Le bouddhisme chinois', in H.-C Puech, *Histoire des religions*, vol. 1, Paris, Gallimard, 1970. E. O. Reischauer, *Ennin's Travels in T'ang China*, New York, Ronald Press Co., 1955.

114. Ch'en, *The Chinese Transformation of Buddhism*, pp. 31, 45.

115. S. Weinstein, 'Imperial Patronage in the Formation of T'ang Buddhism', in A. F. Wright and D. Twitchett, ed., *Perspectives on the T'ang*, New Haven, Yale University Press, 1973, pp. 266–67.

116. Ibid., pp. 284–8.

117. Ibid., pp. 291–305.

118. Reischauer, op. cit., pp. 225–7.

119. *The Brihadaranyaka Upanishad* 4/4/5, trans. Swami Madhavananda, Mayavati, Almore (Himalayas), Advaita Ashrama, 1934 (date of preface), p. 712.

120. S. Dasgupta, *A History of Indian Philosophy*, chap. 4 ('General Observations on the Systems of Indian Philosophy'). J. Sinha, *A History of Indian Philosophy*, vol. 1, Calcutta, Sinha Publishing House, 1956, chap. 6 ('The Common Ideas in Indian Philosophy').

121. Radhakrishnan and Moore, *A Source Book in Indian Philosophy*. p. 247; from K. Misra, *Prabodhya-candroyada*.

122. Radhakrishnan and Moore, op. cit., p. 237; from J. Bhatta, *Tattvopaplavasimha*, chap. 7.

123. E. Deutsch, *Advaita Vedanta*, chap. 6, esp. pp. 86–94.

124. J. Sinha, *Indian Psychology*.

125. B. K. Matilal, *The Navya-Nyaya Doctrine of Negation*, Cambridge (Mass.), Harvard University Press, 1968, p. x. S. C. Vidyabhusana, *A History of Indian Logic*. I. M. Bochenski, *History of Fomal Logic*. C. L. Hamblin, *Fallacies*. D. H. Ingalls, *Materials for the Study of Navya-Nyaya Logic*, Cambridge (Mass.), Harvard University Press, 1951. B. K. Matilal, *Epistemology, Logic, and Grammar in Indian Philosophical Analysis*, The Hague, Mouton, 1971. W. and M. Kneale, *The Development of Logic*, London, Oxford University Press, 1962; unlike Bochenski and Hamblin, confined to Europe. For a contemporary attempt to evaluate Indian epistemology, see N. K. Devaraja, 'What Is Living and What Is Dead in Traditional Indian Philosophy?' *Philosophy East and West* 26/4 (1976), pp. 432–44.

126. For contemporary analyses of ancient Chinese logic, see *The Journal of Chinese Philosophy* 2/3 (1975).

127. Algebra rather than geometry: H. J. J. Winter, in A. L. Basham, ed., *A Cultural History of India*, p. 154. Venturesomeness: M. Kline, *Mathematical Though from Ancient to Modern Times*, New York, Oxford University Press, 1972, p. 199.

128. 'China' 2 ('Chinese Craftsmanship'), in H. Osborne, ed., *The Oxford Companion to the Decorative Arts*, London, Oxford University Press, 1975. M. Medley, *The Chinese Potter*, Oxford, Phaidon, 1976.

129. R. Hartwell, 'A Revolution in the Chinese Iron and Coal Industries During the Northern Sung, 960–1126 A.D'. *The Journal of Asian Studies* 21 (1961–2), pp. 153–62; reprinted in J. T. C. Liu and P. J. Golas, eds., *Change in Sung China*, Lexington (Mass.), Heath & Co., 1969.

130. Ping-ti Ho, *The Ladder of Success in Imperial China*, New York, Columbia University Press, 1962; reprinted New York, John Wiley, 1964, pp. 41–2. 'The Birth of Capitalism in China', in E. Balasz, *Chinese Civilization and Bureaucracy*, New Haven, Yale University Press, 1964. B. Wiethoff, *Introduction to Chinese History*, pp. 66–8.

131. J. R. Levenson, *Confucian China and Its Modern Fate*, vol. 1 Berkeley, University of California Press, chap. 1. B. Nelson, 'Science and Civilizations "East" and "West": Joseph Needham and Max Weber', in R. J. Seeger and R. S. Cohen, eds., *Philosophical Foundations of Science*, Dordrecht, Reidel, 1974. B. Nelson, 'On Orient and Occident in Max Weber', *Social Research* 43/1 (Spring, 1976). J. Needham, 'Poverties and Triumphs of the Chinese Scientific Tradition', in A. D. Crombie, ed., *Scientific Change*, London, Heinemann, 1963.

132. M. Postan and E. E. Rich, eds., *The Cambridge Economic History of Europe*, vol. 2, Cambridge, Cambridge University Press, 1952, pp. 203, 344–6, 435, 439, 461–9. C. M. Cipolla, *Before the Industrial Revolution*, London, Methuen, 1976. A. Pacey, *The Maze of Ingenuity: Ideas and Idealism in the Development of Technology*, Cambridge (Mass.), MIT Press, 1976. P. Rossi, *Philosophy, Technology and the Arts in the Early Modern Era*, New York, Harper & Row, 1970.

133. J. Needham, *Science and Civilization in China*, vol. 1, Cambridge, Cambridge University Press, pp. 109–111 (110 quoted).

134. M. Loewe, *Everyday Life in Early Imperial China*, London, Batsford, 1968, pp. 105–107. See also J. Needham, *Clerks and Craftsmen in China and the West*, Cambridge, Cambridge University Press, p. 230.

135. Needham, *Science and Civilization in China*, vol. 1, pp. 235–7.

136. S. Nakayama, 'The Empirical Tradition: Science and Technology in China', in A. Toynbee, ed., *Half the World: The History and Culture of China*. I have not seen S. Nakayama and N.

Sivin, eds., *Chinese Science: Explorations of an Ancient Tradition*, Cambridge (Mass.), MIT Press, 1973. For India see W. E. Clark's article in *The Legacy of India*, and H. J. J. Winter's more recent one in *A Cultural History of India*. For a fresh, untechnical comparison of surgical medicine in the different civilizations, see G. Majno, *The Healing Hand: Man and Wound in the Ancient World*, Cambridge (Mass.), Harvard University Press, 1975, esp. pp. 310–12.

137. M. Purver, *The Royal Society: Concept and Creation*, London, Routledge & Kegan Paul, 1967.

138. J. Ehrard, *L'idée de nature en France à l'aube des lumières*, Paris, Flammarion, 1970, chap. 2.

139. A. R. Hall, *From Galileo to Newton 1630–1720*, London, Collins, 1963, chap. 5. A. C. Crombie and M. Hoskin, 'The Scientific Movement and Its Influence, 1610–1650', in J. P. Cooper, ed., *The New Cambridge History*, vol. 4, Cambridge, Cambridge University Press, 1970; 'The Scientific Movement and the Diffusion of Idea, 1688–1715', in J. S. Bromley, ed., *The New Cambridge History*, vol. 6, 1970. M. W. Flynn, *Origins of the Industrial Revolution*, London, Longman, 1966. A. E. Musson, ed., *Science, Technology and Economic Growth in the Eighteenth Century*, London, Methuen, 1972.

140. *After Babel: Aspects of Language and Translation*, London, Oxford University Press, 1975, p. 473.

3. *Scriptures, Revelation, and Reason*

1. E. Gilson, *History of Christian Philosophy in the Middle Ages*, New York, Random House, 1955, p. 45.

2. *Saint Augustine's Confessions*, trans. R. S. Pine-Coffin, Harmondsworth, Penguin Books, 1974. See also E. Gilson, *The Christian Philosophy of Saint Augustine*, London, Gollancz, 1961.

3. *On Free Will*, in *Augustine: Earlier Writings*, trans. J. H. S. Burleigh, London, SCM Press, 1953, p. 137.

4. *St. Anselm's Proslogion*, trans. M. J. Charlesworth, London, Oxford University Press, 1965, p. 115.

5. *Cur Deus Homo*, in *St. Anselm: Basic Writings*, trans. S. N. Deane, La Salle, Open Court, 1962, p. 177.

6. Ibid., p. 179.

7. Ibid.

8. Averroes, *On the Harmony of Religion and Science*, trans. G. F. Hourani, London, Luzac, 1961, chap. 2.

9. Averroes, *On the Harmony of Religion and Philosophy*, trans. G. F. Hourani, p. 61.

10. E. Gilson, *Reason and Revelation in the Middle Ages*, New York, Scribner's, 1952, chap. 2.

11. St. Thomas Aquinas, *On the Truth of the Catholic Faith* (*Summa Contra Gentiles*), *Book Two: Creation*, trans. J. F. Anderson, Garden City, Doubleday (Image Books), 1956, chap. 4. See also, E. Gilson, *History of Christian Philosophy in the Middle Ages*, p. 708, note 90.

12. E. Gilson, *The Christian Philosophy of St. Thomas Aquinas*, London, Gollancz, 1957, p. 10. P. Granet, *Thomism: An Introduction*, New York, Harper & Row, 1967.

13. St. Thomas Aquinas, *Summa Theologiae*, vol. 1, trans. T. Gilby, London, Blackfriars, 1964, la/1/1, p. 7.

14. Ibid., pp. 7–9.

15. Ibid., la/1/2, pp. 11–13.

16. Ibid., 1a/1/5, p. 19.

17. Ibid.

18. Ibid.

19. St. Thomas Aquinas, *On the Truth of the Catholic Faith* (*Summa Contra Gentiles*), *Book One: God*, trans. T. Gilby, Garden City, Doubleday (Image Books), 1955, chaps. 2–3.

20. G. E. M. Anscombe and P. T. Geach, *Three Philosophers*, Oxford, Blackwell, 1963, p. 125.

21. *The Mahabharata*, vol. 1, trans. J. A. B. van Buitenen, Chicago, Chicago University Press, 1973, 1/1/190–210, pp. 30–1.

22. Jaimini, *Mimamsa Sutra, Śabara-Bhasya*, vol. 1, trans. G. Jha, Baroda, Gaekwad's Oriental Series, Oriental Institute, 1933–1936, 2/1/13–29 and the commentary of Sabara, pp. 190–9.

23. Ibid., 1/2/1, p. 51. The phrase quoted is from an initial argument that is later refuted; but the phrase itself is characteristic of Mimamsa and is accepted without objection.

24. Ibid., 1/3/9, p. 100.

25. Ibid., e.g., 1/3/29, p. 115.

26. Ibid., e.g., 1/4/1, p. 125; 1/4/29–30, pp. 164–66; 1/22–29, pp. 195–99.

27. *The Tattvasangraha of Śantaraksita with the Commentary of*

Kamalaśila, vol. 2, trans. G. Jha, Baroda, Gaekwad's Oriental Series, Oriental Institute, 1939, chap. 24, sections 2104–5.

28. Ibid., sections 2086, 2346–7.

29. *Tarkasamgraha*, trans. S. K. Śastri, Madras, p. 253. Based on the *Nyaya Sutra* 1/1/7.

30. Ibid., p. 260.

31. *Gautama's Nyayasutras with Vatsyayana Bhasya*, trans. G. Jha, Poona, Oriental Book Agency, 1939, 2/2/13–39.

32. *The Vedanta Sutras of Badarayana with the Commentary of Śankara*, vol. 1, trans. G. Thibaut, New York, Dover, 1962, 1/1/4, p. 22; 2/1/2, p. 295.

33. *Eight Upanishads with the Commentary of Śankaracarya*, 2 vols., trans. S. Gamghirananda, Calcutta, Advaita Ashrama, 1966. See Śankara's commentary on the *Mandukya Karika* 2/32.

34. *The Vedanta Sutras*, vol. 1, 1/1/14, p. 22; 2/1/6, p. 306.

35. For Śankara's criticism of Buddhist Idealism, see, e.g., *The Vedanta Sutras*, vol. 1, 2/2/28–31.

36. *The Brihadaranyaka Upanishad, with the Commentary of Śankaracarya*, trans. S. Madhavananda, Calcutta, Advaita Ashrama, 1965, 2/1/20, pp. 301–2.

37. See Paul's first letter to the Corinthians 1/20–25.

38. Averroes, *On the Harmony of Religion and Philosophy*, p. 44.

39. Ibid., p. 48.

40. Ibid., p. 49.

41. B. de Spinoza, *Tractatus Theologico-Politicus*, trans. R. H. M. Elwes, 2nd ed., London, George Bell and Sons, 1887, chap. 2., pp. 33–34.

42. G. E. von Grunebaum, in Grunebaum, ed., *Logic in Classical Islamic Culture*, Wiebaden, Otto Harrassowitz, 1970, pp. 6–7.

43. See, e.g., 'The Veracity of Scripture from Philo to Spinoza,' in H. A. Wolfson, *Religious Philosophy*, Harvard, Harvard University Press, 1961.

44. J. K. Shryock, *The Origin and Development of the State Cult of Confucius*, New York/London, The Century Co., 1932. D. H. Smith, *Chinese Religions*, chap. 11 ('The State Cult of Confucianism'). D. H. Smith, *Confucius*, London, M. T. Smith, 1973. H. S. Galt, *A History of Chinese Educational Institutions*, vol. 1, London, Probsthain, 1951. C. O. Hucker, *China's Imperial Past*, pp. 362–76, on Neo-Confucianism. W. T. de Bary, 'A Reappraisal of Neo-Confucianism', in A. F. Wright, *Studies in Chinese Thought*,

Chicago, Chicago University Press, 1953. *To Acquire Wisdom: The Way of Wang Yang-ming*, trans. J. Ching, New York, Columbia University Press, 1976, pp. 2–20. L. C. Goodrich, *The Literary Inquisition of Ch'ien Lung*, Baltimore, Waverly Press, 1935.

45. *To Acquire Wisdom*, p. 18.

46. Tu Wei-ming, *Neo-Confucian Thought in Action: Wang Yang-ming's Youth (1472–1509)*, Berkeley/Los Angeles, University of California Press, 1976, p. 161.

47. Goodrich, *The Literary Inquisition*, pp. 88–92.

48. Ibid., p. 35.

49. Ibid., p. 49.

4. *Modes of Argument*

1. J. Passmore, *Philosophical Reasoning*, London, Duckworth, 1961, seems to be unique in considering philosophical argument as it is actually carried on. Although relevant only in part, the history of logic by I. M. Bochenski, which deals with Indian as well as European logic, and that by W. and M. Kneale provide a convenient starting point. C. L. Hamblin, *Fallacies*, with a chapter on India, may also be recalled here.

Perhaps the quickest insight into the strengths and weaknesses of European philosophical argument is by way of the attacks of the sceptics on it. For ancient Greece the obvious beginning is *Sextus Empiricus*, translated in four volumes by R. G. Bury, and published by Harvard University Press and William Heinemann, in the Loeb Classical Library, from 1939 to 1949. C. L. Stough, *Greek Skepticism*, Berkeley/Los Angeles, University of California Press, 1968, makes a good companion to Sextus. A. Naess, *Scepticism*, London, Routledge & Kegan Paul, begins with Sextus and goes on to scepticism in general. The most sceptical Indian philosophers, in a sense, were the Carvaka, some of whose doctrines have been mentioned in the text, while Buddhism, in particular, played a sceptical role in relation to Hindu philosophy and to any belief in the metaphysical reality of the physical world or the self. For China, see the bibliography of the following section.

2. See S. C. Vidyabhusana, *A History of Indian Logic*, and T. Stcherbatsky, *Buddhist Logic*, especially the introduction, and volume 2.

3. For the complexity of the outcome, see, e.g., E. A. Moody, *The Logic of William of Ockham*, London, Sheed & Ward, 1935, and for exercises in sophisms and their solution, J. Buridan, *Sophisms on Meaning and Truth*, trans. T. K. Scott, New York, Appleton-Century-Crofts, 1966. The attitude of Islamic philosophers toward (Greek) logic is represented in F. Rosenthal's anthology, *The Classical Heritage in Islam*, London, Routledge & Kegan Paul, 1975, pp. 75–82, and in the same author's *Knowledge Triumphant*.

4. K. H. Potter, *Presuppositions of India's Philosophies*, pp. 59–92, gives an introduction to Indian logic and *tarka*. A more detailed but not always clear treatment of Indian philosophical reasoning may be found in S. Bagchi, *Inductive Reasoning: A Study of Tarka and Its Role in Indian Logic*, Calcutta, no publisher mentioned, 1953. See also Vidyabhusana, Bochenski, Hamblin, and E. A. Solomon (bib. note 43 to chap. 2).

5. *Milinda's Questions*, vol. 1, trans. I. B. Horner, London, Luzac, 1963, pp. 38–39.

6. J. van Ess, 'The Logical Structure of Islamic Theology,' in G. E. von Grunebaum, ed., *Logic in Classical Islamic Culture*, 1970, Wiesbaden, Otto Harrassowitz, p. 25.

7. K. Battacharya, trans., 'The Dialectical Method of Nagarjuna', *Journal of Indian Philosophy* 1 (1971), pp. 220–21.

8. B. K. Matilal, 'Reference and Existence in Nyaya and Buddhist Logic,' *Journal of Indian Philosophy* 1 (1970), pp. 90, 103. On the 'empty subject' in Indian philosophy see K. H. Potter, 'Realism, Speech-Acts and Truth-Gaps in Indian and Western Philosophy,' *Journal of Indian Philosophy* 1 (1970), pp. 13–21; A. C. S. McDermott, 'Empty Subject Terms in Late Buddhist Logic,' ibid., pp. 22–29; and J. L. Shaw, 'Empty Terms: The Nyaya and the Buddhists', ibid. 2 (1974), pp. 332–43.

9. *The Vedanta Sutras of Badarayana with the Commentary by Śankara*, vol. 1, trans. G. Thibaut, New York, reprinted Dover, 1962, 2/2/28, pp. 420–21.

10. A. C. Graham, 'The Logic of the Mohist Hsiao-Ch'ü', in *Toung Pao* 51(1964), p. 38. See also J. Cikocki, 'on Standards of Analogical Reasoning in the Late Chou', *Journal of Chinese Philosophy* 2 (1975), pp. 325–57.

11. J. Chmielewski, 'Notes on Chinese Logic', *Rocznik Orientalistyszny*, in 6 parts, 1962–66; quotation from part 4, p. 108.

12. A. Waley, *Three Ways of Thought in Ancient China*, London, Allen and Unwin, 1939, p. 194.

13. D. C. Lau, 'On Mencius' Use of the Method of Analogy in Argument,' in *Mencius*, trans. D. C. Lau, Harmondsworth, Penguin Books, 1970.

14. *Mencius*, trans. Lau, 6/A3.

15. E.g., K. Lorenz, *Studies in Animal and Human Behaviour*, vol. 2, London, Methuen, 1971; W. H. Thorpe, *Animal Nature and Human Nature*, London, Methuen, 1974; E. O. Wilson, *Sociobiology*, Cambridge (Mass.), Harvard University Press, 1975.

16. See, e.g., G. E. R. Lloyd, *Polarity and Analogy: Two Types of Argumentation in Early Greek Thought*, Cambridge, Cambridge University Press, 1966; and the same author's 'Analogy in Early Greek Thought', in the *Dictionary of the History of Ideas*, ed. P. P. Wiener. See also ibid., A. Maurer, 'Analogy in Patristic and Medieval Thought'.

17. D. C. Lau, 'On Mencius' Use of the Method of Analogy,' p. 261. See A. C. Graham, note 9 above.

18. Maurer, *Dialectica*, ed. De Ryk, p. 442.

19. Lau, ibid., p. 262.

20. J. S. Cikoski, op. cit., p. 345.

21. Ibid., p. 346.

22. Ibid., p. 354.

23. A. Flew, 'Introduction', *Essays in Logic and Language*, 1951; quoted in C. W. K. Mundle, *A Critique of Linguistic Philosophy*, London, Oxford University Press, 1970, p. 113.

24. G. Ryle, *The Concept of Mind*, London, Hutchinson, 1949, p. 119.

25. *Mencius*, trans. Lau, 6/A4, p. 161.

26. L. Wittgenstein, *Philosophical Investigations*, Oxford, Blackwell, 2nd ed., 1958, paras. 37, 553.

27. Ibid., para. 593.

28. A. C. Graham, 'The Logic of the Mohist Hsiao-ch'ü,' pp. 38–39.

29. A. C. Graham, 'Chuang-tzu's Essay on Seeing Things as Equal,' *History of Religions* 9 (1969–1970).

30. *The Complete Works of Chuang Tzu*, trans. B. Watson, New York, Columbia University Press, 1968, chap. 6, p. 77.

31. Ibid., chap. 2, p. 45. Graham, 'Chuang-tzu's Essay,' p. 147.

32. L. Wittgenstein, *On Certainty*, Oxford, Blackwell, para. 115.

33. Ibid., para. 506.

34. E.g., *The Tattvasangraha of Śantarksita with the Commentary of Kamalaśila*, trans. G. Jha, Baroda, Baroda Oriental Institute, 1939.

35. Chung-ying Cheng, 'On Zen (Ch'an) Language and Zen Paradoxes,' *Journal of Chinese Philosophy* 1 (1973).

36. B. de Spinoza, *Tractatus Theologico-Politicus*, trans. A. G. Warnham, London, Oxford University Press, 1958, chap. 17, p. 153.

37. J. Passmore, op. cit.

38. M. Granet, *La pensée chinoise*, Paris, Albin Michel, 1934, p. 4.

39. Passmore, op. cit., is a notable exception.

40. J. M. Bochenski, 'Logic and Ontology', *Philosophy East and West* 3 (1974), p. 279.

41. Hamblin, *Fallacies*, especially 'The Concept of Argument.'

42. From Descartes' third Meditation, in *Descartes, Philosophical Writings*, trans. G. E. M. Anscombe and P. T. Geach, Edinburgh, Edinburgh University Press, 1954.

43. From the commentary to the 4th century *Padarthadharmasamgraha*, in Radhakrishnan and Moore, *A Source Book in Indian Philosophy*, p. 401.

44. See D. Leslie, 'Argument by Contradiction in Pre-Buddhist Chinese Reasoning', Australian National University Occasional Papers, No. 4, Canberra, 1964.

45. Granet, op. cit., p. 336.

46. From the 3rd century B.C. philosophical encyclopedia, the *Lu Shih Ch'un Ch'iu* 18/4. See Cikoski, op. cit., p. 325.

47. *Mencius* 6/B6, pp. 175–76.

48. *Padarthadharmasamgraha, Source Book*, p. 406.

49. *Phaedo* 76 c-d, trans. R. Hackforth, Cambridge, Cambridge University Press, 1955.

50. *Padarthadharmasamgraha*, op. cit., pp. 404–5.

51. *Mencius* 2/A6, p. 82 (cf. Tau's introduction, p. 18).

52. *Wei Shih Erh Shih Lun*, trans. C. H. Hamilton, New Haven, American Oriental Society, 1938, p. 45.

53. *Sextus Empiricus*, vol. 2, *Against the Logicians*, sentences 73–74, p. 39.

54. *Mo Tzu*, chap. 43 (explanations of the canon, B).

55. *Sextus Empiricus*, vol. 1, *Outlines of Pyrrhonism*, sentences 164–69, p. 95.

56. *Chuang Tzu*, chap. 2. See Watson's translation, pp. 46. 48, and Graham's (note 28, above), pp. 157, 155.

57. For the 'two world's argument', see Passmore, op. cit.

58. *Sarvadarśanasamgraha*, Radhakrishnan and Moore, *Source Book*, p. 231.

59. R. J. McCarthy, *The Theology of Al-Ashari*, Beirut, Imprimerie Catholique, 1953, pp. 20–21.

60. *Chuang Tzu*, Ssu Pu Pei Yao edition, 1/25a/2–3.

61. Nagarjuna, *Vigrahavyavartani*, trans. Bhattacharya (note 6 above), chap. 33, p. 240.

62. *Sextus Empiricus*, vol. 1, p. 11.

63. Nagarjuna, op. cit., chap. 2, pp. 222–23; chaps. 21–22, pp. 232–33.

64. *Chuang Tzu*, chap. 2. See Graham's translation (note 28 above), p. 157.

5. 'Cogito Ergo Sum': Descartes, Augustine, and Śankara

1. Descartes, *Oeuvres philosophiques*, 3 vols., ed. F. Alquié, Paris, Garnier, 1963–1973. *The Philosophical Works of Descartes*, 2 vols., trans. E. S. Haldane and G. R. T. Ross, Cambridge, Cambridge University Press, corrected reprint, 1931–1934.

On the argument at issue the following have been consulted: E. Gilson, *René Descartes, Discours de la méthode*, 2nd ed., Paris, Vrin, 1926, pp. 292–301; and the same author's *Etudes sur le rôle de la pensée médiévale dans la formation du système cartésien*, chap. 2. Lefèvre, *La bataille du 'cogito'*, Paris, Presses Universitaires, 1960, pp. 211–28. L. J. Beck, *The Metaphysics of Descartes: A Study of the Meditations*, London, Oxford University Press, 1965, pp. 77–92. F. Alquié, *La découverte métaphysique de l'homme chez Descartes*, Paris, Presses Universitaires, 1966, pp. 180–200. J. Hintikka, 'Cogito, Ergo Sum: Inference or Performance', in W. Doney, ed., *Descartes: A Collection of Critical Essays*, Garden City (Anchor Books), Doubleday, 1967. G. Rodis-Lewis, *L'oeuvre de Descartes*, 2 vols., Paris, Vrin, 1971, esp. vol. 1, pp. 237–69. H. Caton, *The Origin of Subjectivity: An Essay on Descartes*, New Haven, Yale University Press, pp. 123–25, chap. 5.

2. *Discourse on Method*, part 4: Haldane and Ross, vol. 1, p. 101.

3. *Meditations*, part 2: Haldane and Ross, vol. 1, p. 150.

4. *Principles of Philosophy*, part 1, principle 7: Haldane and Ross, vol. 1, p. 221.

5. 'The Search After Truth' (Eudoxus, close to end): Haldane and Ross, vol. 1, pp. 324–25.

6. On the addition of *existo*, see Gilson, *Discourse*, p. 292.

7. 'Reply to Objections II', 'Thirdly': Haldane and Ross, vol. 2, p. 38.

8. *The Nichomachean Ethics of Aristotle*, trans. D. Ross, London, Oxford University Press, 9/9, 1170a/29–33. See also the similar passage in *De Sensu* 448a/27, which reads, in the Oxford translation, '(If) it is conceivable that a person should, while perceiving himself or aught else in a continuous time, be at any instant unaware of his own existence,—as well as of his seeing and perceiving. . . .' My remark on the Greek sceptics is based on the statement attributed to Pyrrho, 'For we admit that we see, and we recognize that we think this or that, but how we see or how we think we know not'. Diogenes Laertius, *Lives of Eminent Philosophers*, vol. 2, trans. R. D. Hicks, London, Heinemann (Loeb Classics), bk. 10, p. 103.

9. *The City of God*, trans. M. Dods, Bk. 11, chap. 26; in *Basic Writings of Saint Augustine*, vol. 2, ed. W. H. Oates, New York, Random House, 1948, p. 168.

10. *On the Trinity*, trans. A. W. Haddan, rev., bk. 15, chap. 12; in *Basic Writings*, vol. 2, p. 849.

11. F. Copelston, *A History of Philosophy*, vol. 2, London, Burns Oates & Washbourne, 1953, pp. 62–63.

12. To Colvius, Nov. 14, 1640: Descartes, *Philosophical Letters*, trans. A. Kenny, London, Oxford University Press, 1970, pp. 83–84.

13. *Rules for the Direction of the Mind*, rule 3: Haldane and Ross, vol. 1, p. 7. See also Rodis-Lewis, op. citl, vol. 1, pp. 91–92, 169–74.

14. *Rules*, rules 12, 4, 9: Haldane and Ross, vol. 1, pp. 41, 10, 28.

15. For this section see the standard histories of Indian Philosophy, and, for a clear general guide, E. Deutsch, *Advaita Vedanta*. E. Deutsch and J. A. B. van Buitenen, *A Source Book of Advaita Vedanta* contains much pertinent material. The fullest exposition of Śankara in English is P. Deussen, *The System of the Vedanta*. The

Vedanta Sutras of Badarayana with the Commentary by Śankara, 2 vols., has been translated by G. Thibaut, 2 vols, London, Oxford University Press; re-printed New York, Dover, 1962. For some details of Śankara's argument, see N. K. Devaraja, *An Introduction to Śankara's Theory of Knowledge*, Varanasi, Matilal Banarsi Dass, 1962.

16. For a summary of different views of self-perception, see J. Sinha, *Indian Psychology*, vol. 1, chap. 12.

17. On Śankara's date, see T. M. P. Mahadevan, *Gaudapada: A Study in Early Advaita*, 3rd. ed., Madras, University of Madras, pp. 2–16, where it is argued that an earlier date, such as 655–687 A.D., is required to maintain the plausible position that Gaudapada was Śankara's teacher's teacher. Ingalls, too, suggests an earlier date, following the Japanese scholar, Nakamura, who points out that Śankara quotes Dharmakirti, who flourished in the seventh century. D. H. H. Ingalls, 'Śankara's Arguments Against the Buddhists,' *Philosophy East and West* 3 (1954), p. 292, note 3.

18. *Vedanta Sutras* 1/1/1, vol. 1, p. 14.

19. Ibid. 2/2/28, vol. 1, pp. 423–24.

20. Ibid. 2/3/17, vol. 2, p. 14.

21. *Upadeśasahasri*, in Deutsch & van Buitenen, pp. 92–93.

22. Devaraja, op. cit., pp. 177–81.

23. *The Bridhadaranyaka Upanishad with the Commentary of Śankaracharya*, trans. Swami Madhavananda, Mayavati, Almora. Swami Vireswarananda Advaita Ashrama, 1934, 4/3/7, p. 612.

24. Ibid., p. 614.

25. P. Deussen, *The System of the Vedanta*, pp. 71, 136.

26. *Brihadaranyaka Upanishad* 2/4/9.

27. Deussen, op. cit., p. 136. For the 'procession' stated systematically, *Vedanta Sutras*, vol. 1, pp. xxiv-xxv; 1/3/30, pp. 211–13; vol. 2, 2/4/20, pp. 96–98. Another passage stating that Brahman needs no sense organs, ibid. 1/1/5, pp. 50–51.

28. E. Deutsch, *Advaita Vedanta*, p. 51; and N. K. Devaraja, *An Introduction to Śankara's Theory of Knowledge*, pp. 180–82. Devaraja says, 'There can be no doubt that Śankara believed that even the conditioned self had a self-proved existence. . . Śankara sometimes confuses the pure cit with the conditioned self. . . Śankara's recognition of the objectivity of the self is only half-hearted.'

Śankara sometimes uses the word *ahamkara*, which means *I* but does not refer to the cosmic Atman.

29. On Augustine and Plotinus, see E. Gilson, *History of Christian Philosophy*, New York, Random House, 1955, pp. 71–73.

30. E. Bréhier, *The Philosophy of Plotinus*, Chicago, University of Chicago Press, 1958. J. M. Rist, *Plotinus' The Road to Reality*, Cambridge, Cambridge University Press, 1967. R. T. Wallis, *Neoplatonism*, London, Duckworth, 1972. A. H. Armstrong, 'Plotinus', in *The Cambridge History of Later Greek and Early Medieval Philosophy*, ed. A. H. Armstrong, Cambridge, Cambridge University Press, 1967. *Plotinus*, 3 vols., trans. A. H. Armstrong, London, Heinemann (Loeb Library), Plotin, *Ennéades*, trans. E. Bréhier, Paris, Les Belles Lettres, 6 vols., 1954.

31. *Enneads* 6/9/1.

32. Ibid. 1/1/1, 3/9/7, 6/7/36 (On negative definition).

33. Ibid. 5/9/8.

34. Ibid. 3.8/11.

35. Ibid. 3/6/7: Armstrong trans., vol. 3, p. 241.

36. Ibid.: Armstrong trans., vol. 3, p. 242.

37. Ibid. 4/3/18–19, 4/4/1–2.

38. For the Greek terms, see F. E. Peters, *Greek Philosophical Terms: A Historical Lexicon*, New York, New York University Press, 1967. For *epibole*, not included in this lexicon, see *Enneads* 6/7/38/25–26.

39. Bréhier, *The Philosophy of Plotinus*, chap. 7; and 'Les analogies de la création chez Çankara et chez Proclus', in his *Etudes de philosophie antique*, Paris, Presses Universitaires, 1955. R. T. Wallis, *Neoplatonism*, p. 15. A. H. Armstrong, *The Cambridge History of Later Greek and Early Medieval Philosophy*, pp. 7–8; 201, note 1. For bibliography, see J. F. Staal, *Advaita and Neoplatonism: A Critical Study in Comparative Philosophy*, Madras, University of Madras, 1961.

40. E. R. Dodds, 'Traditional and Personal Achievement in the Philosophy of Plotinus', *Journal of Roman Studies* 50 (1960), pp. 1–7; and E. R. Dodds, "Bewusst' und 'Unbewusst' bei Plotin', together with the following discussion, in *Les Sources de Plotin*, Geneva, Foundation Hardt, 1960.

6. *Between Fatalism and Causality: Al-Ash'ari and Spinoza*

1. See, e.g., M. S. Seale, in his *Muslim Theology*, London, 1964, esp. p. 55, who sides with Jahm ibn Safwan against Ahmad ibn Hanbal, and see the scholars opposed to Seale.

2. Of the books meant for the series, the following have appeared: *Crescas' Critique of Aristotle, The Philosophy of Spinoza, Philo, The Philosophy of the Church Fathers*, and *The Philosophy of the Kalam*.

3. 'Nicolaus of Autrecourt and Ghazzali's Argument against Causality', *Speculum* 44 (1968), pp. 234–38.

4. See, e.g., W. J. Courtnay, 'The Critique on Natural Causality in the Mutakallimun and Nominalism', *Harvard Theological Review* 66 (1973), pp. 77–94, an important article.

5. See, e.g., D. B. McDonald, 'Continuous Re-Creation and Atomic Time in Muslim Scholastic Theology', *Isis* 9 (1927), pp. 326–44, in particular for his hint on the possibility of Indian influences. A more elaborate discussion of such influences is given in S. Pines, *Beiträge zur islamischen Atomenlehre*, Berlin, 1936.

6. For the influence of Alexander's *De Fato* on Islamic thought, see J. Guttmann, 'Das Problem der Willensfreiheit bei Hasdai Crescas und den islamischen Aristotelikern', in *Jewish Studies in Memory of G. A. Kohut*, New York, 1935, pp. 326–49 and appendix.

7. H. A. Wolfson, *The Philosophy of Spinoza*, vol. 1, Cambridge (Mass.), Harvard University Press, 1934, p. 417.

8. W. M. Watt. 'Al-Ashari', *Encyclopedia of Islam*, 2nd ed. See also the good biography in M. Allard, *Le probléme des attributs divins dans la doctrine d'al-Ashari*, Beirut, Imprimerie Catholique, 1965, pp. 25–72. 'I never saw', from Ibn 'Asakir, in R. J. McCarthy, *The Theology of Al-Ash'ari*, Beirut, Imprimerie Catholique, 1953, p. 169.

9. *Kitab Maqalat al-Islamiyyin*, ed. H. Ritter, 2nd ed., Wiesbaden, 1963. *Al-Ibana 'an 'usual al-Dianah*, English trans., W. C. Klein, *The Elucidation of Islam's Foundation*, New Haven, American Oriental Society, 1940. *Kitab al-Luma'*, ed. with English trans., R. J. McCarthy, op. cit.

10. From al-Khatib al-Baghdadi, *Ta'rikh Baghdad*, vol. 2, p. 346,

in A. S. Tritton *Muslim Theology*, London, Royal Asiatic Society, 1947, p. 166.

11. *Ethics* 1/32, cor.; 2/48; 5/42, schol. & demonst.

12. Quran 42/49–50, 16/76, 2/28. Here and later I use the translation by N. Dawood, rev. ed., Penguin Books, 1959. For al-Ash'ari on causality, see: McDonald, op. cit. (note 5), pp. 326, 328; W. M. Watt, *Free Will and Predestination in Early Islam*, London, 1948, p. 14; al-Ashari, *Kitab al-Luma'*; and the analysis of *Kitab al-Luma'* in R. M. Frank, 'The Structure of Created Causality', *Studia Islamica* 25 (1966), pp. 13–75.

13. 'Life, power, knowledge', A. J. Wensinck, *The Muslim Creed*, Cambridge, Cambridge University Press, 1932. p. 188. For the Mu'tazilah, see Al-Khayyat, *Kitab al-Intisar*, ed. and French trans., A. Nader, *Le Livre du Triomphe et de la Réfutation d'ibn al-Rawandi l'Hérétique*, Beirut, Les Lettres Orientals, 1957, p. 16 (French trans., p. 8). The confining interpretation, which was ascribed by ideological opponents to the outstanding Mu'tazilite, Abn al-Hudhait al-'Allaf (d. 841 or 850), is not very convincingly waived by the Mu'tazilite author of the book noted just above.

14. McCarthy, op. cit. (note 8), p. 9.

15. Al-Ash'ari, *Kitab al 'Luma'*, sec. 87. For atomism, see Maimonides, *The Guide of the Perplexed*, trans. S. Pines, Chicago, University of Chicago Press, 1963, 1/73. For a good account, see McDonald, op. cit. (note 5). See also Al-Ghazali, *Mishkat al-Anwar*, Cairo, 1343 H., pp. 113–14.

16. Al-Ghazali, *Ihya' Ulum al-Din*, Cairo, 1348 H.. vol. 4, p. 213.

17. M. Fakhry, *Islamic Occasionalism*, London, Allen & Unwin, 1958, p. 77.

18. Al-Ash'ari, *Maqalat*, pp. 549, 313. H. A. Wolfson, *The Philosophy of the Kalam*, Harvard, Harvard University Press, 1976, pp. 550, 581.

19. Ibn Hazm, *Al Fisal fi al-Milal*, Cairo, 1317–1327 H., part 2, pp. 12–17. Wolfson, op. cit., pp. 584–86.

20. Wolfson, op. cit., pp. 586–89.

21. *Cogitata Metaphysica* 1/1, 1/3. *Ethics* 1/11, 2nd proof (W. H. White trans., rev. A. H. Stirling).

22. H. A. Wolfson, *The Philosophy of Spinoza*, vol. 1, p. 198, including note 1.

23. *Ethics* 2/48 & demonst. See also, Wolfson, *Spinoza*, vol. 2, pp. 172–73.

24. A. J. Wensinck, *The Muslim Creed*, p. 211; and *Al-Fikh al-Akbar I*, art. 5, trans. Wensinck, p. 190.

25. *Short Treatise* 2/16, par. 3, note 2.

26. *Ethics* (White-Stirling trans.) 1/11, 3rd proof, schol.; 1/24 & cor. Wolfson, *Spinoza*, vol. 1, pp. 203–204.

27. *Al-Fikh al-Akbar II*, art. 2, trans. Wensinck, op. cit., p. 188.

28. Wolfson, *Spinoza*, vol. 1, pp. 400–410.

29. Muslim, *Kadar*, trad. 16, Wensinck, op. cit., p. 54. Abu Da'ud, *Sunnah*, b. 16, trans. Wensinck, op. cit., pp. 108–109.

30. W. M. Watt, *Free Will and Predestination in Early Islam*, p. 20.

31. H. A. Wolfson, *The Philosophy of the Kalam*, pp. 573–75.

32. For a bibliography and for a brief but full description of al-Nazzam, see H. Laoust, *Les schismes dans l'Islam*, Paris, Payot, 1965, pp. 103–104. For al-Nazzam's views on this subject, see Wolfson, *Kalam*, p. 575.

33. *Averroes' Tahafut al-Tahafut* (*The Incoherence of the Incoherence*), trans. S. van den Bergh, vol. 2, London, Luzac, 1954, p. 65, notes 4 and 5 to p. 90 of vol. 1.

34. See Maimonides (note 15), 1/73.

35. See al-Ghazali, *Tahafut al-Falasifah*, pp. 512, 514; English trans. in *Averroes' Tahafut al-Tahafut* (note 33), vol. 1, pp. 313, 314, and note 4 to p. 313 (vol. 2, p. 173). Wolfson, *Kalam*, p. 572. Abd al-Qahir al-Baghdadi, *Usul al-Din*, Mecca, 1349 H., pp. 169ff.; and al-Iji, *Mawaqif*, ed. Sörensen, Leipzig, 1848, pp. 175ff.

36. *Tractatus Theologico-Politicus*, in *Spinoza Opera*, ed. C. Gebhardt, Heidelberg, 1925, vol. 3, pp. 81, 83–84.

37. Watt, *Free Will* (note 12), p. 20. There is a vast literature on the influence or possible influence of Christianity, e.g., M. S. Seale, *Muslim Theology*, London, 1964, who tries to show the identity of many Islamic with Christian ideas.

38. Quran (Dawood trans.) 18/28, 18/16.

39. Watt, *Free Will*, p. 73. Al-Ashari, *Maqalat*, p. 428.

40. Watt, *Free Will*, p. 74. Al-Ashari, *Maqalat*, p. 401.

41. Watt, *Free Will*, p. 104. Wolfson, *Kalam*, p. 667.

42. The customary attitude is reflected, e.g., in McCarthy, *The Theology of al-Ashari*, p. 58 note 15. The recent analysis I refer to is that of Frank (note 12).

43. Frank, op. cit., p. 25. McCarthy, op. cit., p. 58. Frank, p. 27, quotes al-Baghdadi, *Al-Farq baina al-Firaq*, Cairo, 1948, p. 110,

where the example is given that although Allah is the creator of pregnancy he is not to be called 'impregnator of women'.

44. Al-Ash'ari, *Kitab al-Luma'*, sec. 87, trans. McCarthy, p. 56. Cf. Frank, op. cit., pp. 32, 34.

45. Al-Ash'ari, *Al-Luma*, secs. 107, 96–99, trans. McCarthy pp. 67–68, 62–64.

7. *Two Metaphysical Concepts: Li and Idea*

1. H. Baumann, 'Mythos in ethnologischer Sicht', part 2, *Studium Generale* 9 (1959), pp. 596–97. For old but informative introductions, see 'Names (Egyptian)', 'Names (Indo-European)', 'Names (Primitive)', and 'Words (Sumerian and Babylonian)' in Hastings' *Encyclopaedia of Religion and Ethics*. Further, for the powers of word and name in Egypt, see S. Morenz, *Egyptian Religion*, London Methuen, 1973, pp. 163–66; and R. T. Rundle Clark, *Myth and Symbol in Egypt*, London, Thames & Hudson, 1959, pp. 72–73, 75–80. For India, see L. Renou, 'Les pouvoirs de la parole dans le Rigvéda', in his *Etudes védiques et paninéennes*, vol. 1, Paris, de Boccard, 1955; and D. S. Ruegg, *Contributions à l'histoire de la philosophie linguistique indienne*, Paris, de Boccard, 1963, chap. 1. For Africa, see P. Alexandre, 'Names', in G. Balandier & J. Maquet, *Dictionary of Black African Civilization*, New York, Leon Amiel, 1974. For the Hebrews, see T. Boman, *Hebrew Thought Compared with Greek*, London, SCM Press, 1960, pp. 58–67.

2. S. Kramer, *The Sumerians*, Chicago, University of Chicago Press, 1963, pp. 91–96. See also 'The Myth of Zu', an Akkadian myth of the theft of the Tablets of Destinies by the bird-god, Zu, in J. B. Pritchard, ed., *Ancient Near Eastern Texts*, 3rd ed., Princeton, Princeton University Press, 1969, pp. 111–12.

3. W. Müller, 'Les religions des Indiens d'Amérique de Nord', in W. Krickeberg et al., *Les religions Amerindiennes*, Paris, Payot, 1962, pp. 260 (on the Iroquois of Ontario), 228–29 (on the Algonquins of Canada).

4. Quoted from Haile, 'Soul Concepts of the Navaho', *Annali Lateranensi* 7 (1943), pp. 59–94; in H. Lander, 'Two Athapascan Verbs of "Being," ' in J. W. M. Verhaar, *The Verb 'Be' and Its Synonyms*, Dordrecht, Reidel, 1967, p. 56.

5. To philosophers, the most immediately intelligible and use-

ful introduction is B. K. Matilal, *Epistemology, Logic, and Grammar in Indian Philosophy*, The Hague, Mouton, 1971. Other extensive summaries may be found in R. R. Dravid, *The Problem of Universals in Indian Philosophy*, Delhi, Motilal Banarsidass, 1972; D. N. Shastri, *Critique of Indian Realism: A Study of the Conflict Between the Nyaya Vaiśesika and the Buddhist Dignaga School*, Agra, Agra University, 1964; and J. Sinha, *Indian Psychology*, vol. 1, pp. 163–98.

6. Out of the extensive literature on Plato's Ideas, I have been helped particularly by D. Ross, *Plato's Theory of Ideas*, London, Oxford University Press, 1951; I. M. Crombie, *Plato's Doctrines*, vol. 2, London, Routledge & Kegan Paul, 1963, pp. 247–472; and some of the articles in *Plato: A Collection of Critical Essays*, ed. G. Vlastos, vol. 1, Garden City, Doubleday (Anchor Books), 1971.

7. So far as I know, Prof. D. C. Lau, of the London School of Oriental and African Studies, is the first person to have used the passage in question in order to compare *Li* with *Idea*. He made the comparison in an unfortunately still unpublished paper, which I was privileged to read some years ago. I should like to take this opportunity to thank him for many stimulating talks about Chinese philosophy and philosophy in general.

8. See Fung's *History of Chinese Philosophy*, vol. 1, p. 177; Chan's *Source Book*, pp. 260–61 (to which may be added his more detailed article on *Li* in his *Neo-Confucianism etc.: Essays by Wing-tsit Chan*, New Haven, Oriental Society, 1969); and Liao's *Han Fei Tzu*, vol. 1, London, Probsthain, 1939, pp. 191–95.

9. I have used the *Han Fei-tzu Chi Shih*, edited by Ch'en Ch'i-yu, Shanghai, 1974.

10. For the emendation, see op. cit., p. 370, under 'Tao Hung Ching'.

11. This quotation from the *Lao Tzu*, chap. 1, is translated in accord with the interpretation suggested below. It does not imply that the *Lao Tzu* must be read in this way; but see *Tao Te Ching*, trans. J. J. L. Duyvendak, London, John Murray, 1954.

12. See H. F. Cherniss, 'The Philosophical Economy of Ideas', in *Plato: A Collection of Critical Essays* (cited in note 6, above).

13. *Phaedo* 103d, as translated in R. Hackforth, *Plato's Phaedo*, Cambridge, Cambridge University Press, 1955.

14. See A. Wedberg, 'The Theory of Ideas', in *Plato: A Collection* . . . .

15. *The Republic* 518, 517, as translated by H. D. P. Lee, Harmondsworth, Penguin Books, 1955.

8. 'Dream-world' Philosophers: Berkeley and Vasubandhu

For Berkeley, I have used *The Works of George Berkeley, Bishop of Cloyne*, ed. A. A. Luce and T. E. Jessop, London, Nelson. Page references for *Philosophical Commentaries*, earlier called *Commonplace Book*, are to vol. 1, 1948, while page references to *Principles of Human Knowledge* and *Three Dialogues between Hylas and Philonous* are to vol. 2, 1949.

1. Bu-ston, *The Jewelry of Scripture*, vol. 2 (of 2 vols. in 1 binding), trans. E. Obermiller, Heidelberg, M. Walleser, 1932, pp. 143–44.

2. 'Asanga', *Encyclopedia of Buddhism*, vol. 2, ed. G. P. Malasekera, Ceylon, Government of Ceylon, 1966, pp. 135–36; from *The Life of Vasubandhu by Paramartha*, trans. J. Takakusu, *T'oung-pao* (1904).

3. *Three Dialogues*, 1st dialogue, p. 201.

4. *Wei Shih er Shih Lun or The Treaties in Twenty Stanzas on Representation Only*, trans. C. H. Hamilton, New Haven, American Oriental Society, 1938. The twenty stanzas and excerpts of the commentary are reprinted in Radhakrishnan and Moore, *A Source Book in Indian Philosophy*.

5. *Principles*, sec. 43, p. 58.

6. Ibid., sec. 116, p. 93.

7. *Philosophical Commentaries*, entries 864–65, p. 102.

8. *Principles*, sec. 98, p. 83.

9. *Philosophical Commentaries*, entries 67, 72, p. 14.

10. *Principles*, sec. 75, p. 73.

11. Ibid., sec. 18, p. 48.

12. *Philosophical Commentaries*, entry 823, p. 98.

13. *Principles*, sec. 33, p. 54.

14. Ibid., sec. 30, p. 53.

15. *Three Dialogues*, 3rd dialogue, p. 235.

16. *Principles*, secs. 30–31, pp. 53–54; secs. 146–48, pp. 107–109.

17. *Three Dialogues*, 3rd dialogue, pp. 230–31.

18. *Principles*, sec. 106, p. 87.

19. *Philosophical Commentaries*, entry 433, p. 54.

20. *Three Dialogues*, 3rd dialogue, p. 241.

21. *Philosophical Commentaries*, entry 675, p. 82.

22. Ibid., entry 715, p. 87.

23. Ibid., entry 290, p. 36.

24. *Principles*, sec. 93, p. 81.

25. See Paravahera Variranana Mahathera, *Buddhist Meditation in Theory and Practice*, Colombo, M. D. Gunasena & Co., 1962, p. 458.

9. The Possibility of Knowledge: Kant and Nagarjuna

1. *Immanuel Kant's Critique of Pure Reason*, trans. N. K. Smith, London, Macmillan, 1933, A 760, p. 606.

2. D. Hume, *A Treatise of Human Nature*, ed. L. A. Selby-Bigge, Oxford, Clarendon Press, 1888, 1/3/5, p. 84.

3. Ibid., 1/4/6, p. 252.

4. Ibid., p. 261.

5. Kant, op. cit., A 122, p. 145.

6. Ibid., A 334, p. 323.

7. Ibid., A 828, p. 650.

8. K. N. Jayatilleke, *Early Buddhist Theory of Knowledge*, London, Allen & Unwin, 1963, pp. 445–9.

9. Buddhaghosa, *The Path of Purification (Visuddhimagga)*, trans. Bhikkhu Nyanamoli, Berkeley, Shambala, 1976 (originally Colombo (Ceylon), R. Semage, 1956), 18/22–24.

10. N. Mahathera, *Guide Through the Abhidhamma Pitaka*, 2nd. ed., rev. by N. Thera, Colombo, Baudha Sahita Sabha (Buddhist Literature Society), 1957, pp. 2–3.

11. Nagarjuna, *Mulamadhyamikakarika (Didactic Verses of the Middle Doctrine)*, trans R. H. Robinson, *Early Madhyamika in India and China*, Madison, University of Wisconsin Press, 1967, 7/30, 7/31; p. 44.

For complete translations of this work of Nagarjuna, see F. J. Streng, *Emptiness*, Nashville, Abdingdon Press, 1967; and K. A. Inada, *Nagarjuna*, Tokyo, The Hokeido Press, 1970. On Nagarjuna's philosophy, see: Th. Stcherbatsky, *The Conception of Buddhist Nirvana*, Leningrad, 1927; reprint The Hague, Mouton & Co., 1965. T. V. Murti, *The Central Philosophy of Buddhism*, London, Allen & Unwin, 1955. K. V. Ramanan, *Nagarjuna's Philosophy*, Rutland (Vermont), C. E. Tuttle for the Harvard-Yenching Institute, 1966. M. Sprung, ed., *The Problem of Two Truths in Buddhism and Vedanta*, Dortmund, Reidel, 1973.

12. Nagarjuna, op. cit., 15/9, p. 41.
13. Ibid., 20/16, p. 41; 20/19, p. 42.
14. Ibid., 27/3, p. 44.
15. Ibid., 27/9, p. 45.
16. Ibid., 24/24, p. 46.
17. Ibid., 24/25, p. 46.
18. Ibid., 16/10, p. 47.
19. Ibid., 18/7, p. 59.

Bibliography

The nature of this bibliography is dictated by the fact that it accompanies a critical introduction to comparative philosophy. As befits an introduction, reliable introductory books are pointed out and emphasis is laid on books in the English language; but the need to be critical has led to the inclusion of some of the more important books in French and German. Critical comments have usually been brief, but have now and then been extended when an author with great influence on the subject has been characterized. Heavy documentation would have been inappropriate to the authors' purpose, but the documentation given should be adequate to judge and perhaps extend their statements.

The present, general bibliography is divided into ten parts, as follows: I-Other Comparative Studies; II-Comparative Philosophy; III-India: General Background; IV-India: Religion and Philosophy; V-India: Philosophy; VI-China: General Background; VII-China: Religion and Philosophy; VIII-China: Philosophy; IX-Islam: General Background; X-Islam: Philosophy.

The bibliographical notes contain a number of brief, more specialized bibliographies. Books listed in the general bibliography are referred to in abbreviated form. Likewise, books listed in chapter-section bibliographies are referred to in abbreviated form in the references of the same or immediately succeeding chapter-sections.

I Other Comparative Studies

Although comparative philosophy has been developing rather slowly and in the face of a certain resistance among philosophers, comparative studies have been pursued in many fields during the past few decades. It would seem excessive to take space here to provide even minimal bibliographies in these fields, which include comparative art, comparative literature, comparative mythology, comparative religion, comparative linguistics, comparative law, and comparative or cross-cultural or, as they are sometimes called, transcultural psychology, psychiatry, and sociology. Books in some of these fields will be recalled only later, when they are relevant to the subjects under discussion; but it would ungrateful not to at least mention Max Weber, the most powerful thinker among the comparativists.

Because history furnishes a background for comparative studies of all kinds, including philosophy, it may be best to be a little more specific about it.Apart from the works of Oswald Spengler, which are still sometimes reprinted, and those of Arnold Toynbee, world histories have appeared one after the other. These histories include the *Historia Mundi*, published in Berne; the *Histoire universelle* (part of the *Encyclopédie de la Pléiade*) and the *Histoire générale des civilisations*, both published in Paris; the *Propyläen Weltgeschichte*, published in Frankfurt and Berlin; and the still unfinished *History of Mankind: Cultural and Scientific Development*, published in London for an international commission set up by UNESCO. W. H. McNeill's one-volume synthesis, *The Rise of the West*, published by Chicago University Press, 1963, should also be mentioned.

Of the multi-volume histories, the *Histoire générale*, which stresses culture, is perhaps the best integrated—most of its volumes were written by only one or two authors. The UNESCO *History of Mankind* is organized in sections, including extensive ones on religion and philosophy, that invite comparisons. It often lacks intellectual tension, however. Volume III, *The Great Medieval Civilizations*, London, Allen & Unwin, 1975, with chapters not only on religion and philosophy, but on languages and writing systems, and on learning and education, is particularly helpful.

II Comparative Philosophy

Despite the slow development of comparative philosophy, comprehensive books dealing with it have, of course, been published. There is even a comprehensive bibliography to guide students, J. C. Plott and P. D. Mays, *Sarva-Darśana-Sangraha: A*

Bibliographical Guide to the Global History of Philosophy, Leiden, Brill, 1969. It contains lively comments and 'A Synchronological Chart to the Global History of Philosophy'.

As notable examples of general or comparative histories of philosophy, the following ten, which I put into chronological order, may be mentioned:

1. G. W. F. Hegel, *Lectures on the History of Philosophy*, the three volumes of which appeared in English between 1892 and 1895. Hegel's scholarship was considerable, even, for his time, in Eastern philosophy, though his system of ranking philosophies was obviously Procrustean. He regarded Oriental thought as primarily religious, troubled, and obscure, and the Chinese and Hindus as so abstract in their philosophizing that they were unable to create a determinate, adult philosophy. He read translations of the *Five Classics*, mainstays of Chinese tradition, and of Confucius, Lao Tzu, Chuang Tzu, and Mencius; and he translated or paraphrased into German passages from H. T. Colebrooke's translations from Sanskrit into English.

2. P. Deussen, *Allgemeine Geschichte der Philosophie*, 7 vols., Leipzig, Brockhaus, 1894–1917. Two volumes of this history of philosophy, each over seven hundred pages, were devoted to India and China. The pages on India represented a substantial pioneering effort, while the appendix of some hundred pages devoted to China and India was hardly more than an afterthought. Two volumes taken from Deussen's history have been published in English, *The Philosophy of the Upanishads*, 1906, reprinted New York, Dover, 1966; and *The System of the Vedanta*, 1912, reprinted New York, Dover, 1973.

3. P. Masson-Oursel, *Comparative Philosophy*, New York, Harcourt Brace, 1926. A sketch, translated from the French, with a pioneering quality. Masson-Oursel was a Sinologist with a substantial interest in Indian and in Western thought, and his approach was lucid and rational, though neither detailed nor otherwise intensive. His subsequent book, *La philosophie en Orient*, Paris, Presses Universitaires, 1938, a supplement to Bréhier's *Histoire de la Philosophie*, is very broad in scope and makes a number of interesting formulations, but is too rapid and philosophically thin. This is a pity, because Masson-Oursel seems to have been capable of writing an intelligent comparative history of philosophy.

4. G. Misch, *The Dawn of Philosophy*, London, Routledge & Kegan Paul, 1950, first published in German in 1926. An examination of the beginnings of philosophy in China, India, and Greece, this book stresses the human situations and emotions in which philosophy begins. The projected second volume seems not to have appeared. Misch makes a genuine attempt to see in what the doctrines from the different cultures resemble and differ. He approaches the texts with respectful immediacy, but without specialized knowledge.

5. C. A. Moore, ed., *Philosophy East and West*, Princeton, Princeton University Press, 1944, the record of a conference held at the University of Hawaii. Though a heterogeneous assemblage, it may serve as an introduction to the subject, for it gives a brief and simple sketch of Indian philosophy, and a longer, though equally simple, sketch of Chinese philsosophy, together with essays in comparison. Moore has edited a number of other relevant collections of essays.

6. S. Radhakrishnan, ed., *History of Philosophy: Eastern and Western*, 2 vols., London, Allen & Unwin, 1957. In spite of its name, this work does not attempt any serious comparisons, and its pages on Chinese and Japanese philosophy are so brief that they seem to be there for the sake of no more than a perfunctory courtesy. However, the information given on later Indian philosophy is relatively hard to come by.

7. K. Jaspers, *The Great Philosophers*, 2 vols., New York, Harcourt & Brace, 1962, 1965, translated from the first of three projected German volumes, published in 1957. As the name indicates, this book is not a history; but it is meant to be genuinely comparative and to deal with Eastern philosophers on a par with the Western. Independent, lucid, humane, and easy on the mind.

8. P. T. Raju, *Introduction to Comparative Philosophy*, Lincoln (Nebraska), University of Nebraska Press, 1962. A Neo-Vedantist view, tentative and schematic by turns. The concluding moral is that 'comparative philosophy should recognize the complementary nature of the three dominant attitudes'.

9. H. Nakamura, *Ways of Thinking of Eastern Peoples: India-China-Tibet-Japan*, Honolulu, East-West Center Press, 1964. An unusually learned book that makes many generalizations, it is thought-provoking though not rigorously thought-out. As might

be expected, the section on Japan, which is the longest, is the most interesting.

10. B. Parain, ed., *Histoire de la philosophie*, of the *Encyclopédie de la Pléiade*, vol. 1, Paris, Gallimard, 1970; vol. 3, 1974. Sequential rather than comparative, but lucid, authoritative, and uniquely compact. This is so far the only general history of philosophy to have a fair and competent representation of non-European philosophy. The first volume, edited by B. Parain, contains the major articles on Chinese, Indian, and related philosophy, and on Islamic philosophy. The third, final volume, edited by Y. Belavel, contains compact chapters on later Chinese, Indian, and Islamic philosophy. There are comparative charts, brief bibliographies, and exemplary indices. H.-C. Puech, ed., *Histoire des religions*, vol. 1, Paris, Gallimard, 1970, has much the same virtues as the corresponding history of philosophy. It gives a close, perhaps inseparable background to philosophizing in the cultures dealt with here. P. Demiéville's chapter on Buddhism in China is exceptionally rich, compact, and knowledgeable.

A number of additional books may be mentioned along with the above. Though they deal with limited or special subjects, they make free use of comparisons between East and West:

I. M. Bochenski, *History of Formal Logic*, Notre Dame, University of Notre Dame Press, 1961. For the first time, apparently, a serious history of logic contains a serious summary of Indian logic and an attempt to compare it with the Western varieties.

C. L. Hamblin, *Fallacies*, London, Methuen, 1970, has a clear chapter on 'The Indian Tradition'.

W. Kaufmann, *Religion in Four Dimensions*, New York, Reader's Digest Press, 1976. Kaufmann blends objective description, personal experience, and unafraid appraisal. The book contains many of his beautiful photographs.

T. Ling, *A History of Religion East and West*, London, Macmillan, 1968, is an even-handed and scholarly history of both Eastern and Western religion, perhaps the first single-author history of religion of which this can be said.

T. R. V. Murti, *The Central Philosophy of Buddhism*, London, Allen & Unwin, 1955. Murti makes comparisons with Kant, Hegel, and Bradley in particular.

B.-A. Scharfstein, *Mystical Experience*, New York, Bobbs-

Merrill and Oxford, Blackwell, 1973; as paperback, Penguin (U.S.), 1974.

F. Staal, *Exploring Mysticism*, Harmondsworth, Penguin, 1975. Staal is more favourable than Scharfstein to the metaphysical claims of mysticism, but, like him, insists on maintaining scholarly and intellectual standards. He concentrates on Hindu and Buddhist mysticism.

Th. Stcherbatsky, *Buddhist Logic*, 2 vols, 1932, reprinted 'S-Gravenhage, Mouton, 1958. The author compares freely and perhaps rashly with Leibniz, Bergson; Mach, Mill, Russell; Locke, Kant, Bergson, Russell; Brentano, Mill; Aristotle; and Hegel. The comparisons may not always be convincing, but this is a work of genuine intellectual stature.

Attention should also be drawn to at least three journals that deal with comparative philosophy: *Philosophy East and West*, the *Journal of Indian Philosophy*, and the *Journal of Chinese Philosophy*. The first is published by the University of Hawaii Press, and the two others by the Reidel Publishing Co., Dordrecht, Holland.

III India: General Background

W. T. de Bary, ed., *Sources of Indian Tradition*, New York, Columbia University Press, 1958. A well-edited, newly translated anthology, covering as much of Indian culture, including philosophy, as could be expected in a single volume.

A. L. Basham, *The Wonder that Was India*, London, Sidgewick & Jackson, 3rd ed., 1967. A relatively full account of ancient Indian history and culture, containing many of the author's own translations.

A. L. Basham, ed., A cultural History of India, London, Oxford University Press, 1977. This successor to *The Legacy of India* is fuller and, of course, more up-to-date.

G. C. Garratt, ed., *The Legacy of India*, London, Oxford University Press, 1937.

A History of India, Harmondsworth, Penguin Books. Vol. 1, R. Thapar, 1966; vol. 2, P. Spear, 1965. Brief, clear, reliable.

D. D. Kosambi, *The Culture and Civilisation of Ancient India*, London, Routledge & Kegan Paul, 1965. Kosambi tries to rethink the early history of India in mildly Marxist terms, that is, with attention to economics, sociology, and class structure. Undocumented, but based upon substantial knowledge.

R. Lannoy, *The Speaking Tree: A Study of Indian Culture and Society*, London, Oxford University Press, 1971. An attempt, compounded in almost equal measure of prosaic knowledge and of imagination, to understand India by way of its art, family life, social structure, value system and attitudes, and sacred in relation to secular authority.

R. C. Majumdar et al., *History and Culture of the Indian People*, 6 vols., Banares, 1951–1960. A full-scale history, written by Indian scholars, with substantial attention to culture, including philosophy.

S. A. Tyler, *India: An Anthropological Perspective*, Pacific Palisades (Calif.), Goodyear Publishing Co., 1973. A sketch of Indian history with emphasis on religion and philosophy, continuing with chapters on tribes and peasants, family and kinship, and the caste system.

IV India: Religion and Philosophy

J . N. Farquhar, *An Outline of the Religious Literature of India*, London, Oxford University Press, 1920. A clear, well-arranged, accurate outline with an extensive bibliography. Quite readable.

Die Religionen Indiens, 3 vols., Stuttgart, Kohlhammer. Vol. 1, J. Gonda, *Veda und älterer Hinduismus*, 1960; vol. 2, J. Gonda, *Der jüngere Hinduismus*, 1963; vol. 3, A. Bareau, W. Schubring and C. Fürer-Haimendorf, *Buddhismus-Jainismus-Primitivvölker*, 1963. A comprehensive, scholarly summary of existing knowledge.

L. Renou, J. Filliozat & others, *L'Inde Classique*, 2 vols. Vol. 1, Paris, Payot, 1947; vol. 2, Paris, Imprimerie Nationale, 1953. This compressed, scholarly summary of a great deal that is known of ancient Indian culture lays the stress on religion and philosophy. The second volume is a brief compendium of practically the whole of Indian philosophy. Its extensive section on Buddhist philosophy is especially notable. Parts of this work have been translated into English and published in India by Susil Gupta (India) Private Limited, Calcutta.

R. H. Robinson, *The Buddhist Religion: A Historical Introduction*, Belmont (Calif.), Dickenson Publishing Co., 1970. Brief, lively, philosophically well-informed. Includes Buddhism in China and elsewhere.

India: Philosophy

The larger histories of Indian philosophy cite many books, of course, but the only separate comprehensive bibliography to date is the *Encyclopedia of Indian Philosophies*, vol. 1, K. H. Potter, *Bibliography*, Delhi, Motilal Banarsidass, 1970; published for the American Institute of Indian Studies. This bibliography contains the names (and publication data) alone of relevant books and articles, arranged in classified lists.

There is no satisfactory full-scale history of Indian thought. The two best-known works are those by S. Dasgupta and S. Radhakrishnan. These have been so influential that I give them a somewhat extended characterization.

S. Dasgupta, *A History of Indian Philosophy*, 5 vols., London, Cambridge University Press, 1922–1955. Dasgupta came from a family known for its Sanskrit learning. 'In his early years, between five and eight, while he did not know any Sanskrit, he showed certain remarkable gifts of answering philosophical and religious questions in a very easy and spontaneous manner. He could demonstrate the various Yogic postures (*asanas*); and used to pass easily into trance states, while looking at the river Ganges or listening to some Kirtan song. He was visited by hundreds of learned men and pious saints at his father's residence and was styled 'Khoka Bhagwan' (Child God)'.

Dasgupta was interested, not alone in Sanskrit learning, but also in modern science. At Sanskrit College, in Calcutta, where he studied, he was noticeable for his scholarship and for his personal habits. 'He took no care of his clothes and hair; he studied on a mat with a pillow for a table; and his place was littered with books and papers'. He preferred to learn everything by himself. In Chittagong College, where he taught for many years, 'he continued his studies for fourteen hours or more a day, in spite of the teasing of his friends'.

Urged to go to Europe to study European philosophy, Dasgupta spent some time in Cambridge, where he studied with McTaggert and came into contact with Moore and Ward. As a result, his whole intellectual life changed. 'My mind became more critical', he said, 'not only towards European philosophy but also towards Indian philosophy as a whole. I had thrown off the shackles of Hegel long before I went to England, but Einstein's theory of relativity, and *anekanta* relativism of the Jains, and the realists with whom I came in contact in England, finally drew my mind away from all sorts of Absolutism in philosophy. I was getting sick of Absolutism for a long time but lacked the initiative to make an open revolt. My life in Cambridge invigorated me, and the main fruit that I reaped there was courage'.

In spite of this change, Dasgupta was convinced that 'most of the problems that are still debated in modern philosophical thought occurred in more or less divergent form to the philosophers of India. Their discussions, difficulties and solutions, when properly grasped in connection with the problems of our own times may throw light on the course of the process of the future reconstruction of modern thought'. (*History*, vol. 1, p. viii.)

Dasgupta originally planned his history to be complete in one volume. It began on a scale like Radhakrishnan's, but grew more detailed, and more fragmented, as it proceeded. The subject exerted a stronger and stronger hold on him. He collected material from all parts of India and came upon a mass of both published and unpublished texts, so that the scale of his work inevitably changed. 'He spared no pains and underwent a tremendous amount of drudgery to unearth the sacred buried treasures'.

In a memoir of his life, his wife wrote that during his stay in England and his lecture tours in Europe 'he won the reputation in debate of being an almost invincible controversialist'. Renou, the celebrated Indologist, one of whose books is mentioned above, later wrote to him, 'While you were among us, we felt as if a Śankara or a Patanjali was born again and moved amongst us'. Like Śankara, Dasgupta was sharp in controversy. 'In the meetings of the Aristotelian Society he was a terror to his opponents, his method of approach being always to point out their errors [a method, as one of the chapters of the present book shows, that was characteristic of ancient Indian philosophy]. He inflicted this treatment on many other scholars, particularly Stcherbatsky and Levy'.

Dasgupta suffered from eye trouble and, during the last twelve years of his life, was confined to bed by acute heart trouble; but he continued his painstaking work on his history, often directly from manuscript sources. His history remained unfinished; and he died just after he had begun an extended account of his own philosophy. (The foregoing account is based on the memoir by Dasgupta's wife in vol. 5 of his history, and on his essay, 'Philosophy of Dependent Emergence', in Radhakrishnan and Muirhead, *Contemporary Indian Philosophy*.)

Unlike Radhakrishnan, Dasgupta austerely forgoes comparisons with Western philosophy. Most of the ground in his history is therefore without landmarks for the Westerner. But it contains a substantial proportion of material for which there is no substitute in Western languages. Although, as it progresses, it tends to become a series of almost disconnected paraphrases, this history embodies an extended act of devotion.

S. Radhakrishnan, *Indian Philosophy*, 2 vols., London, Allen & Unwin, vol. 1, 1929; vol. 2, 1931. This history is lucidly written, though parts of the second volume require close reading. The style is generally easy, dramatic, and at times rather rhetorical and even sentimental (see, e.g., vol. 1, p. 353). The second volume is often more detailed than the corresponding part of Dasgupta's history and cites the sources more frequently.

Radhakrishnan, who became a father figure in Indian intellectual life and, furthermore, the President of India, wrote that in his youth he had believed that the political downfall of India was the result of the intellectual incoherence and ethical unsoundness of Hinduism. Depressed by this idea, but curious, he went on to study Indian thought and came to the conclusion that it had really been affirmative and soundly ethical. He therefore denied the usual charge, levelled, for example, by Albert Schweitzer (in his book, *Indian Thought and Its Development*, Holt, 1936) that Indian philosophy renounced the improvement of life and tried to destroy the desire to live. He also argued (in *Eastern Religions and Western Thought*, Oxford University Press, 2nd ed., 1940) that Hinduism was basically tolerant, while Judaism, Christianity, and Islam were by nature destructively intolerant.

The virtues and defects of Radhakrishnan's history have been put in the following words:

'Radhakrishnan's determination to defend Indian philosophy, and the Vedantic system, in particular, provided his work with a coherence and forcefulness that the subject desperately needed at the time, but it also bore an apologetic tone from which his writings are never entirely free. Just as his master's thesis "was intended to be a reply to the charge that the Vedanta system had no room for ethics" (p. 40), naturally all of his subsequent writings are an attempt to establish idealism and Hinduism as a solution to the conflict of philosophical and religious ideals'.

Radhakrishnan was inspired by Tagore's poetic vision, itself inspired by the vision of Maurice Maeterlinck and others, and by Bergson's praise of intuition. He emphasized 'the humanistic character of Vedanta and its cognitive certainty based on intuition'. He interpreted Vedanta and therefore Hinduism at, he believed, its best as an expression of the ideal of integration within the self and of the personal with the universal self. (R. A. McDermott, *Radhakrishnan: Selected Writings on Philosophy, Religion, and Culture*, New York Dutton, 1970. Quotations from pp. 13, 14–15. The account of Radhakrishnan's beliefs in youth is from the first page of his essay, 'The Spirit in Man', in S. Radhakrishnan and J. H. Muirhead, eds., *Contemporary Indian Philosophy*, New York, Macmillan, 1936. For a critique of Radhakrishnan's conception of Indian thought, see P. Hacker, 'Ein Prasthanatraya-Kommentar des Neuhinduismus. Bemerkungen zum Werk Radhakrishnans,' *Orientalische Literaturzeitung*, 56. Jahrgang, Nos. 11/12, Nov./Dec. 1961, pp. 566–76.)

Writing retrospectively of his history, Radhakrishnan acknowledged that 'the writer may at times allow his personal bias to determine his presentation. His sense of proportion and relevance will not be shared by others. His work at best will be a personal interpretation, and not an impersonal survey'. (From 'Fragments of a Confession', in P. S. Schilpp, ed., *The Philosophy of S. Radhakrishnan*, New York, Tudor Publishing Co., 1952, p. 11; as quoted in McDermott, op. cit.)

Radhakrishnan's preference for the Vedanta, which he tended to identify with Indian philosophy in general, led, not unnaturally, to an inadequate account of Buddhist philosophy.

T. de Bary, ed., *The Buddhist Tradition in India, China, and Japan*, New York, Random House (Modern Library), 1969, is mostly drawn from de Bary's anthologies of Indian, Chinese, and Japanese tradition. It contains a good deal of philosophy.

E. Deutsch, *Advaita Vedanta: A Philosophical Reconstruction*,

Honolulu, East-West Center Press, 1969. A well-conceived, lucid, and intelligent account of the philosophy of Vedanta.

E. Deutsch and J. A. B. van Buitenen, eds., *A Source Book of Advaita Vedanta*, Honolulu, University of Hawaii Press, 1971.

E. Frauwallner, *Geschichte der indischen Philosophie*, 2 vols. (more were projected), Salzburg, Otto Muller, vol. 1, 1953; vol. 2, 1956. Frauwallner's intention was to write a continuous history reaching up to the present. Instead of describing the Indian systems of philosophy as a completed dogmatic whole, he made the risky but worthwhile attempt to show their development. He supposed that the creative impulse had been stronger during the period of growth of Indian Philosophy than during the period when complete but mainly retrospective compendia were compiled. The translation into English by V. M. Bedekar, 2 vols, Delhi, Motilal Banarsidass, 1973, is essentially accurate but unfortunately clumsy.

E. Frauwallner, *Die Philosophie des Buddhismus*, Berlin, Akademie Verlag, 1956. The only anthology of Buddhist philosophy, as distinct from Buddhism in general.

M. Hiriyanna, *Outlines of Indian Philosophy*, London, Allen and Unwin, 1932. Recommended. One of the briefer, simpler histories in English.

A. B. Keith, *Buddhist Philosophy in India and Ceylon*, London, Oxford University Press, 1923. A history of Buddhist philosophy as a whole.

K. H. Potter, *Presuppositions of India's Philosophies*, New Delhi, Prentice-Hall of India, 1965, is organized by problems. Formally, it is a kind of introduction, Much of it, however, is more natural to someone who knows a good deal about Indian philosophy but would like to perceive it in a more generalizing, fundamental way. The writing is clear but at times perhaps too compressed or too lacking in examples for a beginner. The exposition of Indian logic is particularly interesting (and, if right, clarifying).

S. Radhakrishnan and C. Moore, *A Source Book in Indian Philosophy*, Princeton, Princeton University Press, 1959. The only even somewhat comprehensive anthology of Indian philosophy.

W. Ruben, *Geschichte der indischen Philosophie*, Berlin, Deutscher Verlag der Wissenschaften, 1954, is, like Zimmer, an interesting, idiosyncratic account. Published in East Germany, it apparently could not avoid calling on Engels, Marx, Lenin, Stalin, and Zhdanov to dispense their materialistic logic among the Upanishadic sages. From his earlier studies, we know that Ruben was interested in Indian materialism and logic before he came under the aegis of German Marxism. Here, in his *Geschichte*, he made the Upanishadic sage, Uddalaka, the champion of 'materialism', and then read the whole of the history of Indian philosophy as a struggle of the followers of Uddalaka, the good Materialist, against Yajnevalkya, another Upanishadic sage, seen as the wicked Idealist. Yet Ruben's knowledge was broad-ranging, and his frequent references to social conditions, his use of extra-philosophical sources, whether literary or medical, and his assumption that philosophy had social motivations and effects, all lend his history, compared with others on the same subject, an air of unrarified reality. He was also capable of brief, clear expositions, notably of some of the logicians. In spite, then, of his egregiously conducted warfare, his history is lively and suggestive.

J. Sinha, *Indian Psychology*, 2 vols., Calcutta, Sinha Publishing House. Vol. 1, *Cognition*, second ed., 1958; vol. 2, *Emotion and Will*, 1961. Sinha, the author of a learned history of Indian philosophy, has organized the content of much of Indian philosophy in a uniquely valuable way. In the first volume, for example, all the Indian theories of perception are compared in one chapter, theories of perception of space and movement in a second, and theories of perception of time in a third. The second volume contains chapters on body and self, on degrees of consciousness, on pleasure and pain, on aesthetic emotion, and so on.

N. Smart, *Doctrine and Argument in Indian Philosophy*, London, Allen and Unwin, 1964. Recommended, along with Hiriyanna, as one of the briefer and simpler histories in English.

A. K. Warder, *Indian Buddhism*, Delhi, Motilal Banarsidass, 1970, is well-informed and compendious, and pays substantial attention to philosophy. It has a good bibliography and an excellent index. In English, at least, it is now the best history of Indian Buddhist thought.

H. Zimmer, *Philosophies of India*, New York, Pantheon, 1951, edited by J. Campbell after the author's death, shows an active, rather Jungian imagination. Zimmer was a scholar, but he tended to replace the sometimes unromantic reality with a modernized expansion of old romantic stereotypes.

VI China: General Background

W. T. de Bary, ed., *Sources of Chinese Tradition*, New York, Columbia University Press, 1960. Parallel to the volume on India. Well-chosen, well-edited, and well-translated.

R. Dawson, ed., *The Legacy of China*, London, Oxford University Press, 1964. On Western conceptions of China, on Chinese culture, and on Chinese influence on the world.

W. Eberhard, *A History of China*, 4th rev. ed., London, Routledge & Kegan Paul, 1977. The author's interests, which have been expressed in wide-ranging research. lead him to make sociological analyses, to stress China's reciprocal relationships with her neighbors, and to be generally curious about the life of the 'common man'.

J. K. Fairbank, E. O. Reischauer and A. M. Craig, *East Asia: Tradition and Transformation*, New York, Houghton Mifflin, 1973. A reworked condensation of two earlier volumes, *East Asia: The Great Tradition* and *East Asia: The Modern Transformation*.

J. Gernet, *Le monde chinois*, Paris, Armand Colin, 1972. A historical synthesis made by a distinguished French scholar.

C. O. Hucker, *China's Imperial Past*, Stanford, Stanford University Press, 1975. Maintains the balance between historical narrative and description of the government, of social and economic life, of thought, and of literature and art.

M. Loewe, *Imperial China*, London, Allen & Unwin, 1966. Clear, concise chapters on political, social, and cultural life.

J. Meskill, ed., *An Introduction to Chinese Civilization*, New York, Columbia University Press, 1973. The history of China, followed by essays, each by a specialist, on different aspects of Chinese civilization.

B.-A. Scharfstein, *The Mind of China*, New York, Basic Books, 1974; paperback, Dell, 1974. An introduction, first to traditional family and political life, and then to China's traditional artists, historians, cosmographers, and philosophers.

L. E. and T. K. Stover, *China: An Anthropological Perspective*, Pacific Palisades (Calif.), 1976. A sociologically oriented sketch of Chinese history, followed by chapters, relating mostly to the recent present, on ecology, economics, politics, kinship, stratification, religion, and world view.

A. Toynbee, ed., *Half of the World: The History and Culture of*

China and Japan, London, Thames & Hudson, 1973. Brief, authoritative chapters, extensively illustrated in colour and black-and-white.

VII China: Religion and Philosophy

K. K. S. Ch'en, *Buddhism in China*, Princeton, Princeton University Press, 1964. A relatively full account.

K. K. S. Ch'en, *The Chinese Transformation of Buddhism*, Princeton, Princeton University Press, 1973.

H. Maspero, *Mélanges posthumes sur les religions et l'histoire de la Chine*, Paris, Musée Guimet (Civilisations du Sud), 1950. Vol. 1, *Les religions de la Chine*; vol. 2, *Le Taoisme*. The work of a distinguished scholar.

J. H. Shryock, *The Origin and Development of the State Cult of Confucius*, New York, the Century Co., 1932. Explains the part played by Confucianism in Chinese history, especially from the standpoint of the Chinese government.

D. H. Smith, *Chinese Religions from 1000 B.C. to the Present Day*, New York, Holt, Rinehart & Winston, 1968. Well-informed, outspoken, somewhat unsympathetic to the popular religions of China. Ignores the revolutionary sects that played so important a role in Chinese History.

L. C. Thompson, *Chinese Religion: An Introduction*, Belmont (Calif.), Dickenson Publishing Co., 1969. Brief, modern, anthropologically oriented.

H. Welch, *The Parting of the Way: Lao Tzu and the Taoist Movement*, Boston, Beacon Press, 1957.

A. F. Wright, *Buddhism in Chinese History*, Stanford, Stanford University Press, 1959. A good sketch.

VIII China: Philosophy

The leading historians of Chinese philosophy are Alfred Forke and Fung Yu-lan. Despite their eminence, neither of them succeeded in writing a satisfactory, full-scale history of Chinese philosophy. I add some particularly necessary words of appraisal to the description of Fung's history.

A. Forke's history was issued in three volumes: *Geschichte der alten chinesichen Philosophie*, Hamburg, Friedrichen, 1938; *Ges-*

chichte der mittelalterlichen chinesichen Philosophie, Hamburg, de Gruyter, 1934; *Geschichte der neueren chinesichen Philosophie*, Hamburg, de Gruyter, 1938. Forke's is the most detailed history we have. Of its three volumes, perhaps that on the 'medieval' period is the most valuable. For all of Forke's great learning, the degree of his precision is not up to contemporary sinological standards.

A. Forke, *The World-Conception of the Chinese: Their Astronomical, Cosmological and Physico-Philosophical Speculations*, London, Probsthain, 1925; since reprinted. A convenient, scholarly accumulation of views that should give considerable help in the study of Chinese philosophy. Some of the views Forke reports are less ancient, it seems, than he believes. His joining of the views he describes in a unified 'world conception of the Chinese' is now recognized to be arbitrary.

Fung Yu-lan, *A History of Chinese Philosophy*, 2 vols, Princeton, Princeton University Press; vol. 1, 2nd ed., 1952; vol. 2, 1953. Like Forke, Fung includes a veritable anthology of excerpts from the sources. These excerpts are especially valuable in the second volume, the contents of which are less well known in the West. Fung wrote his *History* in Chinese and had to include extensive paraphrases of the ancient texts, which were no longer intelligible to the Chinese themselves. In English, however, the translated ancient texts are quite as clear as the paraphrases, which become more or less redundant. At the time he wrote his *History*, Fung was his own kind of Neo-Confucian, with faith in *li* or the Norm, taken to be, at once, metaphysical and moral. Fung has since recanted, or been forced to recant. His history, which quickly became standard, is learned, but rather partial and not notable for its analytic powers. Beginners will prefer his *Short History of Chinese Philosophy*, New York, Macmillan, 1948, which is not only shorter, but also clearer. It also contains some new material.

A word more of introduction to Fung's history. In embodies a concealed polemic against another eminent Chinese scholar, one of the renovators of Chinese literature, Hu Shih. In 1919, Hu Shih published *An Outline of the History of Chinese Philosophy*, vol. 1 (republished Tapei, Commercial Press, 1958), and in 1922, he published what was for its time an important thesis, *The Development of the Logical Method in Ancient China* (republished New York,

Paragon Book Co., 1963). Hu Shih was attracted to the more skeptical and rational elements in Chinese philosophy, and, not inconsistently, became a follower of John Dewey. In his *Outline*, which was written in the then new literary version of colloquial Chinese, and which became popular, Hu Shih complained that Confucianism taught subordination to family and state, and that Taoism taught a socially harmful *laissez-faire*. Fung Yu-lan's reaction was, 'One cannot help but see that for him Chinese civilization has been entirely led astray'. When Fung's *History* came out, Hu Shih attacked it, in turn, as needlessly emphasizing the superstitious rather than the rational elements of Chinese thought. In the context of Chinese thought of the time, Hu and Fung were therefore antipodal. (These remarks are based in part on Paul Demiéville's introduction to the French translation of Fung's *Short History*. Demiéville gives examples of what he takes to be superficial or poorly chosen comparisons made by Fung with Western philosophy. For the debates of modern Chinese philosophers, see O. Brière, *Fifty Years of Chinese Philosophy: 1898–1948*, New York, Prager, 1965. On Hu Shih, see J. B. Grieder, *Hu Shih and the Chinese Renaissance*, Cambridge (Mass.), Harvard University Press, 1970.)

W.-T. Chan, *A Source Book in Chinese Philosophy*, Princeton, Princeton University Press, is the only relatively extensive volume of translations. Chan is a knowledgeable, conscientious translator, at his best, perhaps, in Neo-Confucianism.

——, *Indications for Practical living and Other Confucian Writings by Wang Yang-ming*, Columbia, 1963.

——, *The Way of Lao Tzu*, New York, Bobbs-Merrill, 1963.

——, *Reflections on Things at Hand*, Columbia, 1967.

C. Chang, *The Development of Neo-Confucian Thought*, 2 vols, New York, Bookman Associates; vol. 1, 1957; vol. 1, 1962. Useful as the only history of its kind.

J. Ching, *To Acquire Wisdom: The Way of Wang Yang-ming*, Columbia, 1976.

A. C. Graham: *The Book of Lieh-tzu*, London, John Murray, 1960. Translations combining readability with scholarly precision.

E. R. Hughes, *Chinese Philosophy in Classical Times*, London, Dent (Everyman's Library), rev. ed., 1954. A brief, lively anthology of excerpts reaching up to about the first century A.D.

D. C. Lau, Lao Tzu, *Tao Te Ching*, Harmondsworth, Penguin Books, 1963. Scholarly, readable.

——, *Mencius*, Penguin, 1970.

——, Translation of Confucius is said to be forthcoming from the same publisher.

Legge, J., *Confucian Analects, The Great Learning and the Doctrine of the Mean*, London, Oxford University Press, 1863. Of the older translations of Chinese philosophy into English, those of James Legge have held up remarkably well. A missionary, Legge was the first Professor of Chinese at Oxford. Helped by an expert Chinese assistant, he translated painstakingly and, it must be admitted, in a rather pedestrian way. He shirked no difficulties and always gave justifications for the choices he made in translating. His translations of Confucius and Mencius are still therefore very useful. His translation of Taoist texts, though equally careful, rather misses their spirit, to which he appears not to have been attuned.

——, *The Texts of Taoism*, Oxford, 1863.

——, *The Works of Mencius*, Oxford, 1895. All three books have been reprinted in recent years by Dover Publications.

B. Watson, *Early Chinese Literature*, New York, Columbia University Press, 1962.

——, *Mo Tzu: Basic Writings*, Columbia, 1962.

——, *Hsün Tzu: Basic Writings*, Columbia, 1963.

——, *Han Fei Tzu: Basic Writings*, Columbia, 1964. (All three of the above books are available in one volume).

——, *The Complete Works of Chuang Tzu*, Columbia, 1968.

IX Islam: General Background

A. J. Arberry, *Aspects of Islamic Civilization*, London, Allen & Unwin, 1964. A General anthology, though with a more literary emphasis than Lewis's.

D. M. Dunlop, *Arab Civilization to A.D. 1500*, London, Longman, 1971. Well-informed chapters on literature, historiography, geography and travel, philosophy, and science and medicine.

H. A. R. Gibb, *Islam* (formerly *Mohammedanism*), London, Oxford University Press, 1959 and subsequent editions. Simple, brief, knowledgeable.

J. Schacht and C. E. Bosworth, eds., *The Legacy of Islam*, 2nd ed., London, Oxford University Press, 1974.

G. E. von Grunebaum, *Medieval Islam: A Study in Cultural Orientation*, 2nd ed., Chicago, University of Chicago Press, 1953. An original and influential analysis with sociological leanings. One chapter contrasts medieval Christendom and Islam. Another illustrates creative borrowing in terms of the adaptation in the *Arabian Nights*, not only of plots, but of the concept of love from Greek novels.

J. Gulik, *The Middle East: An Anthropological Perspective*, Pacific Palisades (Calif.), Goodyear Publishing Co., 1976.

P. M. Holt, A. K. S. Lambton and B. Lewis, eds., *The Cambridge History of Islam*, 2 vols, Cambridge, Cambridge University Press, 1970. Volume 2, which can be bought as separate paperbacks, contains essays on Islamic society and civilization, including such subjects as religion and culture, mysticism, science, and philosophy.

B. Lewis, *Islam*, New York Harper & Row, 1974. An illuminating, well-translated anthology from the sources.

B. Lewis, ed., *The World of Islam*, London, Thames & Hudson, 1976. Includes a chapter on 'The Scientific Enterprise', in which philosophy, too, is taken up. Extensively and beautifully illustrated.

D. and J. Sourdel, *La civilisation de l'Islam classique*, Paris, Arthaud, 1968. On Islamic history, religion and society, and economy and social milieu. Well written, based on extensive scholarship, and beautifully illustrated.

X Islam: Philosophy

For reasons made clear in the text, Islamic philosophy is here regarded as fitting, for the most part, into the 'Western' philosophical tradition. The bibliography that follows is therefore extremely brief.

There is no satisfactory, full-scale history of Islamic philosophy. A few of the briefer histories follow:

T. J. De Boer, *The History of Philosophy in Islam*, London, Luzac & Co., 1903; republished, New York, Dover, 1903. Clear, brief, and generally reliable.

H. Corbin, *Histoire de la philosophie islamique*, vol. 1, Paris,

Gallimard, 1964. Perhaps the most satisfactory of the brief histories.

M. Fakhry, *A History of Islamic Philosophy*, New York, Columbia University Press, 1970.

F. Rosenthal, *Knowledge Triumphant: The Concept of Knowledge in Medieval Islam*, Leiden, E. J. Brill, 1970, is in a different category than the other histories here mentioned. More technical than the others, it is an original and spirited exploration of Islamic attitudes toward knowledge, including, specifically, theology, Sufism, philosophy, and education.

W. M. Watt, *Islamic Philosophy and Theology*, Edinburgh, University of Edinburgh, 1962.

There is no extensive anthology of Islamic philosophy. A. Hyman and J. J. Walsh, eds., *Philosophy in the Middle Ages*, New York, Harper & Row, 1967, does, however, contain selections from the most famous Islamic and Jewish philosophers.

Jewish philosophy, which is not directly treated in the present book, is so closely related, in medieval times, to Islamic philosophy that it may be regarded as forming part of the same philosophical context.

E. R. Bevan and C. Singer, eds., *The Legacy of Israel*, London, Oxford University Press, 1927. Will provide those interested with a general cultural background.

J. Guttman, Philosophies of Judaism, New York, Holt, Rinehart, and Winston, 1964. May be consulted for the history of Jewish philosophy; unlike Husik, not confined to the medieval period.

I. Husik, *A History of Mediaeval Jewish Philosophy*, New York, Macmillan, 1916.

Index